Directory of
GRAND PRIX CARS
1945-65

Directory of
GRAND PRIX CARS
1945-65

Mike Lawrence

ASTON PUBLICATIONS

Sole distributors for the USA

Motorbooks International
Publishers & Wholesalers Inc.

Published in 1989 by Aston Publications Limited
Bourne End House, Harvest Hill
Bourne End, Bucks, SL8 5JJ

ISBN 0 946627 46 0

Designed by Chris Hand

Sole distributors to the UK
book trade,
Springfield Books Limited
Norman Road, Denby Dale
Huddersfield, West Yorkshire, HD8 8TH

Sole distributors for the USA,
Motorbooks International
Osceola, Wisconsin 54020
United States

British Library Cataloguing in Publication Data.

Lawrence, Mike
    Grand Prix cars 1945-1965.
    1. Racing cars. Racing. Races : Grands Prix
    I. Title
    796.7'2

    ISBN 0-946627-46-0

Printed in England by The Amadeus Press Ltd., Huddersfield

Contents

Introduction	7
Formulae	9
World Championships	11
A.F.M.	12
A.J.B.	13
A.T.S.	15
Alfa Romeo	16
Alta	22
Arzani-Volpini	26
Aston-Butterworth	27
Aston Martin	28
B.M.W./Bristol	32
B.M.W. Specials	33
B.R.M.	35
B.R.P.	49
Baird-Griffin	50
Behra-Porsche	51
Berkshire Special	52
Bond	52
Brabham	53
Bugatti	59
C.T.A.-Arsenal	61
Cegga-Maserati	62
Cisitalia	63
Clairmonte	65
Clisby	65
Connaught	67
Cooper	77
Cooper Variants: Aiden-Cooper	91
Cooper-Alfa Romeo	92
Cooper-Alta	93
Cooper-Arden	94
Cooper-Aston Martin	95
Cooper B.G.-Bristol	96
Cooper-B.R.M.	96
Cooper-Connaught	97
Cooper-Ferrari	98
Cooper-Ford	99
Hume-Cooper	99
Cooper-Maserati	99
Cooper-O.S.C.A.	100
Coventry Climax	101
Cromard	103
D.A.M.W.	104
D.B.	106
Derrington-Francis	107
De Tomaso	108
Dommartin	111
E.N.B.-Maserati	112
E.R.A.	113
Elios	115
Emeryson	115
Ferguson	121
Ferrari	123
Ferrari-Jaguar	153
Frazer Nash	153
Giaur	154
Gilby	154
Gleed-M.G.	156
Gordini	157
Guérin	161
H.A.R.	162
H.R.G.	163
H.W.M.	164
Honda	169
J.B.W.-Maserati	171
Kharkov	172

Kieft	173		R.R.A.	230
Kurtis-Kraft	174		Rover	231
Lancia	175		Sacha-Gordine	232
Lancia-Ferrari	177		Sadler	234
Lancia-Marino	181		Scarab	234
Lancia-Nardi	181		Scirocco	236
Lola	182		South African Specials	238
Lotus	184		Speed V-8	242
Lotus-Borgward	199		Stebro	243
Lotus-Maserati	199			
M.B.M.	199		Talbot-Lago	243
Maserati	201		Tatra	248
Maserati-Platé	214		Tec-Mec	249
Mercedes-Benz	215		Turner	250
Milano	222			
			V.M.	251
O.S.C.A.	223		Vanwall	252
			Veritas	263
Parnell	225			
Porsche	226		Walker-Climax	264

INTRODUCTION

If this book were devoted to contemporary Grand Prix cars, there would be no need for this introduction because we would all know where we stood, it would cover Formula 1 cars in World Championship races. Apart from the fact that such a Championship did not exist for part of the period covered, in 1952-3 the Championship was run to Formula 2 because there were not enough competitive F1 cars to make a race.

For some obscure reason, in the years 1950-60 the Indianapolis 500 counted towards the World Drivers' Championship, but the only driver who actually raced both in the WC and at Indy was Alberto Ascari in 1952. Ironically, it was after 'Indy' was dropped from the Championship that F1 drivers began to compete there on a regular basis.

Indianapolis may have been a World Championship event, but it was not a Grand Prix and so has been ignored in this book. On the other hand some races which bore the title Grand Prix were nothing of the sort. They might be run for 500cc F3 cars, for example, or for amateurs in sports cars, and were instances of some local club having delusions of grandeur.

Throughout the 20 years under review non-Championship Grands Prix proliferated throughout Europe. This tradition declined with the arrival of the 3-litre F1 in 1966, when the economic structure of the sport changed and non-Championship F1 races became increasingly less viable.

They were usually run over shorter distances than classic Grands Prix and the value of each win has to be weighed against the entry list. On occasion there were some decidedly odd entries. In the 1950 Pescara GP, for example, there were works teams from Alfa Romeo and Talbot, and also on the grid was Alfredo Schwelm in a Jaguar XK120!

There was a time when an F1 race was run each year at Reims and in some years this was designated the French GP. In those years when the French GP was run at, say, Rouen, the Reims race was still run, and it was on a Grand Prix circuit over a full Grand Prix distance, and the field was the same as for a World Championship race. In my book a win at Reims under such conditions does not lose any merit because WC points were not awarded.

Thus, when Jean Behra won at Reims in a Gordini in 1952 he became a Grand Prix winner, even though World Championship statistics say he was not. In the same way Luigi Musso's win at Reims, in 1957, was a victory of equal stature to any included in the Championship.

The World Championship has played a major part in popularizing F1, and these days the two are synonymous, but it has not always been the case. For this reason I have included cars which never raced in any WC event but which did appear in races run to contemporary Grand Prix formulae.

There is little new to be written about such as Mercedes-Benz, Ferrari, Lotus or Maserati, although I like to think I have added a few minor details, but on the whole the best one can hope to do is to provide a handy, condensed history and to put them into historical perspective. A fresh, critical look at some marques is anyway long overdue.

On the other hand there are a host of half-remembered marques which did little more than make up the numbers on a grid. Each one, however, represented someone's best efforts and the sport would have been poorer without them. I have also included a number of projects which never actually made the start of a race, for they too are part of the broad story of racing in the period and add background colour and texture. Sometimes the failures give us a better understanding of, and greater respect for, the successful constructors.

One has to draw the line somewhere, so I have used my judgement when dealing with the grey areas which occurred when, say, 1½-litre F2 cars became elevated to Formula 1 on the stroke of midnight, 31 December, 1960, or when Formula 2 or Formula Junior cars appeared in F1 races.

From quite early on in the 1950s came a series of engine projects intended to serve the small constructor. Some, such as the Speed V-8 and Clisby V-6, were failures, while others helped change the face of motor racing. Success or failure, I have given these projects their own entries. Apart form anything else it saves repetition, particularly in the case of Coventry Climax and B.M.W./Bristol, who provided engines for so many makers.

Again, to save repetition I have assumed that readers will know that until the beginning of the 1960s it was normal practice to make racing car bodies from aluminium and therefore I have mentioned only the exceptions. Wire wheels were also the norm in the same period so, again, it is the exceptions, the cars with alloy wheels, which have their wheels described. In the same way, brakes. Assume drum brakes until 1955 and disc brakes after 1959, with exceptions and unusual arrangements appearing in the text.

A word or warning, many brake horsepower figures quoted are *for amusement only*. I have done my best to moderate the more outlandish claims and have commented on some in the text, but many remain 'unproven'.

During my research, I have drawn on hundreds of sources (books, magazines and, wherever possible, personal interviews), but when I have leaned heavily on one particular work for an entry I have acknowledged it. There are, however, two books to which I constantly referred.

The first is The Formula One Register's *A Record of Grand Prix and Voiturette Racing*. The enthusiasts behind the Register are Paul Sheldon and Duncan Rabagliati and both have generously made available to me their research and even the manuscripts of future volumes of this great work.

The other is *Stirling Moss – My Cars, My Career* by Moss and Doug Nye (published by Patrick Stephens Ltd). Stirling drove more cars of the period than anyone else and is uniquely qualified to make assessments. His view has naturally coloured my own view of many cars included in this book and, I suspect, will be a major influence on all future motor racing historians. Doug Nye's considerable contribution to this joint effort deserves full recognition as well.

I would also like to thank Lynda Springate and her colleagues at the National Motor Museum Library, Beaulieu, who have been of enormous help in the preparation of this book and other books and articles I have written.

Finally I would like to thank Denis Jenkinson, whose influence on modern motor racing historians has been incalculable. Jenks' writing in *Motor Sport* set standards which have not been surpassed, and his guidance, even if sometimes it has been only a sharp intake of breath and a raised eyebrow, has always been appreciated.

Errors of fact, however, remain my responsibility.

Mike Lawrence *Chichester, 1989*

FORMULAE

Although we all use the terms 'Formula 1', 'Formula 2', etc., very few people outside of those intimately concerned with designing racing cars really know the precise definitions of these terms. A simple test to prove the point: what are the precise maximum dimensions for a current F1 car's rear wing? That's not a trick question, for as any designer will tell you the size of a rear aerofoil is a major element in deciding a car's performance.

During the years covered by this book, racing formulae were much less tightly controlled, but few of us carry them all in our heads, so some readers may appreciate this brief résumé of Grand Prix formulae together with a reminder of the precise nature of other formulae which are referred to in this book.

Formula 1

1938-46. Actually called 'Formula A', this was a capacity/weight formula, though in practice cars were either 3-litre supercharged or 4½-litre unblown. Minimum race distance was 500 km (311 miles). A number of races were run in 1946 and these were basically disputed between Alfa Romeo 158s and Maserati 4CLs, with a supporting cast of Delahayes and Talbots, in other words a mixture of pre-war *'Voiturettes'* (the equivalent of Formula 2) and nominal Formula A cars, which were actually often stripped-down two-seaters.

1947-53. Originally called 'Formula A'. Maximum capacity of 4½ litres or 1½ litres supercharged, a decision based on a purely pragmatic basis – the vast majority of existing cars were either one or the other and the experience of 1946 showed that the equivalence was reasonably fair even though 1½-litre cars had dominated the important races.

From 1950, the beginning of the World Championship, minimum race distance was reduced to 300 km (186 miles) or three hours, whichever was the longer. Although this formula notionally remained in force until 1953, after Formula 2 became the World Championship category in 1952, it became a secondary class. The reason for F1 losing its Championship status was that there were too few competitive cars to justify its continuation.

1954-60. Maximum capacity of 2½ litres or 750cc blown. In practice only two types of car raced using the supercharged equivalent and both were failures. Fuel was 'free' until the beginning of 1958, when the use of aviation fuel of 100-130 octane became mandatory. In 1958 minimum race length was reduced to 300-500 km *and* two hours.

1961-65. Minimum capacity of 1301cc, maximum capacity of 1500cc, no supercharged equivalent. Minimum dry weight of 450 kg. Commercial fuel mandatory. Cars had to be fitted with a self-starter and although fuel could be taken on during a race, oil could not.

Formula 2

1948-53. Originally known as 'Formula B', it stipulated a maximum capacity of 2 litres unblown or 500cc blown. In practice the supercharged option was exercised very rarely and never when, between 1952-3, the category was used to decide the World Championship.

1957-60. Maximum capacity 1500cc with no supercharged equivalent. In 1957 commercial fuel was mandatory, but from 1958 onwards aviation fuel was permitted.

1961-63. There was no Formula 2 for these years, but its function was taken over by Formula Junior.

1964-67. Maximum capacity of 1-litre unsupercharged and limited to 4-cylinder engines running on commercial fuel.

Inter-Continental Formula

When the FIA announced that, from 1961 on, Formula 1 would be for 1½-litre cars, British teams tried to block the move, which is why B.R.M. and Coventry Climax were late producing new engines. The 3-litre 'Inter-Continental' Formula was launched as a rival, but it was basically just a chance to run obsolete 1960 F1 cars. After five races, all in Britain, it fizzled out as teams concentrated on their proper business, F1.

Formula 3

1950-60. Maximum capacity of 500cc unsupercharged, minimum weight 200 kg. F3 became an international category in 1950, whereupon a previous rule calling for a minimum ground clearance of four inches was scrapped. In practice this formula declined sharply in importance from 1955-56 and its position as a training ground for young drivers was taken over first by small-capacity sports-racing cars, then by Formula Junior.

1964-70. Maximum capacity of 1000cc unblown and restricted to 4-cylinder production-based engines running on commercial fuel and using only one carburettor. Minimum weight of 400 kg.

Formula Junior

1959-63. A capacity/weight formula for cars using engines derived from production car units. Commercial fuel mandatory, overhead camshafts banned. Maximum capacity of 1000cc unsupercharged with a minimum weight of 360 kg, or 1100cc with a minimum weight of 400 kg. The USA had two other capacity/weight options, but neither caught on. In practice, from 1961 on, most FJ cars used 1100cc engines. The Formula 3 of 1964-70 derived from FJ, but imposed stricter limits on engine tuning.

WORLD CHAMPIONSHIPS

Since its inception in 1950, the Drivers' Championship has been a mixed blessing. It has unquestionably helped spread the sport's popularity by acting as a peg on which the general public can hang its imagination, but it has also distorted the sport. We have seen great wins downgraded because they have not scored WC points. We have seen drivers soft pedal by going for a finish rather than a win in order to build up their points tally. We have seen, too, injustices in deciding the title, such as when Hawthorn won it in 1958 with only one victory and a string of seconds, while Moss was runner-up with four wins.

When Ayrton Senna won the 1988 World Championship he did it with eight wins which beat the previous record of seven wins by Jim Clark (1963) which was equalled by Alain Prost in 1984. Actually, when Rudolf Carraciola became European Champion in 1935 he won *eight* Grands Prix in the season but these apparently do not count because that was before there was a World Championship. Clark, indeed, won 12 Formula One races in 1963 but so far as 'records' go, he won only those which carried WC points even though some of the non-Championship races featured all the major opposition.

So far as WC wins are concerned, we might also remember Alberto Ascari who, 1952-3, won nine races in succession and for a period of just over 12 months won every single WC race. That is a record which nobody has approached, before or since.

From 1950 to 1959 the World Championship scoring system was 8-6-4-3-2, with another point for fastest lap. Until the end of 1957 drivers who shared a car in a race shared the points, but from the beginning of 1958 points were awarded only to a driver who completed the entire distance. From the beginning of 1960 the point for fastest lap was dropped and given to the sixth-placed finisher. In 1961 a win was upgraded to nine points, a weighting which has continued to the time of writing, thus: 9-6-4-3-2-1.

Each year a driver has been able to keep only a specified number of points finishes. In the period covered by this book, it was a given number (between four and six) *over the entire season*, but, excluding the Indianapolis 500, there were never more than ten races in the Championship and, on two occasions, only six.

The Manufacturers' World Championship, now the Constructors' Cup, was instituted in 1958, and during the period under review points were awarded on the same basis as for the Drivers' Championship, except that a manufacturer could count only its highest finisher in each race. With the exception of the first Championship, which was won by Vanwall, the winning manufacturer also built the car used by the World Champion.

A. F. M.

It is quite astonishing how quickly some German enthusiasts were able to build new competition cars after the war, for the difficulties they faced were immense. The country was a smouldering ruin, there were severe restrictions imposed by the occupying powers and even basic components were often hard to come by.

One who did was a former B.M.W. engineer, Alex von Falkenhausen, who set up a small racing and tuning shop in Munich. He began by building some sports cars based on B.M.W. 328 components and made his first single-seater in 1949. This had a tubular chassis with coil spring and double wishbone front suspension and a de Dion rear end suspended by torsion bars. Von Falkenhausen had done a lot of work on the B.M.W. unit and was extracting about 130 bhp from it for racing.

A double reduction drive was fitted between the B.M.W. gearbox and final drive to give a lower seating position, and the brake drums were integral with the cast alloy wheels. As a B.M.W. man, von Falkenhausen was well aware of the advantages of good aerodynamics, and the car was finished with a tight, neat body.

A.F.M.s performed well in German F2 races and provided the chief threat to Veritas. The outstanding A.F.M. exponent was Hans Stuck, the former Auto Union driver and European Hill Climb Champion. Since Stuck had taken Austrian nationality he was able to compete with the car outside Germany, and in the 1950 Monza GP actually won the first heat from Ascari's Ferrari, though he retired in the second heat.

In 1950, a second car was built and this was driven principally by Fritz Riess, who used it to win the Eifelrennen that year, though that was then merely a German national event. In the search for more power, however, the B.M.W. unit became over-stressed and they both suffered frequent mechanical failures.

A.F.M. also made an attempt to market a five-seater touring car using a 2½-litre Opel engine, but this was not a success, and during 1950 von Falkenhausen began to contemplate a return to B.M.W. Before he rejoined the company, however, he fitted one of the cars with a V-8 engine designed by Richard Küchen, which was based on an Abarth design. This was a d.o.h.c. unit of 1993cc (67.3 × 70 mm), which gave about 150 bhp. At first it ran using eight Amal carburettors, but when these proved too difficult to keep in tune, a twin-choke Weber feeding each bank of cylinders was substituted.

Since the whole car was extremely light (about 445 kg) with 150 bhp it had exceptional acceleration, something which Stuck was able to exploit in hill climbs, but it was not very reliable, and the Achilles' heel was the valve gear. Von Falkenhausen closed his workshop in 1951, but Stuck persevered with the car and scored wins and places in German events.

In 1952 he entered the Swiss GP, where he qualified 13 seconds off the pace, and behind Ken Wharton's Frazer Nash-Bristol, and his race ended after four laps. Three B.M.W.-powered cars started the German GP, but none finished.

For 1953 Stuck fitted a Bristol engine to his car, but it appeared in only one WC race, the Italian GP. There it qualified second last, over 20 seconds off the pace, and eventually trailed in 14th, 23 laps down. That was the end of A.F.M.'s racing career, although the Stuck car came to England and raced in Historic events until it was crashed heavily.

Hans Stuck with his V-8 A.F.M. in the 1953 International Trophy race at Silverstone. (Guy Griffiths)

A. J. B.

With his goatee beard, quick movements and beret, Archie Butterworth looks like everyone's idea of a brilliant if eccentric inventor — and so he is, with a long string of patents to his name. After the war he was working at Enfield designing small arms, while designing a Grand Prix car in his spare time. This was to have a 4425cc (89 × 89 mm) air-cooled V-8 engine mounted in an independently sprung frame with torsion bar suspension and four-wheel drive. Braking was to be by hydraulic discs all round (this was in 1947!) and among several patented features was a 5-speed gearbox with a twin-pedal change.

Materials were scarce and, besides, Archie was working alone, so it is no wonder the design was never completed, although the frame was made and is still in existence, but a number of the car's features were made and used in racing.

While he was working on this design, he happened to see Sydney Allard debut his 3.7-litre Steyr-engined special at Prescott and was struck by the similarity in broad layout between the Steyr unit and his own proposed engine. Casting around, he discovered a couple, complete with 3-speed gearboxes, at the Chobham military establishment and he was able to buy the lot for a tenner.

The upshot was the S.2 (he had built a sprint special, S.1, pre-war), though it was never known as anything else but the 'A.J.B. Special'. It was completed in just six months, and while its chassis was crude, with quarter-elliptic springs all round and boxed-in Jeep side-members, its transmission was ingenious. From the gearbox the power was transmitted to a transfer box, which offset the drive to a central differential. From there prop-shafts took the power front and rear to standard Jeep axles, which, of course, were 'live'. It was a fierce device and Archie says, 'It was a terribly dangerous little car, not very good on right-hand corners, for the driver sat on the left. It spent three years trying to kill me, and very nearly succeeded at Shelsley Walsh.'

After one appearance in 1948, still without a body, Archie set to work on the engine. The Steyr's individual iron barrels were replaced by aluminium ones with iron liners and the capacity increased to 4425cc (87.5 × 92 mm). With eight Amal carburettors, alcohol fuel and a compression ratio of 14:1, Archie succeeded in raising the power output from 85 bhp to 260 bhp.

With that amount of power in a rudimentary chassis, the car became an instant crowd pleaser. It was pretty successful too, albeit in sprints and hill climbs, and in 1950 took part in the International Trophy at Silverstone. Unfortunately the aluminium crankcase flexed and it ran its bearings after just one lap. Butterworth entered it in a handful of other F1 races, but on the only occasion it arrived, for the 1950 Jersey Road Race, he failed to qualify.

By the following year, swing-axle front suspension had been fitted and the old 3-speed Steyr gearbox replaced with the 5-speed unit Archie had originally drawn for his Grand Prix car. Only five inches long, it featured two clutch pedals: by depressing one pedal the box changed up a gear, pressing the other changed down while automatically blipping the throttle to synchronize the revs exactly.

During practice at Shelsley Walsh, however, the car got out of control, hit a gully and flipped. That effectively ended Archie's competition career and the car was sold to the American Four Wheel Drive Corporation, which was interested in its ingenious gearbox. In the States Bill Millikin modified the chassis, renamed it the 'Butterball Special' and competed with it a few times. It may now be seen in the 4WD Museum in Cliftonville, Wisconsin.

Meanwhile Archie, who had gone into business on his own account, laid down a new flat-four engine which, by the simple expedient of changing the cylinder barrels, could be made in sizes between 1½-litres and 2½ litres. For the 1952 season he had made up parts for six of these units in 2-litre form (87.5 × 82.5 mm) with the modified Steyr barrels and heads which had been seen on the V-8, though new heads were on his drawing board. As usual, Butterworth specified one Amal motorcycle carburettor per cylinder.

One of these engines went to Kieft and was fitted with Norton barrels (see Cooper-Arden and Kieft), one went to an amateur racer for installation in an early space-frame Tojeiro sports car, one vanished from view, and two went to Bill Aston (see Aston-Butterworth).

Other business commitments kept Archie's racing projects on the back boiler for a while, but the ingenious gearbox was ordered by Jack Brabham. Unfortunately time could not be found to complete it and Brabham's deposit was returned. Then Lotus showed interest in taking over the design, but Chapman insisted on some modifications which Butterworth was against and the result was an exchange of solicitors' letters. Perhaps Chapman should have accepted it as it was for, after all, the transmission had proven capable of handling 260 bhp with complete reliability.

The name 'A.J.B.' next appeared on the racing scene in 1957 with an air-cooled flat-four 1½-litre engine utilizing Butterworth's patented swing inlet valve. The idea was that it allowed uninterrupted airflow into the cylinder and in shape was rather like a French horn. These valves were each mounted on an individual shaft, at the end of which were three thin torsion bars pivoting

around a central torsion shaft. Activation was by a short push-rod which, when it pushed the valve into the combustion chamber, would cause the torsion bars to wind up.

Large sodium-filled poppet valves were used for the exhaust and these had similar valve springing. The torsion shafts limited the number of cylinders to four, though Butterworth laid out an air-cooled flat-eight with desmodronic valve gear. This, he thought, would deliver 600 bhp in 3-litre form, his flat-four gave 148 bhp, which made it one of the most powerful engines of its size in 1957.

Since each cylinder barrel could be easily changed, it was theoretically possible for the engine to be made into a 2-litre or even a 2½-litre unit and Butterworth hoped to see his engine in F1. The 1500cc unit was intended just to prove the concept.

It was fitted in the works Elva Mk 3 sports car and driven by the great Archie Scott-Brown. Unfortunately, while it was very quick when it went, it suffered constant valve failure. Ironically it was the conventional exhaust valves which failed, due to faulty manufacture, but after Archie rigged up a system to cool the valves by oil, the car won a minor race at Brands Hatch.

Relations between Elva and Butterworth had become strained, but Archie Scott-Brown appears to have retained faith in the engine and plans were laid to run him in F2 in 1958 using a 1½-litre A.J.B. in a modified Cooper chassis. The long-term aim was to run an F1 version.

An entry was filed for the Monaco GP, which had an F2 class, but the car was not ready in time, so Scott-Brown instead drove the works Lister-Jaguar at Spa, where he was caught out by a sudden shower, crashed, and died of his injuries.

With Scott-Brown's death, Butterworth lost interest in motor racing and turned his attention to other engineering projects. His ideas had shown a lot of promise, and all were basically sound, but Archie insisted on doing too much by himself and this obsessive degree of personal involvement finally proved counter-productive.

A. T. S.

Ferrari has always been a hot-bed of intrigue, but Enzo Ferrari controlled the factions within his fiefdom with the skill of a medieval princeling. An exception was when Laura Ferrari started to add her 'twolireworth' and began to interfere. In 1961 there were some unhappy men at Maranello, and these included some of the key personnel, who were supposed to be answerable only to the boss. Things reached such a pretty pass that they issued an ultimatum, 'Either we are allowed to work in peace or we go.'

At about the same time, 24-year-old Count Giovanni Volpi di Misturi inherited a title and a fortune from his father and rather than fritter away his wealth on idle pleasure he formed a racing team, Scuderia Serenissima. Before long he decided he would like more control over his destiny than being a customer of other constructors, and he approached two industrialists, Jaime Ortiz Patino and Georgio Billi, who were both toying with the idea of building competition cars. Volpi proposed they should join forces.

Then Italian motor racing was rocked by the news that, after enjoying its first dominant year in F1 for eight years (the Scuderia's 1956 cars were Lancias), Ferrari had suddenly lost six of its top men, including team manager Romolo Tavoni and chief designer Carlo Chiti. This was opportune for Volpi and his colleagues and, a few weeks later, they stepped forward and reached an agreement with the defectors.

In February 1962 a new company was formed, the Societa per Azioni Automobili Turisimo Sport Serenissima, and Chiti got on with the task of designing a new Serenissima F1 car. The plan was to have the F1 cars ready by the end of 1962 and then, as they went on from triumph to triumph, to make a production 2-litre version of the F1 engine to power a GT car which would be sold in ever increasing numbers and then be complemented by other models. Within a few years Ferrari would be brought down to size. So ran the theory, and it was a scenario for an opera with a typically Italian theme of feud and revenge.

Before long, however, Volpi fell out with his partners and left, taking with him the name 'Serenissima' (the old name of the Republic of Venice). The company therefore became Automobili Turismo e Sport or A.T.S.

At the end of 1962 Chiti's new F1 car was displayed, and handsome it was too. He had specified a Lucas fuel-injected 90-degree V-8 d.o.h.c. engine of 1494cc (66 × 54.6 mm) which drove through a 6-speed Colotti gearbox modified by A.T.S. The space-frame chassis was reminiscent of the then-current Ferrari, but that was understandable since that was a Chiti design.

It was a petite car, though its otherwise low, clean lines were a little spoiled by bulges over the carburettors and a proportionally large windscreen. Front suspension was by rocker arms with inboard coil springs, while the independent rear set-up was by double wishbones, links and coil springs. The brakes, discs all round, were mounted inboard and the car in prototype form was neat, purposeful, and nicely finished.

To drive the cars, A.T.S. had attracted former World

Giancarlo Baghetti at the wheel of his A.T.S. in the 1963 Belgian Grand Prix at Spa-Francorchamps; he retired because of gearbox problems. (Nigel Snowdon)

Champion Phil Hill and young Giancarlo Baghetti, who both came from Ferrari.

Then A.T.S. went away to prepare for 1963 and normally would have been expected to have raced in the non-Championship curtain-raisers. But they did not and neither did they appear for the Monaco GP. The team of which much was expected (many would have liked to have seen Ferrari beaten by an Italian team) did not appear until the Belgian GP in early June, and what emerged from the transporter sent some into giggles and left some askance.

The cars were a sorry sight. Gone was the neat bodywork and in its place were rumpled aluminium shells, pock-marked and badly sprayed. Oil and grease marks were everywhere. None of the panels fitted and some seemed to be hanging on by will-power alone. There had clearly been problems in testing and the rear end of the chassis must have been flexing like a sponge, for welded across the top of the engine bay were reinforcing tubes. To change an engine, the frame had to be sawn and, afterwards, new tubes welded into place.

The Ferrari-beaters would have been derided at a banger meeting, where at least nobody presents a car covered with grease and oil. Neither driver could get near the pace in practice at Spa (Hill, the faster of the two, was 11.6 seconds off pole) and both retired in the first half with transmission troubles. They did little better in the next race, the Dutch GP, but at least the cars were tidied up a little and the bracing tubes over the engines were removable. Hill had a rear stub axle break after 15 laps and Baghetti retired two laps later with a blown engine.

The team missed the French and British races, while it struggled to reach the level of a semi-competent amateur outfit. Entries were filed for the German GP, but on the way to the Nürburgring the transporter crashed.

Still they were back, and raring to go, at Monza and there they scored their first finishes. After numerous pit stops Baghetti was 15th, 23 laps down on Clark's winning Lotus, while Hill had a comparatively easy race to finish 11th, only seven laps down.

At Watkins Glen both cars retired after five laps with oil problems, while in Mexico neither car would run properly at the high altitude. Baghetti retired after 10 laps with carburation problems, while Hill survived to two-thirds distance, when a rear wishbone collapsed.

After that, the A.T.S. F1 team was seen no more and nobody regretted its going, least of all the drivers, whose careers were blighted by the adventure. A few A.T.S. GT cars were made and when the company collapsed the remains were bought by Volpi, who used them as the basis for his short-lived Serenissima marque. A 3-litre Serenissima engine was used by Bruce McLaren in F1 on three occasions in 1966 and, in the only race in which he was able to start with such an engine (the British GP), it powered Team McLaren to its first World Championship point.

Some of the remaining pieces of this sad story were refettled as the Derrington-Francis (q.v.) which made a single appearance, at Monza, in 1964. One of the cars is now in the Donington Collection, where it has been restored to the condition in which it should have raced.

ALFA ROMEO

When Alfa Romeo emerged from the Second World War, its car factory was devastated but its racing machinery was intact, for when the war had started to get nasty in Italy, all the cars had been moved into the country and walled up in an old cheese-making plant. It was typical of Alfa Romeo that even while its factory was a ruin, it would decide to set up a competition department which would not only run pre-war designs but would start on new projects.

There were plenty of cars to choose from to mount an attack for, apart from those which had raced before hostilities began, there were two which had developed during the war. One was the Tipo 162 with a 135-degree V-16 d.o.h.c. 'four-valve' engine of 2995cc (62×62 mm), which had given 490 bhp in early testing. This was fitted in a ladder frame with coil spring and trailing arm

front suspension and a de Dion rear end sprung by torsion bars. The other was the Tipo 512, which was the company's intended weapon for the 1½-litre formula which everyone had expected would come into force in 1941. This intriguing mid-engined car, which resembled a scaled-down Auto Union D-Type, had a flat-12 d.o.h.c. engine of 1489cc (54×54.2 mm) which had three blocks each of four cylinders and two-stage supercharging. It gave 335 bhp at 8600 rpm, and drove through a 5-speed gearbox mounted behind the rear axle.

The chassis frame followed Auto Union practice with two elliptical main tubes, and longitudinal torsion bars provided the springing medium, acting on double wishbones at the front and a de Dion rear axle located by fabricated radius arms and a Watt linkage.

It was not to these two cars Alfa Romeo turned,

however, and both remained unraced although the 512 appears later in the story. It also appeared in another guise in 1947, for its designer was Giaocchino Colombo, who went to Ferrari and designed the 'short block' 60-degree V-12, which bore more than a passing resemblance to the engine in the Tipo 512.

Nor did Alfa Romeo decide to resurrect its V-12 Tipo 12C-312 or the V-16 Tipo 16C-316 (not to be confused with the Tipo 160 V-16, which was a 65-degree 'two valve' engine with two crankshafts which derived from two Tipo 158 blocks). There was, too, the straight-eight Tipo 8C-308 with an engine which derived from the Tipo B, and although Jean-Pierre Wimille used one of these to win Grands Prix at Bourgogne, Perpignan and in the Bois de Boulogne, Alfa Romeo decided instead to dust off its Tipo 158 Alfettas, which had been built for *Voiturette* racing.

In 1946 Alfa Romeo had a choice of six distinctly different cars with which to tackle Grand Prix racing, a unique situation. The fact there were six options also suggests a certain amount of confusion, and so there had been.

During the 1930s Scuderia Ferrari had become the Alfa Romeo works team, but neither the company nor the team had been able to do much about German supremacy. This did not go down well in government circles for Mussolini's Italy had been the model for other national socialist movements and Hitler had been Il Duce's pupil. As Mussolini strove to create a new Rome, suddenly the Hun had begun to steal his thunder, including on the race track.

When Alfa Romeo struggled all kinds of pressure was brought to bear and the upshot was that Vittorio Jano, the chief designer, was sacked and replaced by Wifredo Ricart, a man of impeccable political views according to the lights of Mussolini's Italy. In the shake-up Scuderia Ferrari was disbanded and replaced by a works team called 'Alfa Corse'. For a while Ferrari stayed on as team manager, but there was no love lost between he and Ricart and eventually a separation was negotiated, one of whose clauses was that the Scuderia would remain dormant for five years. Thus Ferrari went into general engineering and also set to work on a competition car which he named the 'Auto Avio' in order to by-pass his agreement with Alfa Romeo.

Although Germany dominated Grand Prix racing pre-war, Maserati was successful in *Voiturette* racing and Ferrari saw that in that class lay a chance to put Alfa Romeo into the winner's circle.

Together with Giaocchino Colombo, Ferrari sketched out an overall concept which Colombo realized and thus was created the Tipo 158 Alfetta. Its chassis

The rear-engined Tipo 512 designed by Wifredo Ricart, but not raced. (Alfa Romeo S.p.A.)

resembled that of the Tipo 308C, a tubular frame with trailing arm and transverse leaf front suspension and swing-axle and transverse leaf rear suspension. The straight eight d.o.h.c. 'two valve' engine which Colombo designed was of 1479cc (58 × 70 mm). Initially with a single supercharger, this produced 190 bhp at 6500 rpm, which it delivered via a 4-speed gearbox mounted in unit with the final drive.

In the *Voiturette* 'curtain raiser' to the 1938 Coppa Ciano, Emilio Villoresi (older brother of Luigi) and Clemente Biondetti scored a maiden 1-2 for the type, and while the cars retired in two of the other three races they entered, Villoresi and Martino Severi scored another 1-2 in the Milan GP. Further successes followed in 1939 and the cars were showing a good deal of promise. As a result of this it was decided that the 1939 Tripoli GP would be run to the *Voiturette* formula (Libya was an Italian colony) and six Alfettas were confidently entered.

Then Mercedes-Benz showed its strength and produced the 1½-litre W165 in an astonishingly short time and promptly scored a 1-2, with the best Alfetta, of Emilio Villoresi, third. It was a humiliation and work was immediately put in hand to improve output, resulting in a roller bearing crankshaft which, with other work, increased power to 225 bhp at 7500 rpm. It also had a

redesigned body, which became one of the classic shapes of motor racing.

Designated the Tipo 158B, this model won the Coppa Ciano, Coppa Acerbo and the Prix de Berne in 1939 (the Mercedes-Benz W165s were absent) and in 1940 (Italy was neutral until June that year) took 1-2-3-5 in the Tripoli GP.

Thus the pre-war background to the car which dominated Grand Prix racing between 1946 and 1951. Although Alfa Romeo had six options when it went racing again, the Tipo 158 was clearly the sensible choice. It was a proven design which was reliable, in the absence of the German teams it was superior to anything else, and there were lots of them.

For drivers the team could call on Giuseppe Farina, Jean-Pierre Wimille, Felice Trossi, Consalvo Sanesi and, making a come-back to racing having been cured of morphine addiction, the great Achille Varzi. Alfa Romeo's first appearance was in the St Cloud GP, near Paris, where cars were entered for Farina and Wimille, but both retired with clutch trouble. After this try-out, however, Alfa Romeo was to remain undefeated for five years.

By the GP des Nations at Geneva three months later, the cars had been up-rated to Tipo 158C specification

Giuseppe Farina at the wheel of his Alfa Romeo Tipo 158/46B in the 1946 Grand Prix des Nations at Geneva. Farina finished in first place, ahead of other Alfas driven by Trossi and Wimille.
(Louis Klementaski)

with two-stage supercharging (260 bhp at 7500 rpm) and twin exhaust pipes. The event was run in two heats and a final; Varzi and Farina won their heats and Alfettas filled the first three places in the final (Farina, Trossi, Wimille).

Sanesi replaced Trossi for the Turin GP, but he and Farina retired with transmission problems, while Varzi led home Wimille. Actually it was a stage-managed finish (an all-Italian win in Italy) and Wimille threw a wobbler and so was dropped for the next race, the Milan GP, where the final order was Trossi, Varzi and Sanesi.

It was decided to take part in only four races in 1947 and Farina went off to drive for Maserati. In the Swiss GP the final order was Wimille, Varzi and Trossi. In the Belgian GP it was Wimille, Varzi and Trossi, though Raymond Sommer's Maserati had run in second place until his transmission broke. Two cars were entered for the Bari GP (1st Varzi, 2nd Sanesi), while for the Italian GP there were four cars. Wimille, who was not supposed to have won the Belgian GP, was dropped and his place was taken by Alessandro Gaboardi, one of the racing mechanics. The final order was Trossi, Varzi, Sanesi and Gaboardi.

This was real domination, but Alfa Romeo was not content to rest on its laurels, and in practice for the Italian GP had tried the 158D, which had a larger primary supercharger, a single exhaust pipe, softer springs in the suspension, and 310 bhp. Varzi was given the car for the Swiss GP, the first of Alfa Romeo's four outings in 1948, and in practice, which was wet, he misjudged a bend, the car flipped and he was killed.

Despite this, the team still started and Trossi led Wimille home with Sanesi fourth. In third place, however, was Luigi Villoresi with a Maserati 4CLT/48, the first time one of the team cars had been led at the finish.

For the French GP, the team included Alberto Ascari in his only drive for Alfa Romeo, and the three cars entered came home in the order: Wimille, Sanesi, Ascari, but once again Villoresi's Maserati had been a challenge, holding third place until he suffered plug trouble. The challenge was strengthened at the Italian GP, where three Ferrari Tipo 125s joined the fray. Wimille in a 158D won, but was followed by a Maserati and a Ferrari.

At the Monza GP there were 158Ds for the regular trio and a 158C for Piero Taruffi. Once again a Ferrari gave them trouble and Raymond Sommer ran second until he had to retire with an asthma attack; thereafter the four cars finished in the order Wimille, Trossi, Sanesi and Taruffi.

Alfa Romeo missed 1949 and various reasons have been given. Finance is one reason offered, and certainly the company was not making many cars, while on the other hand it was working on getting its new 1900 series

Reg Parnell, the only British driver to be entered with the Tipo 158, on his way to third place in the 1950 European Grand Prix at Silverstone. The damage to the front of the car was caused by a collision with a hare. (Guy Griffiths)

Views of the cockpit (note the left-hand gear lever operating in an open gate) and the heavily ribbed brake drum of the Alfa Romeo 158. (Guy Griffiths)

in production. Then Wimille was killed in the Argentine in January 1949 in a Simca-Gordini. Thus Alfa Romeo had lost both Varzi and Wimille, its two best drivers. Another suggestion is that the real threat from Maserati and Ferrari and the imagined threat from Cisitalia and B.R.M. caused the Alfa Romeo board to make a tactical withdrawal. The truth is probably a combination of all three.

With the cat away, the mice played, and 1949 saw an interesting season contested mainly by Talbot, Ferrari and Maserati. It was business as usual again in 1950, however, and during its absence Alfa Romeo had continued development work and returned with power increased to 350 bhp at 8500 rpm. It had, too, a new driver line-up consisting of Farina, Fangio and Luigi Fagioli, a veteran of 52 making a come-back after 12 years in retirement. Fangio, at 38, was the kid in the team, whose combined age was 134, but they were boy racers compared with the three Talbot drivers (combined age 145), and the design of the Tipo 158 was 12 years old as well.

The 1950 British GP, the first World Championship event ever, was a walkover. Cisitalia had faded away, B.R.M. was still trying to make the start of a race, Maserati had stopped making GP cars and Ferrari was absent, so the only opposition came from Talbot. Fangio retired and Farina led home Fagioli with Reg Parnell (a pleasant gesture, giving the Brits a Brit to cheer) third.

At Monaco, Farina and Fagioli were eliminated in a first-lap pile-up and Fangio stroked home to win, a lap

ahead of Ascari's Ferrari. Farina led Fagioli home in the Swiss GP (Fangio retired with a dropped valve). Fangio led Fagioli in the Belgian GP, but Farina encountered gearbox problems and had to be content with fourth behind Rosier's Talbot.

Farina retired in the French GP, where Fangio again won from Fagioli. At the start of the Italian GP, the last Championship race of the year, Farina had 21 points, Fangio 26 and Fagioli 24, with the four best results to count. For the first time they faced Ascari and Serafini driving full 4.5-litre Ferraris and the pace of these was soon evident, as Ascari took second place on the grid, only two-tenths off Fangio's pole.

Fangio and Ascari battled in the opening laps, but both retired and took over other cars. Ascari, in Serafini's Ferrari, was to come home second, while Fangio, who took over Taruffi's 158, suffered his second dropped valve of the afternoon. Farina won, and became the first World Champion, and Fagioli finished third. Fagioli ended the season with more points than Fangio, but after he dropped the four he won at Monza, came third in the Championship.

Six races, six wins, and the three regular drivers coming 1-2-3 in the World Championship is real domination. Not only that, but the cars finished first in the San Remo GP (Fangio); 1-2 in the Bari GP (Farina and Fangio); 1-2-3 in the Grand Prix des Nations at Geneva (Fangio, de Graffenried and Taruffi); first and third in the Coppa Acerbo (Fangio and Fagioli; it would have been a 1-2, but Fagioli had the offside front spring break on the last

Juan Fangio at the wheel of his Tipo 159 Alfa Romeo in vain pursuit of Gonzalez' Ferrari in the 1951 British Grand Prix. (T. C. March)

lap); and 1-2 in the International Trophy (Farina and Fangio). In 1950, Alfa Romeo entered eleven races and its final tally was eleven wins, six seconds and four thirds.

The performance of the Ferraris at Monza, however, showed there was no time for complacency and for 1951 the Tipo 159 was introduced. This was a revised 158 with needle roller big end bearings and up to 405 bhp at 10,500 rpm. This power was to be used judiciously, however, since the engine was now very highly stressed and, in fact, it delivered over twice the horsepower of the original car 13 years before. It was a little like a turbo engine in that power was gained at the expense of economy and reliability and drivers were to limit themselves to 8500 rpm for preference, 9500 rpm (385 bhp) if necessary, and only use all the power if desperate. Since the 159 returned only 1½ mpg, additional tanks were available and if all were added (in the cockpit and along the sides) they increased capacity to 75 gallons, but upset handling and made refuelling a much longer process.

It was decided to retain Farina and Fangio as the principals, with support from guest drivers. The team's first appearance was in the International Trophy, which provided an uncanny omen. Tipo 158s won the preliminary heats, but just after the final started there was a downpour of hail and rain of monsoon proportions and Reg Parnell in the 4½-litre 'Thin Wall Special' Ferrari had lapped the entire Alfa Romeo team by lap six, when the race was abandoned. Parnell took the prize money, but officially there was no winner, so Alfa Romeo's winning streak was intact, but another 4½-litre Ferrari on the same circuit would end it.

That was in the future, but not far in the future. In the opening round of the Swiss GP, fuel consumption was giving rise to worry and Taruffi gave Alfa Romeo a hard time. Taruffi took over the new 'twin-plug' Ferrari from Ascari, who was unwell, and he finished second to Fangio, from the Tipo 159s of Farina, Sanesi and de Graffenried and, moreover, he lapped Sanesi once and de Graffenried twice. Before the next major race, Farina had a single car for a couple of races in Britain and he easily won the Festival of Britain Trophy at Goodwood and the Ulster Trophy at Dundrod.

In the Belgian GP Fangio had a Tipo 159A, which had a de Dion rear axle located by an 'A' bracket, larger brakes, and the twin-branch exhaust system. He had the full complement of supplementary tanks and found the car a handful. Fangio, Farina and Sanesi now faced three 'twin-plug' Ferraris (Ascari, Villoresi and Taruffi) and a huge battle ensued. While in the lead Fangio came into the pits, but one of his wheels was jammed on and after all remedies to free it failed, the tyre had to be changed on the existing rim. That cost him 15 minutes, but Farina eventually won with the Ferraris of Ascari and Villoresi not far behind.

A similar duel took place in the French GP at Reims until both Fangio and Ascari had to retire. Fangio took over Fagioli's car and went on to win from Ascari (in Gonzalez' Ferrari). At Silverstone it was Gonzalez in a 1950 spec car (one plug per cylinder) who finally put an end to Alfa Romeo's run of wins. Compared with other circuits, it was a medium-fast track and the Ferrari's torque tipped the balance. Fangio came in second, 50 seconds behind, and some idea of the fierceness of the duel between the two great Argentinians can be gained from the fact that Villoresi (Ferrari) in third was two laps down and Felice Bonetto (Alfa Romeo), in fourth, was three laps down.

In the German GP Alfa Romeo fielded Farina, Fangio, Bonetto and Paul Pietsch, who had driven for Auto Union. Only Fangio finished, second to Ascari, with other Ferraris filling the rest of the top six places. In the Italian GP Tipo 159As were given to Farina, Fangio and Bonetto, while de Graffenried had an ordinary 159. Fangio and Ascari disputed the lead, with Farina in third. Farina's engine blew and he took over Bonetto's car, Fangio's car broke a piston and this left the Ferraris of Ascari and Gonzalez secure in the lead. After further fuel stops, Farina came in third and lapped.

Fangio took a car to a couple of wins in races at Goodwood and then the team ran in its last race, the Spanish GP on the Pedralbes circuit at Barcelona. There Ascari set pole from Fangio, but Ferrari fitted smaller, 16-inch wheels and the resulting high wear rate on the tyres offset the Alfettas' economy handicap. Fangio won from Gonzalez, Farina, Ascari, Bonetto and de Graffenried.

Thus in their last race, four Alfettas started and four finished, and not only did Alfa Romeo win its last race with the car, but Fangio won his first World Championship. The car could not be developed any further and besides it was clear that the day of the supercharged engine was over, which is probably the reason why the mid-engined Tipo 512 was never brought out as everyone had predicted it would be, once the Alfetta had been beaten.

It is curious, but while Alfa Romeo had been so assured and dominant while developing and running its pre-war GP cars, its post-war development and competition programme as a whole had been a shambles, lacking aim and commitment. This continued to be the case over the coming years with every sports car project it undertook floundering. Against that background it is perhaps easy to see why there was no new GP car on the stocks.

When the 2½-litre F1 was announced, however, the flat-12 Tipo 512 was re-examined and a 2483cc (68 × 57 mm) development of it was made with the block cast in magnesium alloy. Instead of the mid-engined layout, it was proposed to put this unit at the front of a backbone chassis, where it would act as a stressed member. Suspension was to have been by coil springs and double wishbones at the front, with a coil-sprung de Dion rear axle located by very long radius arms. It was intended that it would have four-wheel drive (with it possible to disengage the front wheels from the cockpit) and the driver would sit at the very back, behind the rear axle, as on a dragster. Odd though this seating position may seem, it was tried in testing on an Alfetta, and while Sanesi found it extremely uncomfortable, for it was only a test rig and he had no wind protection, apparently he found no difficulty in controlling the car.

This project did not get beyond the experimental stage and for many years Alfa Romeo concentrated on racing and rallying versions of its road cars, which were sold in ever-increasing numbers, for the decision had been taken to become a volume producer. The story of Alfa Romeo in GP racing 1945-65 was not quite over, for modified versions of the 1300cc d.o.h.c. Giulietta engine were popular in South Africa in the early 1960s with the Alfa Special of Piet de Klerk being especially successful.

ALTA

Geoffrey Taylor was a gifted engineer who never had the resources to do justice to his ideas. By all accounts he was a man of fixed views, who could be bloody-minded, but these were qualities he needed to pursue his uphill struggle.

The Alta Car and Engineering Company was established at Tolworth and it was as early as 1929, when Taylor was only in his mid-twenties, that the first Alta sports car appeared, with a 4-cylinder d.o.h.c. engine of 1074cc (60 × 95 mm).

These sold in small numbers throughout the 1930s and Taylor made 1500cc and 2-litre models as well.

Since these had wet cylinder liners in basically the same block, owners could run the same car in 1500cc or 2-litre form as the racing calendar dictated. From 1934 Alta began to make 'off-set' single-seaters, and in sprints, hill climbs and short races they were a viable alternative to the E.R.A. In longer events, however, they tended to be unreliable.

In 1937 an improved *Voiturette* appeared, this time a genuine single-seater with all-independent suspension, and George Abecassis was successful with one of these cars in Britain. Taylor also planned a 3-litre Grand Prix car by putting two 4-cylinder engines on a single crankshaft, but war put an end to that.

One car that did appear was a 2-litre *Voiturette* with all-independent suspension by torsion bars, an advanced idea at the time. Before it could be completed, Europe was in turmoil but, post-war, it raced in the hands of Robert Cowell and Gordon Watson.

Racing was only Taylor's hobby, but Alta was still the first British company to make a post-war Grand Prix car. While B.R.M. lurched along, Taylor found enough spare capacity in his works to make the cars he had planned during the war years. Alta also resumed production of its sports cars, but Taylor's real interest was in racing and he did not press development of his production cars.

The difficulties which faced any engineering company after World War II, which included severe restrictions on basic materials, meant that the GP Alta did not appear until 1948. Overall the design was similar to Taylor's pre-war thinking, but the 4-cylinder d.o.h.c. 1490cc engine had 'square' cylinder dimensions of 78×78 mm. Blown by a single Roots-type supercharger made by Alta, it produced a claimed 230 bhp at 7000 rpm and drove via Taylor's usual choice of gearbox, a 4-speed E.N.V. preselector unit.

The car's chassis was a tubular ladder-frame similar to the one Taylor had made for his last pre-war car, but the all-independent suspension was new, having a system of wishbones and rubber blocks in compression. It was clothed in a strikingly handsome body reminiscent of a Mercedes-Benz W165, but did not live up to its looks. We can only guess how well it might have gone had one been run by a good team intent on a proper programme of racing and development.

All Altas were made to order and George Abecassis took delivery of GP1 in 1948. It made its debut in the British Empire Trophy on the Isle of Man, and though it showed promising speed it retired after two laps with a broken gearbox. Abecassis crashed it in Bremgarten and it failed to finish in either of its other two races that year. He raced it only three times in 1949 and finished only once and then well off the pace. He had intended to complete a full season with the car, but the H.W.M. project, which used Alta engines, otherwise diverted him. Later GP1 was converted into a Jaguar-engined special and its remains have subsequently been reconstructed for the Donington Collection.

A second car, GP2, was completed for Geoffrey

George Abecassis at the wheel of his Grand Prix Alta in the Isle of Man in May 1948. (**Guy Griffiths**)

Crossley in early 1949 and this had an improved gear-change and sleeker bodywork. Crossley took it to Spa for the Belgian GP and, driving cautiously in his first race abroad, brought it home a distant seventh. He continued to race it until the end of 1951, but achieved little success with it. Crossley, anyway, was an amateur who raced for fun and had no pretensions to be an ace. Still, in 1949, he drove it at Monthléry and took records over 50 km, 50 miles and 100 km.

A third car, GP3, was built for Joe Kelly in 1950 and this had the two-stage supercharging which had been part of Taylor's original thinking. Kelly mainly stuck to Irish races, but in the 1952 Ulster Trophy at Dundrod he came home a fine third, beating both Rosier's Ferrari and Etancelin's Talbot.

Kelly knew the circuit well, of course, but was not an ace, and this performance suggests that in the right hands, backed by a properly run team, the Grand Prix Alta might have amounted to something. As it was, the three cars became an opportunity for an amateur driver to taste the big time from the back of the grid. The only time an Alta was even classified as a finisher in a World Championship event was in the 1950 Belgian GP, when Crossley finished ninth, five laps down. Kelly drove in the 1950 and 1951 British GPs and on both occasions was unclassified, and over 20 laps in arrears. Both GP2 and GP3 were later broken up and the parts used to make specials.

Taylor's thin resources did not allow him to develop his GP cars and he was trapped in the spiral which is always the lot of such a builder: no money = poor results = less money = worse results. Besides he quickly lost interest in F1 in favour of the 2-litre F2. His engines had already enjoyed success with the H.W.M. team (q.v.) and in 1951 he showed his first F2 car, which was made for the Australian Tony Gaze.

Its engine followed usual Alta practice in that it had double overhead camshafts driven by twin roller chains,

Geoffrey Crossley at the wheel of his Grand Prix Alta in the paddock at Silverstone for the European Grand Prix in May 1950. (**Duncan Rabagliati**)

In front of the pits at the European Grand Prix in 1950 is Joe Kelly with his Grand Prix Alta. (**Duncan Rabagliati**)

Gordon Watson's Formula 2 Alta in the 1952 International Trophy at Silverstone. (T. C. March)

but its capacity was now 1970cc (83.5 × 90 mm) and in place of the old blower there were four S.U. carburettors. Chassis and suspension was broadly as before, for the rubber block system had caused no problems, and though it had only 130 bhp on tap, and was on the heavy side, the car was undeniably handsome and looked every inch a racer.

Unfortunately its performance did not match its looks, but F2/1 (Gaze's car) and F2/2 (built for Gordon Watson) could attract starting money on the Continent, although the highest finish either achieved in 1951 were Gaze's eighth places in the Christopher Columbus Centenary race at Genoa and in the F2 German GP. Later in 1951, a third car, which had started life as GP4 but became F2/3, was completed for Anthony Stokes.

Since all the post-war Altas were bought by amateurs it is hard to assess their performance. Stokes, however, drove his car in the 1951 Grenzlandring race, which was more or less a flat-out blind on a stretch of autobahn, and the fact that he could do no better than ninth in a field of B.M.W. specials puts the Alta into perspective.

During 1952 Gaze installed his engine in an H.W.M. chassis and sold on the rest of his Alta, which became a Jaguar-engined special. Watson and Stokes continued to race their cars in minor events, where they were also-rans. They were joined in that department by Oliver Simpson, who bought F2/4.

A more serious customer, who was to be Taylor's last for a complete car, was Peter Whitehead, who took delivery of F2/5, which was the only Alta to be fitted with

Cockpit view of Ray Potter's 2-litre Alta in the paddock at Castle Combe in 1965. Note the prominent 'A' on the boss of the steering wheel. (Anthony Pritchard)

alloy wheels. He raced the Alta in the Paris GP at Monthléry, where it retired with gearbox failure, and in the Monza GP, where he came seventh in his first heat (the marque's best overseas result), but retired in the second heat with a broken float chamber on one of the S.U. carburettors.

Whitehead cast around after the race and decided to fit two twin-choke Webers, which were mounted on long inlet pipes for ram effect. In conjunction with a stubby exhaust pipe he achieved a noticeable increase in power, and back at the works Taylor was to record an extra 20 bhp. Whitehead drove the car in the Reims GP, where it retired with gearbox trouble, and lent it to his half-brother Graham for the British GP. There it finished 12th, five laps down, but only a lap behind Peter's Ferrari. That is another performance which, in the absence of an Alta ever being driven by a top-rate driver, helps to put the marque into perspective.

Peter Whitehead then took it over for the Comminges GP, where he finished fourth, but at La Baule he retired with a broken crankshaft. This effectively ended the career of Alta as a marque. The following year Whitehead installed the engine in a Cooper chassis and enjoyed somewhat better fortune.

Taylor was said to be at work on a V-8 engine for the 2½-litre formula, but this was not made, presumably because it was beyond Alta's resources, and anyway he came to an arrangement to supply 4-cylinder engines to Connaught.

There is a paradox in Alta's post-war history in that it failed as a marque and yet made an enormous contribution to the growth of British motor racing, through the H.W.M. and Connaught teams. Both marques are dealt with at length elsewhere in this book, but in the context of the present story it is as well to remember that H.W.M.s with Alta engines were the first British cars to undertake a serious racing programme on the Continent.

It was, too, an Alta-engined Connaught with which Tony Brooks trounced the works Maseratis in the 1955 Syracuse GP to give Britain its first Grand Prix victory for over 30 years. Even when Connaught withdrew from racing in 1957, the Alta story did not end, for both Paul Emery and Geoffrey Richardson installed Alta engines in Cooper chassis.

By the late 1950s, Alta had been wound up and Geoffrey Taylor himself died in 1966, when he was only 63 years old. Ten years later his son, Michael, attempted to revive the Alta name with an unsuccessful Formula Ford car.

ARZANI-VOLPINI

Egidio Arzani and Gianpolo Volpini, both from Milano, had for some years made cars for the International F3 and the Italian 750cc formula. While they had not exactly taken motor racing by storm they had built a reputation for being sound engineers. A wealthy amateur driver,

Mario Alborghetti, decided that he wanted his own F1 car. The two sides combined.

Arzani and Volpini bought one of the Maserati-Milano (q.v.) 1½-litre supercharged cars from the Ruggeri brothers and prepared it for the 2½-litre F1. Its

The Arzani-Volpini, rebuilt from the Maserati-Milano, seen before its ill-fated debut at Pau in 1955. (Corrado Millanta)

4-cylinder d.o.h.c. engine was bored and stroked to 2492cc (94×90 mm) and four Weber 48DOM carburettors replaced the former two-stage supercharging, and this gave a *claimed* 240 bhp, but in fact it is unlikely it had even 200 bhp.

The base car appears to be the second 1950 Milano, which had a ladder chassis made from large oval tubes. Front suspension was by double wishbones and longitudinal torsion bars connected by a link to the lower wishbone. At the rear was a transverse leaf spring and twin trailing arms. The gearbox was mounted behind the differential and the prop-shaft went from the engine and under the diff to the gearbox. Weighing in at 630 kg, it was a little adipose for its available power. Still it was a handsome, well-made car and a credit to its builders.

The car was tested at Modena and the little team prepared to make its début at Pau in 1955. Alas, Alborghetti was not cut out to be a Grand Prix driver and we will never know how good the car might have been. He qualified slowly, behind even Armagnac's 750cc s/c D.B. He made three pit stops early in the race, the reasons for which are not recorded, and on his 19th lap he lost control at Virage de la Gare and ploughed straight on into the straw bales. The crash injured nine spectators and killed the young driver. The cause of the accident is unknown, but most observers felt that it was driver error.

Later that year the Arzani-Volpini was entered in the Italian GP for Luigi Piotti, but it refused to run properly in practice, was withdrawn from the race, and was never seen again in serious racing, but it still exists and appears in Historic events.

In 1958 the name Volpini appeared again, this time on a Formula Junior car. It was a decent effort, but not quite up to the Taraschi and Stanguellini cars. When the British entered FJ in 1960, Volpini disappeared along with the rest of the Italian makers.

ASTON- BUTTERWORTH

For the 1952 F2 season, an amateur called Bill Aston built a near copy of the 'box-section' Cooper chassis, but with swing axles at the rear. Suspension followed the Cooper pattern with transverse leaf springs and lower wishbones. Aston did not wish to follow the herd and install a Bristol engine, so cast around for an alternative. It seems he would have preferred to use an A.F.M. V-8 engine, but A.F.M. was vague about delivery dates and he eventually settled for Archie Butterworth's air-cooled flat-four unit.

This was the interim A.J.B. unit of 1983cc (87.5×82.5 mm), which was fitted with Steyr barrels and heads and produced about 140 bhp. Since this was a much lower engine than the Bristol unit, the car looked distinctly different from its high-bonneted Cooper cousins.

Another feature which marked it off from the Coopers was the use of Borrani wire wheels, which enhanced its already pleasing lines. Transmission was via a 4-speed M.G. gearbox, and to keep the driver-line as low as possible the prop-shaft passed under the chassis-mounted E.N.V. differential, where the power was transferred upwards by a couple of straight-cut spur gears.

As work on the project progressed, a friend of Bill's, Robin Montgomerie-Charrington, thought it looked promising and ordered a car for himself, though he specified bolt-on Dunlop alloy wheels.

Named the Aston-Butterworths (they should properly have been called 'Cooper-A.J.B.s') they were perhaps the lightest cars in F2 and, initially, could match the pace of some of the Cooper-Bristols, but it was beyond the resources of two enthusiastic amateurs to develop the concept. An early modification was to the rear suspension, when double c/v joints were put into the drive-shafts, making them more like Coopers.

Both cars were plagued by unreliability, but without there being any pattern to it. Montgomerie-Charrington scored the best World Championship result in 1952, when, in the Belgian Grand Prix, he managed to qualify 15th of 22 runners, and faster than the Gordinis of Claes, O'Brien and 'B. Bira' and the Ferrari of Louis Rosier. In the race he ran as high as seventh, but when he came into refuel, the wrong mixture was poured into the tank.

In non-Championship events, the best showing was at Chimay in a large field of privateers, and while Aston retired, Montgomerie-Charrington finished third, despite running out of fuel on his last lap.

Before the end of 1952 Montgomerie-Charrington emigrated to the USA, but Aston persevered and was continually modifying both the engine and chassis, but when he turned up for the Italian GP at Monza he could not even qualify.

The following year, Aston made a few unsuccessful

R. Montgomerie-Charrington at the wheel of his Aston-Butterworth in the 1952 International Trophy at Silverstone. (T. C. March)

appearances with his car, and then put it away. Archie Butterworth is of the opinion that Aston lacked the expertise to install the engine properly and keep it supplied with fuel. While Archie is not an impartial witness, it has to be said that when Aston raced it after 1952, it did often suffer from fuel starvation and sometimes caught fire.

In 1959 Aston sold his car to 'Dickie' Metcalfe, who had it converted into a sports car with a Coventry Climax F.W.A. engine and a stunning body made by Maurice Gomm. This car, now with a supercharged 1500cc Ford engine, is still running, while the Montgomerie-Charrington car passed through several hands and was last heard of being rebuilt with a view to running it in Historic events.

ASTON MARTIN

The post-war competition history of Aston Martin is a story of missed opportunity. It had the advantage of a famous name, its cars were handsome and well made, and it often employed star drivers. These combined to give Aston Martin glamour, some of which still clings, but the company's competition programme was woefully mis-managed.

In the 1950s Aston Martin made sports-racing cars designed to compete in the great road races, yet most of their appearances were in British national events. It's true A.M. made a few appearances in the Mille Miglia up to 1955 and, once, even entered a single car in the Targa Florio, but too often it was content to thrash around Silverstone or Goodwood in 20-lap sprints.

Its engines were never on a par with the best opposition, and even when it brought out a new one it was still behind. Although the fortune of David Brown, its owner,

had been founded on gear making, its transmissions were always poor. Its chassis were out-dated and it was still running ladder-framed cars, while Lotus was building space-frames and Jaguar had a monocoque-section on the D-Type.

While Lotus and Jaguar sought, and found, an advantage in aerodynamics, Aston Martins were *styled*. Aston Martin pioneered no advance in any single area of design, and was generally years behind the best opposition.

It is true that Aston Martin won the World Sports Car Championship in 1959, but that was largely by accident in a year when the opposition was fairly thin. Aston Martin had intended to concentrate on Le Mans, but Stirling Moss persuaded the works to lend him the team spare for the Nürburgring 1000 km, with himself paying all expenses. He won, despite his co-driver putting the car in a

Reg Parnell testing with the DB3S single-seater at Chalgrove in late 1955. (**Duncan Rabagliati**)

genius who flattered the cars.

Every time Aston Martin had a chance to make a breakthrough, it fluffed it. It built DB3S coupés for Le Mans, and these proved slower than the open cars. This was discovered at the race because nobody had the nous to take one up the A1 in the early hours to see if the idea worked.

Aston Martin was fundamentally flawed and nowhere better is this sorry tale of incompetence illustrated than in its Grand Prix project. The firm first considered building a Grand Prix car in 1951 using a 2-litre version of the 6-cylinder, 2.6-litre, LB6 engine installed in a modified DB3 (sports-racing) frame. The project apparently got some way, but Robert Eberan von Eberhorst, the chief designer, was offended by the compromise and it was scrapped. John Heath, who had been flying the flag on the Continent with his H.W.M. team, asked to buy the engine, but David Brown refused.

When the 2½-litre formula was announced, Aston Martin again considered modifying an engine and chassis, this time a DB3S, and went some way to completing it. Again von Eberhorst was against the idea. Then in 1955 Reg Parnell asked if he could complete it and take it to New Zealand. Originally intended to have a 3-litre supercharged LB6 engine, this was changed to a 2.5-litre normally aspirated engine when the blown engine broke in testing. In practice for the New Zealand GP it threw a rod and was withdrawn, while, with a new engine, Parnell could do no better than fourth in the

ditch. After Aston Martin won Le Mans by being reliable, thanks to Moss' Nürburgring performance it found itself with a chance of clinching the title if it entered the Tourist Trophy at Goodwood. Again, Moss' virtuosity won the day, and the Championship.

In fact all its major victories, with the exception of Le Mans, were won by Moss and/or Brooks, two drivers of

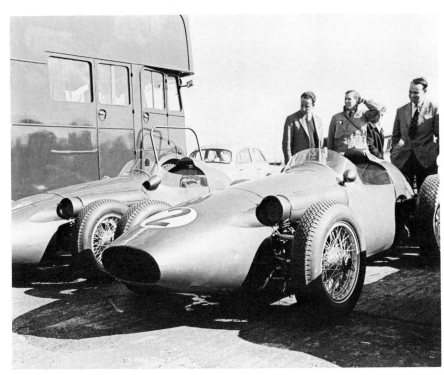

The DBR4s in the paddock at Silverstone in May 1959 for their debut in the International Trophy race. (**T. C. March**)

A cockpit view of the DBR4. (T. C. March)

Lady Wigram Trophy. This chassis later formed the basis of the second R.R.A. (q.v.).

When work began on the Aston Martin DBR1 in 1956 a parallel F1 project began using the improved 6-cylinder RB6 engine, which debuted at Le Mans that year in 2½-litre form. As usual with Aston Martin it took an age to complete, but it was ready for testing late in 1957. This means it took two years to complete an obsolete chassis to take an existing engine and gearbox.

During that same two-year period Lotus had dominated the 1100cc class with the Lotus Eleven, entered F2, won the Index of Performance at Le Mans, set several International speed records, started production of the Seven, introduced the Elite, and was preparing for its F1 debut. In his spare time, Chapman had also designed a chassis for Vanwall and sorted out the B.R.M. P25. 'Nuff said.

Although the DBR4/250 was ready to tackle the 1958 F1 season, it was put on ice for a year while Aston Martin tackled the WSCC, which consisted of all of six events in which Aston Martin filed a total of 12 entries. How the team ever thought it could lose a year of development, even if it had not been overtaken by the rear-engined revolution, remains a mystery. The car, a parts bin special begun in 1956, was ready to race in 1959.

Aston Martin's team manager, John Wyer, has claimed that his car was faster than the Vanwall which won six of the ten 1958 World Championship rounds. If, however, we look at the practice times for the two races where comparison is possible, Zandvoort and Monza, we find that the *slowest* time set by a Vanwall in 1958 was quicker than the *fastest* Aston Martin in 1959, and at Monza the difference was 2.5 seconds.

The DBR4/250 had a conventional, if overweight, triangulated space-frame and the prototype was first fitted with unequal-length wishbones and torsion bar front suspension similar to that used on the DBR3 (which raced only once), but by the time the cars appeared in competition a coil spring and wishbones set-up, similar to the DB4 road car, had been adopted in its place. Rear suspension was similar to the DBR1, with a three-piece

Roy Salvadori with DBR4/3 which he retired with valve trouble in the 1959 Italian Grand Prix at Monza. (British Petroleum)

In the 1960 British Grand Prix Roy Salvadori struggled round with his DBR5 before retiring with handling problems. Note the attitudes of the four wheels. (T. C. March)

de Dion tube sprung by longitudinal torsion bars and located by twin trailing arms and a Watts linkage. Its one claim to distinction was that it was the last new Grand Prix design to have a de Dion axle.

The engine was a 2493cc (83 × 76.8 mm) version of the d.o.h.c. RB6 engine fed by three double-choke Weber 50 DCO carburettors and it used the A1.95-degree twin-plug cylinder head. Its maximum power, 250 bhp at 7800 rpm, was fed through a 5-speed trans-axle and Girling disc brakes were fitted outboard all round.

Two cars, in the hands of Carroll Shelby and Roy Salvadori, made their debut in the 1959 International Trophy and Salvadori came second to Brabham's Cooper and set a new lap record. It looked a promising start, but the engines had been revving to 8000 rpm and the big end bearings wore rapidly. Shelby retired with bearing failure and Salvadori's would not have lasted much longer.

This was a mystery, since the 3-litre sports car version had always been reliable. Months were spent working on the problem, during which time the drivers were limited to 7000 rpm, before the problem was easily solved by boring the holes through which oil circulated in different places in the crankshaft.

In the Dutch GP both drivers qualified well off the pace and retired with con-rod failure due to the bearing problem. Aston Martin missed the French race, but re-appeared for the British GP at Aintree. After practice Salvadori sat on the front row, having equalled Brabham's pole time, while Shelby was sixth fastest and just ahead of Moss' B.R.M. Shelby eventually retired with a broken valve, while Salvadori came home sixth. Ominously, three of the five cars ahead of him, including the winner, were Coopers.

Portugal was next, and on the Monsanto circuit both cars started near the back, a full 11 seconds off the pace. Still they soldiered on and Salvadori finished sixth with Shelby eighth, three and four laps respectively down on Moss' winning Cooper. At Monza again they were at the rear end of the grid, considerably off the pace, and while Salvadori retired with a broken valve, Shelby finished tenth, two laps down on Moss' Cooper.

Some teams might have noticed that so far as the front-engined Grand Prix car was concerned, the writing was on the wall – in block capitals. Colin Chapman, for example, went away and designed a whole range of rear-engined cars, which changed motor racing once and for all, and even Ferrari began work on a rear-engined car.

Some teams might have grasped that all other things being equal, a heavy car was slower than a light one and a car with a large frontal area was slower than one with a small frontal area.

Aston Martin, however, vigorously met the challenge with another obsolete car, the DBR5/250. True, the space-frame was smaller and lighter, and the gear-change was improved, by adopting the Maserati 5M-60 trans-axle (so much for David Brown gears), but it was still a hopelessly dated design. The original torsion bar front suspension was fitted to both the DBR4 and the DBR5, there was a two-piece prop-shaft to lower the drive train, and a new de Dion tube went in front and not behind the final drive.

While most of the effort was being pursued down a blind alley, time was found to sketch out a rear-engined car which got as far as a chassis frame. This was not a new design, but a cut-and-shut DBR4. Naturally, it was not completed.

For 1960, new 80-degree cylinder heads were fitted, but the design office made a huge error in the inlet porting and the result was a drop in power. Instead of reverting to the 95-degree heads which were still available, it was decided to try to get around the problem by using fuel injection for the first time. A Lucas system was installed on the first DBR5 and this had the effect of increasing power, so it was only 5 bhp *down* on the previous year. This is the team which thought it could have beaten Vanwall and Maserati....

One of the DBR4s (still fitted with Webers) and the first DBR5 appeared at the 1960 International Trophy for Salvadori and Trintignant. Salvadori's race ended after four laps with a misfire, while Trintignant could do no better than tenth. Salvadori was entered in the DBR5 in the Dutch GP and returned a practice time which would have seen him on the last row of the grid. The organizers had invited 21 cars and promised starting money to the fastest 15, of which the Aston Martin was not one. Instead of accepting its place as a make-weight, Aston Martin withdrew its entry.

Nothing daunted, for the British GP at Silverstone Aston Martin abandoned fuel injection and brought out a new DBR5 with independent rear suspension. Far from being an improvement this made matters worse and Salvadori did well to qualify in mid-field (five seconds off the pace), though he eventually retired with steering problems. The earlier DBR5 was entered for Maurice Trintignant, and he brought it home 11th, five laps down.

So ended the sorry story of Aston Martin's F1 project. It was not a case of a good car appearing too late, the fact is that Aston Martin's racing department moved with elephantine slowness and could not keep up with a new quick-witted generation of constructors epitomized by Cooper and Lotus. No matter when a new Aston Martin appeared, it was likely to be out of date.

Ironically, when versions of the DBR4 have appeared in Historic racing, they have often given a good account of themselves against the likes of 250F Maseratis and their performance appears to back up the claim that they could have been contenders. They have, however, invariably been fitted with 3-litre 'Tasman' engines.

Acknowledgements to Chris Nixon's *Racing With The David Brown Aston Martins* (Transport Bookman Publications Ltd), while stressing that Chris Nixon does not necessarily share this writer's view of the marque.

B.M.W./BRISTOL

As a maker of cars, B.M.W.'s history began in 1928, when it marketed the 'Dixie', an Austin Seven made under licence. In 1933 came its first 6-cylinder design, the 303, and by degrees B.M.W. began to make a name for itself as a maker of medium-sized saloons and sports cars. From 1934 onwards its 319 sports model began to appear in competition results, first as a 1½-litre car, then as a 2-litre, and this led the firm to look seriously at competition and to explore ways of increasing performance.

One of its main designers, Fritz Fiedler, was put in charge of chassis development, while Rudolf Schleicher looked for ways to improve engine performance. Since the company was still making its way, Schleicher was constrained by economics and the need to use existing components. His solution was to create a new cylinder head, cast from aluminium, which gave most of the advantages of a d.o.h.c. head but without major re-tooling.

It used the existing camshaft, which had been driving a conventional push-rod valve system, to activate six push-rods to short rockers which operated the inlet valves (inclined at 100 degrees to the exhaust valves). Another six push-rods went to rockers which then operated short push-rods across the top of the head (in alloy tubes) to another set of rockers which activated the exhaust valves.

In 1936 this engine of 1971cc (66 × 96 mm) was fitted to Fiedler's revised chassis and so was born the B.M.W. 328, a car which established new standards in the 2-litre class. By 1939 these units were delivering a reliable 130-140 bhp in racing trim and special 328s swept their class in racing and won the 1940 Mille Miglia (Brescia Grand Prix) outright.

Pre-war A.F.N. Ltd, makers of Frazer Nash cars, had been the British B.M.W. importer and had, in fact, marketed them under the name Frazer Nash-B.M.W. During the war, H. J. Aldington of A.F.N. Ltd reached an agreement with Sir George White and Reginald Verdon-Smith of the Bristol Aircraft Company to join forces and market a new 'Bristol' car once hostilities ceased.

Aldington was a member of one of the war reparations panels which went to Germany and brought back useful pieces of technology which Britain could exploit. These trips delivered various B.M.W. components, which would form the basis of the Bristol 400 coupé, among them the 328 engine. Aldington was also able to have Fritz Fiedler released from custody, and he came to England to work for A.F.N.

The arrangement between Bristol and A.F.N. was short-lived, one reason being that Bristol was content with 80 bhp while A.F.N. wanted about 50 per cent more. As part of their severance agreement, Bristol agreed to supply A.F.N. with FNS (Frazer Nash Special) versions of the engine, which had been developed by Fiedler. This was supposed to be an exclusive arrangement, but somehow FNS-spec engines managed to leak from Bristol to selected customers.

While the Bristol engine was essentially the B.M.W. 328, they were not identical in every detail for, as one of the world's leading aircraft makers, Bristol knew a thing or two about engineering and the B.M.W. drawings first went through the Bristol drawing office. Still, whether the engine was called Bristol or B.M.W., it provided the power for a lot of British and German 2-litre sports and F2 cars

Although B.M.W. was in no position to make 328 engines in the immediate post-war period, that part of the company which found itself in East Germany did continue to make pre-war B.M.W.s, which were marketed under the name E.M.W. (Eisenacher Motoren-Werke), so it was possible to obtain new B.M.W. 328 engines before B.M.W. resurrected the unit for its stop-gap model, the 501 introduced in 1952. Eventually B.M.W. took its East German cousins to court on an issue of copyright (E.M.W. was using the B.M.W. logo but with red quarters instead of blue) and E.M.W. changed its name to I.F.A. and built a version of the D.K.W. Sonderklasse, which eventually transmuted into the Wartburg.

There is a small irony in the Bristol/B.M.W./A.F.N. link. The 328 had been so successful that B.M.W. had become profitable enough pre-war to be able to progress some way to a no-compromise unit, a d.o.h.c. 2.5-litre straight six and, post-war, had already come to regard the 328 as obsolete. Aldington had tried to interest Bristol in this engine, but Bristol had invested too much effort in the 328 to be interested. B.M.W. itself was in no position to fund development.

That engine, had it been adopted, would have been a much better bet in competition than the 328. Stroked, it might have been a decent F2 engine and it might even have helped a few teams into $2\frac{1}{2}$-litre F1. Bristol itself built a team of racing coupés which it ran at Le Mans and Reims with considerable success and in 1955 the company was planning an F1 car, but after the Le Mans tragedy it withdrew from racing.

B. M. W.   SPECIALS

Long before Germany was re-admitted to international motor sport (a ban insisted upon by France, the only country to sign an armistice with Hitler) German enthusiasts were organizing races and building cars. Between 1948 and 1954 there were annual series of F2 races in both parts of Germany, and while details remain tantalizingly fragmentary, cars derived from B.M.W. 328 components enjoyed a virtual monopoly. Some pre-war cars, notably a couple of Maseratis, were also raced and Cisitalias and, even, a Ferrari began to appear in 1949.

There are enormous gaps in the history of those early German F2 races, which were conducted under difficult circumstances and for which nobody bothered to keep records or even results, let alone entries and practice sessions. There was not, either, a specialist German motor sport magazine to keep a tally.

Two makes using B.M.W. components, Veritas and A.F.M., enjoyed success not only in Germany but also in other parts of Europe, while a third maker, D.A.M.W. (*aka* E.M.W. and A.W.E.), made probably the best B.M.W.-based cars of all, but politics meant that they only ever raced in the two parts of Germany and in

Eastern Bloc countries. These makers receive separate entries.

Some constructors merely gave their cars the name 'B.M.W. Special', which is not a great deal of help to an historian. We cannot even be sure which of the cars that raced in some F2 races were single-seaters or, even, merely stripped-down B.M.W. 328s. Within the terms of reference of this book it does not matter what was racing in East Germany in 1948, but despite our best efforts, details of some cars which appeared in European Grands Prix in 1952-4 remain hazy.

For the record, the following are among the B.M.W. Specials which appeared in International F2 and, even, F1 races up to the end of 1954.

Grifzu

Strictly speaking this falls outside the remit of this entry, but is mentioned because the East German driver Paul Grifzu was a considerable figure in German motor racing post-war. His special was the most consistently successful East German car in 1951 and the early part of 1952, when Grifzu himself was killed in a race at Dresden. The car continued to be entered by Grifzu's widow for other drivers and was still enjoying success as late as 1954.

Heck

A rear-engined special (*Heck* means 'rear' or 'tail' in German) driven by Ernst Klodwig in the 1952 and 1953 German Grands Prix. On both occasions it qualified at the back of the grid, over two minutes off the pace, but it did manage to finish in the latter year, three laps down in 15th place.

Jicey

Announced in 1948, this was a French attempt to build a production F2 car and even before the first had been completed, a British agent was appointed. It used a B.M.W. 328 engine together with a French gearbox and these were installed in a welded deep-section chassis made of light alloy. Front suspension was by Lancia-style sliding pillars while the independent rear layout used double wishbones.

At least two cars were built but their racing careers were spasmodic. Georges Berger ran his in the 1950 German (F2) Grand Prix and finished ninth, three laps behind Ascari's Ferrari, but that seems to be the *marque's* only appearance in a major race.

Eugène Martin had another Jicey and his best showing was fifth in the 1952 Pau GP, but 10 laps down. The ex-Berger car was still appearing in minor races as late as 1954 when it ran in the GP des Frontières at Chimay (driver, Roger Meunier, retired first lap) and the Circuit de Cadours where Marcel Balsa finished fifth, last, and lapped, in his heat and retired in the final with a broken shock absorber.

Monnier

Maurice Monnier built this wire-wheeled single-seater in 1950, but it only occasionally appeared in races and perhaps its best result was Monnier's ninth in the 1953 Avusrennen by which time it was fitted with a Bristol engine. Others also drove it, someone called Noreille came fifth in a minor race at Monthléry in May 1953 and Georges Mulnard drove it in the 1953 Grand Prix des Frontières where it failed to make any impression at all. The following year it was entered in the same event by its new owner, Pierrre Bastien where it was over a minute off the pace and retired around half-distance with a broken oil pipe.

Orley Special

A Veritas. Adolf Brudes, a pre-war driver, raced it in the 1952 Eifelrennen, but retired with engine trouble after three laps.

R. G. Special

Named for its owner, Roger Gerbout, this started life in 1950 with a Lombard engine and was an occasional, unsuccessful, entrant in F2 races. Fitted with a B.M.W. unit, it appeared in the 1954 Grand Prix des Frontières where it qualified last by a big margin and retired early in the race.

Reif

East German special driven with some success by Rudolf Krause in his home championship. It ran in the 1953 German GP, where Krause qualified it ahead of, among others, a couple of private Ferraris, but lasted only three laps in the race itself.

B. R. M.

When B.R.M. made its debut at the 1950 International Trophy, Raymond Sommer let in the clutch and the car lurched forward — for a few inches. A drive-shaft had snapped. As it was wheeled away, the huge crowd which had gathered to see the British 'wonder car' hooted and jeered, and some threw pennies at it. The press had a field day and made much of the fact that children had contributed their pocket money towards the dismal failure, an inaccurate reference to a fan club, the B.R.M. Association. It became the butt of cartoons and music hall comedians enshrined it along with Wigan Pier.

One problem was that because of the name, many assumed it was an official British project, like the French national efforts. That did a lot of damage to British racing, yet also on the grid for the International Trophy was the H.W.M. team which had just come back from its first Continental raid with honour.

Something which was overlooked was that the car failed not because of a design fault but because the drive-shaft had been made wrongly by the company which donated it, and that fact points to one reason for failure. The team was dependent on the generosity of outside suppliers.

During World War II, Raymond Mays and Palin 'Peter' Berthon, who had collaborated on the E.R.A. project, had planned a new British GP car to take on the world and formed a company, Automobile Developments Ltd, as a starting point. When peace returned Mays hawked his idea around British industry and obtained some support. Even the government lent moral support to the idea and *The Times* ran a leader in praise of it.

One thing about the B.R.M. project which is fequently missed is that the excitement surrounding it was of enormous benefit to the embryo British motor racing tradition which was growing after World War II. The very idea that the Brits could build a world-beater was novel, and the fact that the government supported the idea of such a scheme smoothed the progress of others with more limited ambitions.

In 1947 the British Motor Racing Research Trust was set up to guide the project and help with cash and/or components. Mays converted some outbuildings at his home in Lincolnshire into a design office and from it emerged a very interesting design.

Nobody who has heard it will ever forget the exhaust note from the 1496cc (49.53 × 47.8 mm) supercharged 135-degree V-16 d.o.h.c. engine, but it was a seriously flawed unit. Auto Union and Alfa Romeo had both made V-16 GP units, but they had years of experience and vast resources. It was beyond the competence of the small team at Bourne.

The B.R.M. engine was designed in four blocks of four cylinders with a half-speed power take-off in the centre, where the drive for the two-stage centrifugal supercharger was also situated. It was designed to deliver up to 600 bhp, but it took years to achieve even 440 bhp and there were several reasons for this.

The first is that the engine's breathing was more restricted than had been expected, and to compensate for this, the supercharger had to be run at a higher speed than had been anticipated. Fuel injection had been planned, but this proved a failure and the car raced only on three-inch S.U. carburettors, which were more restrictive than it was thought injection would be.

Development of the engine took longer than expected partly because the firms supplying the project were many and it only took one to be late or half-hearted and everthing was held up, and it also proved very difficult to machine the cast-iron wet cylinder liners with enough precision to prevent coolant leaking into the cylinders. These problems were compounded by poor management at B.R.M.

The engine was installed in a frame with twin parallel main members braced by sheet steel and it drove through a 5-speed gearbox mounted transversely at the rear. Suspension was similar to the E Type E.R.A., being twin trailing links at the front (à la Auto Union), but these were sprung by Lucas air struts, which also sprung the de Dion rear axle which followed the layout of the late pre-war Mercedes-Benz cars, with a rotating tube located laterally by a sliding block in the differential housing and longitudinally by torque arms. The 14-inch three-shoe drum brakes were made by Girling.

It was not until late in 1949 that a T15 first ran and it looked very smart with its smooth bodywork and small air intake. Testing, however, showed up severe cooling problems and when the cars raced they had a much larger radiator, which did nothing for the aerodynamics, and louvres cut everywhere.

Testing must also have demonstrated the desperately narrow power band and far less than the vast amount of power that was hoped for. In 1950 the engine produced 330 bhp at 10,250 rpm. One quite often hears that a narrow power band was inevitable when running with a centrifugal supercharger, but above 25 lb boost a centrifugal system has more potential than a Roots-type blower and as boost increases so the power band widens

Unfortunately it was not until 1953, four or five years too late, that the engine was running on 56 lb boost and producing a reasonable curve with usable power between 5500 and 11,000 rpm. Then, in racing trim, the

Raymond Sommer at the wheel of the V-16 B.R.M. on its debut at the International Trophy at Silverstone in 1950. To the right of the car are Raymond Mays and Peter Berthon. **(Guy Griffiths)**

unit was developing 440 bhp at 11,000 rpm, which was little better than the normally aspirated 4½-litre Ferrari, which had much better torque.

The figures I have quoted may surprise some, for quite often one reads that the engine gave 550 or even 600 bhp at 12,000 rpm. I have taken my figures from a booklet Laurence Pomeroy wrote in 1953 with access to works testing figures, and these are somewhat different to those quoted in PR handouts. If the engine was indeed capable of up to 600 bhp in 1953 it would have reflected in the cars' performance and they would not have had any trouble coping with the Vandervell Ferrari, at least along the straights.

The project lurched along, constantly threatening to appear and constantly disappointing, and to make matters worse there had been much hype about the project. Had there been less talk of a 'world-beater' there would have been less reaction when it failed, but when it did fail the reaction was predictable and not unjustified. Two cars were entered for the 1950 International Trophy, but in testing both suffered cracked cylinder liners. Aware of the enormous pressure upon them, B.R.M. put in an enormous effort and got one car to the start. It was a close run thing and it was too late to practice, but Sommer started from the back of the grid and then, as mentioned earlier, let in the clutch and humiliation followed.

Five weeks later there was a glimmer of hope when

Reg Parnell used the car to win two short races at Goodwood, but against negligible opposition. The popular press, however, raised hopes and the car was a 'world-beater' again. Public pressure caused the team to enter the Spanish GP at Barcelona and Parnell was terrific for just over a lap, when the drive to his supercharger sheared. Peter Walker in the other car stalled on the line, but was up to fifth when he retired with a leak from the gearbox.

The B.R.M. Trust squabbled and proved the rule that the collective intelligence of a committee equates to the IQ of the least intelligent person minus one point for each person present. There was not enough money to do the job properly and there was not enough experience and competence. 1951 was supposed to be the big year, but the cars only appeared once, at the British GP. That was the fourth race of the WC season, but there were so many problems with the car that B.R.M. did not even enter a race until the French GP in July, and scratched from that. At Silverstone both cars had to start from the back of the grid because they had not practised. Driven by Reg Parnell and Peter Walker they finished fifth and seventh, five and six laps respectively behind the winner. Both drivers were in poor condition at the end, for their feet were burned and blistered by the exhaust − and that after five years of the project.

The cars turned up for the Italian GP, when the

Reg Parnell on his way, painfully, to fifth place with the V-16 B.R.M. in the 1951 British Grand Prix at Silverstone. (Guy Griffiths)

A view of the crammed bonnet of the V-16 B.R.M. This photograph was taken in 1952. (Guy Griffiths)

organizers rightly refused to accept the entry of the works tester, Ken Richardson, a man with no racing experience. Hans Stuck then tested the car, but the trans-axle seized. On the grounds of safety it was decided to scratch both entries. As a result the FIA decided to make F2 the World Championship class, for without B.R.M. there would otherwise be only Ferrari and one team can't make a race.

Thus B.R.M. effectively ended its own career. Over the next four years the cars improved, a Mk II version was made and run, disc brakes were fitted, and B.R.M.s were often successful in club races provided there was only amateur opposition. It was a farce, and while Tony Vandervell, a former supporter, went off and created the Vanwall, which really was a world-beater, B.R.M. lurched along.

Stirling Moss is on record as saying it is the worse car he has ever driven and apart from unpredictable handling, poor steering, and its peaky engine, it did not even give the driver enough room to work in. Other top-line drivers such as Fangio and Gonzalez also tried taming the beast, without success, and with talent like that behind the wheel B.R.M. had no excuses.

Sir Alfred Owen, head of the large private company Rubery Owen, had been a long-time supporter of the project and eventually he bought the company outright. It remained under the direction of Mays and Berthon.

Mays was well-intentioned and nobody can take away from him the personal effort and sacrifices he made to try to get Britain on top, but wishing something is not the same as doing it. In a later book, packed with factual howlers, Mays declared that one of the problems the project had to contend with was too much publicity, but the fact is that he generated most of it.

While B.R.M. amused itself winning races at Turnberry and Snetterton, it turned half-heartedly to the 2½-litre F1. Nearly four years after the announcement of the category, it was ready to race, with the usual excuses that it was dipping its toe in the water. In the meantime B.R.M. bought a Maserati 250F, which it fitted with disc brakes, but even this ran only ten times in three years.

It was not until the *Daily Telegraph* Trophy at Aintree on 3 September, 1955, that it was ready to race its new car. In contrast to the T15, the P25 was a simple device. It had a 4-cylinder d.o.h.c. engine of 2497cc (102.87×74.93 mm), designed by Stuart Tresilian, which initially gave 248 bhp at 9000 rpm. It was installed in a space-frame with front suspension by double wishbones and oleo-pneumatic struts and a de Dion rear axle suspended by a transverse leaf spring and oleo-pneumatic struts and located by twin radius arms.

Why on earth Bethron felt that an otherwise conventional design would be improved by dispensing with metal springs when his previous design had been so appalling remains a mystery. Even more of a mystery is why he decided to complicate the issue by stipulating that rear braking should be by a single disc brake mounted on the back of the combined 4-speed gearbox/final drive.

Peter Collins should have made the start at Aintree, but he crashed in practice and so did not debut the car until three weeks later, at the Oulton Park Gold Cup. He was not particularly quick in practice, but in good company he slotted his car into third after four laps, and retired soon after when his oil pressure fell. Later it was said that the gauge had been faulty. B.R.M. had at last made its debut in the 2½-litre formula, but let it be noted that it had had exactly the same notice as everyone else and in the meantime Mercedes-Benz had come in, raced a bit, and had withdrawn, having redefined the parameters of the sport.

For 1956 B.R.M. was able to sign up Hawthorn and Brooks, both Grand Prix winners, who had been in their first season of club racing when the 2½-litre formula was announced. It also replaced the original Dunlop disc brakes with Lockheed discs.

Their first race was the Richmond Trophy at Goodwood and Hawthorn stormed into the lead from third place on the grid, but was soon overtaken by Scott-Brown's Connaught and Moss' Maserati. Still, he held third until a wheel came off and the car rolled over, fortunately without harming him. Brooks retired early on with no oil pressure. Hawthorn led the Aintree 200 for a lap or so and then his brakes failed completely, but Brooks brought the other car home second to Moss' Maserati, albeit a lap down with fading brakes.

A single car was entered for Hawthorn in the International Trophy at Silverstone; he led the race for the first 13 laps, and broke the lap record, but then coasted to a halt with a sheared magneto drive.

Two cars appeared for the Monaco GP, where they were over-geared and would not run cleanly. Worse, their brakes were giving trouble, so having qualified near the back of the grid they were withdrawn. Entries were filed for the Belgian and French, but B.R.M. scratched from both because two and a half years into the formula they were still not ready to race. At Monaco it was discovered that the large sodium-filled valves had distorted and so they were replaced by solid valves, which restricted the engine to 8000 rpm.

Ron Flockhart joined the team for the British GP (he retired after two laps with stripped timing gears) and Hawthorn's car had three inches added to its wheelbase. For five laps Hawthorn and Brooks led, but then Brooks started to fall back and Hawthorn's race ended after 23 laps with oil leaking from his transmission. In the meantime Brooks' throttle broke and he called in to have it fixed. Going through Abbey on lap 40 the throttle stuck open, Brooks went into a slide, the car hit the bank, throwing the driver out, and then had the good manners to burn out.

After that Brooks refused to have anything further to do with the beast and Hawthorn was thoroughly cheesed off as well. B.R.M. withdrew for the rest of the year, and when they reappeared in 1957 the cars had the longer wheelbase and high stressed sides around the cockpit. Flockhart and Salvadori were signed on and the cars made their first appearance at the Easter Goodwood Meeting. Salvadori's race lasted less than a lap, when his brakes seized. Flockhart managed third place, a lap down to Lewis-Evans' Connaught, after surviving two spins caused by a partly locked rear suspension.

B.R.M. then called in Colin Chapman to advise and, surprise, surprise, he recommended coil springs all round. There was not enough time to implement the improvements for the Monaco GP, where the cars still suffered from locking brakes. Salvadori just failed to qualify and he joined the exodus from B.R.M. Flockhart,

however, made the start and was fifth after 60 laps, and behind Brabham's 2-litre Cooper, when his engine's timing gears stripped.

At Rouen the young American Herbert MacKay Fraser was brought in and he was running seventh when the engine broke. Flockhart had gone long before when he slid on some oil and crashed heavily. Poor MacKay Fraser was to die in the F2 race at Reims the following week.

With Flockhart injured, B.R.M. desperately sought drivers for the British GP and suffered the humiliation of being turned down by Archie Scott-Brown, who desperately wanted a drive, but not at any price. Eventually Jack Fairman and Les Leston were employed and they were predictably slow until they retired with engine trouble.

Then Jean Behra did a deal with the works to allow him a car for the Caen GP, where serious opposition was conspicuously absent. B.R.M. sent two cars, and when Harry Schell's Maserati packed up he was loaned the second. Behra's experience was invaluable in fine-tuning the car and he and Schell entertained the crowd by swapping the lead. Schell eventually retired with engine

Mike Hawthorn with the B.R.M. P25 in the 1956 International Trophy at Silverstone. He led but retired when the engine cut out. (T. C. March)

trouble, but Behra went on to win by eight seconds from Salvadori's 2-litre Cooper.

B.R.M.'s next race was the International Trophy at Silverstone, where, against negligible opposition, Behra, Schell and Flockhart scored a 1-2-3, but the best one can say is that they finished, for, in practice, Tony Brooks had lapped 1.4 seconds faster than any of them in a 2-litre Cooper. Flockhart and Bonnier drove in the Modena GP and both retired. Then Flockhart and Trintignant were entered in the non-Championship Moroccan GP, which had a full WC field, and although Flockhart retired, Trintignant finished a strong third – ahead of Fangio's Maserati.

At last there was a glimmer of hope, and since Maserati had withdrawn there were good drivers on the market. For 1958 B.R.M. was able to sign Behra and Schell and, moreover, the stipulation that cars be run on Av-gas was an advantage to teams running a 4-cylinder engine. A new space-frame was designed and the front suspension changed so that it worked in better harmony with Chapman's modified rear. In addition the engine was redesigned with a five-bearing crankshaft instead of the previous three-bearing crank.

1958 saw the team start in better shape, but disappointment came at its début at Goodwood. Behra and Schell had been quick in practice, but both went out early with brake failure; in Behra's case it involved the demolition of the chicane. Behra was quick in the Aintree 200, but again retired with brake trouble. This was cured by discarding the servo system (which was prone to sticking) and mounting the fluid reservoir on a flexible mounting.

This seemed to have a positive effect and Behra actually led the International Trophy at Silverstone until a stone smashed his goggles. He pitted to get a new pair and have some of the glass removed from his face and went on to work his way up from 11th to fourth at the end. It was a moral victory. While Behra had been in the pits, Flockhart had led until being taken out by a back marker.

Behra led the Monaco GP until a brake pipe fractured and Schell finished sixth after a carburettor float chamber had stuck open. In the Dutch GP Schell and Behra finished second and third, and Schell took fifth in the Belgian, with Behra retiring with loss of oil pressure. They were fast but out of luck in the French GP at Reims (Behra with fuel pump trouble after leading, Schell with overheating and Trintignant with a broken oil pipe).

In the British GP, Behra found his handling awry and retired. It was discovered that he had hit one of the Silverstone hares and a leg bone from the deceased had pierced a rear tyre. Schell, second fastest in practice, was a little tired and could only make fifth, but now fifth was 'only'. Both cars retired from the German GP, Behra was fourth and Schell sixth in the Portuguese, all three failed to finish the Italian GP (Bonnier had joined the team) and for the Moroccan GP B.R.M. had four cars with Flockhart back in the fold. He and Behra both retired,

Jack Fairman, a hasty recruit to the B.R.M. team, in the 1957 British Grand Prix from which he retired with engine problems. (T. C. March)

but Bonnier and Schell came fourth and fifth.

It had been a mixed season and Cooper finished ahead of B.R.M. in the inaugural World Manufacturers' Championship. Behra would have won the International Trophy, which had a very strong field, but for the shattered goggles, and while the cars retired too often, at least they were at the sharp end of the field.

Behra, who had contributed a lot to improving the cars' handling (Moss has called the B.R.M. P25 the best-handling front-engined F1 car of all), had had enough of their unreliability and joined Ferrari, and in his place came Jo Bonnier. Stirling Moss arranged to have a B.R.M. engine in a Cooper chassis and also agreed to drive a P25 on occasion. Late in the day B.R.M. was slowly discarding its rotten reputation.

During 1958 the cars' engines had often suffered overheating and loss of power and these problems were tackled, but not cured, over the winter months. It was not until the end of 1959 that B.R.M. discovered faults in the cooling system which caused this problem. It had not been apparent during the few races run in 1955-57, because then the cars used alcohol-based fuels, which have inherent cooling properties. For 1959, Dunlop disc brakes were re-adopted and the bodywork tidied up to give reduced frontal area.

Schell and Bonnier came third and fourth in the Richmond Trophy at Goodwood, retired in the Aintree 200 and missed the International Trophy at Silverstone, where Moss and Flockhart drove instead. Moss led the

first three laps and then the brakes failed completely and he had to spin it to a stop. Flockhart, however, had a trouble-free race and finished a strong third, lapping Phil Hill's Ferrari. Schell, Flockhart and Bonnier all retired from the Monaco GP with brake problems, without ever threatening the leaders, but at Zandvoort Bonnier drove superbly, setting pole and never running below second, to score B.R.M.'s first major victory.

The euphoria was deserved, and enjoyed, but it was short-lived. It was the single swallow which does not make the summer. Flockhart came sixth in the French GP, Schell fourth in the British and Bonnier fifth in the odd German GP run in two heats at Avus. Then Schell was fourth in Portugal and all three cars were unplaced at Monza. Bruce Halford joined Flockhart for the Silver City Trophy at Snetterton and there Flockhart won from Brabham's Cooper with Halford third. That ended the works team's year, since B.R.M. decided not to enter the US GP.

Thus B.R.M. ended 1959 with its solitary win and without showing similar form in any other race. Moss, however, had been impressed by the car he had driven at Silverstone and proposed a deal whereby he had one for selected races in 1959, but it was entered by B.R.P. B.R.M. accepted gladly, but the implication was clear: Moss did not trust B.R.M. to prepare the car properly, and after his close shave in the International Trophy few blamed him.

Thus a P25 in the bright near-yellow green of B.R.P.

B.R.M.'s first major win did not come until the 1959 Dutch Grand Prix at Zandvoort where Joakim Bonnier drove this car to victory. (**Autosport**)

appeared in the French GP. As an aside, there is no such colour as British Racing Green outside of a paint catalogue and *any* shade of green represents Britain. Equally, Scots teams which paint their cars blue and white are wrong to use Austria's racing colours. Scotland's racing colour has always been green, for the Scots count as British.

At Reims Moss ran as high as second, and set fastest lap, but eventually the clutch went. Then, running third and attempting to take second, he made a rare unforced error and spun and, without a clutch, could not get going again. He drove the car in the British GP at Aintree, was delayed by a slipping clutch, a long stop to change tyres and fuel feed problems, but brought it home second. Hans Herrmann had the car at Avus and not long into the second heat the brakes failed (again) and he crashed. Herrmann was thrown out unharmed, but the car rolled and rolled and destroyed itself. Thus the B.R.M.-B.R.P. collaboration lasted for just three races.

Although B.R.M. had lagged behind in technical innovation, at least that which actually worked, midway through 1959 it had seen the writing on the wall for the front-engined GP car and set to work to make a rear-engined car.

For 1960 B.R.M. retained Bonnier and also signed

up Graham Hill and Dan Gurney. Only Bonnier and Hill were entered in the Argentine GP, both in P25s. They were quick in practice and even ran 1-2 for a time before Graham dropped out with a broken valve spring. Bonnier not only led, but lapped the entire field, and then suffered a broken valve spring with victory only minutes away.

In the Richmond Trophy at Goodwood B.R.M. fielded a P25 for Bonnier and new P48s for Gurney and Hill. The P48 is interesting because it was a converted P25, literally, with the older chassis reworked to put the engine at the rear and the old de Dion axle giving way to an independent system using McPherson struts. Much later, when Historic racing came into vogue, existing P48s were converted back to P25 spec, and oddly enough this was accepted, although it is a little like a grown man trying to pass himself off as a schoolboy on the grounds that once he was. In Historic racing bogus P25s became the biggest kids in the playground.

At Goodwood Gurney collided with another car, Bonnier finished sixth and Hill, who discovered that the car was unstable unless driven on the optimum racing line (tricky when you are dicing), came home fifth and lapped, and that in a fairly weak field.

Hill was the only B.R.M. to finish in the International

Graham Hill took the lead with his rear-engined B.R.M. in the 1960 British Grand Prix, but spun out of the race because of a locking brake. (**David Phipps**)

Trophy at Silverstone, in third, for the old problems, brakes and engine, eliminated Bonnier and Gurney. Only Bonnier finished in the Monaco GP, fifth and 17 laps down. He had led but, like Gurney, had a rear hub casing fracture. Hill managed third in the Dutch and the Belgian races, but none finished in the French round. The cars had been quick in qualifying, but for 1960 the big problem, apart from brakes, had been valve springs. 1960 was the *seventh* year of the 2½-litre formula and still B.R.M. had not worked out how to slow its cars. B.R.M. had been fortunate not to have killed drivers through its incompetence in tackling this fairly basic requirement.

Against this background of gloom, the performance of Graham Hill in the British GP was even more surprising. He stalled on the line and drove through the field to take the lead after 55 laps. Unfortunately his brakes began to fail (again) and with just six laps to go he spun and stalled.

The season limped on, Hill came second in the Silver City Trophy at Brands Hatch and third in the Oulton Park Gold Cup, Bonnier took third in the Lombank Trophy at Snetterton, fifth at Oulton Park and fifth in the US GP. A total of eight WC points, and place finishes in some minor races, was a disgraceful result for a team running three top drivers.

At Snetterton a new car, the Mk II (or P48/57), ap-

peared, and this had a lighter chassis, a smoother body, coil spring and double wishbone rear suspension and, at long last, conventional outboard rear brakes. With five weeks of the 2½-litre formula to run, the engine had fuel injection, something which Connaught had used in 1953. Needless to say it would not run properly and did not make the start, but Hill used it to take third at Oulton Park.

Only two cars were entered during 1961, for Hill and Tony Brooks. In common with other British makers, B.R.M. had resisted the new 1½-litre F1 and so faced the year with its new car some way from being ready. As a stop-gap it used Mk IIs fitted with Coventry Climax FPF engines, but B.R.M. naturally received no special attention from Climax and these engines seem not to have been of the best – Tony Brooks once told me that during the whole season he never once got the rear wheels to spin.

It is not surprising then that, despite employing two superb drivers, B.R.M.'s season was pretty thin. In WC events it amounted to Hill coming sixth in the French GP and fifth in America, and Brooks taking fifth in the Italian and third in the US GP in his final race before retiring. Thus B.R.M. finished a clear bottom of the Manufacturers' Championship table with just seven points.

When you've hit bottom there's only one way to go if

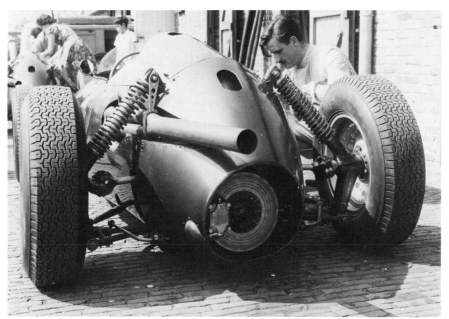

Graham Hill working on his rear-engined B.R.M. at the 1960 Italian Grand Prix. Note the single rear transmission disc brake.

In 1961, with the advent of the 1500cc Grand Prix Formula, B.R.M. raced the 1960 chassis with the Mk 2 FPF Coventry Climax engine. This is Graham Hill in the British Grand Prix in which he retired because of valve spring trouble. (David Phipps)

you stay in the game, and for B.R.M. there was a real possibility of not staying in, for Sir Alfred Owen made it quite clear that 1962 had better produce at least two wins or it would be the last season of his frittering away his money. In practice for the Italian GP, however, came hope for the future in the shape of the first P57, which received a very respectful reponse when it appeared.

It was a neat little car, a lower, lighter and slimmer version of the Mk II with, at its heart, a 90-degree V-8 d.o.h.c. engine of 1498cc (68.5 × 50.8 mm) with Lucas direct injection and transistorized ignition. As it first raced it produced 188 bhp at 10,250 rpm (in 1962 the Climax FWMV's output was 186 bhp at 8500 rpm). With the troublesome single disc brake on the transmission gone, it was possible to add another gear into the casing, and although it was 84 lb over the minimum weight limit, it offset this slight disadvantage by being very reliable.

Graham Hill remained on the strength, and he was joined by Richie Ginther, who while not of the top drawer as a racer was outstanding as a development driver. Another development for 1962 was that B.R.M. started to supply other teams with engines and this was the beginning of what was to be a thriving business for the company throughout the 1960s and early 1970s. Two Mk IIs fitted with V-8 engines were sold to the privateers, Tony Marsh and Jack Lewis, who competed mainly in non-Championship events.

Hill gave the car its debut in the Brussels GP and won the first heat, but a fault in the starter motor led to a push-start and that to his disqualification. Hill finished second to Clark in the Lombank Trophy at Snetterton and then won the Richmond Trophy at Goodwood. He and Ginther followed Clark in the Aintree 200, but both retired, and then came the extraordinary International Trophy.

It rained at Silverstone and, late in the race, Clark eased off to stroke home to an easy win, but Hill put in a

At the start of the 1962 season the B.R.M. team raced the new V-8 cars with 'stack' exhaust system. Here, in the International Trophy race at Silverstone, Graham Hill won by the narrowest of margins. Hill has lost three out of four 'stack' pipes on the offside. (T. C. March)

tremendous effort and on the very last corner passed the Lotus, sideways, to win by a couple of feet. It was one of the most dramatic finishes ever in F1 and it set the pattern for the season, which was to be Clark (Lotus) versus Hill (B.R.M.), with the rest as the supporting cast.

With two wins, a second, and a heat win before the season even started properly, B.R.M.'s prospects looked bright. Hill duly doubled B.R.M.'s total score of WC wins by taking the Dutch GP and appeared to have the Monaco GP sewn up when his engine let go a few laps from the finish and he had to be content with sixth. He finished second to Clark in Belgium, second to McLaren in the Reims GP and appeared to have the French GP in his pocket when the fuel injection broke, but at Rouen Ginther took third.

Hill then came fourth in the British GP, won the German (two WC wins, B.R.M. was saved!), came second in the Oulton Park Gold Cup, won the Italian GP (with Ginther second) and came second in the US GP. With only one race left Clark still had a chance of the title, but only because Hill had to drop points, and they went to East London with Hill on a gross total of 43 to Clark's 30. It would have been cruel luck if the scoring system had denied him the Championship, but Clark dropped out and Hill won, taking not only the Drivers' title but the Manufacturers' as well.

From bottom in the tables to top in one easy bound.

Berthon and Mays finally saw their dream realized after 17 years of effort and one reason for everything finally coming right was that Tony Rudd was chief engineer.

At the start of the season the cars had a distinctive 'smoke-stack' exhaust system with eight individual pipes curving up from the bodywork, but these caused unwanted turbulence, and 'low-line' systems were used from the Belgian GP onwards. Six-speed Colotti gearboxes were also used during the season as well as the B.R.M. unit, but work was in progress on B.R.M.'s own 6-speed transmission.

1963 started with the same cars and drivers and Hill opened the score by winning the Lombank Trophy. He and Ginther both retired in the Richmond Trophy, but came first and fourth in the Aintree 200. Hill retired from the International Trophy at Silverstone and then opened up his WC score with the first of his five wins at Monaco, with Ginther a close second.

It appeared as though B.R.M. might continue the dominance it had shown the previous year, but 1963 was the year of Jim Clark and the Lotus 25. In the Belgian GP, Ginther had the new B.R.M. 6-speed transmission and finished fourth, while Hill, who had set pole and run second, retired with gearbox trouble.

At the Dutch GP a new B.R.M., the P61, appeared in the paddock. Designed by Tony Rudd it had a monocoque central section of duralumin. Beyond the front

Graham Hill again, with the P61 V-8 B.R.M. in the 1964 British Grand Prix at Brands Hatch where he finished second. (T. C. March)

bulkhead was a tubular structure which carried a new inboard front suspension with the upper wishbones acting as rocker arms. Rear suspension was as on the P57, but bolted on to the back of the engine was the new B.R.M. 6-speed transmission. Hill and Ginther elected to drive the older cars and Hill was in third spot when his car overheated, but Ginther finished fourth, a lap down.

Hill used the new car to finish third in the French GP (Ginther retired with a holed radiator) and, apart from the works cars, Scuderia Centro-Sud also had a P57 for Lorenzo Bandini. The works ran P57s at Silverstone, where Hill finished third, Ginther fourth and Bandini fifth. Bandini took fourth in the Solitude GP and Ginther third in the German GP, with Hill retiring with gearbox trouble.

The season was not going B.R.M.'s way, but Bandini took third in the Mediterranean GP and Ginther (P57) second in the Italian with Hill (P61) retiring with clutch trouble after contesting the lead. Still, driving P57s, Ginther and Hill came second and third in the Oulton Park Gold Cup and then Hill led his team-mate home for a B.R.M. 1-2 in the US GP. Ginther was third and Hill fourth in the Mexican GP and Hill took third in the team's last race of 1963, the South African GP.

The year had been completely dominated by Clark's Lotus, but Hill and Ginther followed him, admittedly at some distance, in the final WC table.

Testing had shown that the monocoque/tubular subframe layout of the P61 was not satisfactory and so it was replaced by the P61/2, which retained the same central-section but had stressed sections front and rear. Power had risen steadily and would continue to rise to 212 bhp

at 11,500 rpm by the end of 1965. Declaring its faith in the new car, B.R.M. sold two of the 1963 works car to Scuderia Centro-Sud. Hill and Ginther were retained as the main drivers, while Richard 'Dickie' Attwood was also entered on occasion.

Apart from the Centro-Sud and works cars, some old 48/57s were still around and B.R.M. engines were very much in evidence in other cars, notably the leading Lotus and Brabham privateers. In some races over half the field was equipped with the B.R.M. P56 engine, so quite apart from the works team, B.R.M. made a significant contribution to F1 in the period 1962-65.

Thus, when Innes Ireland won the first F1 race of 1964, the *Daily Mirror* Trophy at Snetterton, there was a B.R.M. engine in the back of his B.R.P. Hill led the *News of the World* Trophy at Goodwood, but the rotor arm in his distributor broke with victory in sight and he had to settle for fifth. Attwood came fourth after being affected by gearbox trouble.

In both the Aintree 200 and the International Trophy at Silverstone, Hill came second to Brabham, but in the Monaco GP he led home Ginther for another 1-2. Fuel vaporization kept Hill in fourth place in the Dutch GP. Ginther and Hill came fourth and fifth in the Belgian GP, while in the French, Hill was second and Ginther fifth. Hill was also second in the British and German GPs and Ginther was second in the Austrian GP and fourth in the Italian.

Hill then won the US GP, with Ginther fourth, but they retired from the Mexican race, which concluded B.R.M.'s season. When the points were tallied, Hill and B.R.M. actually had the largest gross number in their

In practice for the same race Richard Attwood drove the experimental four-wheel-drive B.R.M. P67. The project was soon abandoned, but resurrected by Peter Lawson who used the car to win the RAC Hill Climb Championship. (David Phipps)

respective Championships, but the scoring system meant they both had to drop points, and thus Surtees and Ferrari carried off the honours with Hill and B.R.M. honourable runners-up.

Having so often been a latecomer in F1, B.R.M. decided to take the initiative for the forthcoming 3-litre formula and began exploring four-wheel drive, it being felt that a doubling in engine size would require a radical solution. In 1964 it built the P67 with a monocoque similar to that of the P61/2, and suspension from the P57, the engine turned through 180 degrees and the driving position slightly offset to the right to accommodate a drive-shaft running through the left-hand side of the cockpit.

The four-wheel drive system itself came from Ferguson, was similar to that used on the Ferguson P99, and was run with a 50/50 torque split. The system proved trouble-free, but did impose a weight penalty of 150 lb, or 15 per cent of the car's total dry weight, which was too much for 200 bhp to cope with. Attwood carried out preliminary testing in June 1964 and he was entered for the British GP at Brands Hatch. In practice he managed a best time of 1 m 45.2 s, which compares to Graham Hill's 1 m 38.3 s. It was decided not to start the race.

Other considerations kept it from being developed further for F1 (it would have needed a complete redesign to make it light enough for the 1½-litre formula), but both Peter Westbury and David Good later used it for hill climbing. In 1968 Peter Lawson used it in the RAC Hill Climb Championship, which he won. By then it had a 2.1-litre 'Tasman' engine and was running with a 70/30 torque split with a bias towards the rear. Had B.R.M. persevered, it might just have made the P67 into a reasonable proposition for F1.

Among other developments which B.R.M. had pursued was a collaboration with Rover to make a turbine-powered sports car, which ran reliably at Le Mans in 1963 and 1965. One has to presume that this too was considered for F1.

B.R.M. also tried four-valve-per-cylinder heads, but when these failed to meet expectations, a two-valve-per-cylinder head was made along the same lines, with the exhaust pipes within the vee. Hill used this engine at Monza, but the clutch stuck open at the start and he could not get it off the line.

In 1965 Ginther went to lead the Honda team, and was rewarded with his only WC win. In his place came a youngster called Jackie Stewart, fresh from a year of

A superb photograph of Graham Hill with the P61 in the 1965 British Grand Prix at Silverstone. He again finished second. (T. C. March)

dominating F3 with a Cooper. The season began with the South African GP on New Year's Day and there Hill finished third with Stewart playing himself in and finishing a sensible sixth. By the Race of Champions at Brands Hatch in March, however, Stewart was in his stride and he finished second, albeit aided by the retirement of many of the front runners.

No excuses were needed at Goodwood and the *Sunday Mirror* Trophy, where Stewart set pole but suffered a broken camshaft in the race. Hill, however, finished second to Clark. Hill led the International Trophy at Silverstone and then suffered another broken camshaft, but Stewart came through to win his first F1 race ahead of Surtees' Ferrari.

As was becoming usual, Hill won the Monaco GP, with Stewart third, but the young Scot really came to the fore in the Belgian GP, where he finished second to Clark in a very wet race and was the only driver not lapped. Hill, who finished fifth in Belgium, a lap behind his young team-mate, occupied the same position in the French GP on the difficult Clermont-Ferrand circuit, but again Stewart finished a strong second to Clark.

Clark won the British GP with Hill second and Stewart fifth. Stewart finished second in the Dutch GP, with Hill fourth, but it was Hill's turn to come in second to Clark in the German GP. Stewart had been threaten-

ing to win a race all year, but Clark's reliability record held until the Italian GP, where Stewart won from Hill. Graham, however, won the US GP (Stewart retired with a broken wishbone), but neither man finished the last race of the 1½-litre formula in Mexico.

1965 had been Jim Clark's year, but B.R.M. had done pretty well too with three wins and six seconds. In fact, B.R.M. grossed more points than Lotus in the Manufacturers' Championship, but had to be content with second place again, while Hill was runner-up in the Drivers' Championship for the third successive year and Stewart was third in the table.

In the period 1962-65, B.R.M. not only came good but was sufficiently successful and consistent to bury the unenviable reputation it had gained during the preceding 12 years. Unfortunately it was never to enjoy such success again as first it struggled with a 3-litre H-16 engine which was heavy and complex and never gave the power which was hoped for it. Later, under new management, it built a V-12 which could have been much more successful than it was had the team been allowed to maintain its engines properly instead of making and mending and using tired and repaired parts.

Eventually B.R.M. once again became something of a joke and when it eventually disappeared in the mid-1970s nobody missed its passing.

B. R. P.

The British Racing Partnership was formed in 1959 by Alfred Moss and Ken Gregory who were, respectively, Stirling Moss' father and manager. The team ran a pair of Cooper-Borgwards in F2 and, on occasion, a B.R.M. P25 for Moss and Hans Herrmann. In 1960 B.R.P. ran F1 Coopers under the banner of its sponsor, the Yeoman Credit finance company, and the following two years saw the operation running cars for a rival finance company, United Dominions Trust.

Thus B.R.P. brought a degree of commercialism into the sport, but also won a reputation as a serious team employing good drivers, and indeed, Innes Ireland won the inaugural, non-Championship, Austrian GP in 1962 at the wheel of a B.R.P.-entered Lotus 24.

Both finance houses withdrew from racing at the end of 1962 and B.R.P. faced the usual problem of the privateer: it was never able to get its hands on the latest cars, but had to buy customer models, which were always behind the works cars. So, to redress the situation, it took the decision to build its own cars.

Tony Robinson was in charge of design and his first essay was a copy of the Lotus 25's monocoque, though made of thicker-gauge aluminium, with suspension copied directly from one of the team's Lotus 24s. Apart from that, the main difference between a Lotus and a B.R.P. was the choice of a B.R.M. P56 V-8 engine and a 5-speed Colotti gearbox.

It was one thing to make a copy of a Lotus 25, it was quite another to tweak the best out of it, and B.R.P. had not the expertise to set the car up to a standard where it could match the Lotus 24, which was always user-friendly. A similar thing happened when Chapman introduced ground effect; everyone copied it, but few really understood how it worked.

A single car, for team leader Innes Ireland, was entered in the 1963 Belgian GP, while the team's other driver, Jim Hall, used a Lotus 24 throughout the season. Ireland qualified it in seventh place, which was a respectable debut, but actually below his average place on the grid with a Lotus 24, and he retired with gearbox trouble.

In the Dutch GP he again qualified seventh and this time finished fourth, but thereafter the team made little progress, though it did take third at Solitude. In both the German and Austrian rounds, Ireland reverted to his Lotus 24 and qualified it fourth in Austria, a position which the B.R.P. was never to make. An accident kept Ireland out of the last races of the year, so the car raced only six times, taking fourth at Monza on its last appearance.

Things did not improve very much in 1964, although a second car was built and Ireland was joined by Trevor Taylor, another ex-Lotus driver. Nowhere were the cars particularly impressive, although Ireland did win the

In the 1963 Dutch Grand Prix Innes Ireland with the B.R.P.-B.R.M. is passed by Graham Hill's B.R.M. Ireland finished fourth. (Nigel Snowdon)

Daily Mirror Trophy at Snetterton against a strong field, but the race was run in very wet conditions. Innes had the skill to exploit the situation and, for once, had the run of the luck. It was a popular win, for he was well liked and many felt he deserved a better car.

It was more due to the drivers than anything else that Ireland took third in the Mediterranean GP, against decent opposition (Taylor actually qualified second but retired with a broken radius arm), and fifth in the Austrian and Italian Grands Prix. Taylor's best result was

sixth at Watkins Glen, which must have seemed light years away from his early performances with Lotus in 1962.

Having demonstrated that it could not build a car as good as the obsolete Lotus 24, and having crept ever further down the grid during the 18 months it had run its own cars, B.R.P. decided to turn its attention to the lucrative USAC scene, and for 1965 built cars with Ford customer V-8 engines, which were pretty hopeless, and the outfit soon folded.

BAIRD-GRIFFIN

When it was announced that from 1952, the World Championship would be run for F2 cars, one of the people it caught wrong-footed was the Ulster enthusiast Bobby Baird. Baird was heir to a large printing concern which included *The Belfast Telegraph* and was a bit of a tearaway in his youth. To try to exercise some control over him, his father would not allow him to buy new cars so instead he set up a good, and large, team to modify and run 'pre-owned' racing cars, of which he owned a large number. Ironically this was probably a more expensive way of doing things than buying new.

Baird bought the first post-war Emeryson and ran it with a 4½-litre Duesenberg engine but could never find a strong enough transmission. Intriguingly, he once filed an entry for a Maserati-engined car called the 'Tornado'

but this never appeared in any F1 race. During 1951 he laid plans for a new F1 car using Maserati components. When the FIA sensibly switched the World Championship formula Baird decided to go ahead with his project with the idea that, should it prove successful, he would make a second car for F2.

The Baird-Griffin was built around a simple ladder frame with Simca front suspension (lower wishbone, upper link and torsion bars) while at the rear was a de Dion axle located by long fabricated radius arms and suspended by Morris torsion bars. Its engine was based on a Maserati 4CLT unit with many of its major components (block, crankshaft, crankcase and con-rods) being made new in Ulster and it drove through a rear-mounted 4-speed gearbox. The engine was built by Dennis Griffin,

Bobby Baird with the 4CLT Maserati-based Baird-Griffin at Eniskerry Hill Climb in 1952.

an engine tuner from Dublin, hence the name.

By the time it appeared, at the 1952 Easter Monday Goodwood Meeting, interest in F1 had already waned considerably and it quickly became nothing more than glorified Formule Libre. The Baird-Griffin appeared in a handful of minor events, mainly hill climbs, where it performed well against amateur opposition but from the beginning it was outclassed in even British national racing. At Goodwood, for example, Baird could do no better than ninth in a small field and in the Ulster Trophy at Dundrod he was disqualified for dropping oil.

When Baird's father died and he inherited the family firm, he bought a Ferrari 500, which was streets ahead of any other F2 car, so plans for an F2 Baird-Griffin were shelved.

Bobby Baird was practising for a race at Snetterton in 1953 when he crashed and was thrown from his sports Ferrari. He felt himself uninjured, shrugged away offers of assistance, and made back to the pits. He had walked a hundred or so paces when he dropped dead from a punctured lung.

BEHRA-PORSCHE

Before Porsche got around to building a single-seater, Jean Behra commissioned Valerio Colotti to design him one based on RSK components. The resulting car had a space-frame chassis, Porsche trailing link and torsion bar front suspension, coil spring and double wishbone rear suspension and was finished by a pleasing body, not unlike Porsche's later 718 F2 car.

Contractual conflicts and then a fatal crash meant that Behra himself never raced the car, though it went well in other hands. After his death it was taken over by the American Camoradi team, who ran it in a couple of F2 races in 1960, but it failed to finish on either occasion.

It did, however, appear in two World Championship races, the 1960 Argentine and Italian GPs. At Buenos Aires, Masten Gregory qualified 16th from 22 starters, ahead of two 2½-litre Cooper-Maseratis and some local Maserati 250Fs and, though four laps down at the end, he was 12th and a classified finisher. Fred Gamble drove it at Monza, where he was extremely slow, finishing not only nine laps down, but seven laps behind the leading F2 car. Behra's memory deserved better.

Fred Gamble drove the Behra-Porsche in two 1960 World Championship events, but perhaps was not the driver who could demonstrate the car to best effect. Here, at Monza, the combination proved embarrassingly slow. (**LAT**)

51

BERKSHIRE SPECIAL

Among the entries for the 1955 Easter Monday Meeting at Goodwood was the Berkshire Special, the work of Geoffrey Crossley, with Bruce Adams and John Lloyd. It had a ladder-frame chassis with transverse leaf and lower wishbone front suspension, a Riley live back axle suspended on quarter-elliptics located by radius rods, and a 2½-litre Lea-Francis engine, which gave all of 130 bhp.

In essence, it was a club special which happened to be eligible for F1 and had cost a mere £1200. Geoffrey Crossley himself was an experienced amateur who had campaigned an Alta in F1 and he tested it and reported that it handled well. A couple of small problems prevented it from taking part in the Richmond Trophy and, with a young family and pressure of work, Crossley decided to pursue the project no further and sold it on. Nothing further was heard of it.

Photographs of the unraced Berkshire Special are rare indeed. Here the car is seen in practice at Goodwood in 1955.

BOND

Laurie Bond was a maverick designer who created the odd, but commercially successful, Bond Minicars, the Berkeley sports car and the Bond Équipe, and who every so often essayed a design for racing. Among his best known were a front-wheel-drive 500cc F3 car, which ran on tiny wheels, and a front-engined Formula Junior car with a glass-fibre monocoque, but neither achieved any success.

In the early 1950s Bond designed an air-cooled V-8 Formula 1 engine with rotary valves. On paper it looked promising and Connaught experimented with the design. A single-cylinder experimental engine was made on a J.A.P. bottom end, but the rotary valve system proved impossible to seal and the project was abandoned. Bill Wareham, who oversaw its trials at Connaught, says, 'It produced a lot of oil smoke but not much power.'

BRABHAM

Jack Brabham had not only won two World Championships for Cooper, but he had virtually become the designer. It was natural that he should nurture his own ambitions and, in 1961, announced his intention of building his own cars. Later it would not be uncommon for a driver to make this move, but at the time it was a radical move. Previously, constructors had built up a business and graduated to Formula 1. Brabham started at the top and built up a business beneath him.

His move reflected the changing nature of the sport. With his reputation he was able to secure fuel and tyre contracts, and he knew, too, that the sport could take a new maker of production racing cars. Obtaining competitive engines and reliable transmissions, very difficult only four years before, was now simple and indeed he had a choice of Coventry Climax or B.R.M. There was, too, a network of sub-contractors who could make chassis, tanks and bodywork. Brabham thus became the first of the modern racing car constructors. The first frames, in fact, were made under conditions of secrecy by Buckler, the pioneer of kit cars and space-frames, for Brabham was still under contract to Cooper and was playing his cards close to his chest.

From Australia he recruited an old friend, Ron Tauranac, who had designed a successful FJ car, the Lynx, and he produced a similar car which ran in 1961 under the name 'M.R.D.' Officially the new company was, and is, Motor Racing Developments, but since M.R.D. is pronounced in France as 'merde', the cars were known as 'Brabhams'.

Two separate facilities were set up; the production racing car side, Brabham Racing Developments, was under the direction of Ron Tauranac, and this also designed and built the F1 cars, which were sold to the Brabham Racing Organisation. B.R.O. was under the direction of Brabham himself and was the entrant of the works F1 cars.

The start of the 1962 season saw the first Brabham F1 car some way from completion, so B.R.O. ordered a Lotus 24 as a stop-gap. It was not until the end of April that Jack's new Lotus arrived and he had very little luck with it apart from a second to Surtees in the Mallory Park 2000 Guineas' race. There were a couple of other top six finishes, but more often than not he retired. Without Cooper behind him, Brabham was beginning to look decidedly lacklustre, but, World Champion or not, he was running a private car and one cannot imagine that the Lotus suited his rugged driving style.

It was not until the German GP in August that the Brabham BT3-Climax appeared (BT for Brabham and Tauranac), although the FJ cars were already selling steadily and making a reputation for themselves as an ideal customer car, easy to set up and maintain, and forgiving to their drivers. The first F1 car followed that broad philosophy and was an uncomplicated machine built around a space-frame with an engine bay similar to the Lotus 24.

Front suspension was outboard by coil springs, single lower wishbones, upper single transverse arms and a long upper radius arm. It was an asymmetrical layout with the bottom wishbone pivots set forward of the centre of the axle line. At the rear were coil springs, single lower wishbones, transverse links and twin radius rods, a system similar to that used by Lola. Outboard Girling disc brakes were used all round and the engine was in unit with a 6-speed Colotti-Francis gearbox.

It was too new and unsorted to perform well at the Nürburgring and, anyway, Brabham suffered a wrecked engine in practice and had to cobble together a unit to complete his mandatory five laps. He qualified last but two and retired after nine laps with a broken throttle linkage. Brabhams were always to suffer more that their fair share of engine and throttle failures and it is difficult to pinpoint why. It may, however, be traced to the subtle art of engine installation, which was not fully understood at the time.

The new car was better sorted when it arrived for the Oulton Park Gold Cup, for there it qualified fifth and, after a troubled run, finished third, albeit three laps down. A dispute with the organizers over starting money saw him absent from the Italian GP, but at Watkins Glen he qualified sixth and came home fourth, a lap in arrears. In the non-Championship Mexican GP, however, he led in the early stages until overhauled by Jim Clark, who had taken over Trevor Taylor's car. Still, a second in Mexico and fourth in the last race, the South African GP, were decent results with which to end the season.

For 1963 Brabham engaged Dan Gurney, who began his season at Monaco, but it was to be the year of Jim Clark and the Lotus 25. In the British curtain-raisers Brabham looked as though he would at least take second in the Richmond Trophy at Goodwood, but was delayed by a loose wire. He had qualified second fastest for the Aintree 200, but had a piston break before the race, so was a non-starter, while in the International Trophy at Silverstone he was hampered by his engine cutting out. At Silverstone Brabham had a new 5-speed gearbox made by Mike Hewland in a VW casting. It was a development of the transmission already used on the Brabham FJ car and was to become Brabham's main gearbox. More than any other team, Brabham put Hewland on the map.

Jack Brabham on the debut of the first Formula 1 car to bear his name, the BT3 with V-8 Coventry Climax engine, in the 1962 German Grand Prix. He was eliminated by throttle linkage problems. (**David Phipps**)

The troubles the team had in the non-Championship races continued in the first Championship round, Monaco, where both Brabham and Gurney had engines blow in practice. Colin Chapman lent Brabham the spare Lotus 25 so that he could make the start, but he was all at sea in the car. Gurney had the new BT7, which had a longer wheelbase and other detail refinements, which included revised rear suspension with the single wishbone now the upper element and the transverse link the lower. Through meeting Malcolm Sayer, Jaguar's aero-dynamacist, Tauranac had re-thought the shape of his car and had tested the results in a wind tunnel. As a result the nose dipped downwards at the front and this helped prevent under-car air turbulence.

One point worth noting is that from the start Brabham tended to take second place in the team, so the new car was handed to Gurney while he patiently waited for the second chassis to be built. Gurney, who was as quick as anyone, qualified sixth at Monaco and was running seventh early in the race when his crown wheel and pinion broke. At Spa, Gurney qualified second and looked like finishing second when the heavens opened and, no lover of Spa in the wet, he eased off to finish third.

As the season progressed so the team improved. In the Dutch GP Gurney came second despite a pit stop when a chassis member broke. He had one of the new flat-crank FWMVs and the engine bay had been modified to accept it. The tube which broke had a fuel pipe on it, and needed to be taped up. Brabham, driving a BT7 for the first time, held second place until a throttle spring broke, again.

Less than a year after the marque's debut, Brabham was a top team. Both drivers qualified in the first five at Reims, where Brabham finished fourth and Gurney fifth, and both were on the front row at Silverstone and led the opening laps until the inevitable Clark spoiled their fun, but both retired with engine problems. Brabham took a single car to Solitude and won, but the cars were unhappy at the Nürburgring and Jack had to be content with seventh, while Gurney retired with gearbox failure.

At the Kanonloppet, a BT3 was entered for Brabham's protégé, Denny Hulme, who finished fourth in one heat, fifth in the other, and fourth overall, while Jack had the pleasure of heading Clark and Taylor in the works Lotuses in the first heat only to have his engine cut out, but he got going again and finished third. The overall result was decided on a points basis with aggregate time being used as a tie-breaker. Before the second heat it started to rain heavily, so Lotus went for a safe finish and did not challenge Brabham, who narrowly beat Taylor and Clark. All three, however, had equal points. Clark and Brabham each had a first and a third (1 + 3 = 4), while Taylor had two seconds (2 + 2 = 4), but when the *times* were added, Clark won from Taylor with Brabham third.

In the Mediterranean GP at Enna Brabham qualified slowly, and retired, but he won the non-Championship Austrian GP. Gurney led the Italian GP, but retired with a fuel feed problem while Brabham finished fifth after a stop for fuel. Neither driver was too happy in the Oulton Park Gold Cup, though Jack took fourth, and he took fourth too in the US GP, while Gurney, who had been battling for second, retired with a broken chassis frame.

Gurney held second in the Mexican GP (now a Championship race) until he untaped a fuel tap to change over to another tank and fuel flooded the cockpit, necessitating a pit stop that dropped him to sixth, but the Guv'nor inherited the spot and came home second. Dan made amends by taking second in South Africa, while Brabham spun out of fourth.

For a first full season it had been a good showing, with Gurney finishing fifth in the Drivers' Championship and Brabham seventh, and the team third in the Manufacturers' Championship behind Lotus and B.R.M. The company had done well with its customer cars, too, and of 16 important Formula Junior races, nine went to Brabham BT6s. Most successful of the Brabham Junior drivers was Denny Hulme, who, in 1964, was to win seven of his 14 starts with a works car.

The prototype BT3 was sold to Ian Raby, who installed a B.R.M. engine, and he enjoyed his usual season concentrating mainly on non-Championship races, while a new BT11-FWMV was sold to Bob Anderson. Brabham's own BT7 was modified at the rear to accommodate the new breed of fatter Dunlop tyres. The 1964 car, the BT11, was a refinement of the BT7, and the broad outline remained the same but was generally tidied up. It is interesting that the first BT11 went to a customer, while the works drivers continued with adapted 1963 cars, but while most constructors let the customer buy last year's technology, Brabham was always happy to sell current cars.

Still, the works Brabham BT7s worked very well with the new Dunlops and, in 1964, had a decided edge on the field. Jack spun and crashed in the very wet Lombank Trophy at Snetterton, but gave notice of his car's improvement by taking pole in the *News of the World* Trophy at Goodwood, disputed the lead with Clark and

had second place in the bag until a broken wheel caused him to crash. He then won the Aintree 200 after a battle with Clark which ended when Clark, in second, tangled with some inept back markers.

In the International Trophy at Silverstone Gurney and Brabham took the first two places on the grid and Gurney led until half-distance, when he retired with rear brake failure, whereupon Brabham took the lead. Hill's B.R.M. then moved up and the two men had an enormous dice for most of the second half of the race. It was resolved on the last corner when Brabham went on the outside at Woodcote to win by two feet with the time-keepers unable to separate them.

Those early races demonstrated that the Brabham team was now a force in the land and the production car business was doing nicely as well, particularly since a new Formula 2 began that year. Brabhams dominated F2 in 1964, winning ten of the 17 races, in contrast to a poor season in F3.

While others were busily copying the monocoque of the Lotus, and often creating problems for themselves, nobody thought to copy Brabham, which stayed with space-frames and would eventually win two World Championships with 'out-dated' designs. At the start of 1964, the Brabham BT7 was the class of the field with enough edge to give its drivers wins even though, gifted as both were, neither had been touched by the gods in the way Clark had been. Perhaps the secret was that the Brabhams were user-friendly whereas the Lotus 25 needed a genius like Clark to get the best from it. Jack Brabham was more skilled at tailoring a car to a circuit than anyone else around.

In 1964 the World Championship series opened at Monaco, where Brabham shared the front row of the grid with Clark. Clark made his usual lightning start, but Brabham and Gurney lay second and fourth with Hill's B.R.M. in between. Both the BT7s, however, were to retire, Brabham first, with a fuel injection problem, and Gurney with a broken gearbox. Gurney put his car on pole for the Dutch GP and ran strongly until his steering wheel broke, and the team had no spare in the pits. Jack had a very tight wallet and would never splash out money on spares which might not be used.

Gurney took pole again in the Belgian GP and pulled out a huge lead and then started to run out of fuel — and the team had none in the pits. On the very last lap he ran dry, and then so did Hill's B.R.M., which had taken the lead. Jim Clark, who had been delayed by overheating, then took the flag, and promptly ran out of fuel on the slowing-down lap. It was cruel luck, but typical of Brabham's history. Gurney's fine effort was scarcely rewarded by sixth place, but Brabham did make third. In

Because of unreliability, few successes came Brabham's way during the years of the 1500cc Formula. Here Dan Gurney is on his way to a rare victory with the BT7 in the 1964 French Grand Prix at Rouen. (**David Phipps**)

the French GP at Rouen, Clark was on pole from Gurney, but when the great Scot retired with a broken piston, Gurney stroked home to win, with Brabham third. It was the American's first WC win, and the first for the Brabham Racing Organisation, and both were long overdue.

In the first running of the British GP at Brands Hatch, both works cars were quick in practice and there were no fewer than seven Brabhams in the field, and this from a marque which had yet to celebrate its second birthday in F1. Apart from the works cars, and those of Raby and Anderson, Jo Bonnier had his Rob Walker B.R.M.-powered BT11, Jo Siffert had a similar car and Frank Gardner had an F2 BT10, which qualified faster than some of the F1 entries. This show of strength could, however, produce nothing better than a fourth place for Jack Brabham and then after a couple of pit stops.

In 1964 some of the non-Championship F1 events dropped away and were replaced by races for the new one-litre F2. Apart from the British series, most of the rest of Europe started to look thin as regards non-Championship F1 races. In the Solitude GP Anderson came third in a very wet race. In the German GP at the Nürburgring the cars were very competitive, and Gurney looked as though he was going to win as he took the lead on lap four and pulled away. Then the Brabham luck struck; waste paper caught in the nose of his car and caused overheating and he finished tenth. Jack suffered a

broken crown wheel and pinion, but Siffert brought his car home fourth and established a claim to be noticed.

Siffert strengthened that claim in the Mediterranean GP at Enna, where he set pole and won. It was not a class field, but it included the Lotus team, and while Clark was only a tenth behind at the flag, he was still behind, and Siffert had beaten him in a private car. It has been suggested, in jest, by a member of the team that it was as well the organizers did not check the size of Siffert's engine. Fie upon the thought!

The remaining races of the year were all for the World Championship, apart from the Rand GP, which Brabham did not enter. At every circuit the cars qualified well and Gurney was always in the top four. In the races they ran at the sharp end of the field, but every time, save one, they retired or were hampered by some fault, here a collapsed front suspension, there a flat battery. There was no pattern to the troubles and it seemed as though luck had deserted the team.

The exception was the Mexican GP, when Jim Clark appeared to have the race, and the Championship, in the bag when his engine blew on the last lap. Gurney slipped by to win, a victory which went almost unnoticed as Surtees came in second to clinch the title for Ferrari. It was tough on Clark and Lotus, but Gurney and Brabham had endured more than their share of bad luck during a year which had started so well.

Although he had taken two wins, Gurney finished

only sixth in the Championship, one place lower than the previous year, when he had taken no wins at all. Only Clark scored more than two wins that season and he was placed third in the series. In fact, Gurney scored points in only three races, the two he won and that sixth place at Spa, which should have been a win but for a cock-up by the team.

For 1965 the works team ran BT11s, but while Gurney and Brabham were front-runners, they had lost the edge they'd enjoyed the previous year. The team did less testing and development than their rivals, partly due to parsimony, partly because the production car business sapped too much time and energy.

Again Brabham suffered more than its fair share of retirements and again there seemed to be no pattern to them. Perhaps the drivers made excessive demands on their cars, for neither possessed the relaxed fluidity of the truly great. Perhaps, too, Brabham was stretching himself too thinly, for apart from driving in F1, he was supervising his team and driving in F2 as well.

Eight Brabhams were entered for the South African GP, which started the 1965 season, and while some were

F2 cars, Frank Gardner had John Willment's (ex-Rob Walker) BT11-B.R.M., Anderson had his BT11, and Rob Walker entered an ex-works BT7-Climax for Bonnier and a BT11-B.R.M. for Siffert. Brabham qualified third and ran third until problems saw him slip to finish eighth, while Gurney was an early retirement with ignition trouble.

Despite the disappointing results, history was made in that race, for Gurney's car had Goodyear tyres. Goodyear had been traditionally second to Firestone in the States, but had decided on a competition programme which grew into one of the most dedicated in racing history. The new tyres appeared to be competitive in the dry, but Goodyear still had something to learn about wet-weather racing.

In the Race of Champions at Brands Hatch, Gurney finished second to Clark in the first heat and led the second, when Jimmy made an uncharacteristic mistake while trying to pass on the first lap. Gurney's engine went sick soon after, but Brabham looked as though he had the race sewn up until his engine lost its oil.

Jo Bonnier in Rob Walker's BT11-B.R.M. took fourth

Dan Gurney at the wheel of the BT11 in the French Grand Prix at Clermont-Ferrand in 1965. He retired because of engine trouble. (David Phipps)

in the Syracuse GP, where Siffert had put in a tremendous drive to lead the works Ferraris, and the race, when he happened to snatch fifth gear as his car went over a bump and the revs soared sky high and wrecked the engine with only ten laps to go. Brabham came third in the *Sunday Mirror* Trophy at Goodwood, where Gurney had seemed set for a win until he lost oil pressure. Then Brabham appeared set to win the International Trophy at Silverstone until a broken gearbox caused his retirement.

Like Jim Clark, Dan Gurney missed the Monaco GP to concentrate on the Indianapolis 500 and his place was taken by Denny Hulme, who had been quick, but unlucky, in F2 driving a works BT10. At Monaco, Brabham had a four-valve FWMV and he was second to Hill in practice, while Hulme, making his WC debut, did an excellent job to qualify eighth. Despite his front-row position Brabham was only fifth on the first lap, but he took the lead at one-third distance. Then his rev counter broke and he over-revved his engine. Hulme finished eighth, driving slowly because of a loose wheel.

The Belgian GP was run in very wet conditions and Gurney, who had qualified fifth, had to struggle with both his dislike of Spa in the rain and an ill-handling car, for his Goodyears were not up to scratch. He finished tenth, two laps down, while Brabham came home fourth, a lap down on Clark and Jackie Stewart who, in only his third WC race, was posting notice of his greatness.

Since Hulme knew Clermont-Ferrand from F2 (he had beaten Stewart and Rindt in winning the 1964 race), Brabham stood down from the French GP in favour of his protégé and Hulme rewarded his confidence by being quickest on the first day of practice and eventually finishing fourth in the race. Gurney had run third in the early stages, but retired with engine trouble before half-distance.

The marque's reliability record was poor. Brabham himself was approaching his 40th birthday and not only had he no answer to Clark, but the arrival of Stewart pushed everyone one rung lower in the notional ratings. It seemed that Brabham was ready to bow out to concentrate on the running of his team.

Thus when, at the British GP, Gurney's four-valve engine broke, Jack handed over his car even though he could have told Denny Hulme to step down. Gurney's lanky frame was a tight fit in the Guv'nor's cockpit and he had an unhappy time, eventually finishing seventh, while Hulme retired with a broken alternator belt.

Brabham stood down in favour of Hulme at the Dutch GP as well, where both cars used two-valve engines. Still, Gurney ran a close second to Clark until Stewart passed him and he had to be content with third with Hulme in fifth place.

Brabham was back for the German GP, where he could qualify no higher than 14th, 22 seconds off Clark's pole time, 15 seconds slower than Gurney and 2.6 seconds slower than Hulme. Gurney had another good race, finishing a strong third, and, while Hulme retired with a fuel leak, Brabham came in fifth.

Hulme and Brabham represented the works in the Mediterranean GP at Enna in Sicily, and while they finished only fourth and sixth, Jack Brabham must have been pleased with the race, for in third place was Frank Gardner in the Willment car, while the winner, for the second year in succession, was Jo Siffert in Rob Walker's BT11-B.R.M., and again Siffert beat Clark – this time by just three-tenths of a second.

In the Italian GP Jack Brabham again stood down and the team ran Gurney, Hulme and yesterday's man, Giancarlo Baghetti, who had one of the old BT7s. None of the cars were able to qualify in the top ten, and Gurney's engine was decidedly tired. Still, while Baghetti retired with a broken con-rod and Hulme with front suspension trouble, Gurney managed to come home third.

Only two races, both in North America, remained of the 1½-litre formula and for both the team consisted of Gurney and Brabham. In the US GP they came second and third respectively, while in the Mexican race, Gurney finished second, within two seconds of Ginther's Honda, while Brabham retired with an oil leak.

Thanks to his end-of-season performances, Gurney was placed fourth in the World Championship behind Clark, Hill and Stewart, while Brabham finished third in the Manufacturers' series behind Lotus and B.R.M., who between them won every race that year. In the lesser formulae, Brabham took six wins in F2 and 15 in F3. By the end of only its fourth year in business, M.R.D. had sold over 120 cars.

Looking at the early years of Brabham one sees two pictures. One is the establishment of a new breed of racing car constructor which was immediately successful both in terms of cars sold and the number of wins they took. It was no mean achievement, either, to create a Formula 1 team which established itself as one of the four top outfits within months of its first car turning a wheel. In Brabham's first three full seasons in F1 it won a total of 99 World Championship points, and while this was a long way short of Lotus or B.R.M., it compares well with Ferrari's 102 points over the same period.

One the other hand, the works team should have done much better than just two Grand Prix victories and four non-Championship F1 wins. From the beginning of 1964, it had potentially the best car on the grid, but too often was let down by unreliability and, in 1965, insufficent development. It may have been a case of concentrating so hard on the pennies that the pounds never got a look in.

Brabham, however, had become a well-founded company and had built up a good overall reputation. This led to it being able to put together engine deals for 1966 which saw it win all but one race in F2 (with Honda) and successive World Championships with Repco.

At the end of 1965 Brabham was ready to hang up his helmet and run Gurney and Hulme but Dan went off to found his own team so he continued. In 1966 he became the first driver to win the title in a car of his own making. He was close to the crown as well in 1967 and in 1970 when he finally called it a day.

Brabham returned to Australia leaving Tauranac in charge but before long Ron sold the firm to Bernie Ecclestone and 'retired' until boredom set in. To keep himself amused he started making cars under the name 'Ralt' (Ron and Lewis Tauranac after an early special he had made with his brother) and this hobby has grown into a considerable manufacturer of production racing cars.

BUGATTI

In 1947, Ettore Bugatti's last design was unveiled to the public. It was the Type 73A, a small sporting saloon with a 4-cylinder, d.o.h.c. engine of 1488cc (76 × 82 mm). A supercharged version, the Type 73C, was made and this gave a promising 250 bhp. Two single-seater chassis were prepared with a view to returning to Grand Prix racing, but Bugatti faded and the project was forgotten. With his death faded the car-building side of the business, though a handful were made to pre-war designs over the next few years. In its attempt to recover from the ravages of war, the company turned to general engineering and received a boost from military contracts when France entered a bloody, unsuccessful, colonial war in Indo-China (later Vietnam).

Bugatti prospered to the point where the new regime felt itself able to commit the company to a return to Grand Prix racing. It was a resonable enough decision to take both in terms of the company's glorious history and as an advertisement for its engineering products. Further, it secured the services of none other than Gioacchino Colombo, the man responsible for the Alfa Romeo 158, the Ferrari V-12 'short-block' engine, and the Maserati A6GCM, the direct forebear of the 250F. On paper the whole project looked right and it seemed France was again on the threshold of racing success.

Work began in 1953 with the intention of running a team the following year, but progress was slow, and when the Indo-Chinese war ended the following year, it became slower as Bugatti's profits took a dive. Eventually a prototype was shown to the press in November 1955.

Colombo had essayed a radical car, but was apparently working to a concept created by Ettore Bugatti before his death. For a start, it was rear-engined with a transversely mounted d.o.h.c. straight-eight unit of 2431cc (75 × 68.8 mm) with hairpin valve springs. The engine was cast in magnesium alloy and made in two units each of four cylinders and each with its own crankshaft. Between the two halves was a cluster of spur gears which both synchronized them and took the drive to a 5-speed gearbox with Porsche synchromesh mounted directly to the back (side?) of the engine.

Colombo believed that it would be possible to bolt together the two halves of the engine in different planes, which would affect the balance, firing order and, hence, induction pulses of the engine. By careful calculation it would therefore be possible to create one version for twisty circuits, where torque is of the essence, and another for high-speed circuits.

The chassis was a properly triangulated space-frame, but had rigid axles front and rear, a Vintage concept, but one with which Ferrari experimented as late as the mid-1970s. Front and rear axles were both de Dion tubes, which were located by twin radius rods. At each hub there was a push-rod connected to a rocker arm, at the other end of which were long coil spring/damper units angled at 45 degrees diagonally across each other to mounting points on the lower frame. As shown and raced the car had drum brakes, but in practice for the 1956 French GP a car was briefly fitted with Bugatti-designed discs each housed in a casing fitted with a hot-air extractor. The bodywork was particularly neat, although the choice of pannier fuel tanks made the car look a little chubby and, at 750 kg, it was the heavyweight of the field in 1956 by more than 2 cwt, but its aerodynamics were sound.

In testing the engine was kept in a low state of tune, so that it should be reliable while the chassis was developed. Thus, while 275 bhp was predicted, the

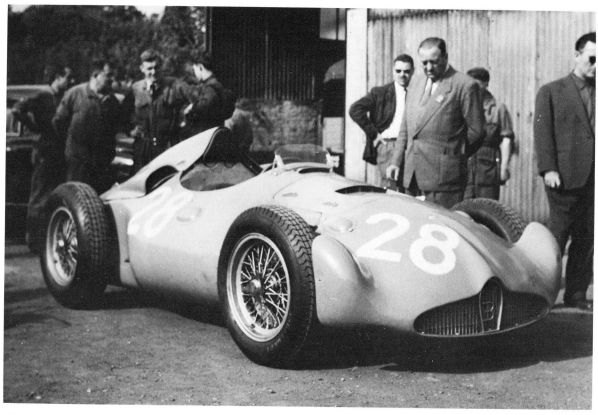

The second of the two Type 251 Bugattis, the car not raced in the 1956 French Grand Prix at Reims. (LAT)

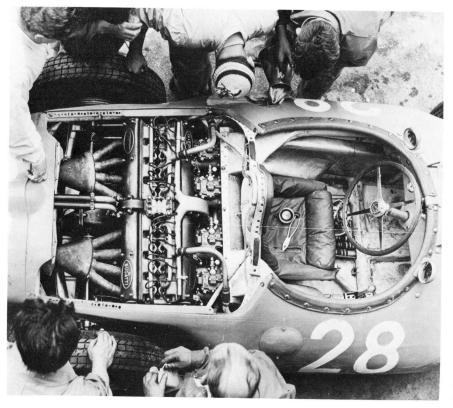

The transversely mounted straight-eight engine of the Colombo-designed Type 251 Bugatti.

Bugatti T251 never ran with more than 230 bhp, which was a little below par. Maurice Trintignant was entrusted with testing and he discovered that the rearward weight bias gave reasonably good road-holding, excellent traction and thoroughly unpredictable steering. It was hard to keep it in a straight line, while, under braking, the front end became very difficult indeed.

While it was nowhere near ready to race, the organizers of the 1956 French Grand Prix applied so much pressure to Bugatti that it reluctantly agreed to enter. To try to sort out the handling problems, a second car with a longer wheelbase and a slightly different treatment to the nose panels was created. This ran in practice at Reims, but Trintignant elected to race the prototype. It was a hopeless cause and he started 17th on the grid from 19 runners and 18.7 seconds off the pace. In the race he was running in 14th place when, on lap 18, he began to experience a sticking throttle caused by dirt getting into the mechanism, and he retired.

At the time of the French race the intention was to continue with the programme and there was even talk of making a sports version to run at Le Mans. It was soon clear, however, that it would require much more money to develop than the company could afford, and so the project was shelved; both T251s eventually ended up in the Schlumpf collection. As Pierre Marco, the works manager, said once it was all over, 'We made a complicated car when we should have made a simple one.'

C.T.A.-ARSENAL

Having been humiliated by government-backed German cars before the war, the French nurtured the idea of a national racing car which could take on, and beat, the world. In 1946 the Centre d'Études Techniques de l'Automobile et du Cycle (C.T.A.) received a grant to create a car to fly the *tricolor* and it employed Albert Lory to design it. Lory had been responsible for the 1½-litre Delage of 1927, which had swept all before it and, indeed, had remained competitive for many years. The hyphenated 'Arsenal' of the name was not a tribute to the great soccer club but an allusion to the fact that the car was constructed in a former arsenal at Châtillon, near Paris.

Lory drew a 90-degree V-8 of 1482cc (60 × 65.5 mm) with two-stage supercharging; the two banks of cylinders were staggered, the iron block had non-detachable heads, the five-bearing crankshaft ran in roller bearings, and twin magnetos provided the sparks to the two plugs per cylinder. Power output appears to have been around 266 bhp at 7500 rpm, which was

Raymond Sommer at the wheel of the ill-fated C.T.A.-Arsenal at the French Grand Prix at Lyon in 1947.

61

very close to what Alfa Romeo was achieving with its Tipo 158.

Although the engine appeared promising, the rest of the car was less so. While the body was probably quite efficient, its ground clearance was on the high side and the handling was never up to scratch. The chassis was a simple ladder frame with boxed sections in which the engine was angled at 8 degrees, and power was delivered via a prop-shaft which went under the driver to a 4-speed gearbox in unit with the final drive. Suspension was independent all round by a system of vertical slides, transverse links and longitudinal torsion bars. To gain optimum weight distribution, fuel was stored in no fewer than five separate tanks.

In early September, 1947, Raymond Sommer took the wheel for the car's first trials at Monthléry and had no difficulty in controlling his enthusiasm. Word was that it needed 'development', whereas it needed a new chassis, for its handling was dreadful. With the grant from the government came pressure for the car to start in the French GP, which was held only a couple of weeks after the initial, unsatisfactory, test session.

So it was the C.T.A. arrived at Lyon, and quite apart form the fact that it would not hold a straight line at speed, it was having to conduct its shake-down tests in public. On the starting grid, the clutch seized and when Sommer released the pedal the power of the engine snapped a drive-shaft. The car did not even make it to the start/finish line.

A second car was completed and both were entered at Reims the following July, but after the first day of practice it was clear they were completely outclassed and so they were withdrawn from the race and put away.

For some reason Tony Lago bought both cars, but apparently did nothing with them, and they stayed in a corner of the Talbot works for some years. One now tours museums in France.

CEGGA-MASERATI

The most complicated thing about this 1962 F1 car was the name, which was an acronym of the builders: Claude Et Georges Gachnang of Aigle in Switzerland. The brothers had previously built Bristol and Ferrari-engined sports cars and like their earlier efforts their single-seater had a simple space-frame and all-independent suspension. It was fitted with a 4-cylinder Maserati 150S engine and a Maserati 5-speed gearbox.

It was entered for Maurice Caillet in the non-Championship Pau and Naples Grands Prix, but on both occasions failed to qualify. Later it was used for hill climbing, where it fared somewhat better.

CISITALIA

Cisitalia was formed in 1946 by Piero Dusio, a wealthy industrialist and amateur racing driver who had finished third in the 1938 Mille Miglia. Alongside him from the beginning was Piero Taruffi, a leading driver and a gifted engineer. While a series of Fiat-based road cars was being readied for production, Cisitalia decided to spread its name through competition and attacked on two fronts.

The first was a run of D46 single-seaters based on 1100cc Fiat components, and the idea of these cars was to create a low-cost single-seater formula. A run of 500 was envisaged, but in the event only two or three dozen were made. These days that is not a great number, but then it was huge amount and, moreover, the cars were successful in their class and continued to appear in races, albeit with diminishing returns, until 1953.

In 1947, with financial backing from Switzerland, Cisitalia formed a 'circus' of 15 cars. The theory went that they would be transported to a major race and top drivers would each draw a car and engage in a one-make curtain-raiser to the main event. It was a sound idea, but to get it off the ground a series of races were organized in Egypt, a nation not noted for its motor racing tradition. After the first event, at Cairo, which was won by Taruffi, the venture lost so much money that it was abandoned and the cars sold on.

An altogether more serious proposition was the Type 360 Grand Prix car. After the war the remnants of the famous design studio founded by Dr Ferdinand Porsche

The Porsche-designed rear-engined 12-cylinder Cisitalia seen in the Cisitalia works soon after the first car had been completed.

The engine installation of the rear-engined Cisitalia.

were operating from an old wood mill in Austria and denied access to its headquarters in Stuttgart. Engineers who had once designed the Auto Union Grand Prix cars, the Volkswagen, and a wide range of military vehicles, found themselves repairing cars and making barrows. Dr Porsche himself had been invited to Paris to advise on the new Renault 4CV, and after the perfidious French had picked his brains, they imprisoned him and close colleagues on trumped-up charges of war crimes. Eventually the colleagues were released, but a ransom was demanded for Ferdinand Porsche.

Then in 1947 Dusio approached the studio with a commission to design him a Grand Prix car, and since the money on offer would ransom the founder, the commission was eagerly accepted. Work began under the studio's chief engineer, Karl Rabe, and the design was finalized in a matter of months.

Despite the restrictions in time and materials, the 360 represented perhaps the biggest advance in racing car design ever seen. For a start the chassis was the first true space-frame ever designed for a Grand Prix car and this was constructed from chrome-molybdenum steel tubing. Suspension was independent all round by torsion bars and hydraulic dampers, and the frame was covered by a tight, neat, slipper body with a tiny air intake. Dry weight of the car was 1583 lb with a 48/52 distribution. Under the skin there were more surprises. For a start the flat-12 engine was mounted in the rear, the layout favoured by the Porsche studio for its Auto Union designs, but the power from the engine was driven to all four wheels. A 5-speed gearbox, then not at all usual, was used and this featured a new style of synchromesh designed by Leopold Schmid. In terms of Porsche's long-term prosperity this was an important feature, for a refinement of Schmid's system was eventually to be licensed to car makers all over the world.

Karl Rabe's engine was a supercharged d.o.h.c. flat-12 unit of 1492cc (56 × 55.5 mm) and it was unusual in being 'over-square', though Gioacchino Colombo had followed a broadly similar route with the V-12 engine he had just completed for Ferrari. Initially three Roots-type superchargers were specified, but later they were replaced by two parallel Centric compressors. Computed output was 300 bhp at 8500 rpm, but the engine was designed to exceed 10,000 rpm.

Dusio had called for the car to be ready by the end of 1947, and intended to have six complete cars at his disposal. Meanwhile Cisitalia had started production of its road cars and Nuvolari very nearly won the 1947 Mille Miglia in one, but was delayed by water getting into the electrical system.

Even had conditions been normal, it would have been a miracle if Dusio's deadline on the 360 had been met; as it was the prototype was nearing completion in November 1948, only 16 months after the commission. Dusio, however, had sunk too much of his money in the project and was facing a financial crisis. He had commissioned other, commercial, designs from Porsche and was able to persuade President Juan Perón to give his support to a new company, Auto Motores Argentinos (Autoar), which would be set up in the Argentine.

Dusio was forced to sell up in Italy when his workers took him to court to settle their unpaid wages and, in 1949, he moved his company to the Argentine. When the first 360 was complete, in 1950, it was sent to the Argentine, but it was no longer a top priority, and while the design mouldered away, the formula for which it had been built came to an end at the end of 1951.

The car was brought out for the 1953 Buenos Aires (Formule Libre) Grand Prix, but practice for the race served only to show that it needed an extensive development programme. Apart from the fact that it was well below par in terms of power, a more pressing, practical, problem was that the gearbox had been designed to pass through neutral in every shift but had a habit of staying in neutral. The originators of the project were thousands of miles aways, making Porsche cars, so it was withdrawn from the race.

It had been developing only 280 bhp, little more than half of what it should have been, but work by Autoar raised this to around 360 bhp. It was decided to attack the South American flying kilometre record with the car, and local ace, Clemar Bucci, took the wheel for the attempt in the middle of 1953. Despite the engine holing a piston on the second run, he managed a small improvement on an obscure record which had stood at 140 mph. Bucci's best run was only 146.6 mph, which could have been topped by an over-the-counter Jaguar C-type, and apart from being neither here nor there in terms of international records was a long way short of the 210 mph which had been originally projected by the Porsche studio.

The car was put under dust sheets and left to rot, but later was discovered by Porsche's team manager, Huschke von Hanstein, who was in the Argentine for the 1959 Buenos Aires 1000 km race. The car was bought by Porsche, rebuilt, and is now in the company's museum in Zuffenhausen. A second, incomplete, car turned up in Switzerland in 1970 and is now in the Donington Collection.

CLAIRMONTE

Although this car never raced in single-seater form, it is interesting because it was Colin Chapman's very first single-seater and was originally designated the Lotus Mk 7. During the winter of 1951/2, two brothers named Clairmonte approached Chapman and commissioned an F2 car. This was a space-frame design with double wishbone front suspension and a de Dion rear axle and was intended to be fitted with a 2-litre E.R.A. engine.

Before the car was completed, the E.R.A. engine was destroyed and the Clairmontes, whose finances could not stand the blow, took delivery of just the bare body/chassis unit. Since it had not been completed, and was not finished until some time after, Chapman did not regard it as a Lotus and its designation was held in abeyance to be used much later to name the Mk 6's replacement, which is why, in Lotus terms, 7 follows 12. Eventually the brothers converted the chassis into a sports car and installed a Connaught-modified Lea-Francis engine. It enjoyed a successful career in club racing, and is still in existence.

The Clairmonte was originally a Colin Chapman-designed Formula 2 car designated the Lotus Mk 7. It only raced in sports car form and then under the name of its owners. It is seen at the Midland Motor Enthusiasts' Club meeting at Silverstone in June 1953. (Guy Griffiths)

CLISBY

In late 1962 news reached Europe of an intriguing new engine project taking shape in Australia. At that time Australia was a place where last year's F1 cars were taken to compete in the Tasman series on a one-way ticket, and even although a number of fine drivers had emerged from the Antipodes, Australasian motor racing was still tied to Europe and was the passive recipient of cast-offs. The new Clisby engine was meant to reverse the trend and be an active contribution to F1.

Harold Clisby was the owner of a successful group of engineering companies, and a part-time racer and special builder, who had been on a European tour in 1960, when he had visited a number of famous factories. While he was impressed by the best of what he saw, he was surprised at the standards of some, and this encouraged him to try his hand at fulfilling an ambition, the construction of his own F1 engine.

Clisby chose a 120-degree V-6 layout and created a state-of-the-art engine with twin overhead camshafts driven by spur gears, markedly 'over-square' cylinder dimensions (73×58.8 mm = 1476cc), and two plugs per cylinder serviced by Clisby-modified Bosch distributors. Each bank of cylinders had a triple-choke Weber carburettor, though apparently there were plans to create a new Clisby triple-choke carburettor in much the same way that transistorized ignition was also a future possibility.

Measuring only 20 inches in length, and only 17 inches high, it was a neat, compact unit cast in aluminium. Lubrication was by a wet sump system, but a dry sump remained a possibility, if needed, and a great deal of care and attention went into cooling the areas around the valves, which were the only parts not made in-house by Clisby Industries.

All in all it looked a serious piece of kit, with a competitive 175 bhp being predicted when using an 8.5:1 compression ratio, while there were plans to increase this to 10:1, if necessary, at which point 200 bhp at 10,000 rpm was expected. Dry weight of the engine was estimated to be 260 lb.

Tom Hawkes, who was running Ausper cars in Formula Junior, expected to take delivery of the first engines for a works team of F1 Ausper-Clisbys. If the engine proved successful, customer units would be available to others and the asking price was expected to be less than the £3500 that Climax and B.R.M. demanded. Interest in the new unit was heightened by the fact that shortly before news of it reached Europe, Coventry Climax had announced it was probably going to withdraw from motor racing.

Having spent over 10,000 man hours on the engine, one can imagine the team's disappointment when it was discovered that the block was porous. To rectify that would have taken a major re-design and since there were other, more pressing, priorities for the company, the project was quietly shelved.

In 1965 an entry was filed for the Australian GP for an Elfin-Clisby for Andy Brown, but it did not even appear for practice.

CONNAUGHT

In the 1930s, the Chelsea College of Automobile and Aircraft Engineering had on its roll two students who were later to play a significant part in the post-war British motor racing renaissance. One was John Heath, later of H.W.M., and the other was Rodney Clarke, of Connaught. Both were individuals who held firm views on engineering, but Clarke was, by far, the more complex man. He had the potential to be one of the handful of truly great racing car designers, and he explored a number of advanced ideas years before anyone else, but his entire output amounted to just two completed designs.

Clarke's great strength, and ultimate weakness, was his insistence on doing everthing correctly. While Heath 'designed' his cars with tubing and a welding torch, Clarke employed draughtsmen, and at one time Connaught had eight in its drawing office, a number only recently surpassed by most Formula 1 teams. One detail which highlights this attitude is the fact that Connaughts are still raced using their original alloy wheels, 35 years after being made, while contemporary Cooper-Bristols are raced on modern alloy wheels because their original equipment long ago became unsafe.

While it is admirable that Clarke's cars were so well made, a racing car exists to win over a season or two, and does not have to be *that* well made. Clarke's problem was that he so concentrated on detail that, given the resources at his disposal, his ideas progressed at a very slow rate and so his ideas, which included a mid-engined GT car (in 1950!), anti-lock braking, self-levelling suspension and a rear-engined monocoque F1 car eight years before the Lotus 25, rarely came to fruition.

Clarke did not intend to become a racing car designer and indeed drifted before joining the RAF as a pilot in 1935 when he was 19 years old. When war broke out he flew bombers, but sinus trouble had him invalided out of the service. In 1943 he set up his own motor business, Continental Cars Ltd, which dealt in high-performance machines, with Bugattis a speciality.

After the war he was joined in the business by one of his customers, Mike Oliver, who had been an RAF pilot himself and who, though not formally trained, was a natural engineer. To Continental Cars, Kenneth McAlpine brought his ex-Whitney Straight Maserati 8CM to be prepared and Clarke and Oliver tackled the job with a professionalism which was then rare. They not only bolted it together properly, but conducted a careful development programme. McAlpine was impressed and when Clarke announced he was to build his own sports car, he put his name at the top of the customer list.

At the time Continental Cars had a problem in that there were very few new cars to sell, since most British cars were earmarked for export, and a hoped-for Bugatti agency did not materialize since Bugatti had virtually ceased production. On the other hand, it was possible to buy complete chassis, and Clarke bought these from Lea-Francis and had them re-bodied, while Oliver re-worked the engines. The result was a sports car with good performance and impeccable road manners with which McAlpine, Clarke and Oliver all enjoyed some success. A total of 14 LeaF-based sports cars were made.

McAlpine was a wealthy man (heir to McAlpine, the building firm) and even before the first sports car was completed he commissioned Clarke and Oliver to build him an F2 car. At the same time he began to trade under the name Connaught Engineering (the name deriving partly from an Irish kingdom, partly from CONtinental AUTomobiles). Clarke designed a ladder frame with two large (3¾-in) main tubes and three cross-members of the same size. Where it differed from most other similar designs was in the detail work (the front cross member doubled as a 3½-gallon oil tank) and careful weight distribution.

Since McAlpine intended to run only in British sprint events, fuel capacity was kept to 19 gallons, stored in two pannier tanks. Independent suspension all round was by double wishbones and torsion bars and the wheels were bolt-on and made from magnesium alloy. High-grade materials were in short supply and their supply was restricted by the government, but Connaught's works foreman was a man of great resource....

Mike Oliver, working in a Nissen hut which was to become a very well-equipped engine shop, took the LeaF engine apart and re-engineered it. The block itself was one of a batch Lea-Francis had cast in aluminium with the original chain valve drive replaced by gears. As fitted to A1, it kept its original size of 1767cc (75 × 100 mm), but Oliver specified new valves, crankshaft, camshafts, valve springs, pistons and rocker covers and converted it to dry sump lubrication. Fitted with four Amal carburettors, it gave 130 bhp, which was twice the original output, but further development was always to be hampered by the valve gear, which achieved a hemispherical chamber by twin camshafts high in the block driving short push-rods. Power was transmitted through a Wilson 4-speed preselector gearbox after Oliver conducted tests which proved that such a box did not waste power.

The car made its debut at the Castle Combe Meeting in October 1950, where, over ten laps, McAlpine finished second to Stirling Moss' H.W.M., but in fact it was a thin field and whatever the merits of the Connaught A-series,

Dennis Poore drove a magnificent race with this A-series Connaught to finish fourth in the 1952 British Grand Prix at Silverstone. (Guy Griffiths)

This view of the rear end of the A-series shows clearly the mounting of the de Dion tube and the high level of engineering. (Guy Griffiths)

it would have had to have been spectacular for McAlpine to have beaten Moss.

From the start, Clarke had conceived the idea of changing the rear suspension for different circuits, and while this was typical of the way Clark's mind ran, it was felt to be impractical. For 1951, however, Connaught A1 was fitted with a de Dion rear axle with the tube itself mounted nearly vertically and located by a compound linkage running from the nearside hub to the chassis frame and a short radius arm, mounted on rubber blocks to the top of the differential.

McAlpine enjoyed his short season and the car appeared nine times in British races and gave trouble on only two occasions, when the throttle linkage broke due to the strain put on it by the four springs that activated the Amals. Its performances were not extraordinary, but it picked up a few places, and one win, in minor races without ever upsetting the form book.

It was a learning year, but progress was slow largely due to the fact that Clarke insisted that everything should be done in a very thorough way. At the end of 1951 he suddenly woke up to the fact that while Maserati was planning to incorporate 50 modifications to its cars over the winter, Connaught had not made a single car in 1951, yet everyone was working flat out. From then on things moved at a more rapid pace though without sacrificing quality.

In Britain, the up-grading of F2 to the World Championship formula coincided with growing prosperity, an easing of restrictions, and an enormous increase in the popularity of motor racing. Connaught Engineering soon had orders and a further eight A-series cars were to be built.

In preparation for the new season, Oliver increased the size of the engine to 1960cc by increasing the bore to 79 mm, but this made the sealing of the cylinder head extremely weak and no adequate solution was ever found for the problem. A four-branch exhaust replaced the separate pipes of A1 and it was found that there was an improvement in power if the four Amals were mounted on 10-in ram pipes, and since these then protruded through the bodywork they were encased in a plenum chamber. To make it easier to remove the engine, the wheelbase of production cars was increased by an inch to 7 ft 1 in.

Ken Downing, a gentleman amateur who had been very successful in his Connaught L2 sports car, took delivery of A3 (for some reason there was never an A2), and he and McAlpine went to test at Goodwood, where both lost oil pressure and seized their engines and so missed the Easter Monday Meeting. In the International Trophy at Silverstone, Downing managed fifth in Heat One and a fortnight later at Silverstone took a couple of wins in club races.

He then took his car to Chimay and the Grand Prix des Frontières, but since that coincided with the Monaco (sports car) GP there were no aces present. Still he dominated the race until the last lap, when, lacking guidance from his pits, he eased off too much and was passed by Paul Frère's H.W.M.

By the time of the British GP, there were four cars ready to do battle and with an increase in the compression ratio, they now had around 145 bhp and Downing managed to qualify fifth behind the works Ferraris and Manzon's Gordini. In the race itself it was Dennis Poore (A4) who drove most strongly and he held third for some distance, ahead of Taruffi's Ferrari, until a botched fuel stop dropped him back. Still he finished fourth, with Eric Thompson's new works car (A5) fifth, Downing ninth and McAlpine 16th.

In third place at Silverstone was Mike Hawthorn's cheap and cheerful Cooper-Bristol, which, with other Coopers and H.W.M.s, had been making a brave show in Europe. By contrast most Connaughts were driven by gentleman amateurs, who raced for amusement when they had the time, and consequently the British GP was the marque's debut race at a serious level.

For the most part Connaughts raced in minor British events, including hill climbs, where they frequently figured in the results. Downing took his car to the Dutch GP, where it retired, but the marque's first serious continental raid came at the Italian GP. There cars were entered for Poore, McAlpine and Stirling Moss. Moss managed to qualify ninth, by slipstreaming Ascari's Ferrari, and he was in ninth in the race after a push-rod broke. McAlpine retired with broken rear suspension and Poore finished 12th, six laps down.

Six cars had been made by the end of 1952 and the tally for the season was six wins, five seconds, three thirds, four fourths, six fifths and two sixth places, but most of these results were gained in British club events. They were fulfilling the function for which they had been made: providing a car for the patron and for like-minded amateurs, but it was clear they could not compete against the best opposition.

The standards to which the cars were built made them an attractive proposition for such a driver, for they were extremely safe and handled well, but that peace of mind was secured at the penalty of weight and they never were as light as they might have been. A Cooper-Bristol was a good 100 lb lighter.

During 1952 Clarke toyed with the idea of a lightweight space-frame car with two 998cc V-twin J.A.P. engines in the rear, and this reached the stage of a model frame. Some progress, too, was made towards making a d.o.h.c. head for the LeaF engine and this was designed at Lea-Francis, but Clarke went cold on the idea when someone in the works copied the drawings and sold them.

Stuart Tresilian, an engineer who did some work for Connaught, offered the team the drawings of a sturdy, d.o.h.c. 'over-square' 4-cylinder engine, but the money did not exist to make it. Later Tresilian worked for B.R.M. and was able to make his engine, as the P25. While on engines, McAlpine had been racing in F3 and decided that a multi-cylinder unit might beat the Nortons. Clarke thought that a lot of little diesel engines used for model aircraft on a common crankshaft might be the answer and actually sketched an X-32 (500cc, 32 cylinders!), but settled on a d.o.h.c. V-12. To test the theory a single-cylinder unit was made by a specialist firm, but by the time it was delivered, interest in the project had waned.

From America came two new tweaks for 1953, Hilborn-Travers fuel injection (which was fitted to two cars, A8 and AL10) and nitromethane. This fuel had the same effect as turbocharging, and adding it to racing fuel increased power but at the expense of economy, so Connaught used a 30 per cent mixture for sprint races and 15 per cent for longer events. A great deal of secrecy surrounded the 'discovery' of the new fuel, but in 1952 Mike Hawthorn had been equally secretive when he had used it to such good effect and it was not for many years that his use of it was confirmed.

When Roy Salvadori appeared in A8 at the Easter Monday Goodwood Meeting and set pole ahead of de Graffenried's Maserati, everyone looked at the fuel injection system and nodded wisely, but nobody suspected the fuel. In fact, fuel injection did not add much to the power, but was a simpler device than the four Amals. No fewer than seven Connaughts raced at Goodwood and Salvadori appeared to have the F2 Lavant Cup in the bag until, on the last lap, a connecting rod in his accelerator broke, and as he coasted towards the line, de Graffenried just pipped him. Still, with Tony Rolt (A3) and Kenneth McAlpine (A1) coming home in third and fourth behind Salvadori it was reckoned a good showing, even if it was only a 17-mile race.

During 1953 two cars with 7 ft 6 in wheelbases were made (AL9 and AL10) and the latter had a rear roll bar which was adjustable from the cockpit. It *may* have been the first time such a device appeared on a racing car, but since it did not make its debut until the August, with only weeks remaining of the formula, it was a case of a bright idea appearing too late to be assessed.

As before, most Connaught appearances were in

Roy Salvadori with his fuel injection A-series at Goodwood in April 1953 after the throttle linkage broke. To Salvadori's left is Gregor Grant, editor of Autosport. (**Guy Griffiths**)

British national events, where they were very successful but where, too, the opposition was thin. By the end of the year, Connaughts had taken 21 wins, 12 seconds, ten thirds, three fourths, six fifths and two sixth places, with Tony Rolt in Rob Walker's car (A3, bought from Ken Downing, who had retired) being the most successful driver with ten wins.

By contrast, when the cars appeared in World Championship events the results were somewhat different. In the Dutch GP, Moss in A8 could get no higher than ninth on the grid, nearly nine seconds off the pace, and though he ran as high as seventh, and finished ninth, he was seven laps in arrears after a pit stop to have a fuel lead reconnected. André Pilette (A4) managed 11th in the Belgian GP and he was seven laps down, too, which is no surprise, for in practice he had been 57 seconds off the pace. In the few races they did at the top level, the story was always the same, for the team lacked experience and were always short of money. The year's best showing in WC events was Peter Walker's drive at Silverstone (A3), where he held fifth until eliminated by a broken half-shaft, and the same race provided the year's best result, when 'B. Bira' finished a lacklustre seventh, eight laps down.

On the horizon, however, was the 2½-litre F1 and Connaught needed an engine. It experimented with Laurie Bond's air-cooled V-8 (q.v.), which did not work, and then Clarke, Oliver and Bill Warham made drawings for a Connaught rotary valve engine, but that progressed no further than pencil on paper. Another engine, a d.o.h.c. four, reached the stage of having castings made, but since the team could not risk money on an unknown quantity, it was dropped.

In the pipeline, however, were two outside projects which might have given Connaught the power it needed, the Coventry Climax 'Godiva' and the Speed V-8. It is clear from Clarke's own papers that he was keeping alive the possibility of their appearance right up to the end of Connaught Engineering. Indeed, in a memo written in April 1957, a month before the team folded, he refers to the fact he had once considered taking over the 'Speed' project and had in the works a mock-up of the 'Godiva'.

Since the 'Godiva' unit appeared the more promising, he designed a radical new car to use it. This was designated the 'J5', though it is sometimes referred to as the Type D. Drawings show that it looked not unlike the later B.R.M. P57, with its rear engine and alloy wheels with knock-off hub nuts. At the front it was to have a beam axle with torsion bar springing, located by radius rods and a Panhard rod, and the disc brakes would have been mounted outboard. At the rear was a sub-frame carrying the engine, transmission and a de Dion rear axle

with inboard disc brakes. This was to be bolted to the centre-section by tapered bolts, so the whole assembly could be removed, in the same way as the later Lola Mk 3.

The transmission itself was a 5-speed preselector epicyclic gearbox/final drive unit with the gearbox behind the final drive, and one of these was actually made together with parts for a further five, but the only time the one was used was in Paul Emery's Cooper-Connaught (q.v.). Most startling of the car's many unusual features was the centre-section, which was to be a monocoque, or, as John Bolster described it in *Autosport*, a 'geodetic' structure, in other words a tubular construction with a stressed skin. This was under construction at the beginning of 1954, but when Coventry Climax failed to release the 'Godiva' engine, it was eventually scrapped.

Although A-series cars continued to be successful in club racing, and five of them appeared in the 1954 British GP, Connaught faced the 2½-litre formula with neither car nor engine. Clarke did a deal with Alta for an exclusive supply of 2½-litre engines and Oliver set about re-working them, and he finished up changing as many components as he had on the old LeaF unit.

By the time they were ready to race, Oliver had coaxed 240 bhp at 6400 rpm. This was on a par with contemporary Maserati and Ferrari engines and belies the story that Connaughts were underpowered. Unfortunately, even with Oliver's best attentions, the 2470cc (93.5 × 90 mm) engine was unable to sustain high-speed running with reliability.

Together with his chief draughtsman, 'Johnny' Johnson, Clarke began work on a new car in July 1953, and the first chassis was complete by that September. It had a simple ladder-frame with coil spring and double wishbone front suspension and a de Dion rear axle located by long single radius arms and a compound linkage and suspended by torsion bars. As before, transmission was through a 4-speed preselector gearbox and about the only innovation under the skin was the use of outboard Dunlop disc brakes all round.

In one stride Clarke had gone from designing the most advanced car of the 2½-litre formula to actually making one which most politely might be called 'conservative'. The B-series cars were anyway only intended as a stop-gap until the 'Godiva' engines arrived and it was safe to proceed with the J5.

One thing which had puzzled the team was the fact the Cooper-Bristols had always had a higher top speed and this was identified as an aerodynamic problem. Accordingly, Connaught rigged up a wind tunnel, powered by a Ford V-8 engine, and was probably the first F1 team to have one of its own.

The result of practical experimentation, together with advice from a friendly aircraft aerodynamacist, Eric Hall, led to the creation of a startling fully enveloping body. It was not shown to the public until August 1954, the delay being due to the time it took to make the Alta engines into viable units, and so although it appeared after the Mercedes-Benz W196, it had been conceived and developed concurrently with it. The streamliner body worked well, but was dropped for a practical reason: the top half was made in one piece and was very light. When it was removed at a race meeting there was often a problem of finding a space to put it, and a further problem was preventing damage to it if the day happened to be windy.

It was not until the 1955 Easter Monday Goodwood Meeting that B1 was ready to race, in the hands of Tony Rolt. By that time the original Borrani wire wheels had been replaced by Dunlop alloy disc wheels and the SU fuel injection had given way to a system of Connaught's own making, though, by mid-season, two twin-choke Webers were more usual. Rolt finished fourth in the Formule Libre race, but in the Richmond Trophy for F1 cars, he retired with a broken throttle.

A second car (B2) was ready for Jack Fairman to drive at the International Trophy and he and McAlpine (B1) ran third and fourth, but a broken throttle side-lined Fairman and a broken fuel union eliminated McAlpine.

Leslie Marr took delivery of B3 and Rob Walker bought B4, but insisted on open-wheeled bodywork. All four were entered for the British GP at Aintree, with Rolt proving the fastest qualifier, in 13th place but 6.2 seconds off the pace. Fairman's car did not start and the other three all retired.

For the rest of 1955 they appeared only in British events and the nearest one came to making a mark was

Body off – Jack Fairman's B-series Connaught in the paddock at Silverstone at the International Trophy in 1955. The body shell is held by three mechanics. (Leslie Marr)

Kenneth McAlpine at the wheel of the streamlined B-series Connaught in the 1955 International Trophy. He retired because of a broken fuel union. (T. C. March)

Rodney Clarke cleans his goggles before testing one of his own designs – the streamlined B-series, B1. (Leslie Marr)

in the *Daily Telegraph* Trophy at Aintree, where Reg Parnell (B2) led Moss' Maserati. After Moss retired Parnell seemed to have the race in the bag, but its engine ran a bearing. For the rest, there was a class win at Shelsley Walsh hill climb (Marr) and a Formule Libre victory at Snetterton (Peter Walker in B4), which was hardly the big time.

It looked as though the end was in sight for Connaught, for the cars were not getting results and, having married, McAlpine had hung up his helmet and no longer had the same incentive to continue. Clarke tried to interest the motor industry in using Connaught as a consultancy, but without success.

Then came an invitation from the organizers of the Syracuse GP, and their offer of £1000 starting money per car was too good to miss. A problem was finding a couple of competent drivers (not stars, they would want money) and eventually Connaught chose Les Leston and a young dental student called Tony Brooks, who had raced an A-series car a couple of times.

Brooks was allowed only 15 laps in practice and given a strict rev limit, but still he qualified B1 on the front row of the grid and in the race trounced the works Maseratis of Musso, Schell and Villoresi. It was Britain's first Grand Prix win for 31 years, so the joy can be imagined, especially since it was unexpected.

It secured Connaught's future for the time being, but was really a lucky win, not in the sense there had been any fluke in Brooks' driving, he had wiped the floor with the Maserati team, but it was a stroke of luck that the youngster selected because he was competent, available, and cheap had turned out to be a genius.

Another great driver, Archie Scott-Brown, was given his chance in the Boxing Day Brands Hatch meeting and he obliged by giving B1 a second win. Scott-Brown was born deformed, with a withered right arm which ended in a thumb and vestigial palm, short legs and club feet, and it had been a battle for him to gain a licence at all. As it was his entries were often rejected by overseas organizers and yet his was an extraordinary talent.

In the Richmond Trophy at Goodwood, Scott-Brown diced with Moss' Maserati 250F (recently fitted with fuel injection) and was in the lead from Moss, and the B.R.M.s of Brooks and Hawthorn, when his brakes began to fade and then a piston broke. Both B.R.M.s retired and Moss stroked home ahead of Salvadori's Maserati with three Connaughts in the next three places.

Desmond Titterington (B1) and Piero Scotti, who had bought B6, both entered the Syracuse GP, but there was to be no repeat of Brooks' great triumph and both retired. Scott-Brown (B2) led the Aintree 200 before

another piston broke, but in the International Trophy at Silverstone he finished second to Moss' Vanwall, with Desmond Titterington (B1) third. McAlpine could look down the entry list at Silverstone and feel some satisfaction at the part he had played in British motor racing, for there were nine Connaughts on the grid.

For financial reasons, the works decided to concentrate on non-Championship meetings, where the starting money was good and where there was a better chance of picking up places and prize money. Piero Scotti raced in the Belgian GP, where he retired, and shortly afterwards there was a dispute over money (Scotti was buying his car by instalments) and the car was returned to the works. It now sits in the Science Museum, one of the few truly original racing cars of the period in existence.

Scott-Brown (B7) set pole for the Aintree 100, but retired while leading. He was the quickest Connaught (B7) in practice for the British GP, but that was only tenth on the grid and four seconds off the pace. In the race he lost a wheel, Titterington (B2) had a con-rod break, while Fairman (B5) came home fourth, but two laps down. Archie in B7 was one of only six starters in the Vanwall Trophy at Snetterton and led until retiring with a loose oil pipe.

While Brooks' Syracuse win is often regarded as Connaught's finest hour, some from the works point to the 1956 Italian GP. Scott-Brown's entry was rejected, so three works cars were entered for Leston (B1), Fairman (B5) and Flockhart (B7). None qualified quickly, but in the race, while Leston was an early retirement with a broken torsion bar, the steady speed of the remaining cars, aided by sweet-handling chassis and Dunlop tyres, meant they did not suffer the spate of blow-outs which delayed so many and Flockhart came home third with Fairman fifth. Connaught's 1956 season came to an end with the BRSCC F1 race at Brands Hatch, where Scott-Brown (B7) led home Stuart Lewis-Evans (B5) in his first F1 race, while only Salvadori's Maserati in third prevented a whitewash, for Leston (B6) and Fairman (B1) were next up. It was, however, only a 'clubbie'.

It was clear that the Coventry Climax Godiva engine was not forthcoming and that McAlpine could not continue to pour money into stop-gap cars. Clarke therefore designed a new car, similar in layout to the B-series but with a space-frame. As usual, it was late in arrriving.

In order to keep the team afloat in 1957 it was decided to run two two-car teams and survive on starting money, a desperate move. Ivor Bueb (B5) and Les Leston (B1) were entered in the Syracuse GP, but Leston retired and Bueb could only finish fifth, five laps down. In the Pau GP both qualified well and finished third and fifth, but Bueb was three laps in arrears and Leston four laps.

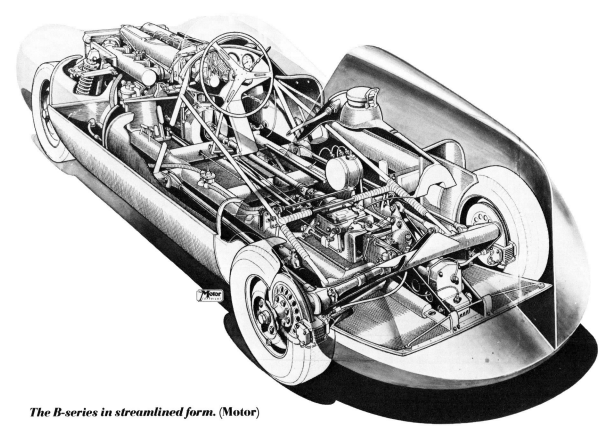

The B-series in streamlined form. (Motor)

Jack Fairman drove this Connaught B-series 'Syracuse' into fourth place in the 1956 British Grand Prix. (T. C. March)

In the Glover Trophy at Goodwood, Stuart Lewis-Evans had B3, which had been re-bodied with a curious, wedge-shaped shell which was immediately nicknamed the 'toothpaste tube'. With the retirement of Scott-Brown (B7), Salvadori (B.R.M.) and the Vanwalls of Moss and Brooks, Lewis-Evans came home to head a Connaught 1-2 with Fairman (B4) trailing in second.

Lewis-Evans had B5 for the Naples GP and there he qualified fifth, but over six seconds off the pace, and his race ended with a broken front hub. So to Monaco, where Connaught entered cars for Lewis-Evans (B3) and Bueb (B2), and while Bueb retired, Lewis-Evans came fourth, albeit three laps down.

A few days later Connaught Engineering was wound up and its effects were sold by auction that October. It is a bitter irony that within weeks of Connaught's retirement Vanwall won its first World Championship race and began the British domination in F1.

One car which did not go under the hammer was the prototype C-series car, with its space-frame, long wheelbase and 'toothpaste tube' body. This was later sold to Paul Emery, who entered it for Bob Said in the 1959 US GP, but Said crashed it on the first lap. Later it was bought by some enthusiasts who supercharged the engine and tried, without success, to qualify for the Indianapolis 500.

At the time Connaught folded Clarke had already thought beyond the C-series and was planning another rear-engined car, this time with an Alta engine, a more conventional space-frame and the 5-speed transaxle.

Clarke returned to the motor trade, specializing in high-performance cars, and died in 1979. Mike Oliver had kept up to date with flying throughout his time at Connaught, became a distinguished test pilot and now lives in Devon. It remains a tragedy that the pool of expertise which was Connaught was allowed to disperse, for the British motor industry could have used it.

Stuart Lewis-Evans with the 'toothpaste tube' B-series at Ardmore in 1958. The car retains the abbreviated nose with which it ran at Monaco in 1957. **(Barry Mckay)**

COOPER

One of the enduring myths of motor racing is that Charles and John Cooper took the front suspension of two Fiat Topolinos, built a simple chassis between them, added a J.A.P. engine and went out and cleaned up 500cc racing, which had started just after the war. A second car was made for Eric Brandon and since this too was successful it led them to become constructors. Like many myths it is broadly true, but the real story is a little more complex, and a lot more interesting. The first 500cc Cooper was initially not as successful as the pace-maker in the class – Colin Strang's special which mated a Vincent-HRD engine to a Topolino chassis. Strang, however, made only one car, while the Coopers decided to make a lot.

They realized that their car performed better than most and was better made and finished than many, and there were a lot of people who fancied trying the new category but who had neither the time nor the expertise to build their own cars. There was a market if they could lay down a production run. In the early post-war days that was easier said than done, for there were severe restrictions on materials, but the Coopers were nothing if not resourceful.

A scrapyard, Coley's of Kingston, was full of redundant military aircraft, some not completed. It had, too, loads of gear from wartime 'shadow' factories: cables, Jubilee clips, nuts and bolts, sheets of aluminium and, if you felt so inclined, crates full of Rolls-Royce Merlin engines. Coley's provided aluminium for the bodies and, melted down and cast, for the wheels. Brakes were a problem, but another scrapyard provided 8-in wet liners from marine diesel engines and these were sawn up to make brake drums.

The Coopers bought up a number of Morrison air raid shelters (a sort of steel table to provide protection from falling masonary in the home), and the tops of these became the fabricated castles which held the Fiat-style transverse leaf springs front and rear, while the legs were used to make welding jigs.

One of the people interested in buying a car was a steel broker and from this source came those chassis tubes which other scrapyards could not source. Once the Coopers had shown the way, other special builders followed, and so the same scrapyards supplied H.W.M., Emeryson, Alta and a host of special builders.

Instead of being just two Coopers there were suddenly 14. One of them was bought by a teenager named Stirling Moss. Another batch of 12 followed and then another. Cooper swamped the field and became the first British large-scale maker of single-seater racing cars as well as changing 500cc racing, so it ceased being the preserve of the special builder and became a serious class

for drivers with their eyes on better things. The success of 500cc racing, due in no small measure to Cooper, led to the FIA recognizing it as Formula 3, the first time that a British series had become an international class.

The Coopers had their rivals, but also had luck on their side. First Alf Bottoms threatened with his J.B.S. cars, but poor Alf was killed in the 1951 Luxembourg GP and the project fell apart. Had he survived, motor racing history might have been very different. Then Kieft marketed a bought-in design which was clearly superior, but the cars Kieft made were of poor quality and another opportunity was lost. Cooper Cars sailed on to success after success.

Charlie Cooper was an irascible character, an ex-racing mechanic who had set up a garage in Surbiton. John, his son, is an easy-going man, who was born with a spanner in his hand. They were shrewd, practical men who were ideally suited to the 1950s, when makers did not have a vast network of sub-contractors and suppliers to draw upon. They thought on their feet, responded to change and got things done at a rapid rate. As engineers they were really cunning blacksmiths, but the word 'cunning' is chosen for all its nuances, including clever craftsmanship, and 'blacksmith' implies the honest worker, a man who not only knows his metal but loves it and can talk to it.

The Coopers *stumbled* upon innovative design and had the nous to exploit their discoveries. By the end of 1951 Cooper Cars had built up its production of 500cc cars to the rate of better than one a week, an unprecedented rate for single-seaters, and it also built a number of front-engined sports cars.

When F2 became the WC category, some 500cc racers thought they would like a crack at the big time. They had raced on the Continent and had made a living from starting and prize money, and they knew they could make even more by running an F2 car provided it was inexpensive and reliable. The Coopers set to work and came up with a chassis not unlike their Mk V F3 car but with the engine in the front. This had drilled box-section main members with a parallel tubular structure. Front and rear suspension still followed the old Topolino layout with transverse leaf springs and lower wishbones, but these were fabricated by Cooper. In the early days of the 500cc movement Topolinos 'condition no object' had become sought after and all baby Fiats in England lived in fear of meeting a special builder.

Of the few available 2-litre engines, the rugged Bristol unit was easily the best bet. It produced no more than 125-30 bhp, a good 35-40 bhp down on Ferrari and Maserati, but it was available and it was reasonably

Mike Hawthorn with his Cooper-Bristol at the hairpin before the pits at Spa in the 1952 Belgian Grand Prix. He drove a magnificent race to finish fourth. (LAT)

priced and could come complete with a Bristol 4-speed gearbox. The Coopers used these units in conjunction with an ENV differential and the resulting car was the T20 or, as it is usually called, the Cooper-Bristol Mk I.

It was finished with a simple body, designed in the usual Cooper way by tossing ideas and sketches around in the workshop, and had bolt-on alloy wheels with cast-in brake drums of the style which the Coopers had made first as an expedient. One snag was that the Bristol engine was very tall and the car never had balanced lines, but the Coopers unwittingly built a vehicle with very good under-car air flow, which made it quick in a straight line.

Jimmy Richmond, an enthusiast who had run a private F3 team in a professional manner, arranged with Cooper Cars for Ecurie Richmond to run the works F2 team. This was more or less a courtesy title which enabled Richmond to negotiate better starting money for his drivers, Eric Brandon and Alan Brown.

While the first three cars were being built, Brandon kept an eye on their progress and made sure that the best parts were used on the works cars, while the other car, for

Bob Chase, got third choice. When the cars tested pre-season on Lasham airfield, however, it was Chase's car which was easily the quickest, for behind the wheel was a youngster called Mike Hawthorn.

He did, however, have an edge, for his father, Leslie, knew all about nitromethane, since he had a lot of experience of tuning motorcycle engines. Adding this to the fuel made a huge difference, as Connaught discovered the following season. Having found an advantage, the Hawthorns were not about to share it with anyone, so Mike's effortless superiority in the early races of 1952 was not entirely due to his talent, although that was considerable.

The cars made their debut at Goodwood and in the six-lap Lavant Cup for F2 cars, Hawthorn led home Brown and Brandon for a Cooper 1-2-3. Then Hawthorn won the Formule Libre race and finished his day's work by hounding Gonzalez in the 'Thin Wall Special' in the F1 event. The following day he was a household name. Wins in minor races followed and then Hawthorn won his heat of the International Trophy at Silverstone and led the final until his gear lever became deranged.

The Richmond team set off for the Continent with their F3 and F2 cars and Alan Brown managed fifth in the Swiss GP to win Cooper's first WC points, but he was three laps down. Hawthorn entered the Belgian GP and came fourth, with Brown sixth and Brandon ninth. None of the cars enjoyed much luck in the French GP, but Hawthorn finished second to Taruffi in the 'Thin Wall' in the Ulster Trophy at Dundrod.

By the time the British GP came around, there was a total of seven Cooper-Bristols and five were in the race. Hawthorn came a fine third ahead of all the Connaughts, which must have been pleasant, for he had tested for Connaught and been turned down. Since Reg Parnell in another Cooper could finish only seventh, Hawthorn's reputation was burnished further.

Then in the 200-mile F1/F2 race at Boreham, which was run in a downpour, Hawthorn built up a lead of 40 seconds over the works 4½-litre Ferraris of Luigi Villoresi and Chico Landi until his engine began to misfire and the track dried. Still he finished third and winner of the F2 class by a country mile. It was a performance which owed everything to talent and nothing to Mike's secret edge in the fuel tank. In the Dutch GP, Hawthorn was a sensational third in practice and fourth in the race behind three works Ferraris, and in the Italian GP he slipstreamed Taruffi's Ferrari until his distributor drive sheared. As a result of his brilliant season, Hawthorn landed a Ferrari test drive and a contract for 1953.

For 1953, Cooper brought out a Mk II (T23) version and a number of the Mk Is were converted into sports cars (most have since been re-converted to F2 form for reasons not unassociated with market values). It was a more thoughtful version of the Mk I rather than a radical departure, with a lighter tubular frame with the parallel longitudinal members further apart, narrower front and rear tracks, larger brake drums, and the use of magnesium alloy in some components to save a little weight.

Externally, the main difference was a sleeker body without the characteristic bonnet scoop of the Mk I. Owen Maddock, Cooper's chief draughtsman-cum-design co-ordinator, had split the radiator core and spread the two halves into an 'A', which allowed cool air for the carburettors to pass between them. Between 14 and 16 Mk IIs were built (Cooper was too busy building cars to keep track), but on the whole they did not perform as well as the Mk Is, not because they were inferior but because the opposition (which now included Maserati) had moved ahead and none of the cars was driven by a talent like Mike Hawthorn.

In the Syracuse GP, the Ferraris all retired, but Rodney Nuckey led home Brandon and Peter Whitehead (who used an Alta engine) for a Cooper 3-4-5 behind de Graffenried's Maserati and Chiron's O.S.C.A. Ken Wharton's Mk II (with an ENV preselector gearbox) qualified on pole and finished second to Hawthorn's Ferrari in his heat of the International Trophy at Silverstone, but a misfire dropped him to fifth in the final. Soon afterwards he came second to Hawthorn's Ferrari in the Ulster Trophy at Dundrod.

Wharton entered the Dutch GP, but was slow in practice and retired with a broken wishbone. He missed the Belgian GP, but reappeared for the French, where he

The Mk 2 tubular-chassis Cooper-Bristol entered by Bob Chase for Eric Brandon in the 1953 International Trophy at Silverstone. **(Guy Griffiths)**

again retired, this time with run bearings, but Bob Gerard in another Cooper-Bristol finished eighth. Wharton also finished eighth in the British GP, but Alan Brown scored Cooper's best result in 1953 WC races with a sixth in Germany, although the best performance of all was put up by Moss in a Cooper-Alta at Monza, where he ran as high as fifth. After Hawthorn's brilliant season, 1953 was a let-down and the whole year brought only a handful of wins, all of them in minor British races. The cars continued to appear with decreasing frequency over the next few years and even appeared in the 1954 and 1956 British Grands Prix, but in a serious sense the Cooper-Bristol had its time in 1952.

The Coopers continued to be successful racing car makers and still dominated F3, but as always were on the lookout for new gaps in the market. Cooper was one of the makers which had approached Coventry Climax and had set in motion the 'Godiva' V-8 engine, which, had it been released, would have seen Cooper in F1. John Cooper has told me that the car the company would have built would have most likely been along the lines of the Cooper-Bristol, but that engine did not appear and Cooper had to wait a little longer before it would become a major international force. In the meantime it made the chassis for the first Vanwall.

Cooper started the rear-engine revolution in modern racing and it happened in a roundabout way. Coventry Climax had made its splendid little 1100cc FWA engine and the rule of the 1950s was that when a good engine appeared there would quickly grow up a class to use it. The Coopers realized that an 1100cc sports car would find a ready market and had appreciated the performances which the aerodynamic Lotuses had put up. They knew that if they were to compete with Lotus they had to take aerodynamics equally seriously.

Cooper had built a couple of fully enclosed 500cc cars for record breaking and had even raced one of them. John consulted a pal who was an aerodynamacist with Hawker, he consulted his boss, the great Sir Sydney Camm, and it emerged that a scaled-up 500cc record-breaker's body would serve their turn. Camm also suggested that the long tail be cut off and a concave panel replace it.

Cooper called this a 'Camm' tail (while joking that it was cut off to make the car fit the transporter), but by an extraordinary coincidence it fitted the theories of the German scientist Dr Wunibald Kamm, so 'Camm tail' or 'Kamm tail', both are correct.

John Cooper tried the record breaker ballasted to reproduce the weight of the Climax engine and proposed gearbox and the tests proved satisfactory. Since the record breaker was a central-seater, the sports car would have the driver in the middle, just like some Veritas and Kieft sports cars. Having chosen the shape the car was designed beneath it, hence the engine in the rear, driving through a modified Citroën gearbox, and the large-tube curved frame. It was not a true space-frame, for it was not properly triangulated, but it was light and stiff and, still using the old Topolino-style suspension, in 1955 Cooper had the edge on Lotus in the burgeoning 1100cc sports cars class.

It was this car, the T39 'Bobtail', which was the true start of the rear-engine revolution in motor racing.

At the beginning of 1955 an Australian called Jack Brabham arrived in England to try his hand at European racing. He had been successful back home in a variety of motor sports and had made his name with his 'RedEx Special', which was a Cooper-Bristol Mk 1 with sponsorship.

He made a false start by buying Peter Whitehead's Cooper-Alta and then seemed to *merge* into Cooper Cars, turning up and turning his hand to anything and doing it all well. The 'Bobtail' was doing so well that it was proposed to put a 2.2-litre Bristol engine into the back of one and try it in F1. Brabham quietly got on with the task of building the car, though it never did get a 2.2-litre engine as the organizers of the 1955 British GP knew only too well, but they nodded it through because it was a good thing to do. The first rear-engined F1 Cooper (T40) had the old 1971cc engine, which gave all of 140 bhp, and it was no surprise to see Brabham way off the pace, for the car had been hastily finished and he had to start from the back of the grid with a broken clutch.

Later in the year, with the teething troubles solved, Brabham had a terrific dice for third place with Moss' Maserati in the RedEx Trophy at Snetterton. Moss won the dice, but his performance convinced Brabham both of his future as a driver and the potential of the Cooper chassis. Brabham took the car 'Down Under' for the winter (summer) season and won the Australian GP. He sold the car on and returned to Europe, where he was to become an important element in the restructuring of motor racing. A second T40 was built for Bob Chase, who entered Mike Keen in it as a sports car, but Keen rolled it in the Goodwood Nine Hours Race, was killed, and the car burned out.

When Chapman introduced the Lotus Eleven sports-racer, Cooper suffered a reverse in the 1100cc class, but fitted with s.o.h.c. 1½-litre Coventry Climax FMB engines, the cars continued to give a good account of themselves. On the horizon, however, was the 1½-litre F2, and Coventry Climax was preparing its d.o.h.c. FPF engine. Cooper was the first in the field with an F2 car, which was, in essence, an open-wheeled version of the

T39 'Bobtail'.

Cooper was the most prolific and successful maker of F2 cars in the 1½-litre formula, and when F2 Coopers began to appear in non-Championship F1 races early in 1957, it became apparent that even giving away a litre these nimble cars could embarrass F1 cars on twisty circuits. It would be only a matter of time before Cooper would request a 2-litre FPF engine and try its hand at F1. Such a car, a collaboration between the works and Rob Walker, made its debut in the 1957 Monaco GP with Jack Brabham in the cockpit, and he was in third place with just five laps to go when the fuel pump mounting broke. Still, Brabham pushed the car from the tunnel to the finish to take sixth. Brabham drove the car next in the French GP at Rouen, but collided with a Maserati on lap five. In the Reims GP he had no way of compensating for being over 100 bhp shy of the opposition and trailed in a long way last, but the car had survived a full GP distance.

Brabham and Salvadori both had 2-litre cars for the British GP and were joined on the grid by Bob Gerard's Cooper B.G.-Bristol (q.v.). Neither were on the pace, but while Brabham retired with clutch trouble, Salvadori took fifth, albeit five laps down and having to push his car over the finishing line with a shattered gearbox. Still, he gave Cooper its first WC points of the 2½-litre formula and Coventry Climax its first ever. It was also the first time that a rear-engined car had ever scored WC points. Salvadori followed this with a second place in the Caen GP behind Behra's B.R.M. and ahead of a number of private Maseratis. The next time that an F1 Cooper appeared was at the International Trophy at Silverstone, where Brabham finished second in his heat to Schell's B.R.M. and retired in the final with a broken oil pipe. Brabham and Salvadori both ran in the non-Championship Moroccan GP and both retired.

So ended Cooper's first F1 season. The cars were

Jack Brabham's rear-engined Cooper-Bristol holds up Hawthorn's Ferrari in the 1955 British Grand Prix at Aintree. (T. C. March)

only make-weights, but they had shown potential on the more twisty circuits. At the end of 1957, however, F1 was to change dramatically. Vanwall was already on top, Maserati withdrew from racing, and there was a switch to Av-gas in place of 'free' fuel. This narrowed the gap between the 2-litre FPF and 2½-litre engines and, besides, Cooper had been ascending a steep learning curve and one of the fruits of that was a stronger Citroën-ERSA gearbox with a new casing designed by Brabham.

The 1958 cars (T45) also had coil spring and double wishbone front suspension and an additional top wishbone at the rear. This latter was a modification Brabham had carried out on the 'Bobtail' Cooper-Bristol when he had taken it to Australia (the Walker cars had additional top radius rods). Disc brakes became usual equipment (previously most production cars had drums) and there was a new front anti-roll bar and a wider body. Later the works would have the use of two special 2.2-litre engines prepared for them by Coventry Climax.

The 1958 season began with the Argentine GP in January, but it was a late addition to the programme and Vanwall refused to send cars, and since B.R.M. wasn't ready the sole British representation was Moss in Rob Walker's 2-litre Cooper. Most of the field consisted of Maseratis, which were unhappy on Av-gas and were overheating, and Moss had no difficulty passing them and harrying the Ferraris. Then he took the lead, but Musso, in the leading Ferrari, did not press him, believing that he would have to change tyres, and the Cooper

had bolt-on wheels. This impression was reinforced by Rob Walker's pit apparently preparing for a pit stop. Too late did Musso realize that Moss intended to drive the whole way on one set of tyres. It was marginal, but Moss brilliantly conserved his tyres by driving on the lines with the most rubber and oil on. He crossed the line with the canvas showing through and Musso still 2.7 seconds behind.

It was one of the greatest drives in history and was not only the first WC win for Cooper and Climax, but also for Dunlop tyres and a rear-engined car. It was, too, the first time a privately entered car had won a WC event.

At the next WC race, Monaco, Coopers occupied third, fourth and fifth positions on the grid behind Brooks' Vanwall and Behra's B.R.M. It was a race of attrition and before half-distance Maurice Trintignant in a Rob Walker car fitted with a 2015cc engine, and Borrani wire wheels all round, was in the lead, with the remaining Ferraris unable to do anything about him. Behind the Ferraris sat Brabham (2.2-litre), who had been delayed after stopping to fix a loose anti-roll bar.

It was incredible. It meant that British cars, Vanwall and Cooper, had won four WC races in succession, yet ten months before Britain had not won a single WC race. Coopers had gone well in the pre-WC season races as well with Brabham and Salvadori second and third to Hawthorn's Ferrari at Goodwood, a 1-2-3-4 in the Aintree 200, where Moss beat Brabham by a whisker with Brooks (F2) third and Salvadori fourth, while Salvadori

In the 1958 British Grand Prix Salvadori with his works 2-litre Cooper-Climax took a fine third place.
(T. C. March)

82

Stirling Moss drove this Cooper with 2.5-litre Climax engine to first place in the Richmond Trophy at Goodwood, Easter Monday, 1959. (British Petroleum)

Jack Brabham on his way to victory with the 2.5-litre Cooper-Climax in the 1959 British Grand Prix at Aintree. (LAT)

had finished second to Collins' Ferrari in the International Trophy at Silverstone.

As the season got into its stride the position changed, but the Coopers still performed strongly on the slower circuits. Salvadori was fourth in the Dutch GP, Brabham sixth in the French at Reims, and Salvadori third and Brabham sixth in the British GP. Along the way Moss also won the Caen GP against a small but sturdy field.

Salvadori and Trintignant were second and third in the German GP, where young Bruce McLaren finished fifth on the road and winner of the F2 section. The cars were out of luck in Portugal, but Salvadori finished fourth on the road in the Italian GP and though too far behind to be a classified finisher he still took his three WC points. Finally the cars were out of the picture in the Moroccan GP, but Cooper finished third in the new World Manufacturers' Championship and Salvadori was fourth in the Drivers' Championship.

The little cars were now being taken very seriously indeed, especially since they were easily the most successful marque in F2, and there was a full 2½-litre engine waiting in the wings. Moreover, Moss, without a drive following the withdrawal of Vanwall, decided his best chance lay with a Cooper, although he hedged his bets by having a B.R.M.-engined car made.

Since Moss was under contract to BP, and Cooper to Esso, and petrol companies picked up most of the bills, the car was supplied to Rob Walker without the usual Citroën-ERSA gearbox and hence Moss turned to his old friend Valerio Colotti, who had left Maserati to set up his own design studio. The Colotti gearbox was to cost Moss the World Championship and lead not only to a lot of trashy newspaper headlines ('Moss Jinx Strikes Again') but to a completely unwarranted reputation as a car breaker. You do not win over 200 races, considerably more than anyone else who has driven at the top level, by breaking cars. There was, incidentally, little wrong with Colotti's design and the fault lay with the sub-contractors who made the parts.

The 1959 cars (T51) were virtually the same as the 1958 (T43) version except that the full 2½-litre Coventry Climax FPF was available, although some teams used other power units, notably the 4-cylinder Maserati 250S engine. Owen Maddock also began a collaboration with gearbox specialist Jack Knight to start work on a new transmission to replace the Cirtroën-ERSA unit. Salvadori went to Aston Martin and enjoyed a pay day, but little success, while Cooper would run a three-car team for Brabham, McLaren and Masten Gregory.

Since F2 was now awash with Coopers, which, typically, accounted for over 80 per cent of any race's entry list, it was decided not run a team from the works but to entrust a works-assisted team to an ex-Cooper privateer, Ken Tyrrell. Thus Brabham, McLaren and Tyrrell, three names which would resound in the world of F1 years after Cooper left, were directly associated with the company in 1959.

The season kicked off with the Richmond Trophy at Goodwood, where Moss led home Brabham. The Ferraris of Behra and Brooks scored in the Aintree 200 after Gregory had led the first stages until retiring and Moss has retired the Cooper-B.R.M. after taking over the lead, but McLaren was third, and not far behind, in his 2.2-litre car. Brabham then won the International Trophy at Silverstone against nearly a full WC field. The writing was on the wall, Ferrari had no answer to Cooper, and if Ferrari had no answer then it was not even worth putting the question to B.R.M., Lotus or Aston Martin.

Moss led most of the Monaco GP until his transmission broke and then Brabham won and there were three Coopers among the five classified finishers. Gregory led the early stages of the Dutch GP until encountering gear selection problems, Bonnier's B.R.M. then led, but Moss had led only to retire with another gearbox failure. B.R.M. had finally won a major race, the third British team to win one in less than two years, but Brabham was second and Gregory third. In the French GP at Reims, the straight-line speed of the Ferraris saw the team grab its chance while it could − it entered five cars and was rewarded with a 1-2-4, but even at Reims Brabham was third, and McLaren was fifth, and both were on the same lap as Brooks' winning Ferrari.

Moss had driven a B.R.M. at Reims and elected to do the same at Aintree for the British GP, but Brabham led from pole to flag and Moss only just managed to beat McLaren to take second. The season, however, was still wide open, as for some silly reason it was decided to hold the German GP on the extraordinary Avus circuit in Berlin, which consisted of two stretches of autobahn, an ill-designed banking and a flat-out curve. In the race Brooks' Ferrari set fastest lap of 149.14 mph, which compares to the then Silverstone record of 105.37 mph, and that was at a time when Woodcote was a very fast corner.

In the interests of safety (stemming from tyre wear rate) it was decided to run the race in two heats and it resulted in a Ferrari 1-2-3, with Trintignant the best Cooper in fourth. In no way was it a serious Grand Prix race (Grands Prix are not run in heats on a circuit with no corners) and just as Musso's win at Reims in 1957 should be recognized as of equal value to any WC race win, so the 1959 Avusrennen should be mentally deleted from any sensible reckoning.

Sanity returned at the Portuguese GP on the Monsanto circuit at Lisbon and there Moss' gearbox held together and he won emphatically, lapping the entire field, just to remind everyone that he was the greatest driver of the day, and when a race was run on a proper circuit, and Italian gear makers were up to scratch, nobody else need bother even considering the possibility of a win. Brabham had held second until tangling with a local amateur, Mario Cabral, who was driving a Cooper-Maserati in a typical 'starting money' deal, and he was lucky not to have sustained serious injury. Masten Gregory upheld works honour by coming second, and as for Ferrari, it might as well have stayed at home, for in practice no Ferrari driver could get within five seconds of Moss' pole.

Ferrari was fairly confident at Monza, however, but Moss pulled another of his strokes of genius by having his Cooper fitted with knock-off wire wheels at the rear. The implication was clear that he was expecting a pit stop to change tyres and, indeed, tyre wear was marginal, but it was the inside front tyre which was the problem. The Walker team obtained a sports Dunlop cover with a deeper tread and fitted that. Moss completed the entire distance without stopping, while the Ferraris had to change tyres. Ferraris filled four of the top six places, but the one which mattered went to Moss, and Brabham came in third.

Moss then won the International Gold Cup at Oulton Park from Brabham and Chris Bristow, who was making his F1 debut in one of the Yeoman Credit (B.R.P.) Coopers, and Brabham finished second to Ron Flockhart's B.R.M. in the Silver City Trophy at Snetterton. With these diversions out of the way attention concentrated on the US GP, the final round of the WC and a race which would decide the title, for Moss, Brooks and Brabham all had a chance.

Moss set pole by a 3-second margin, this time with coil spring and double wishbone rear suspension, and led the race, but then his gearbox failed on lap six. Brabham then led until he ran out of fuel on the very last lap and this let young McLaren into the lead, and he scraped home 0.4 seconds ahead of Trintignant's Cooper. Brooks had been shunted in the rear at the start and had called in at the pits to have his car checked, and that may have cost him the title, for he finished third. Brabham was fourth, however, and that was enough to clinch the title.

In the Manufacturers Championship, Cooper came first from Ferrari and it was an achievement which cannot be underestimated. Some enthusiasts from a Surrey garage were Champions of the world, when all they had initially set out to do was to have some fun and cheap racing with some Fiat Topolino bits and a J.A.P. engine.

Why, they had not even run in F1 three years before and it was less than 29 months since a British car had first won a WC event, and that was the result of years of dedicated effort by a millionaire industrialist. This was *Boys' Own Paper* stuff.

For 1960 Cooper decided to run just two works cars, for Brabham and McLaren, and the season began with the Argentine GP and victory for McLaren, but it was a lucky win and the Cooper team went home perplexed. True, Moss (Cooper) had sat on pole by a clear 1.6 seconds and 3.0 seconds faster than any other Cooper, but Moss was not quite of this world. The problem was the second man on the grid, Innes Ireland. Although he had finished only sixth after a multitude of problems, he had led the race and he had led it in the new Lotus 18, which was, one might say, a Cooper made with applied science.

Ideas for a new car began being considered before the Cooper team left the Argentine and John once told me that back at the workshop Jack Brabham put a seat on the floor and started arranging tubes about it, but perhaps that was just to demonstrate a point. Certainly Brabham's input into the new car was considerable and must have started him thinking of making cars for himself. The upshot of the usual Cooper collaborative design effort was the T53 or 'low-line' works cars (customers had to make do with the older T51 and some ran with the old Topolino-style suspension).

As the name suggests, the 'low-line' was a much sleeker car and its chassis more closely resembled a conventional space-frame with straight main tubes. Coil spring and wishbone suspension was used all round and it had 5-speed Cooper-Knight dry sumped transmission. It would debut at the International Trophy at Silverstone, but before then Ireland would make headlines by beating Moss at Goodwood in the new Lotus 18. Rob Walker immediately bought Moss a Lotus.

Moss still had his Cooper for the International Trophy at Silverstone, which had virtually a WC field, and while he sat on pole by over two seconds, and led until a wishbone broke, it was Ireland who won by 1.9 seconds from Brabham's 'low-line', which had not turned a wheel until arriving at the track. Moss won the Monaco GP in his new Lotus, but Coopers figured strongly and McLaren finished second.

During practice for the Belgian GP, a weld in the steering column broke on Moss' Lotus and he crashed heavily, and with multiple fractures he missed several races. In the GP itself, Chris Bristow in one of the B.R.P. Coopers made a mistake and paid for it with his life and so the short career of a man Moss had tipped as a future World Champion was over. It was a wretched weekend,

Another victory in the British Grand Prix for Brabham and Cooper followed in 1960, this time with the 'low-line' car. (T. C. March)

for Mike Taylor's F1 career also ended with a practice shunt and another promising young Brit, Alan Stacey, died at the wheel of his Lotus. It all overshadowed the fact that Brabham and McLaren scored a 1-2 with Gendebien in a B.R.P. Cooper in fourth.

Although Reims had never been kind to Cooper in the past, the French GP saw a Cooper 1-2-3-4 as Brabham led home Gendebien, McLaren and Henry Taylor (B.R.P.). Then Brabham won the British GP, after Graham Hill in one of the new rear-engined B.R.M.s had spun out of the lead. He followed this with a win in the Silver City Trophy at Brands Hatch against teams from

Ferrari and Lotus.

Brabham was having a terrific season. It is true that Moss was out of action, so everyone had moved up a notch, and it is equally true that B.R.M. and Lotus were often faster but failed to finish. Brabham, however, had not only made an important contribution to the design of the car he drove, he also was expert at setting it up for individual circuits, and this expertise was a big factor in Cooper's greatest year.

Moss was back for the Portuguese GP at Oporto, where he drove a Lotus, but Brabham sat on pole position and he won, with McLaren second, after John

Surtees, who seemed to have the race sewn up in his Lotus, crashed. It was Cooper's fifth successive WC win and it clinched Brabham's second World title.

The British teams boycotted the Italian GP on the grounds that the use of the Monza bankings was unsafe and the next time the works cars raced was in the International Gold Cup race, where Moss won in his Lotus with Brabham second. Moss won the US GP as well, from Ireland's works Lotus, with McLaren third and the confirmed World Champion fourth after an early stop to investigate loud bangs caused by fuel from an overflow igniting on the exhaust pipe.

When all the points were added up, not only was Brabham World Champion, but McLaren was runner-up and the team won the Manufacturers' title by a huge margin. Team Cooper was on top of the world, but would never again taste success approaching that of 1960 and from then on would go into a decline.

The double World Champions faced 1961 without a suitable engine, but with plenty of customers for cars which, since they had less fuel to carry, were slimmer. The works cars were designated T55 and had the engine canted over further in the frame to give a lower rear deck and had 6-speed gearboxes. Customer cars, which were versions of the 1960 works cars, were designated T53P.

Things began well in the early non-Championship races, with Surtees winning the Lombank Trophy at Snetterton in a Parnell-Yeoman Credit 'low-line'. Then Brabham set pole for the Pau GP, but, ominously, Clark's Lotus led all the way and Jack had no answer to the young Scot in the few laps he completed before his fuel pump drive broke. Then Surtees won the Richmond Trophy at Goodwood and Brabham the Brussels GP and the Aintree 200. The appearance of the new Ferrari 156 at Syracuse, however, pointed the pattern for the season for the race was won by Giancarlo Baghetti on his F1 debut and Brabham could do no better than fourth, behind the Ferrari and two Porsches.

The Monaco GP was all about Moss and the Ferraris and Brabham was anyway flitting to and fro across the Atlantic making history by driving a Cooper in the Indianapolis 500, where, although giving away 1½-litres, he finished ninth and sowed the seeds of the rear-engine revolution in the States. As World Champion Brabham was guaranteed a start at Monaco, but he began from the back of the grid and retired with ignition failure. McLaren, meanwhile, could do no better than seventh in qualifying and sixth in the race.

Those same positions also applied to Brabham at the Dutch GP – the World Champions were suddenly midfield runners. They were further back for the Belgian GP, where both retired. McLaren managed fifth in the French GP at Reims, but only after most of the front runners had dropped out. Things were not much better in the British GP, although Brabham came fourth. In non-Championship races when the works Porsches or Lotuses appeared even Brabham usually had to pick what crumbs they left.

At the German GP, however, Brabham had the first example of the new V-8 Coventry Climax FWMV engine, which was fitted into a modified T55 and became the T58. Brabham was second fastest in practice at the Nürburgring, but slid off on the first lap. The race was again all about Moss and the Ferraris with Surtees the highest-placed Cooper in fifth. As for the rest of the season, the non-Championship races belonged to Lotus. McLaren inherited third in the Italian GP, but drove strongly in the American GP (Ferrari absent) to qualify, and finish, fourth. Brabham, with the V-8, retired from both races with overheating, but in the States he did set pole and lead quite handsomely before the water pump drive broke. At the end of the year Brabham left to run his own company, which he had got under way during 1961, and McLaren was promoted to team leader with the young South African, Tony Maggs, alongside him.

The works did not appear in 1962 until the Easter Monday Goodwood Meeting, where McLaren won the Lavant Cup for 4-cylinder F1 cars and, with a V-8, came second in the Richmond Trophy for all F1 cars. He came second to Clark's Lotus in the Aintree 200 (ahead of Phil Hill's Ferrari) and was fifth, and first 4-cylinder car, in the International Trophy at Silverstone.

For the Dutch GP McLaren had a new car, the T60, to which he had made a significant input. It had a narrower, lighter and stiffer frame, revised suspension geometry, a higher roll-centre (and softer springs to compensate), 13-inch front wheels, and a new constant-mesh 6-speed gearbox developed by Maddock and Knight especially for the FWMV engine. At Zandvoort Maggs made his works debut and finished fifth in an older T55, while McLaren retired when the quill shaft broke in his transmission, but he had been second at the time.

For Monaco McLaren had a 4-speed version of the gearbox and he drove a cool and intelligent race to win, while Maggs retired with gearbox problems. It was a sign of the times, however, that only two Coopers were entered for Monaco (there had been ten just two years before), but eight Lotuses were entered. McLaren qualified second for the Belgian GP, and briefly led, but both he and Maggs, who also had a T60, retired. In the non-Championship Reims GP, however, he came home first with Maggs again retiring. It was to be Cooper's last F1 win for more than four years.

Tony Maggs inherited second in the French GP with

Like all the British constructors, Cooper used the Coventry Climax FPF Mk 2 4-cylinder engine in 1961. This is John Surtees with his Yeoman Credit-entered car in the Belgian Grand Prix. He finished fifth. (David Phipps)

Jack Brabham with the first Cooper, indeed the first car, powered by the V-8 Coventry Climax in the 1961 German Grand Prix. He retired early in the race. (David Phipps)

McLaren fourth and plagued by gearbox problems. For the rest of the season: McLaren was third in the British GP; fifth in the German GP; third in the Italian and US GPs; and second in the South African, with Maggs just behind in third. McLaren finished third in the Drivers' Championship and Cooper third in the Manufacturers' series, but the rot was setting in.

Cooper missed the experience of Brabham, and McLaren, brilliant engineer that he was, was only 25 years old and still learning his craft.

For 1963 the works had the T66, which was a further evolution of the 1960 'low-line' but was lighter, slimmer and stiffer than its predecessor and had revised front suspension to prevent the pitching to which the T60 had been prone. Rob Walker bought one of the ex-works T60s for Jo Bonnier and, later, a T66, but their best result was fifth, three laps down, in the Mexican GP. The works did not have a much better season and one of the reasons was that John Cooper was out of action for some time following a serious road accident in a twin-engined Mini he had been developing. With Charles suffering ill-health, Ken Tyrrell stepped in to help the team.

McLaren began the year by finishing fourth in a thin field in the Lombank Trophy at Snetterton, finishing second in the Richmond Trophy at Goodwood, fifth in the Aintree 200 and a good second, to Clark, in the International Trophy at Silverstone. This was followed by a third

at Monaco (Maggs fifth) and second in the Belgian GP, where the cars had still slimmer bodies with very small air intakes. That result meant that McLaren led the World Championship table, but then the season fell apart and, other than a fine second by Maggs in the French GP, the Coopers failed to finish in the points until the Italian GP, where McLaren took third. The team struggled and quite often had engine failure and the only other finish of note was McLaren's fourth, and lapped, in the South African GP. Cooper finished fifth in the Manufacturers' Championship, and it must have been bitter to see Brabham, in its first full season, third in the series.

McLaren went Down Under at the end of the European season with a pair of special cars run under the banner 'Bruce McLaren Motor Racing Ltd', a straw in the wind. As usual, he had a successful time, but on that trip his young team-mate, Tim Mayer, who was to be the works No. 2 in 1964, was killed. Tim was the brother of Teddy Mayer, who, years later, would control Team McLaren. In his place came former World Champion Phil Hill.

For 1964 Cooper designed a base car to cover all single-seater classes, and while Jackie Stewart and Warwick Banks had a fabulous year in F3, which led to Stewart being taken up by B.R.M. in 1965, the F1 team had a miserable time.

The T73 was slim and neat, with inboard front

South African Tony Maggs with his Cooper-Climax V-8 in the 1963 Belgian Grand Prix. He was eliminated by an accident. (David Phipps)

In 1964 the Cooper team had a thoroughly miserable season. This is Phil Hill on his way to sixth place in the European Grand Prix at Brands Hatch. (**British Petroleum**)

suspension by rocker arms and, at the rear, was a lower wishbone, top transverse link and a long radius arm. Thirteen-inch wheels were used all round and the engine was bolted rigidly to the frame to act as a semi-stressed member.

McLaren drove a T66 when he finished third in the Lombank Trophy at Snetterton behind Ireland's B.R.P. and Jo Bonnier's Rob Walker T66, but it was not until the Dutch GP that a works Cooper was a classified finisher in a race, when McLaren came seventh (two laps down) and Hill eighth, a further two laps behind. McLaren inherited second in the Belgian GP and he and Hill were sixth and seventh in the French. Hill took sixth in the British GP, but the only other top six finish in any race that year was McLaren's lucky second in the Italian GP.

The season was an instance of a team spiralling out of control as it lost direction and faith in itself. It should also be said that it had run out of ideas, and was following Lotus and Brabham instead of taking the initiative. McLaren was not being listened to and the others were out of their depth against Chapman and Brabham-Tauranac.

After one disastrous weekend in Austria, when Phil

Hill crashed two cars (one possibly as a result of a breakage), there was a frank and fiery exchange of views and Hill was fired, though he later returned. It had been building up for some time and one reason was that Hill was not as quick as he once had been, another was that his car was never as well prepared as McLaren's. Since Cooper was no longer a top team, it was perhaps not getting the very best from Coventry Climax and that added to the spiral as time and again engines failed.

While the team was struggling in the US GP (both cars retired early in the race) Charles Cooper died and responsibility fell on John, who was still not fully recovered from his road accident. Through Roy Salvadori, who would become team manager in 1965, he began to look for buyers for the company who could inject capital.

Since it was the last year of the 1½-litre formula, the only major difference to the 1965 cars was a wider front track, but McLaren, already planning to leave and start his own team, was joined by Jochen Rindt. The brightest spot in a miserable season, when the cars were outclassed and unreliable, was McLaren's third place in the Belgian GP in the wet. The Brabhams were unhappy on their Goodyear tyres, so that eliminated part of the threat, but the result was largely due to Bruce's driving and if nothing else it demonstrated he had not lost his edge as results might otherwise suggest. Later Rindt would finish a good fourth in the German GP, which was a case of a brilliant driver flattering his car on a driver's circuit.

The Cooper story was not quite over and it would enjoy a brief Indian Summer in the early days of the 3-litre formula, but most of the thrust had already gone. One might even say it went when Brabham departed. Its contribution to British motor racing over its 20-year life was, however, incalculable and this brief sketch does not do it justice. On the other hand, Doug Nye's magnificent history, *Cooper Cars* (published by Osprey), does.

COOPER VARIANTS

Aiden-Cooper

Mrs Louise Bryden-Browne was the patroness of Anglo-American Racing, which entered cars for, among others, Stirling Moss and Dan Gurney. One of its mechanics, Hugh Aiden-Jones, was reckoned to have a few sharp ideas about car design and was allowed his head. He used as his base a 1962 Cooper T59 Formula Junior chassis fitted with a Coventry Climax FPF engine driving through a Cooper 5-speed gearbox. So far, it was the sort of special anyone could make, but the big tweak was the bodywork, which had a pointed nose and side radiators, a first in F1, although, before the end of the season, a front mounted radiator was used.

Ian Burgess drove the car and he made the grid for the Pau GP (nearly seven seconds off the pace set by Clark), and though he finished eighth he was five laps down. In the Aintree 200 Burgess started from the back of the grid and, after a troubled run, finished 17th, and unclassified. The car turned up again for the International Trophy at Silverstone, where Burgess qualified last by a considerable margin and crossed the line last, nine laps down and not classified. With only ten cars allowed on the grid, and 17 cars at the circuit, it hardly seemed worth Burgess' trouble turning up for the Naples GP, but he qualified, and finished fifth, two laps down in a field which was pretty thin apart from a couple of works Ferraris.

In the Mallory Park 2000 Guineas Burgess was last, but in the Kanonloppet he managed fifth from six finishers. He took fifth, too, in the Danish GP after the aggregates of three heats were combined, and while there were only 11 starters, some were stars and at least he was not lapped. Finally the car appeared at the

The Aiden-Cooper of Ian Burgess at the Gold Cup race at Oulton Park in 1962. The original side radiators had been replaced by a conventional one in the nose. (T. C. March)

Oulton Park Gold Cup, where Burgess qualified 15th from 24, but suffered a broken oil pipe in the race.

Burgess was nobody's idea of an ace, but was a man who charmed his way into some good drives at a time when that was possible. In 1963 Aiden-Jones became design consultant to Scirocco, another lost cause, and designed the unsuccessful Shannon F3 car, which, with a 3-litre version of the Coventry Climax 'Godiva' engine, figured briefly in the 1966 British GP.

Cooper-Alfa Romeo

In 1953 Bob Chase installed an Alfa Romeo 1900 engine in a Cooper Mk II (T23) chassis, modified the rear to take a de Dion axle and clothed it with a body which copied the Ferrari 500. It was an unmitigated disaster, slow and ill-handling. Its short and ill-starred career ended at Goodwood, when Duncan Hamilton tried to take it off the line and the back axle dropped out.

Much later a number of rear-engined Coopers with modified Alfa Romeo Giulietta engines were raced in South Africa.

Paul Emery with the Équipe Anglaise Cooper Alfa Romeo at the back of the grid for the Lavant Cup at Goodwood on Easter Monday 1953. Alan Brown (in overcoat) is on the right. (Duncan Rabagliati)

Cooper-Alta

In the search for more power a number of drivers tried the Alta engine in 1953. Peter Whitehead reversed the trend, for he already had an F2 Alta and in his case he was looking for a lighter car and bought a Mk II Cooper together with a Bristol gearbox. Most of his racing was in British events, with the odd trip abroad to take in minor events.

Whitehead was no ace and the engine was probably no improvement over a Bristol unit, but he still managed a fifth in the Lavant Cup at Goodwood, in a decent field of privateers, fifth in his heat in the International Trophy at Silverstone, and ninth in the British GP, but 11 laps in arrears. He retained his car for 1954 and had the engine enlarged to 2½-litres, but it was a disaster. He made the start for just four races and was able to complete only 36 racing laps with the car all year.

Jack Brabham bought the car when he came over from Australia, but quickly realized his mistake and installed a Bristol engine.

Tony Crook had a similar Cooper-Alta, but had no luck with it at all. In the British GP he qualified very slowly, and Crook was no slouch, and then had fuel feed problems on the line, so did not even get started. Later in the year he got it going quite well in British club events, but then the clutch exploded at Snetterton and caused him to crash. After that he had the car converted into a '1½-seater' sports car with a skimpy body and a Bristol engine and in this form it was astonishingly successful in British races.

An altogether different type of car was Stirling Moss' 'Cooper-Alta Special', which apart from its Cooper Mk II frame had very little of Cooper about it. It was a collaboration between Ray Martin and John A. Cooper (Technical Editor of *The Autocar*), who had previously worked on the Kieft 500 car with which Moss had enjoyed some success. It was built by Alf Francis and Tony Robinson.

In place of the Cooper all-independent suspension by

The Cooper-Alta Special of Stirling Moss in the 1953 International Trophy at Silverstone. (T. C. March)

Peter Whitehead with his Atlantic Stable-entered Cooper-Alta in the 1953 British Grand Prix.
(T. C. March)

lower wishbones and transverse leaves, there was coil spring and wishbone front suspension and a de Dion rear end suspended on coil springs. Girling disc brakes were used at the front and the rear drum brakes were mounted inboard. It was finished with an attractive body, which would prove to be the most pleasant aspect of the car.

Some attempt was made to persuade Jaguar to supply one of its XK100 engines, an experimental 4-cylinder d.o.h.c. 2-litre unit which had been considered for production and which had been used to power 'Goldie' Gardner's record-breaking car when he set a new class record at 176.96 mph. It was not the first such request made to Jaguar, a lot of people had eyed the unit with envy, but as always Jaguar said 'no'. Hence a dry-sumped Alta engine with Weber carburettors was installed together with a 4-speed Alta gearbox.

It first ran in the Lavant Cup at Goodwood, finished seventh, and was found to be lacking in many areas. The chassis was too flexible, the brakes were not in balance and the car was extremley twitchy. Work between its debut and the International Trophy at Silverstone improved matters, but while Moss was able to finish second in his heat, and set fastest lap, it was apparent to him that the car was underpowered. Problems in the final saw him finish only ninth.

In its next three races, the Coronation Trophy at Crystal Palace, the Eifelrennen and the Rouen GP, it was completely outclassed and finally the clutch exploded in the French GP at Reims and Moss was lucky not to

sustain serious or, even, fatal injury. That was the last straw and the car was pensioned off. The circle of well-intentioned friends which had successfully essayed an F2 'Cooper-beater' had showed their limitations at the top level of the game.

That left Moss with a problem but the Coopers rallied round and let Alf Francis use the works chassis jigs to make a modified Mk II. These modifications were not startling, but were necessary to accommodate the ENV pre-selector gearbox which had been chosen. In other ways it was a standard Mk II Cooper, except that it was built from scratch in eleven days and ran on nitromethane.

On the test rig at Barwell Engineering an incredible 200 bhp was seen. This made all the difference, and more, and Moss qualified 12th from 34 starters in the German GP and came home sixth in the first car which was not a Ferrari or Maserati. Third in the Sables d'Olonnes GP followed and in September he entered the Italian GP. After two laps Moss was lying fifth and in front of some works Ferraris and Maseratis. It was too good to last and after 20 laps one of his tyres threw a tread because they were unused to having to work so hard and the Cooper had bolt-on wheels. . . .

Other thrown treads followed, and then the fuel tank began to leak, so 13th place, ten laps down, was poor reward for a splendid performance. Moss rounded off the year with a win in the London Trophy at Crystal Palace, a class win at Prescott, a second to Salvadori's Connaught in the Madgwick Cup at Goodwood and fourth in the Formule Libre race at the same meeting, where he was headed by the 'Thin Wall Special' and two V-16 B.R.M.s.

The car was then bought by Ecurie Richmond, which had Barwell Engineering prepare the engine for the 2½-litre formula. It never went as well again and its best result, in a short and dismal season, was sixth in the Lavant Cup at Goodwood.

Cooper-Arden

One of Archie Butterworth's first batch of flat-four engines was bought by Kieft, who fitted 500cc 'double knocker' Norton barrels to the crankcase. This work was undertaken by Ron Mead, with support from Norton, and the 2-litre A.J.B./Kieft/Norton engine was run in a beefed-up F3 car. Kieft had in the back of his mind an F2 car and a team of sports-racers to take on Porsche, but, unfortunately, the works could never properly cool the engine.

It stayed in the Kieft workshops for a few years and, at one time, there was a scheme to install it in the second Lister F2 car. Eventually the unit reached the hands of Graham Eden, who turned it over to Jim Whitehouse of Arden Conversions. By using Norton 350cc barrels, Whitehouse was able to make an engine which complied with the 1½-litre F1 and it was installed in a Cooper chassis with a view to running in selected F1 races.

Called the Cooper-Arden, Eden ran the car just once, in a club race at Silverstone. There it encountered some minor problems with the camshafts which were really just a matter of adjustment. Eden, however, had run out of money and abandoned the project.

Later the engine was converted back to 2-litre form and was used by Ian Richardson in a sprint motorcycle. Running on alcohol, it apparently gave 210/220 bhp, a figure which increased to about 260 bhp when the engine was blown. Richardson enjoyed much success with his machine, 'Moonraker', for several seasons. The engine still exists.

Cooper-Aston Martin

There were only six starters for the 1956 Vanwall Trophy at Snetterton and among their number was a Cooper T23 powered by an Aston Martin engine. Driven by Leslie Hunt it qualified last, and finished last, covering only 11 laps of the 15. Later in the year, in the BRSCC F1 race at Brands Hatch, it returned an identical performance.

Nothing for certain is known about the driver, car or engine. Doug Nye's *Cooper Cars* suggests the chassis might have been Tony Crook's ex-F2 Cooper-Bristol Mk I, which had been converted into a sports car nick-named 'Mucky Pup' and been written off in a crash.

It sounds as though the hand of Paul Emery *may* be detected here, since he was just the sort of chap to make something of a pile of scrap nobody else would touch and he had also bought a number of sub-standard Aston Martin engines from the scrap merchant with the contract to take them away. He had converted one of them to 2-litre form and it is just *possible* that this was used in Hunt's car.

This was not, however, the only Cooper-Aston Mar-tin. In 1954 Eric Brandon bought the ex-Moss Cooper-Alta (the standard Cooper Mk II chassis, not the Cooper-Alta Special) and after Barwell Engineering had succeeded in making the car go slower, he had Bernie Rodger prepare an Aston Martin LM6 engine to 2½-litre spec.

Most of the work was supervised by Rodney Nuckey who, like Brandon, drove for Ecurie Richmond. This seems to clear up one little mystery, Nuckey's announcement (*Motor Racing*, December 1953) that he was to build an F1 car using a Lagonda LM6 engine in a Cooper chassis. Lagonda had been taken over by David Brown in order to obtain its W.O. Bentley-designed engine for Aston Martin. Lagonda or Aston Martin, it was the same engine with different names stamped on the cam covers.

Brandon entered it in the August Bank Holiday meeting at Davidstow but the engine blew up during practice. The project died there and then and the chassis was immediately sold on to Bob Chase who fitted it with a Bristol engine. In this form it ran in the September Goodwood meeting with Mike Keen at the wheel.

Cooper B.G.-Bristol

In 1957 Bob Gerard bought a production rear-engined Cooper Mk II F2 car (T44) which he had modified to take a special ex-works Bristol engine of 2246cc previously installed in his front-engined Mk II Cooper-Bristol. It made its debut at the British GP at Aintree, where Gerard was in penultimate place on the grid. He was still running at the end, though eight laps down, but there had been so many retirements he was classified sixth. He raced it again in the International Trophy at Silverstone but it was very slow and he finished the final three laps down (of 35) and well beaten by a number of F2 cars.

He bought it out again for the 1958 International Trophy the following May, but the story was the same and he retired in the race. It was the last international formula race in which Gerard competed and while it was a low-key performance it should be remembered that in the immediate post-war period Gerard was perhaps the most successful British driver and his triumphs included a fine second in the 1949 British GP at the wheel of his venerable B Type E.R.A.

Bob Gerard at the wheel of the Cooper-B.G.-Bristol in the 1957 British Grand Prix at Aintree where he finished sixth. (T. C. March)

Cooper-B.R.M.

The beginning of 1959 saw Stirling Moss without a works drive. Vanwall had withdrawn and he did not fancy any of the other options open to him, so he strengthened his relationship with Rob Walker.

On paper the most potent combination appeared to be the mating of a B.R.M. 258 engine to a Cooper T45 chassis. Walker was able to buy a Cooper, Sir Alfred Owen of B.R.M. loaned an engine and the car was built under the direction of Alf Francis. Due to conflicting fuel contracts, Cooper supplied the car *sans* gearbox, so a Colotti Mk 10 transmission was bought.

The finished car looked subtly different to any other Cooper, for the rear was longer, the air intake larger to accommodate a larger radiator, and the B.R.M. exhaust system snaked from the left-hand side of the car (it was on the right on Climax-powered cars). Behind the cockpit the Cooper's normal curved tubes were replaced by straight ones and the frame was beefed-up with gussets.

It was entered for the 1959 Aintree 200, but Moss found it difficult to drive, particularly since the front end shuddered under heavy braking, and he could only

qualify seventh. Despite his misgivings, Moss made a lightning start which saw him up to second. He eventually inherited the lead, pulled out a safe margin and broke the lap record. Then a tab washer in the gearbox broke and that led to the car's retirement.

It was taken to the Monaco GP, but was found to be unstable and underpowered, so Moss drove his Cooper-Climax instead. The engine was returned to B.R.M. and the chassis sold on to Paul Emery who used it in his Cooper-Connaught.

Cooper-Connaught

In 1959 Paul Emery and Geoff Richardson cobbled together a deal using the ex-Walker Cooper-B.R.M. chassis, and into the back of it Emery installed an ex-Connaught Alta engine. The most interesting feature of the car, however, was the 5-speed transaxle, which was the unit Connaught had made for its aborted J5 rear-engined car but which had not been previously used.

The car did not race often and when it did it was mainly in sprints and hill climbs, when it was driven by Roberta Cowell. It did, however, appear in the 1959

The Cooper-Connaught in the paddock for the Gold Cup race at Oulton Park in September 1959. It was driven by Paul Emery.
(Duncan Rabagliati)

Oulton Park Gold Cup with Emery at the wheel. The combination proved terribly slow and Emery was over 20 seconds off the pace in practice. He finished the 55-lap race, but nine laps down and unclassified. The following year Richardson again fitted an Alta engine in a Cooper T43 and the story of this car is told under 'R.R.A.'

Cooper-Ferrari

Scuderia Eugenio Castellotti was named in memory of the young Italian driver who appeared set for stardom until he was killed while testing at Modena in 1957. The basic plot of the cars, which were entered as 'Cooper-Castellottis', was the mating of Cooper T51 chassis with Ferrari 555 *SuperSqualo* engines (with downdraught carburettors so the engine could fit into the frame) and Colotti gearboxes. It was actually a ploy by Ferrari to surreptitiously gain some experience of rear-engined cars.

Giorgio Scarlatti was entered in one in the 1960 Monaco GP, but failed to qualify. Two cars, for Scarlatti and Gino Munaron, were entered for the French GP, but Scarlatti's was not ready, and while Munaron just qualified (15 seconds off the pace), engine problems meant he missed the start. Scarlatti's car was still not ready for the British GP, but Munaron qualified in last place and was classified 16th, seven laps in arrears.

Castellotti's memory deserved better than this, but both cars made the grid of the German GP, where they were extremely slow, and while Munaron finished 13th,

five laps adrift, Scarlatti retired with gearbox trouble after a single lap. In the Italian GP, however, the two cars occupied the second row of the grid, driven by Giulio Cabianca and Munaron, but that was a race boycotted by all the British teams, so apart from the works Ferraris the rest of the field was made up of F2 cars and even a private Maserati 250F. Munaron retired, but Cabianca finished fourth, two laps down. The team's final appearance was due to be in the Oulton Park Gold Cup, but on the way the transporter crashed, and since it did not enter the last race of the 2½-litre Formula, the American GP, that was the end of the experiment.

Pete Lovely, a South African domiciled in the USA, who had become well-known for his 'Pooper' (a Cooper 500 powered by a Porsche 356 engine), appeared in the 1960 US GP with another Cooper-Ferrari. This was a T51 chassis with a Ferrari 625LM engine. He qualified near the back of the field, but plugged around to finish six laps down in 11th place.

Two rare birds at Monza, 1960, on the left Gino Munaron, Cooper-Castellotti and on the right Fred Gamble, Behra-Porsche. The memory of Eugenio Castellotti and Jean Behra deserved better than the performance of these cars. (LAT)

Cooper-Ford

In 1963 Bob Gerard entered his protégé, John Taylor, in a Cooper T59 powered by a 1500cc version of the Ford 105E engine. In the main Taylor ran in club races, but he was able to qualify it tenth in the Aintree 200, although unclassified at the finish. It ran, too, in the International Trophy at Silverstone, but retired.

The following year the car was fitted with a 1500cc Cosworth MAE engine, and in the Aintree 200, which at-tracted a very strong field, he finished fifth, albeit three laps down. In the International Trophy at Silverstone, which again had a strong field, he qualified 14th from 22 starters and finished fifth. The car ran in the British GP and again he did not disgrace himself in practice, putting three V-8 B.R.M.-powered cars behind him, but had a troubled race. Soon afterwards Gerard took delivery of a Cooper T60-FWMV.

Hume-Cooper

This special began life as Chris Bristow's T39 'Bobtail' centre-seat sports car and was converted to an FPF-powered open-wheeler by John Hume, who had been one of the earliest of Cooper's mechanics. It was a bulbous car with a rather tatty body, in shape resembling the Porsche 718. Bristow had a lot of success with it in British club races in 1958-9 and even the odd pukka F2 race in good company. Since it was a special (actually not that much different to a Cooper F2 car) it drew attention to Bristow's forceful driving style and launched him on a (tragically brief) career in F1. It passed through other hands and reappeared in 1961, when it was entered by Team Salvatore Evangelistica in three non-Championship F1 races driven by John Langton and Ronald Wrenn. It retired once and twice finished last.

Cooper-Maserati

In 1959-60 some thought it a good idea to install 4-cylinder Maserati 250S engines and 5-speed gear-boxes in Cooper chassis. The engine itself was a d.o.h.c. unit of 2490cc (96 × 86 mm), which was more usually made in 2 and 3-litre forms for the Tipi 60 and 61 'Bird-cage' sports cars. It was reputed to give 236 bhp, but since that was less than the 2½-litre Coventry Climax FPF, which anyway had a much better power curve, there was no advantage except that it was available, and there was no guarantee that the FPF would be at the start of the season.

On the other hand it was perhaps 40 bhp more powerful than the stretched 2.2-litre FPF that Cooper and Lotus had used in 1958 and so it did look a reasonable bet, and it was not only a light and compact unit but it came complete with the Maserati trans-axle, which was normally a reliable unit.

Tommy Atkins' High Efficiency Motors fitted one in a Cooper T45 frame, and driven by Roy Salvadori and Jack Fairman it raced five times in 1959, taking fifth in the International Trophy at Silverstone (Fairman) and fourth in the Oulton Park Gold Cup (Salvadori). In the French and Italian Grands Prix it was near the back of the field and retired on both occasions with a broken piston. At the end of the season it was sold to Gilby Engineering, but raced only twice in 1960. In the Richmond Trophy at Goodwood Keith Greene was slow in practice and retired after 15 laps, and in the Silver City Trophy at Brands Hatch, where Greene finished tenth, three laps in arrears.

The Italian team, Scuderia Centro-Sud, ran up to three Cooper T51-Maseratis, often employing good second-level drivers such as Masten Gregory and Maurice Trintignant. The 1960 season began promising-ly with the Argentinian, Carlos Menditeguy, finishing fourth in his home GP, and this was followed by Gregory taking sixth in the International Trophy at Silverstone, which had virtually a full WC entry.

Running three cars proved too much for the team, however, and as soon as the season got under way in earnest, the rot set in. All three cars failed to qualify for the Monaco GP, they withdrew from the Dutch GP after practice since they were not among the top 15 who would receive starting money, and were very slow in the French GP at Reims, with the finishers, Gregory and Ian Burgess, being too far behind to be classified. The rest of the season was just as bad and the cars either retired, usually with gearbox trouble, or else finished a long way behind. The team's best finish from May onwards was von Trips' ninth, three laps down, in the US GP.

Masten Gregory with a Scuderia Centro-Sud-entered Cooper-Maserati in the 1960 International Trophy at Silverstone. (T. C. March)

For 1961 a less ambitious programme was undertaken with just two cars, which were fitted with Maserati 150S engines (one with a Colotti gearbox, one with a Cooper unit), and the principal driver was Lorenzo Bandini. Bandini managed third in the Pau and Naples GPs, and his best WC finish was eighth at Monza.

Other Cooper-Maseratis were run briefly by the Scuderia Serenissima (best finish: Nino Vaccarella, third, Coppa Italia), the Pescara Racing Club (driver, Renato Pirocchi, no good result) and a couple raced in South Africa, where their best F1 result was Doug Serrurier's sixth in the 1961 Natal GP.

Much later the Coopers were to have 3-litre V-12 Maserati engines, but that is a different story altogether.

Cooper-O.S.C.A.

Alejandro de Tomaso fitted a 2-litre O.S.C.A. engine in a Cooper T43 chassis and entered it in the 1959 US GP. About the best which can be said for it is that it had pretty alloy wheels. In practice it was 28 seconds off the pace and it retired after 13 laps with brake trouble. Later de Tomaso used the chassis as a model for his own cars.

In 1961-2 Walter Breveglieri, who used the pseudonym 'Wal Ever', put an O.S.C.A. MT4 engine in a Cooper T43. It appeared at only three races and the only time it qualified, in the 1962 Mediterranean GP, it was last on the grid and retired after two laps with engine trouble.

COVENTRY CLIMAX

In one sense Coventry Climax was an unlikely outfit to revolutionize motor racing, since its main line of business was fork-lift trucks, industrial engines and fire pumps. On the other hand, in the early 1950s its chief engineer was Wally Hassan, who had a long and distinguished association with motor sport, and he had recruited Harry Munday from B.R.M.

A government contract for a light and powerful fire pump engine designated 'FW' (Feather Weight) had helped Climax become fairly prosperous and when the 2½-litre F1 was announced the head of the company, Leonard Lee, was able to listen sympathetically when Connaught, Cooper, H.W.M. and Kieft approached him with a joint plea to supply them with an engine with which to go F1 racing.

Against bespoke racing engines the Alta, Bristol and Lea-Francis units which most British formula cars had to use were pretty feeble, so when Lee gave his go-ahead in late 1952, it was a ray of hope. Since he did not have the full backing of his board, Lee insisted that it should be a semi-secret project and so the designation FPE (Fire Pump Engine) was chosen as an in-joke, but usually it has been known as the 'Godiva'.

Hassan and Munday decided on a d.o.h.c. short-stroke V-8 of 2477cc (76.2×67.9 mm) with four twin-choke downdraught Solex carburettors, although SU fuel injection soon replaced them. It was a compact, light (340 lb) engine and by 1953 was producing over 250 bhp with exceptional torque and a wide power band.

Alas, Coventry is a long way from anywhere (George Eliot used it to exemplify provincialism in 'Middlemarch') and although Climax had a potential world-beater on its hands it believed the exaggerated power claims of Italian makers and thought it would be shown up. Thus the engine was never released. Had it been made available, Connaught, Cooper, H.W.M. and Kieft would have used it in F1 (Connaught and Kieft had designed cars to take it) and perhaps Lotus would not have been far behind. Perhaps the car Chapman and Costin designed for Tony Vandervell would have been the F1 Lotus-Climax instead. It could have been taken out to 3 or even 4.4 litres, and might have inspired a whole range of sports cars (the Lister-Climax instead of the Lister-Jaguar?). It was poised to change the face of motor racing and remains the most tantalizing 'what if' in racing history.

Much later the FPEs were acquired by Paul Emery, who converted one to 3 litres with Jaguar pistons and Tecalemit-Jackson fuel injection. In this form it gave 312 bhp, a figure which has been doubted, but the author has seen the dyno reports from the Dodge facility and can

confirm them. It appeared twice in races in 1966, once in the back of Hugh Aiden-Jones' Shannon F3 car, once in a B.R.P., and on both occasions the result was embarrassing.

Coventry Climax was still to change the face of racing, but it was to take longer and the springboard was to be the little FW (Feather Weight) fire pump engine, which was originally the result of a government contract. While still waiting for the 'Godiva' to be released, for which he had a completed car ready, Cyril Kieft persuaded Climax to enlarge one of the s.o.h.c. 1020cc units to 1098cc (72.4×66.7 mm) by increasing the bore, replacing the standard cast iron crankshaft with one of forged steel, increasing the compression ratio, adding twin S.U. carburettors and, of course, paying attention to the porting.

Fitted into one of Kieft's rather crude sports cars, it appeared at Le Mans, where it suffered from oil surge, but it was not long before similar units were in demand from such as Lotus and Cooper. Between 1955 and 1959 1100cc sports car racing became the most important junior category in Britain, because the FWA (Feather Weight Automotive) engine was powerful, reliable and available.

It was not long before the engine was giving about 85 bhp and cars using it wiped the floor with the opposition in 1100cc racing. From the FWA came the 1460cc (76.2×80 mm) FWB which took Cooper and Lotus to successes in 1½-litre sports car racing and powered both makers' early F2 cars. Coventry Climax was now well and truly involved in motor racing.

From the FPE came the FPF, which was in essence one bank of the 'Godiva' V-8 with, initially, a capacity of 1475cc (81.2×71.1 mm), in which form it gave 141 bhp with an excellent power curve. Designed by Hassan and Munday (his last work before becoming Technical Editor of *The Autocar*), this was a light, durable engine which Cooper in particular was able to use to good effect in F2.

During 1957 a 1960cc version (86.4×83.8 mm) which gave 176 bhp appeared in the back of the works Coopers in some World Championship events, but they did not particularly shine. When, in 1958, the rules stipulated Av-gas for F1 the FPF came into its own. Stirling Moss had one in a Rob Walker Cooper when he won the Argentine GP, a feat matched by Maurice Trintignant in a similar car in the Monaco GP. On most circuits, however, it was inadequate against full 2½-litre engines, but the works did produce four engines enlarged to their absolute limit, 2207cc (88.9×88.9 mm) for use by Cooper and Lotus. This version, which had a spacer between the block and head, produced 194 bhp, which was between 60 and 90 bhp down on the opposition, but it gave Cooper some respectable place finishes in World Championship events and both 2.0- and 2.2-litre engines took wins in non-Championship events.

Meanwhile Wally Hassan and his new right-hand man, Peter Windsor-Smith, set to work on a Mk II version with a completely new block and a capacity of 2495cc (94.0 × 89.9 mm), and this gave 240 bhp, had excellent torque and was extremely reliable. The increased power was enough to tip the balance in favour of the Cooper and Lotuses, which were much lighter than the opposition, and in 1959 and 1960 the engine won 13 of the total of 17 World Championship races and won virtually all the non-Championship events as well.

British constructors hoped to force the FIA to rescind its decision to introduce the 1½-litre F1 in 1961, but when they failed Climax belatedly set to work on the FWMV V-8 engine and at the same time provided uprated 1½-litre FPF Mk II units as a stop-gap. These had a slightly longer stroke than the first 1½-litre Mk II engines and revisions to the valve gear and porting increased engine speed by more than 1000 rpm to 8200 rpm, at which point they gave 152 bhp.

Although this was 30 bhp less than the Ferrari 156, Moss was able to beat the Ferraris at Monaco and the Nürburgring and Innes Ireland had one in his Lotus when he won the US GP (Ferrari was absent), which was the last occasion that a normally aspirated 4-cylinder engine won a World Championship race.

Since FPFs were popular in the South African 'Gold Star' races, the last appearance of a 1½-litre FPF was in the 1965 South African GP, 2.7-litre versions were also made, and Jack Brabham used one in his Cooper in the 1961 Indianapolis 500 and they reappeared as stop-gaps in 1966, when the 3-litre Formula 1 came into force. No fewer than 273 FPFs were made between 1957 and 1965 and without them it is hard to see how the sport could have continued to grow.

Coventry Climax revolutionized motor racing because it gave everyone an opportunity to build a sports or formula car which would have a competitive, reliable engine, something which had always been the main problem for the likes of H.W.M. and Connaught. The V-8 FWMV series of engines was not to be produced in anything like those numbers because Climax wanted to undertake the rebuilding of this more complicated unit, and since that restricted numbers, the company was fairly selective when it came to deciding who might buy them.

Climax had produced an efficient little s.o.h.c. fire pump engine of 645cc, which was re-worked as the 745cc FWM (Feather Weight Marine) with a view to us-

ing it as a marine engine. From this came the FWMA, which was eventually developed into the Hillman Imp engine. In 1960 Hassan and Windsor-Smith devised a d.o.h.c. head for the FWMA and almost immediately this unit, the FWMC, gave 83 bhp or 111 bhp/litre. Lotus ran one in an Elite at Le Mans in 1961, and although it retired with oil pump failure after ten hours, it was leading the Index of Performance at the time.

Since it had already been decided to use a V-8 layout for the new F1 engine, the FWMC became the base from which the work developed, though the V-8 had different engine dimensions, blocks, heads and a five-bearing crankshaft in place of the three-bearing crank of the FWMC. Still, the little engine contributed a lot of the details and the designation of the new engine, FWMV (Feather Weight Marine V-8), acknowledges its ancestry. It was to appear in seven different types in the period 1961-65, and a further two in 1966 when enlarged to 2 litres. A total of 33 engines was used in racing during 1961-65 and they won 22 World Championship races (19 of those were won by Jim Clark in a Lotus) and dozens of non-Championship events. By contrast, Mercedes-Benz had a float of about *seventy* engines when it returned to racing in 1954-5.

These figures say a lot not only about two different styles of approaching the sport, but a lot about the reliability of the Coventry Climax engines. Typically a team would take two cars and a spare engine to a race. Leaving aside the Mk I unit which did have a few problems, the Mk II won 14 F1 races in 1962, the year of its introduction.

The Mk I version of 1961-2 had a capacity of 1495cc (63 × 60 mm), was fitted with four Weber 38DCNL carburettors and gave 181 bhp at 8500 rpm. The first two engines were loaned to Brabham and Moss in 1961. In 1962 came the Mk II with slightly larger inlet valves, which gave an increase in power (186 bhp) and torque. The Mk III of 1963 was a short-stroke version (67.94 × 51.56 mm) with Lucas fuel injection and this upped power to 195 bhp at 9500 rpm at a very small cost in bmep and torque. It was popularly know as the 'flat crank' engine.

In 1964 came the Mk IV, which had an even shorter stroke (72.39 × 45.47 mm, 1497cc), which increased power to 200 bhp at 9750cc with again a fractional loss of bmep and torque. The thinking behind this engine was to increase the top area of the pistons, and hence combustion chamber, in order to accommodate a four-valve-per-cylinder layout. The Mk V was a one-off with slightly enlarged inlet valves and gave 203 bhp.

Mk VI and Mk VII were one-off 'four-valve' engines with a small difference in the size of the inlet valves. One engine was supplied to Brabham in 1965 and one to Lotus. Brabham always seemed to suffer an unusual number of engine problems (possibly due to installation), while Clark won five World Championship races in succession with his engine. The Mk VI produced 212 bhp at 10,300 rpm, the Mk VII 213 bhp at 10,500 rpm but with lower torque and bmep figures.

Between 1963 and 1964 Climax designed and built one other engine, the flat-16 FWMW, but since the V-8s were winning and the development of the four-valve heads was consuming time and effort, work proceeded slowly and eventually there was no point in racing it. Unlike most 16-cylinder engines designed for racing, this was actually a fairly simple design with four cylinder heads, four exhaust systems and a central power take-off. It was, naturally, a d.o.h.c. unit, with two valves per cylinder and the shortest stroke of any F1 engine with dimensions of 54.1×40.64 mm. It was, too, a very compact engine, only an inch longer than the V-8 and slightly narrower, and only a few pounds heavier.

The design team felt it might give between 220 and 240 bhp at 12,000 rpm, but at the point when development stopped the best figure was 209 bhp. That would have seen it competitive against everything except Climax' own 'four-valve' engines. Lotus built a car, the 39, to use it and this was used by Clark in the Tasman series fitted with a 2.5-litre FPE.

As the 3-litre formula approached, Hassan considered the 1500cc supercharged alternative using the V-8 or the flat-16 as a base, but he realized that turbocharging was the only sensible route and there was no suitable turbo available. Climax had been taken over by Jaguar, and this is sometimes quoted as the reason why Climax withdrew from racing at the end of 1965. Wally Hassan, however, is adamant that the real reason was that the racing programme was becoming a drain on the company in terms of personnel and if continuing might jeopardize the firm's commercial projects. So Climax made a clean break from the sport apart from making a handful of 2-litre versions of the FWMV to see Lotus through 1966.

Its contribution to the sport had been immense and it powered cars which won 40 WC races, four Drivers' Championships, four Constructors' Championships, and thousands of wins in other events ranging from five-lap handicaps at Goodwood to the Index of Performance at Le Mans via F2, non-Championship F1, the Tasman series, the South African 'Gold Star' Championship and the Inter-Continental Formula.

Wally Hassan was later to make an important contribution to Jaguar's magnificent V-12 engine, which in recent years has been so successful in Group C sports car racing. Add to that his work on the Jaguar XK engine and his work for Climax and his stature becomes apparent.

Coventry Climax's importance in the history of motor racing and its contribution to the British renaissance cannot be over-stated. It changed the face of motor racing and tipped the balance of power in Britain's favour.

With acknowlegements to *Climax in Coventry* by Wally Hassan and Graham Robson (Motor Racing Publications Limited).

CROMARD

Bob Spikins was head of the Laystall Engineering Company and an inveterate special builder who enjoyed some success with his cars. The Cromard, named after one of Laystall's trade marks, began life with a 1½-litre Lea-Francis engine mounted in a modified Amilcar chassis fitted with VW suspension. By 1951, however, it had evolved out of all recognition.

In its final form it had a tubular chassis with dual 2-in tubes as side members which was designed and built by Raybern Engineering. This featured VW front suspension, and transverse leaf and swing-axle rear suspension located by fabricated, drilled radius arms. Its engine was an alloy block 1750cc Lea-Francis with four Amal carburettors fitted with S.U. float chambers, and this fed its 120/30 bhp through an ENV-Wilson 4-speed pre-selector gearbox.

It was a neat little car which went quite well in 1951, although the swing-axle rear suspension gave some problems. In the normal course of events this would have been rectified, because Spikins constantly modified his cars, but he was unfortunately killed in a sports car race in Belgium.

At the time of his death Spikins was pressing ahead with an entirely new 2-litre engine for F2, but this came to nothing. The Cromard was then bought by Peter Clarke, the instigator of the H.R.G. F2 car, and like the H.R.G. it made a single appearance in F2 in 1952. In the International Trophy at Silverstone it was driven by Mrs Joyce Howard, who raced it regularly in Ireland, but was completely outclassed.

D. A. M. W.

Deutsches Amt für Material und Warenprufung was a government-funded research outfit operating in East Germany after WW2 in 1950-1 and was associated with E.M.W., which was that part of B.M.W. in East Germany when the fighting ceased. D.A.M.W. instigated a number of projects which were taken over by E.M.W. in 1952. One of these projects was developed into the E.M.W. sports-racing cars, which were notable for their advanced aerodynamics and the power from their straight-six d.o.h.c. 1500cc engines derived from the B.M.W. 328. International politics meant these cars only once competed outside of the two Germanies and the Eastern bloc, but they were successful on circuits as diverse as Avus and the Nürburgring.

D.A.M.W. built two F2 types and they could not have been more different. One was a front-engined car using a d.o.h.c. version of the B.M.W. 328 engine with its crankshaft set in roller bearings and two plugs and one carburettor per cylinder. It had a ladder-frame chassis with double wishbone and torsion bar front suspension and, at the rear, a de Dion axle sprung by torsion bars and located by an A-frame. Since the same chassis was also used for the slim E.M.W. sports-racers, it had an offset driving position (to the left). D.A.M.W. appears to have raced initially with one car driven by Artur Rosenhammer, who won a race at Leipzig in 1951, but

retired from the Eifelrennen. Three cars for Rosenhammer, Theo Fitzau and Josef Ortschitt appeared in the Avusrennen, but the best finish was Ortschitt in seventh, and unclassified.

In 1952 the name was changed to E.M.W., and the team was led by Edgar Barth, who later drove for Porsche. After the death of Paul Grifzu in May 1952, Barth became the leading East German driver, and he appears to have won the majority of East German races during the next two years. They appeared in West Germany only rarely in that period. Barth finished fifth in the 1953 Eifelrennen, but he was out of luck in the German GP, where he qualified down among the B.M.W. specials, over 1m 40s off the pace, and he retired with a blown engine without making an impression.

At least one car appeared in the 1952 (Formule Libre) Brno GP in Czechoslovkia and no doubt they raced in other Eastern bloc events. Even in these days of *glasnost* this remains a grey area.

The name of these cars constantly changed: they began as D.A.M.W., spent most of their racing life as E.M.W. and, in sports car form, they finally appeared as A.W.E. following a court case when B.M.W. contested the right of the company to use the name E.M.W. The name of the team changed too, so there was a time when they were entered by the *I.F.A. Rennkollectiv*, when E.M.W.

A very rare photograph of the D.A.M.W. in monoposto *form driven by Edgar Barth at the Nürburgring in 1952.*

began making I.F.A. cars, which were a version of the D.K.W. Sonderklasse before the company transmuted into Wartburg.

As if this were not confusing enough, information is not to hand as to when they raced in open-wheeled form and/or with sports bodies in the East Germany races, since it was quite common in Germany to run 'dual-purpose' cars, and whereas in most countries this meant putting wings and lights on an offset single-seater, in Germany it quite often meant removing unnecessary road equipment from a sports car with an enveloping body, for the Germans had a liking for high-speed races (Avus, the Grenzlandring, etc.), where an enclosed body was an advantage.

The other D.A.M.W. F2 car is a matter of contention and some will argue it is not a D.A.M.W. at all but an Auto Union. This is a car currently in the Donington Collection which *appears* to have derived from the Auto Union E-Type, which was planned for the 1½-litre supercharged F1 due to come into force in 1941. This advanced design has a rear-mounted *unsupercharged* V-12 engine of 1995cc (62 × 56 mm), which suggests both an

Auto Union base to the design and also Formula 2. In other words, a post-war adaptation of a pre-war design.

The chassis follows Eberan von Eberhorst's thinking with the Auto Union D-Type, i.e. a ladder-frame, trailing arm and torsion bar front suspension, a de Dion rear axle sprung by torsion bars and located by lower wishbones and a A-bracket, and near 50/50 weight distribution.

The engine appears to have suffered from lubrication problems and, before they could be solved, the rug was pulled out from beneath it. Exactly how much of this car is pure Auto Union and how much was D.A.M.W. (post-war but probably with ex-Auto Union engineers involved) is still a mystery, but two, at least, were made and they remain an intriguing 'What if'.

When the 1½-litre F2 was announced, E.M.W./A.W.E. was set to enter it, for, by 1956, the political situation had sufficiently eased to make an international programme possible and the 1500cc sports car engine seems to have been very powerful indeed. Then some commissar or bureaucrat said 'nein' and a team of gifted engineers was put to work on Wartburgs.

D. B.

In 1936, Charles Deutsch and René Bonnet bought a works rent-a-drive in the French Grand Prix, which that year was run for sports cars. In the event, their car was withdrawn, which was probably no bad thing, because neither had much racing experience, but, miffed, they decided from then on to be in control of their own destinies and build their own cars.

It was not until 1939 that their first Citroën-based specials were ready to run, and so they were able to take part in only a few club events before the Second World War intervened. Still, even during the German occupation, and at some risk to themselves, they worked away at a new Citroën-based design. This was ready in 1946 and was remarkable for its low weight, highly tuned engine, and advanced aerodynamics; in fact, it looked not unlike the later Porsche 550. These three elements, low weight, aerodynamics and a modified production engine were to be the hallmark of all the partners' designs.

The two men's talents complemented each other admirably, for Deutsch was an imaginative theorist with a particular flair for aerodynamics, while Bonnet was the pragmatic mechanical engineer who could translate his friend's ideas into practical reality. Before long they had established themselves as among the best of French special builders.

When the British 500cc racing formula began to catch on, D.B. made a 500cc single-seater using a box-section chassis and a modified Panhard engine and transmission (it had front-wheel drive and the engine was forward of the front axle line). Front suspension was by Panhard dual transverse springs which was so light that the rear suspension was by only a pair of telescopic dampers acting on the solid axle. About the best that can be said for this D.B. is that it was the most successful French 500cc F3 car, and that is not saying much.

Using a 750cc engine Elie Bayol drove one in a number of F2 races, where it was comprehensively outclassed. D.B. also built up and tested a four-wheel-drive F2 car with a Panhard engine and gearbox at each end of the car. It began life with a pair of 750cc engines with the idea of substituting 850cc units should testing be successful. Since Bonnet was obtaining 60 bhp from a fully tuned 850cc engine, this would have equated to 120 bhp in a car weighing less than 1000 lb, so there was some foundation for the theory. Testing proved, however, that the car's performance did not justify further development.

In common with other European countries, the French quickly tired of losing to the British in the new F3 and so looked for an alternative. D.B. came up with one; it took its F3 design, gave it an 850cc Panhard engine, and created the 'Monomille novices' series. You paid a fee, drew a car, and you raced it.

There it might have ended except with the coming of the 2½-litre F1 in 1954 and this had a proviso for supercharged cars of 750cc. Deutsch and Bonnet dusted off a couple of their Monomilles, and fitted them with supercharged 746cc (79.6×75 mm) engines. These delivered only about 85 bhp, but were expected to haul a car of only 350 kg compared with the 600 + kg of most of their contemporaries.

The F1 D.B. had a simple box-section chassis with transverse leaf and wishbone ifs and and trailing arm and torsion bar irs. Special cast magnesium-alloy wheels and front disc brakes were made by the French aviation firm Messier, while, since the car was front heavy, drum brakes were used at the rear.

While the body shell was slippery, the ground clearance was typically Monomille (i.e. *enormous*) and the driver sat high in the airstream. Two cars were entered for the 1955 Pau Grand Prix against middling opposition. Neither could make any sort of impression since the engine lacked both torque and bhp. For all its lightness, the D.B.'s power/weight ratio worked out at roughly 250 bhp/ton, while most of its rivals had a ratio of better than 400 bhp/ton.

One driver, Claude Storez, threw in the towel, while the other, Paul Armagnac, soldiered on to finish 16 laps down. After that single race at Pau the design was put away, but when Formula Junior became an international category in 1959 out came the old Monomille again. For a short time they did not exactly disgrace themselves, but when the likes of Cooper and Lotus entered the class, the concept was finally laid to rest.

DERRINGTON-FRANCIS

Vic Derrington, a British pioneer of performance accessories, was persuaded by Alf Francis that it would be possible to resurrect and fettle the remains of the 1963 A.T.S. F1 project. Derrington was intrigued and put up the money, while Francis did a deal to buy some of the redundant parts.

He created a new space-frame which had a wheelbase just over six inches shorter than the A.T.S., clothed it in a new body, and used A.T.S. parts for the rest. The lacklustre Portuguese driver Mario Cabral was persuaded to part with money to run it in the 1964 Italian GP and, true to its antecedents, he qualified it on the back row of the grid and retired with ignition problems before one-third distance. The car was never run again.

The A.T.S. V-8 engine as it appeared in the Derrington-Francis in the 1964 Italian Grand Prix. (LAT)

Mario Cabral drove the Derrington-Francis, actually a re-fettled A.T.S. in the 1964 Italian Grand Prix. In qualifying he was nearly a minute off pace and in the race retired with ignition trouble. This car did not appear again. (LAT)

DE TOMASO

Alejandro de Tomaso is an Argentine domiciled in Italy whose relationship with specialist Italian constructors goes back over 30 years. As a driver he achieved some success in 1958 with O.S.C.A. when he co-drove the 750cc cars which won the Index of Performance at both Sebring and Le Mans. De Tomaso tried running a stripped-down 'desmodronic' sports O.S.C.A. in F2, with a conspicuous lack of success, and then hung up his helmet.

When Formula Junior got under way he built a copy of an FJ Cooper which was given the name 'Isis', but it showed no sign of being favoured by any deity and about the only thing it did was to upset the Coopers. In late 1960 he showed an O.S.C.A.-engined F2 car, which followed the general lines of the Isis (i.e. it was still a Cooper which did not work), but it did not race. The following year it became eligible for F1 and de Tomaso was to make a total six of these cars, most of which were sold to amateurs.

These had space-frames with independent suspension all round by coil springs and double wishbones.

They were pretty little cars, their looks enhanced by special cast-alloy wheels, and in 1961 were available either with a d.o.h.c. O.S.C.A. engine or an enlarged Alfa Romeo Giulietta unit with a special two-plug head, both of which drove through a de Tomaso 5-speed gearbox.

The marque made its F1 debut at the 1961 Naples GP, where two O.S.C.A.-engined cars were driven by Roberto Bussinello and Giovanni Alberti. Neither car was particularly fast, though Alberti did run in sixth place until retiring just after half-distance with a blown engine, while Bussinello finally inherited fifth, but four laps down, and that in a small field of largely second-string cars and drivers.

Giorgio Scarlatti drove the Scuderia Serenissima's Alfa Romeo-powered car at the French GP, where he qualified last, 23 seconds off the pace, and retired with engine problems after 15 laps. Bussinello drove that same car at the Solitude GP, where only Peter Monteverdi's ill-starred M.B.M. was slower in practice and, again, it retired with engine problems.

No fewer than three de Tomasos appeared in the

De Tomaso's attempt at building F1 cars was a disaster. This prototype appeared in the paddock at the 1960 US Grand Prix and, as can be seen, it was a Cooper-copy with pretty wheels. (**LAT**)

Here Roberto Bussinello is seen during practice for the 1961 Italian Grand Prix in a de Tomaso-O.S.C.A. He was 25 seconds off the pace and the engine went on the first lap of the race. (LAT)

Despite the fact that de Tomaso could not even copy a Cooper properly, it originated this car which used a new de Tomaso engine and transmission. Its entire competition career consisted of one lap of a minor race where it was slower than a pushrod Ford-engined O.S.C.A. (LAT)

Italian GP, and at Monza Nino Vaccarella managed to qualify 20th, only to retire after 13 laps when the Alfa Romeo unit let go. Roberto Lippi (Alfa Romeo) and Bussinello (O.S.C.A.) qualified even further back, but both were out with engine trouble after the first lap.

De Tomaso's best result came in the Coppa Italia at Vallelunga, where Bussinello qualified his Alfa Romeo-engined car in fourth spot, but there were only ten starters and those were at best second-string cars. He managed to finish fifth in the first heat and fourth in the second, on both occasions a lap down. On aggregate he was classified fourth from seven finishers, with Roberto Lippi, in an O.S.C.A.-engined car, fifth after taking fourth and fifth in the heats, again a lap down.

While it was clear that the de Tomaso was a completely lost cause, Lippi was back in 1962, where he failed to qualify at Naples but finished sixth on the road in the Mediterranean GP at Pergusa. There were only 13 starters and Lippi was unclassified at the end, six laps down.

Il patrone had both wealth and ambition and had built around him an experienced team, which included Alberto Massimino. While many of us would reckon that an outfit which could not even copy someone else's design properly was not worth supporting, de Tomaso pressed on and built his own engine. It appeared during practice for the 1962 Italian GP and was a water-cooled d.o.h.c. flat-eight with two plugs per cylinder and dimensions of 68×51 mm, which was fed by four twin-choke downdraught Weber DCM carburettors. It was fitted in a chassis which was broadly similar to previous cars, but the physical layout of the engine allowed extra cross-bracing over the top of it and the rear of the frame was reinforced by double tubing which acted as a bulkhead. Output of the engine was claimed to be 170 bhp, though its performance installed in a car suggests that figure is over-optimistic. Even 170 bhp was not enough by the end of 1962, and what power there was fed through a de Tomaso 5-speed gearbox.

Massimino had devised Maserati's 1948 inboard front suspension, a concept which Colin Chapman had taken and refined. It was therefore no surprise to see that Massimino leap-frogged Chapman and came up with a copy of a copy of his own design. At the rear was a version of the system which Lotus and Lola had used with lower, inverted, wishbones, upper transverse links, and radius rods except that the transverse links had been made into rocker arms for the inboard rear suspension.

Girling disc brakes were mounted outboard at the front, while the outboard rear discs were made by Amadori. It was an ambitious project and de Tomaso won admiration for being one of only four teams in the 1½-litre formula which built an entire car, including the engine and gearbox. Unfortunately that was the car's only claim to distinction apart from a sleek body made by Fantuzzi.

At Monza it was entrusted to an Argentinian stock car driver, Estefano Nasif, but it would not run properly and failed to qualify by over four minutes. Lippi, too, entered his car, but was painfully slow and failed to make the race. That was the end of de Tomaso's effort in 1962.

One would have thought that the message would

De Tomaso claimed 170 bhp for this flat-eight engine, but its mediocre performances suggest this may have been optimistic. (LAT)

have filtered through and de Tomaso would have done the decent thing and folded, but apparently he began to plan a V-12 engine and a car with a monocoque central-section cast in light alloy, but neither was built.

Oddly enough, when the marque next appeared in an F1 race, in the Rome GP at Vallelunga in May 1963, it was represented by no fewer than six cars. Lippi (F1-002) and Gastone Zanarotti (F2-001, the prototype chassis) both had Maserati 150S engines in their cars, Nasif had the flat-eight (F1-801), 'Condor' had an Alfa Romeo engine in F1-003, Rovero Campello an O.S.C.A. in F1-001, while Franco Bernabei had a Holbay-Ford unit in a new chassis, F1-005.

Nasif managed to qualify the flat-eight eighth from 19 starters, only to retire after a single lap with clutch trouble. It was Bernabei who was to give the marque its one brief moment of glory. He qualified third behind de Beaufort's Porsche and Anderson's Lola and took the lead of the first heat on lap five. He stayed there for the next 22 laps, apart from a brief interlude when Anderson led, but his race came to an end after 27 laps with run bearings in his engine. Lippi eventually finished fourth on aggregate, two laps down, with Zanarotti eighth, 12 laps down.

An entry was filed for the British GP for Nasif and the flat-eight, but it did not arrive in time to race. Thus the engine's total competition history comprised one lap of a minor race, where it was shown up by a similar car using a modified Ford Anglia engine. Oddly enough, despite his scintillating performance it was the only time that Bernebei or the works de Tomaso-Ford started in an F1 race.

At the Mediterranean GP Lippi appeared with a 65-degree Ferrari 156 engine in his car but despite that, he failed to qualify both there and in the Italian GP and that was the last time any of the cars appeared in an F1 race.

When the 1-litre F2 was announced, de Tomaso built a flat-four engine for it, based on the flat-eight, and for a while it seemed as though the British engine tuning concern, Holbay, was to develop it, but the announcement of the Cosworth SCA engine knocked that idea on the head.

When one takes into account the fact that six de Tomasos were built, and one had the use of a Ferrari engine, the marque must qualify as the absolute lemon of the 1½-litre formula, beating even the dreadful A.T.S. for that unenviable distinction.

DOMMARTIN

In the 1930s a subscription was set up to build a semi-official national racing car and the result appeared at the French GP in June 1935. Called the S.E.F.A.C. (la Société d'Études et de Fabrication d'Automobiles de Course) it was drawn by former Salmson designer Émile Petit and its engine consisted of two 4-cylinder d.o.h.c. units, each with its own crankshaft, housed on a common crankcase, running in opposite directions and geared together, and blown by a single large supercharger.

The total capacity of this engine was 2771cc (70 × 90 mm), but it only produced 250 bhp, making it the least powerful unit of any 1935 GP car. Worse, it weighed in at a massive 931 kg. By comparison, the Mercedes-Benz W25, the most successful car of the year, had 402 bhp and weighed 750 kg, which gave it a power/weight ratio almost exactly twice as good. The S.E.F.A.C.'s power was transmitted via a Cotal electro-magnetic gearbox, front suspension was by forward-facing links and coil springs, and coils also suspended the live rear axle.

When it appeared in the French GP it was thrown out for being overweight. Over the next two years it appeared in practice at a couple of events, but was always withdrawn before the race. When it did finally make the starting grid, for the 1938 French GP, it blew up after two laps. It ran at Pau the following year and again retired.

You would have thought that this catalogue of disaster would have convinced anyone that the car was never going to be honed into a winner, but in 1948 a new company called Dommartin announced it was in the business of building racing cars and proudly unveiled its first product. It was the S.E.F.A.C. with a new body, with the supercharger removed and its engine bored out to 3619cc (80 × 90 mm). Thirteen years after its debut it maintained its record of being heavier and less powerful than any of its rivals.

Before the Dommartin could embark on its career of inevitable fiasco, money ran out and the beast was put away.

The S.E.F.A.C. seen in practice for the 1935 French Grand Prix. Designer Émile Petit is standing in the foreground.

E.N.B. - MASERATI

In 1962, the Équipe National Belge cobbled together the remnants of their Emeryson F1 cars which the team had systematically wrecked over the previous season. Thus was created the 'E.N.B.-Maserati', which used the Emeryson chassis No. 1001, retained the old Maserati 150S engine, which had been a lost cause even before the arrival of the British V-8 engines, and had a new body shell with a twin nostril air-intake which parodied the 1961 Ferrari 156.

Needless to say, the new body was fitted without any regard to aerodynamics and could hardly even be said to

be an aesthetic improvement. Lucien Bianchi was entrusted with the 'new' car in the 1962 Grand Prix de Bruxelles, where he practised nearly half a minute off the pace and retired in the first heat with a broken engine. He then appeared with it in the Pau GP, where it qualified in mid-field, and crashed, and in the German GP, where he qualified last, nearly *two minutes* off the pace, and finished last. Then it was bought by the Belgian Nicholas Koob, who enjoyed some success with it in hill climbs.

E. R. A.

E.R.A. (English Racing Automobiles) was a project financed by Humphrey Cook together with Raymond Mays, whose friend, Peter Berthon, was its chief designer. Conceived for *Voiturette* racing, the first E.R.A.s appeared in 1934 and were very successful both before and after the war, by which time a change in the regulations had made them into Grand Prix cars.

Some of these pre-war models did extremely well in post-war racing, especially in the hands of Bob Gerard, who managed third place in the 1948 British GP and second the following year, as well as wins in the British Empire Trophy and Ulster Trophy in 1947 and the Jersey Road Race in 1948. In the immediate post-war period Gerard was the outstanding British driver, though his talent rarely now receives proper recognition.

Most pre-war E.R.A.s have enjoyed a continuous competition career for over 50 years, for by the time they finally stopped appearing in 'main-stream' events, they were old enough to take part in Historic racing, where they have continued to win races, and at the rate they are going it is likely they will celebrate their centenary by still winning races.

In 1939 E.R.A. produced a new car, the E Type, which was an ambitious attempt to create a state-of-the-art racer. Like all E.R.A. engines, it was a 6-cylinder unit which betrayed its Riley ancestry by having twin camshafts mounted high in the block activating short pushrods, but its 1488cc was achieved with a much shorter stroke than other E.R.A.s (63 × 88 mm). With a Zoller supercharger it delivered around 230 bhp through a 4-speed synchromesh gearbox, unlike other E.R.A.s, which had pre-selector boxes.

Earlier E.R.A.s had had Vintage-style chassis and suspension, but the E Type had independent front suspension by trailing arms and torsion bars (à la Auto Union), while the de Dion rear was also sprung by torsion bars – just like Mercedes-Benz! It was a very sleek and handsome car, but too much was expected from it straight from the box, and when it failed to deliver, Humphrey Cook withdrew his support, having underwritten the project to the tune of over £90,000.

Mays continued to support E.R.A. alone and attempts were made to get the car race-ready. It was extremely quick, and it apparently handled well, but it suffered its share of teething problems, in particular a tendency to overheat. Some progress was made, and the prototype appeared in a few races, but war broke out and it was put away for the duration.

After the war, E.R.A. decided it would not return to racing and the prototype, and a second car which had been built up, were sold to Peter Whitehead and Leslie Brooke, but neither car ever performed satisfactorily and suffered all kinds of troubles and breakages.

In late 1947, E.R.A. Ltd was bought by Leslie Johnson, a gifted amateur racer, and was moved to Dunstable to become a Research and Development consultancy. He bought Brooke's E Type and had his firm work on it. Some progress was made, but it was still too complex a design to sort out easily and was anyway ageing rapidly. Eventually Whitehead's car snapped a driveshaft, which punctured the fuel tank, and the car was burned out. The second car was sold to Ken Flint, who fitted a Jaguar engine and made a reasonable sports car from it.

In common with every other British enthusiast, Leslie Johnson was appalled at the failure of Mays and Berthon's second project, the B.R.M., and he decided to finance his own Formula 1 car and to enter it under the E.R.A. name, even though there was no direct link with the pre-war team.

His idea was to prepare for the 2½-litre F1 and to that end he instigated a design study into a water-cooled straight-six engine based on the Norton 'double-knocker' motorcycle unit. By the end of 1952 an experimental single-cylinder engine was showing promise and appeared capable of achieving what was then the engine builder's Holy Grail, 100 bhp/litre. In the meantime he decided to enter F2 with a Bristol-engined car. As an experienced racer he was under no illusions about the Bristol engine when compared with the likes of Ferrari, but his was a long-term project and the G Type E.R.A. was to test the water and gain competition experience.

For a while after the war, E.R.A. had employed the ex-Auto Union designer Robert Eberan von Eberhorst, and from his pen had come the Jowett-E.R.A., which had been put into production as the Jowett Jupiter sports car. Eberhorst's assistant on that project, David Hodkin, was put in charge of the new E.R.A., and so it is not surprising that the result reflected von Eberhorst's general thinking.

Its ladder chassis featured two large oval tubes and four cross-members, made from magnesium alloy, and was extremely stiff. Front suspension was by coil springs and double wishbones, while at the rear was a coil spring-suspended de Dion axle, located on trailing links which could be adjusted to alter the car's handling. Brakes were inboard at the rear, the wheels were of cast alloy, and the 4-speed Bristol gearbox was in unit with the final drive to aid weight distribution and achieve a high polar moment of inertia.

The Bristol engine was a particulary high unit, so was dry-sumped in order to achieve a lower profile. With

The G Type E.R.A. in the paddock at the 1952 British Grand Prix at Silverstone. (**Guy Griffiths**)

all front-engined single-seaters, the drive-train is the designer's biggest headache and Hodkin tackled the problem by making a fairly wide car with the driver seated to the right of the car between the main tubes, with the prop-shaft running alongside him. Unfortunately this did little for the car's frontal area.

Although the G Type has sometimes been dismissed as a low-budget special, that is far from the case. Parts for three cars were laid down and Johnson was able to secure Stirling Moss to drive the first one. Had that proven successful, it is likely a second car would have been entered. In the event, it was not a success. It made its debut at the 1952 Belgian GP, where Moss found it steered and braked well, but was slow, over half a minute off the pace. A piston broke in practice, a spare engine was flown out and a gudgeon pin let go on the first lap, causing the car to crash. It was rebuilt around a spare chassis, but in the British GP was again off the pace, two seconds a lap slower than Hawthorn's Cooper-Bristol and nine seconds

off pole. At Silverstone it overheated and misfired and, to compensate, Moss drove too hard and spun.

It took third at Boreham in heavy rain, practised last in the Dutch GP and retired with engine trouble. In a race at Goodwood it was rammed from behind and crashed, but Moss was able to take part in a second event when he finished fifth. It ended its season, and its life as an E.R.A. with outings in two minor races at Castle Combe and Charterhall, but on both occasions suffered problems with its steering, possibly a legacy of its Goodwood accident. It retired at Castle Combe and finished fourth at Charterhall.

The G Type was abandoned at the end of 1952 and the project was sold to Bristol Cars, but E.R.A. still continued to research a 2½-litre F1 car until Johnson suffered a heart attack in 1953 and, on medical advice, retired from business. E.R.A. Ltd was sold to Solex Carburettors, and still operates in Dunstable as an engineering consultancy, and although the initials

'E.R.A.' now stand for 'Engineering Research Association' the old E.R.A. logo is retained.

After taking over the G Type project, Bristol examined the design, substituted a steel frame for the magnesium alloy chassis (the steel one turned out lighter!) and discarded the adjustable links on the de Dion rear axle. Fitted with an aerodynamic body, the G Type became the Bristol 450, which finished 1-2-3 in the two-litre class at Le Mans in 1954 and 1955. That was some distance removed from Leslie Johnson's dream of an F1 team to add lustre to a famous name, but it was an honourable enough conclusion to the type's career.

ELIOS

On 10 September, 1961, the Coppa Italia was held at Vallelunga, which was a 'last-minute' event to decide the Italian Championship. The title was disputed between Lorenzo Bandini and Giancarlo Baghetti, but it was known that Bandini would be engaged elsewhere on that day so, not surprisingly, Baghetti clinched the title.

Among the cars entered was the 'Elios', entered and driven by one Mario Pandolfo. Despite the best efforts of the Formula One Register and the author, no information at all has been unearthed about this car, not even what sort of engine it used. Pandolfo qualified last of ten runners and retired with engine trouble in both heats.

EMERYSON

Behind most successful constructors you will find a partnership, a designer and someone to count the beans. Colin Chapman had Fred Bushell, while Enzo Ferrari was essentially a bean counter with a gift for attracting the right designers and stylists, but Paul Emery was always a loner. He could generate ideas like few others and physically turn his hand to anything; leave him alone in a workshop with the materials and through its doors would eventually emerge a racing car, but one thing he lacked was business acumen. He had charisma, and people who worked alongside him, and got their hands dirty, will use the word 'brilliant' in every second sentence. On the other hand, those who tried to help him in business will tell you he was impossible.

Confusingly, 'Emeryson' was used to name three distinct lines of car: specials built by Paul's father, George; some 250cc single-seaters made by his brother, Peter; and those made by Paul himself.

Pre-war, George Emery ran a race-preparation business and Paul served his apprenticeship under his father and Geoffrey Taylor, who ran Alta, going back and forth between the two after blazing rows. In the quiet times they built up several specials, one of which was for Paul to race, and this was the first 'Emeryson'. It was a modified G.N. chassis fitted with a 1020cc Gwynne engine and with it Paul enjoyed some success.

Post-war, son and father (the order had changed) built a new special. It created quite a stir when it appeared in Britain's second post-war race meeting (Gransden Lodge, 1947), for even though it had no body, Eric Winterbottom won a race in it and was timed at over 136 mph. The car was intended for Paul, but money had run out, and to earn some to complete it, the Emerys hired it out.

It had a robust ladder-frame, modified Singer coil spring and trailing arm front suspension, an Alta-type independent rear layout with torsion bars, a 1934 d.o.h.c. Lagonda Rapier engine reduced to 1087cc, an E.N.V. pre-selector gearbox and two-stage supercharging achieved by mating a Marshall supercharger with a second-hand compressor of the sort used to pressurize World War II bombers.

Interviewed at the time of the car's debut, the Emerys talked of building an F1 car with an 'air-cooled flat-12 engine with hydraulically operated valves and something very special in the way of boosting – if the finance becomes available.' Finance never did become available, but Winterbottom continued to hire the car and put up some respectable performances in it.

Then Emery came across the 4½-litre straight-eight Duesenberg engine from the ex-Whitney Straight car, tuned it by raising the compression ratio and fitting eight Amal carburettors so it gave, he says, nearly 400 bhp and fitted it to the car. A share in it was sold to Bobby Baird,

who raced it occasionally but never achieved any success, for it had a habit of devouring gearboxes.

With no suitable transmission on the horizon Emery turned to 500cc racing and made a number of pretty, front-engined front-wheel-drive cars which had all-round independent suspension sprung by rubber bands. These sold in small numbers and were capable, for a time, of winning races. One interesting innovation was a disc brake on the works car – and that was in 1950! Then the new F3 began to become too professional for Paul's liking and, unable to afford the fees of the best tuners, he packed it in and built an F2 car in 1953.

It was a neat design, basically a scaled-up '500', with a tubular 'box' frame, coil springs and wishbone front suspension and a de Dion rear end located by twin trailing arms and suspended on coil springs. To keep the drive train as low as possible, a short prop-shaft led to the gearbox and then a longer shaft went under the backwards-facing differential to a reduction box. It was clothed in a particularly pretty body, which had the usual Emery hallmark of a small but efficient air intake.

At first Paul used a second-hand Aston Martin LB6 engine linered down to 2 litres obtained in a typically Emery way. Aston Martin used to sell its sub-standard components, including whole engines and gearboxes, to a scrap merchant with whom Paul was friendly. This 2-litre engine proved woefully unreliable since it needed a host of new components to complement the reduction in bore, and Emery eventually bought a second-hand Alta engine. At first the car had an Aston Martin gearbox, but Emery soon switched to an E.N.V. pre-selector unit.

It was while fitted with an Aston Martin engine, however, that Colin Chapman had his only race in an F1 car. This was in the 1954 International Trophy at Silverstone, where he sat last on the grid in his heat (over a minute off the pace and 39 seconds slower than the H.A.R., which was second last). He managed to finish his heat, however, as last classified runner in 12th place. In the final he completed 27 laps to the winner's 35 and finished 17th and unclassified. In every race which it finished the Emery-Aston Martin was at the back of the field, generally with the Turner and H.A.R.

When the 2½-litre F1 came into force, Emery bored out the Alta engine to 2471cc (93.5×90 mm) and entered a number of minor British F1 events. On slow to medium tight circuits the car and driver gave a fairly good account of themselves, and at Crystal Palace in 1956 Emery had a fine dice with Moss' Maserati, though he eventually had to be content with second place.

The one major race he entered was the 1956 British GP at Silverstone, and though he qualifed 13 seconds off the pace he was still higher on the grid than the Maseratis of Maglioli, Godia-Sales, Rosier and Brabham, and the Gordini of da Silva Ramos, a creditable performance for a three-year-old special. His race, however, lasted just four laps before he retired with ignition trouble.

During 1957 Emery developed a Jaguar 2.4-litre engine which he dry-sumped and fitted with his own fuel injection made from a CAV diesel injection pump. In this form it appeared in only one F1 race, the Richmond Trophy at Goodwood, where, while it was near the back of the grid, it was at least quicker than a couple of private

Bruce Halford (Emeryson) leads Tony Brooks (B.R.M.) and John Campbell-Jones (Cooper) in the International '100' race at Goodwood on Easter Monday 1961. (Duncan Rabagliati)

Maserati 250Fs. After only four laps it retired with engine trouble. Driven by Roberta (previously Robert) Cowell in hill climbs, however, it was a winner in the Ladies' Class.

Eventually it was sold, converted to a sports car, abandoned, rediscovered, restored to original form and is now in France. Emery also recalls building a second car for an American customer who wanted to use it in USAC racing. This was fitted with a glass-fibre body, taken from the original shell, and fitted with a super-charged 2½-litre Alta engine. Unfortunately, he is unable to supply any more details and the author has been unable to find any other reference to it.

In the meantime Emery had installed a Jaguar engine in an Aston Martin DB3 chassis, which he occasionally raced, worked for while on a water-cooled flat-four F2 engine which was test-run in a Morris Minor, but lack of money meant that it got no further, and installed a 2½-litre Connaught-developed Alta engine into the back of an F1 Cooper to create the Cooper-Connaught (q.v.). He also fettled the unraced Connaught Type C and entered it in the 1959 US GP for Bob Said.

Connaught had been taken over by Alan Brown, and in 1960 he sponsored a new company, Emeryson Cars

Ltd, based at the old Connaught works at Send, to build a range of F1 and FJ cars. The result was a single space-frame design, with the frames built by Lister. Front suspension was by coil springs and double wishbones, while the independent rear was by reversed lower wishbones, coil springs and twin radius rods. It was a low car with a pretty glass-fibre shell and, of course, a tiny air intake. Colotti 5-speed gearboxes were mated to Climax FPF engines.

The prototype, then an F2 car, was debuted by Ron Flockhart at Brands Hatch in August 1960, but created no upset since it qualified well down and retired with a broken oil pipe. At Monthléry, however, in the hands of John Turner, a little-known amateur, it excited some attention. Turner spun, lost two laps, and then proceeded to haul in the leaders. On the strength of this performance, Équipe Nationale Belge approached Emeryson with a view to running a team of F1 cars in 1961. The deal, for three F1 cars and one FJ car, was concluded, but perhaps E.N.B. might have been less forward had it known that Turner's progress was assisted in no small measure by the fact that, every so often, he missed out a chicane at the back of the circuit!

The handover of the Emerysons to Équipe Nationale Belge in 1961 with, left to right, Paul Emery, Dick Claydon (Connaught director), Alan Brown, Mauro Bianchi (at the wheel) and Joe Lievin (Secretary General of E.N.B.). (Duncan Rabagliati)

E.N.B. took delivery of three Emerysons fitted with the 4-cylinder d.o.h.c. 1484cc (81×72 mm) Maserati 150S engine, which had about 140 bhp on tap. Driven by Oliver Gendebien and Lucien Bianchi, they qualified quite well at Pau, but both drivers crashed heavily. That set the pattern for the season, and indeed one car was even damaged being taken from the transporter.

E.N.B. entered three cars in the Brussels GP, where they were slow. Bianchi was placed fourth on the aggregate of three heats, but only because he had survived the afternoon. He was entered in the Aintree 200, but was nearly eight seconds off the pace and crashed on the first lap. Gendebien had one for Syracuse, was slow, and retired with transmission trouble.

Only one World Championship race, Monaco, was entered, but neither car qualified. E.N.B. immediately ordered Lotus 18s, but retained the Emerysons and entered them in several races, but generally did not turn up. On the two occasions they did, they need not have bothered, for the cars failed to qualify.

The prototype car was sold to André Pilette, who fitted it with a Coventry Climax FPF engine, but in the one race for which he managed to qualify, the Austrian GP, he finished a long way last.

Emeryson ran a Mk 2 works car for Mike Spence in a few non-Championship events. Spence, who went on to be a works driver for B.R.M. and Lotus, had made his name by winning the 100-mile Commander Yorke Trophy race at Silverstone, the only important race the FJ Emeryson won. On his F1 debut at Solitude, against a strong field which lacked only Ferrari, he enhanced his reputation by running seventh while holding his car in gear, but soon retired.

Later Spence finished second to Tony Marsh's B.R.M. in the Lewis-Evans Trophy at Brands Hatch, which was a race for F1 privateers, since all the big boys were in North America. The interesting thing is that there were 16 entries and it was only a British national event.

A sports version of the F1 car was made for Ray

Fielding, and this proved the most successful version of the design as Fielding won his class in the 1961 RAC Hill Climb Championship.

At the end of 1961 Hugh Powell, a wealthy American teenager, bought into Emeryson Cars Ltd, and shortly afterwards Alan Brown and the rest of the board resigned, although Emery stayed on as designer. In 1962 Powell ran a two-car team for his guardian, Tony Settember, and John Campbell-Jones.

For 1962 Emery proposed building a 4WD car using 750cc mototcycle engines fore and aft, and still feels he should have been allowed to build it. Instead he came up with a Mk 3 car and, had he not had second thoughts about the expense and weight, it would have had a glass-fibre monocoque. As it was, he essayed a more conservative design, which was slimmer and lighter than the earlier cars and which had a semi-monocoque section, for its pannier fuel tanks were contained in a stressed mid-section. Its most startling feature, however, was the nose section, for the radiator was almost horizontal and air passed under the car and up through the radiator. Athough unusual, this layout never gave any problems.

The Mk 3 was a huge improvement on the early cars, but was never able to show its potential, for it cried out for one of the new V-8 Climax or B.R.M. engines, which it never received. It was too small for Tony Settember to fit into, even though he tried hard, once taking a hacksaw to the problem! Relations within the team became strained when, with it, Campbell-Jones proved easily the quicker driver but he would still have been quicker had they swapped cars. He finished sixth in the Aintree 200 and in the International Trophy he qualified tenth from a field of 24. Had he not had problems, he would have finished higher than his final 11th place.

The cars appeared in occasional WC races, Campbell-Jones finished 11th (and last) at Spa, having qualified nearly 30 seconds off the pace. Settember was 11th in the British GP, four laps down, and he also managed to qualify (last) at Monza, where he retired with a failed head gasket. Before the end of the season, however, Emery left the team, which continued to appear in 1963 under the name 'Scirocco' (q.v.) with new chassis fitted with V-8 B.R.M. engines.

Emery turned to other projects, including a twin-

Mike Spence helps unload the Emeryson with which he made his F1 debut at Solitude, 1961. On his right is designer Paul Emery. (**LAT**)

The Emeryson-Climax of John Campbell-Jones in the paddock at Snetterton in April 1962.
(Duncan Rabaglati)

engined Mini and an Imp-engined GT car, but he was not finished with F1, and later prepared a 3-litre version of the Coventry Climax 'Godiva' engine, which appeared a couple of times in 1966.

Around the same time Emery laid down plans for an intriguing F1 car, with four-wheel drive and a flat-eight turbocharged two-stroke engine based on two Hillman Imp blocks. Lack of money meant it was never built, but it is interesting to note that he conceived a turbo F1 engine 11 years before Renault debuted its pioneering design and he had also latched on to the idea that the ultimate form of turbocharging is with a two-stroke engine.

He then found success in preparing Hillman Imps for racing, and in driving them, became a pioneer of turbocharging (with a rallycross car) and then discovered Midget Oval racing, where he enjoyed great success as a tuner and driver. In his fifties he became a national champion in Midgets for five successive years and, for the only time in his life, found himself making money from the sport.

FERGUSON

If ever a car deserved closer attention than it actually received, it was the Ferguson P99, which remains the only four-wheel drive car to have won an F1 race. Four-wheel drive goes back to the early years of the century, and the first 4WD car was shown as early as 1904, but it is only in recent years that it has found public acceptance.

In the 1960s 4WD F1 cars were built by B.R.M., Cosworth, Lotus, McLaren and Matra, but all were failures. By 1969, when there was a sudden rush to make 4WD cars, advances in tyre technology and aerodynamics negated its advantages, but when the Ferguson P99 was made, in 1960, it represented a significant advance in design, but one which was ignored by other makers.

To find the roots of the Ferguson we have to go back to 1939, when two men who were both gifted drivers and engineers, Freddie Dixon and Tony Rolt, got together to research 4WD with a view to applying it to motor racing.

It was a bold move, for previous attempts to race 4WD cars, mainly by Bugatti and Miller, had been conspicuous by their failure.

The first result of this collaboration was a special called 'The Crab', which not only had 4WD and a backbone chassis, it also had four-wheel steering! The Second World War meant it was never developed and indeed it was far from flawless, but the problems it presented were useful experience to the partners.

After the war, Harry Ferguson, creator of the Ferguson tractor and a mutual friend, decided to fund them and he established Ferguson Research Ltd. Throughout the 1950s Ferguson tried to interest the motor industry in his research and there were, too, frequent reports of a Ferguson saloon car which would revolutionize production car design. Prototypes were built and shown to the press, but the project got no further than that.

In 1960 Ferguson Research Ltd began to build a rac-

Stirling Moss with the Ferguson-Climax on his winning drive in the 1961 Gold Cup race at Oulton Park, the only time a four-wheel-drive car has won a Formula 1 race.

ing car which would be both a research vehicle and to demonstrate that 4WD was a viable proposition for road cars, and did not necessarily carry a weight penalty or waste engine power. Designed by Tony Rolt and Claude Hill, a former technical director of Aston Martin, the Project 99 was a front-engined car built around a triangulated space-frame made of small-gauge tubing.

By the time the first tubes were cut, even Ferrari had joined the 'rear engine revolution', so apart from anything else, the P99 was the last front-engined F1 car. Since the drive was going to all four wheels, it did not matter which end of the car took the 1½-litre Coventry Climax FPF, but it was easier to install the transmission at the front.

To reduce frontal area, the engine was canted to its right. It drove through a 5-speed gearbox developed by Ferguson and Colotti, which was to the left of the centre-line. From the gearbox a set of transfer gears took the drive to a small central differential and from there one prop-shaft went forward to a differential left of centre, while the rearward prop-shaft angled in slightly, alongside the driver, to the rear differential, which was, again, left of centre.

Suspension was independent all round by coil springs and double wishbones. Because power was distributed evenly to all four corners, narrower rear tyres and wheels, and lighter rear drive-shafts, could be used, so the finished car weighed no more than its opposition. The brakes, mounted inboard all round, were fitted with Dunlop's 'Maxaret' system. This was a pioneering form of ABS which Dunlop had developed for aircraft, but while the system was tried in testing it was not used during the car's short life in racing.

For it debut, the Ferguson P99 was fitted with a 2½-litre Coventry Climax FPF engine and entered in the 1961 International Trophy at Silverstone, which was run as an Inter-Continental race.

Tony Rolt had offered the car to an entrant from his driving days, Rob Walker, who nominated Jack Fairman as driver for Silverstone. Fairman was a decent journeyman driver, but unable to explore the new techniques the car required and he never showed particularly well in a wet race which should have suited the Ferguson. He retired with engine trouble with the theoretical advantages of the car remaining unproven.

Fairman was back in the cockpit for the British GP at Aintree, where he qualified a lacklustre 20th. In the race he soldiered around, while team-mate Moss in a Lotus hounded the Ferraris until he retired. Fairman was then brought in so that Stirling could drive the car and he was soon the fastest man on the flooded track though a long way down the order. Then the black flag was shown to Moss, not for any infringement on his part but because Fairman had earlier received a push-start after a pit stop. The irony is that had Moss started in the Ferguson he might have won.

Moss elected to drive the car in the non-Championship Oulton Park Gold Cup, which attracted the best of the non-Ferrari runners and, in difficult conditions, he brought it home a winner. It remains the only occasion a 4WD car has won an F1 race.

Despite a promising, if short, first season nobody else was interested in taking up the Ferguson concept, so it was put away until the end of 1963, when Jo Bonnier drove it in the Ollon-Villars hill climb, which he won. It was then shipped Down Under for the Tasman series. In the hands of Graham Hill and Innes Ireland the Ferguson usually finished in the top three, which was a creditable performance for so old a car.

Meanwhile Andy Granatelli, the Indycar entrant, commissioned Ferguson to build a couple of cars to take his straight-eight Novi engines and Bobbie Unser qualified sixth for the 1964 Indy 500, but was involved in an accident on the second lap. Unser ran as high as seventh the following year until retiring with an oil leak. Four-wheel drive became something of an Indy feature over the next few years, until it was outlawed, though the best result for such a car was Bobbie Unser's third in a Lola in 1969.

Ferguson later designed a second car which was also front-engined and it was intended to fit a Coventry Climax FWMV. Because the normal exhaust system could not be easily accommodated in a front-engine installation, Climax developed the 'flat crank' version of its engine specifically for the Ferguson, which was never to be completed.

Peter Westbury had the use of P99 for the 1964 RAC Hill Climb Championship, which he won easily. Westbury proved the advantages of 4WD for hill climbing, but the rest of the motor racing establishment, apart from B.R.M. remained unconvinced until the natural time for four-wheel drive had passed. Although the B.R.M. P67 was never raced in F1, Peter Lawson used it to win the 1968 RAC Hill Climb Championship.

The Ferguson P99 remains one of the most interesting cars of its period and is presently in the Donington Collection.

FERRARI

Ferrari is an Italian maker of racing cars who enjoyed a great deal of success in F1 in 1951-3, 1961 and in the 1970s, but has been hobbled by the fact that never in its history has it originated a new idea. There are some who maintain that Grand Prix racing would not be Grand Prix racing without Ferrari and they are right – up to a point. Ferrari embodies the romantic spirit of motor racing, but for long stretches of F1 history whether or not Ferrari turned up for a race would have made no difference at all to the result.

Ferrari was so emotive a name, and his cars are so lovely to behold, that such a statement reeks of heresy, but the fact remains that his early reputation rests largely on his sports-racing cars, a lower level of racing. During the 12 years 1954-65, Ferrari-originated F1 cars won 16 WC events, while Ferrari sports-racers won 42 Championship sports car events, or just over 59 per cent of all races, and that included seven wins at Le Mans with that race's unique prestige.

One can say that 16 WC wins is more than any other team except Lotus and deserves special credit on the grounds that Ferrari made almost every part of its cars itself. On the other hand, an average of less than 1½ WC wins per year is not the performance of a top team. The truth lies between the two extremes and while this chapter will not add anything to the history of the marque perhaps it will achieve a balanced perspective.

Too much starry-eyed garbage has been written about Ferrari and about the only book waiting to be written is *Great Recipes From The Works Canteen*. Given the level of objectivity of some authors even that would lead to: 'Giuseppe had allowed the pasta to burn and the pan was a carbonized mess. Years later carbon would be used to construct the monocoque which ...'

Ferrari has competed over a longer period than any other maker, but it has not been as successful as it should have been, given its resources and driver and design talent. Many times I have heard rival team managers and designers say, 'Ferrari should win *everything*.'

Central to the story is Enzo Ferrari, whose conduct of his team has been like a medieval Doge ruling a turbulent city-state with its plotters, poisoners and stiletto artists, and keeping them all supplied with blade and venom, Scuderia Ferrari is Italian and operatic, full of gestures and passion and while this is enjoyable to behold, it is not neccessarily the way to win races.

Enzo Ferrari was born in 1898, the son of a metal worker-cum-engineer. He flunked an engineering course and spent the First World War in the Italian army shoeing mules. Afterwards he hung about in those cafés and bars where the racing set congregated and by degrees became a test driver and industrial spy for Alfa Romeo. This led to a short and quite successful career as a racing driver, which ended after a nervous breakdown. Then came the Scuderia Ferrari, which began as a consortium of private owners, developed into a works-related team for Alfa Romeo and then became the works team itself, as Alfa Romeo officially turned its back on racing to keep its shareholders happy.

When Alfa Romeo failed to meet the threat of the German teams, scapegoats had to be found, for it was unthinkable that Mussolini's Italy could be beaten by cars from the state ruled by his pupil, Hitler. Among the heads which rolled were those of Vittorio Jano, greatest of all Italian designers, and Ferrari. Alfa Romeo decided not to farm out its works team to Scuderia Ferrari, but to enter its own cars under the name 'Alfa Corse'. In a typically Italian way, Ferrari was employed to run it. He did not, however, get on with Jano's successor, Wifredo Ricart, whose case for appointment had been strengthened by his holding impeccable (for Italy, 1938) political views. Eventually a severance was agreed and, as a result, Ferrari set up his own light engineering company, but was constrained from using the name Scuderia Ferrari for four years. In his wake he left Alfa Romeo with the Tipo 158, which he had conceived with Gioacchino Colombo, although the actual design was Colombo's.

Thus Ferrari unwittingly ensured Italian dominance in immediate post-war Grand Prix racing as the Alfa Romeo *Voiturette* went on to successes beyond the wildest imagining of its conceivers and also set the standard at which Ferrari itself had to aim.

It was not long before Ferrari's new firm, Societa Auto Avio Costruzione, Modena turned its hand to car-making. Alberto Massimino created a 1½-litre straight-eight engine based on two Fiat blocks in tandem. Called the Auto Avio 815, to avoid conflict with the severance agreement from Alfa Romeo, two of these cars were entered in the *soi disant* 1940 Mille Miglia, where both retired. Shortly afterwards Italy entered World War II, which was a time of prosperity and growth for Ferrari as his company made parts for whichever power held the upper hand, and when peace returned the works had quadrupled its size. In 1946 the name of the company changed to Auto Costruzione Ferrari, Modena.

Just to make sure that nobody suffered a dearth of prosperity, the Americans rushed in with the Marshall Plan, which subsidized the industrial rebuilding of the aggressive nations. In motor racing terms, this meant that Ferrari had war damage repaired and was set up so he could commission a new design while British constructors picked over ex-WD materials in scrapyards.

At the end of the war titles and honours awarded under the Fascist regime were held null and void, but recipients could apply for their restoration. Ferrari, who had picked up the title *Commendatore* for winning the 1924 Coppa Acerbo (which is a little like the organizers of the International Trophy at Silverstone throwing a knighthood into the prize fund), elected not to do so and has hence been plain 'Signor' ever since.

Ferrari employed Colombo to design a new car and he was keen to make a version of the mid-engined Alfa Romeo 512. Ferrari replied that the horse had always pulled, not pushed the cart. Given the difficulties encountered by Auto Union this was not an unreasonable attitude at the time. Having coined a pleasant aphorism, however, Ferrari kept repeating it, even when it was plain silly.

Colombo drew a 60-degree V-12 engine of 1497cc (55 × 52.5 mm) with s.o.h.c. heads and valves operated by hairpin springs which derived from the flat-12 engine he had created for the still-born Alfa Romeo Tipo 512. Apparently Ferrari was not so mindful of the Alfa Romeo unit, but had fallen in love with the Packard V-12 at an early age!

This engine initially gave 128 bhp in racing trim and drove through a 5-speed gearbox. The chassis chosen for the first sports Ferraris was a simple cross-braced ladder-frame with two oval main tubes and front suspension by

unequal wishbones and a transverse leaf spring, with the live rear axle sprung by a transverse leaf and located by single radius arms. With various sizes of engine Ferraris were very successful in sports car racing, but largely because they were the first post-war design and raced against cars up to ten years old.

The fact that a new car *should* beat a ten year old car, seems often to have been ignored by some historians. In the same way, the fact that a new design failed to beat the ten year old Alfetta is also ignored.

Ferrari had announced his intention to enter Grand Prix racing and the V-12 was an ideal starting point. Fitted with a single Weber carburettor and a Roots-type blower, it developed 225 bhp at 7500 rpm, but although it was designed to rev to 10,000 rpm, it would not exceed 7500 rpm due to higher than expected frictional losses and the poor breathing from the s.o.h.c. heads. It was, however, unusual in that it was the first 'over-square' GP engine for over 40 years.

Although it was not competitive with the Alfa Romeo Tipo 158, Ferrari went ahead and made a single-seater to use it with similar front suspension to the sports car but with swing-axle rear suspension sprung by torsion bars. Before long the torsion bars gave way to a transverse leaf spring.

The Tipo 125 made its debut in the 1948 Italian GP at Turin, where three cars were driven by Raymond Som-

First British appearance of the works Ferrari team was in the 1949 International Trophy at Silverstone. Luigi Villoresi drove this Tipo 125 1.5-litre supercharged car into third place. (Guy Griffiths)

mer, Giuseppe Farina and 'B. Bira'. Sommer pressed the Alfettas early in the race, but had to be content with third behind Wimille's 158 and Villoresi's Maserati, while Farina crashed and Bira retired with transmission trouble. In the other two important races of the year, the GPs of Monza and Penya Rhin (Barcelona), no Ferrari finished. The usual reason for retirement was transmission trouble, but Bira was at least leading in Barcelona when his car called it a day. Farina, however, managed to win the Circuit of Garda against negligible opposition.

They had not been crowned with success, but then Ferrari had a stroke of luck. First Maserati withdrew from running a works team following the departure of the Maserati brothers, and then Alfa Romeo also withdrew. In 1949, Grand Prix racing came down to private Maseratis, which were ageing fast, lumbering old Talbot-Lagos, other privateers in such as Altas and pre-war E.R.A.s – and Ferrari.

Conditions were right, therefore, for Ferrari to make its reputation, and although its GP performances had not amounted to much, cars were sold to Peter Whitehead and Tony Vandervell, who had been instrumental in sorting out some of the problems with bearings on the engines. Despite the fact that the level of opposition was thin, and Ferrari signed both Luigi Villoresi, the established ace, and Alberto Ascari, the 'coming man', it still did not take GP racing by storm.

In the first major race they contested, the Belgian GP, the Ferraris were quick, but Rosier's Talbot, aided by making no fuel stop, won from Villoresi, Ascari and Whitehead. The lesson of this defeat was not lost on Ferrari and soon work began on an unsupercharged, more economical, 4½-litre engine.

Ascari and Villoresi, however, made amends by scoring a 1-2 in the Swiss GP, when the cars ran with a revised rear suspension layout with the leaf spring relocated. It was the marque's first important single-seater victory. A single car, for Villoresi, was entered for the French GP and it retired with transmission problems, although Whitehead's car came third to a Talbot and a Maserati. In the Dutch GP, Ascari retired with a broken stub axle, but Villoresi won, and then Ascari won the International Trophy at Silverstone with Villoresi third.

Aurelio Lampredi had joined Ferrari and together with Colombo he set about converting the Tipo 125's engine to both two-stage supercharging and twin overhead camshafts driven by gears instead of the earlier chain-drive. This engine delivered 310 bhp, which brought it closer to the benchmark set by Alfa Romeo and the car's wheelbase and track were increased. The year ended with Ascari winning the Italian GP with one of the new cars and with Whitehead winning the

Czechoslovakian GP with his private car.

It had been a mixed first full season and there was a lot wrong with the cars, as Tony Vandervell had been quick to point out when he had returned his first one in disgust, accompanying it with a list of constructive criticisms. Many of the problems stemmed from the materials Ferrari had to use; he may not have had to scrounge round scrapyards, but Italian metals were not of a high quality. Still, Ferrari really should have done better than it did. Being twice defeated by Talbots, a pre-war design, was not good and neither was the fact that Farina's private Maserati could still beat works Ferraris, as he demonstrated at Lausanne and Pau.

Although the opposition of 1949 did little more than grow a year older in 1950, Alfa Romeo was poised to return with a three-car team in the hands of Fangio, Farina and Fagioli, one of the strongest driver line-ups in motor racing history.

The first confrontation between the two teams came in the San Remo GP, where Ferrari fielded five cars, but the only one still showing at the end was Villoresi's in second place. Ferrari missed the British GP, the first race of the new World Championship, and in the Monaco GP Ascari finished second to Fangio's Alfetta, but a lap down.

While the new 'long-block' V-12 was progressing under the guidance of Lampredi (Colombo had left), the Scuderia produced an interim car for the Swiss GP, with a shorter wheelbase, a de Dion rear axle suspended on a transverse leaf spring and located by twin radius rods, and the 4-speed gearbox in unit with the final drive. This was driven by Villoresi, who retired with back axle failure, while Ascari in a conventional car had an oil pipe break.

The season limped on with the Ferraris not impressing. The irony is that Alfa Romeo with a pre-war design created by Colombo was vastly superior to Ferrari's post-war design created by Colombo. In the meantime, Ferrari's reputation was growing as it was highly successful in sports car racing. Even though the supercharged Ferraris were failures in GP racing (that 1949 season against thin opposition flattered them) the Ferrari mystic was growing and one still meets people who believe Ferrari was successful in F1 in its early days.

Political and economic conditions had not sufficiently eased to allow the potential opposition to display itself. Not every country had had the good fortune to be able to surrender to the Americans and then bask in Yankee largesse. Ferrari had an opportunity to produce a wonderful car and had basically plonked a fairly inept version of the Alfa Romeo 512 engine into an amateurish chassis which won few accolades from its drivers. It was,

Alberto Ascari with the 4.1-litre unsupercharged Ferrari on its debut in the 1950 Grand Prix des Nations at Geneva. The car was retired with water running out of the exhaust pipes. (Louis Klementaski)

in short, a failure, completely outclassed by Alfa Romeo's pre-war Tipo 158.

The first expression of Lampredi's 'long-block' V-12 was entered in the Belgian GP. The Tipo 275F reverted to single overhead camshafts and had a capacity of 3322cc (72 × 68 mm). Initially it produced 300 bhp at 7200 rpm. It derived from Colombo's engine, but you cannot simply scale up an engine, and while its bare specification was similar, it was different in detail. Readers wishing to know more are referred to *Ferrari* by Hans Tanner and Doug Nye. One of these engines was installed in a swing-axle chassis for Ascari to drive at Spa and he brought it home a distant fifth, behind three Alfa Romeos and a Talbot. At the Grand Prix des Nations at Geneva, Ascari had a Tipo 340 with a 4101cc (80 × 68 mm) version of the engine which had 310 bhp and a much better torque curve, and there he ran a strong second to Fangio, and ahead of the rest of the Alfa Romeo team, until his engine boiled dry. Villoresi crashed his 3.3-litre car when in fifth place.

By the Italian GP the Tipo 375 was ready with full-sized engine of 4493cc (80 × 74.5 mm) which delivered 330 bhp. By then Ferrari was committed to the new engine and two cars were entered for Ascari and Dorino Serafini. Ascari disputed the lead and when his engine gave way he took over Serafini's car and tigered up from sixth to second. It was a turning point in motor racing, for it signalled the end of the supercharged engine. Alfa Romeo missed the GP at Barcelona and there Ascari and Serafini filled the first two places with 4.5-litre Ferraris,

while Piero Taruffi was third in a 4.1-litre version. It is at this point that Ferrari's brief career of great success in Grand Prix racing begins.

As raced in 1951, the cars had the 4½-litre engine driving to a 4-speed all-synchromesh gearbox in unit with the final drive. A twin-plug cylinder head, introduced early in the year, helped raised output to 380 bhp at 7000 rpm. Its suspension system was unchanged, but, at 7 ft 6 in, its 'standard' wheelbase was slightly shorter than the blown cars and its front and rear tracks were slightly narrower. There were, however, variations at almost every race, and again readers wishing to know exactly who did what, and with which, and to whom, are referred to the Tanner/Nye book.

Running with single-plug heads, and with a combination of chassis, including those with swing-axle rear suspension (when all is said and done, Ferrari was a special builder who happened to make all his own parts), Ferraris had an easy time in the opening non-Championship races of 1951 and won at Pau, Syracuse and San Remo. It was not until the Swiss GP that Ferrari met Alfa Romeo and there Ascari and Taruffi had full 1951 specification cars, while Villoresi had a 'single-plug' version. Ascari had been burned in the F2 curtain-raiser and it was a wonder he raced at all, let alone finish sixth. Villoresi crashed, but Taruffi finished second to Fangio's Alfa Romeo and ahead of Sanesi and Farina's Alfettas.

Although the power of the Ferrari was now close to the Tipo 159, the Alfetta was faster in a straight line, while

Ascari's twin-plug 4.5-litre Ferrari lined up with the other works cars in front of the pits before the 1951 British Grand Prix at Silverstone. (Guy Griffiths)

the Ferrari had superior torque. Thus Farina's Alfa won the Belgian GP, with Ascari and Villoresi in hot pursuit, and Fangio won at Reims in Fagioli's car, but Ferraris filled the next three places. The crunch would come at Silverstone, then regarded as a medium-fast circuit.

There the newcomer to the team, Froilan Gonzalez, was given a 'single-plug' model and the man the Press dubbed 'The Wild Bull Of The Pampas' (a daft tag, for he was actually a sensitive man and driver) surprised everyone by setting pole. He led from pole to flag to give Ferrari its first WC win and thus inflicted on Alfa Romeo its first defeat since early in 1946. Ferrari had finally beaten the car he had instigated 13 years before and was moved to say, 'I killed my mother today', which sounds like a line from an opera, *written on a bad day*. More to the point, it was the object of the exercise and his 'mother' had not so much been killed but had grown feeble with age.

Moving away from libretto for a moment, it is as well to record that only Fangio finished on the same lap as Gonzalez and Villoresi's third-placed Ferrari was two laps down. It had, indeed, been a passionate duel.

Then Ascari won the German GP from Fangio, with Gonzalez third and Villoresi fourth, Taruffi fifth and Fischer sixth. Alfa Romeo was on the run, it was hobbled by its fuel consumption (about 1.5 mpg in 1951) and its engines were unable to match Ferrari on the slower circuits. Ascari then led Gonzalez to a 1-2 in the Italian GP with other Ferraris fourth and fifth.

It would have been possible for Ascari to have won the World Championship at the last race, the Spanish GP, but Ferrari fitted the smaller wheels which had been successful at Monza. They worked well in qualifying (Ascari took pole by two seconds), but were a disaster in the race as the cars chewed up their tyres. Perhaps Ferrari had a duff batch, as Lampredi has suggested, but more likely, given the track surface and the temperature, fitting the smaller wheels was simply a mistake. Thus it was that Fangio won for Alfa Romeo with Gonzalez' Ferrari second, and the great Argentinian won his first World Championship. It was fitting that Alfa Romeo was able to retire from F1 on a winning note, for the company had done so much to make the category popular.

After proving the superiority of unblown engines,

Whoops! Froilan Gonzalez on the grass during his winning drive with the single-plug Tipo 375 car in the 1951 British Grand Prix. (Guy Griffiths)

Ferrari was robbed of the edge it had worked so hard to enjoy. With Alfa Romeo out and B.R.M. unable to keep appointments, the FIA decided to run the World Championship to Formula 2 for two years with the 2½-litre formula to follow.

This change did not cause Ferrari to falter, for it already had the best F2 car on the grid. In fact it had the *only* bespoke F2 car on the grid. Its V-12 Tipo 166 had been virtually unbeatable during 1949-51, but not content to rest on its laurels, Ferrari introduced the 4-cylinder Tipo 500.

By contrast, the British contestants were special builders using whatever engines they could lay their hands on, the French were summed up by one word, 'Gordini', the German builders were running out of steam with their B.M.W.-based cars and Maserati was not yet ready to rejoin racing.

Lampredi liked simple designs and the Tipo 500 was as simple as successful racing designs come with a 4-cylinder d.o.h.c. engine of 1985cc (90 × 78 mm) which produced 165 bhp at 7000 rpm. It was fitted into a chassis which was a smaller and lighter version of the 4½-litre car with wider front and rear track.

The main drivers were Ascari, Villoresi and Farina, but it was Piero Taruffi, brought in because Ascari was driving a 4½-litre car at Indianapolis and because Farina had been injured in the Millie Miglia, who scored the first WC win, in the Swiss GP. When Ascari returned from his unsuccessful attempt on Indy, he won the rest of the Championship races, the Grands Prix of Belgium, France, Britain, Germany, Holland and Italy, Ferrari also

took second in every race except the Italian GP, where Gonzalez' Maserati interloped and Ferrari drivers took the first four places in the Championship: Ascari, Farina, Taruffi and the Swiss privateer Rudi Fischer, who tied with Mike Hawthorn (Cooper-Bristol). In addition, Ferrari entered ten non-Championship races (Syracuse, Pau, Marseilles, Naples, Paris, Monza, Reims, Sables d'Olonne, Comminges and Modena) and won nine of them. The only defeat was at the hands of Jean Behra, who took his Gordini to a brilliant win at Reims, but 16 F1 wins from 17 races was a fabulous effort.

For 1953 the cars remained much the same apart from some modifications to the engines to improve their breathing. New to the team, however, was John Michael 'Mike' Hawthorn, who had performed miracles in 1952 with his Cooper-Bristol.

So far as the WC was concerned, Ascari won the Grands Prix of the Argentine, Holland and Belgium, and thus scored nine consecutive Championship wins, a run without equal in racing history. The French GP at Reims, however, saw a titanic battle between Hawthorn and the Maserati of Fangio, with the young Englishman winning by a second. In third place was Gonzalez' Maserati and Ascari was fourth, with less than five seconds covering the first four cars.

Ascari won the British GP and was dominating the German, but he was robbed of a fourth consecutive victory at the 'Ring when a wheel came off. He made it to the pits on three wheels and a brake drum and rejoined with a new wheel. Then Nello Ugolini, Ferrari's team manager, called in Villoresi and he and Ascari swapped cars, but Ascari soon retired with a blown engine. Farina went on to win for Ferrari with Hawthorn third.

Ascari won the Swiss GP and was battling for the lead on the last lap of the Italian GP when he made a rare mistake (or was nudged by Marimon's Maserati) and crashed on the last corner while holding a narrow lead. Fangio won, to give Maserati its first important victory for some years, and Farina came second, 1.8 seconds behind. Thus Ferrari was denied a second clean sweep, although Ascari won his second title, from Fangio, and Ferrari drivers Farina, Hawthorn and Villoresi filled the next three places.

The Scuderia also raced in the non-Championship events at Syracuse, Pau, Bordeaux, Silverstone (the International Trophy), Naples and Dundrod (Ulster Trophy) and won all of them except Syracuse. There all retired with engine trouble caused by a batch of faulty valve springs and victory went to de Graffenried's Maserati. Thus the F2 World Championship ended with Ferrari winning 28 of the 31 races it contested, and 14 of the 15 WC events, with Ascari winning 11 of those.

One race the team missed was the Modena GP on its own doorstep. At the Italian GP Ferrari announced he was to pull out of racing, for he could no longer afford it.

To emphasize the point Ferrari missed the Modena GP. It was, of course, one of Ferrari's periodic ploys to drum up more money. Soon afterwards, the racing world was rocked to hear that Ascari and Villoresi had joined Lancia. At the root of the defection was the fact that Ferrari had complacently decided to enter the new 2½-litre F1 with what was basically an enlarged F2 car. Mercedes-Benz were known to be returning to F1 and the way it had tackled sports-car racing with its 300SL coupés in 1952 was enough to convince everyone except Enzo Ferrari that it would be a formidable return. Possibly, too, Ascari had not been impressed by Lampredi's urging of a 2½-litre V-twin engine!

Ferrari was to race two models in 1954, the Tipo 625, which was the old F2 car fitted with an engine enlarged to 2490cc (94 × 90 mm) which began the season with 230 bhp and ended it with 245 bhp. This was intended to be a stop-gap, with the car of the future being the Tipo 553, which, with a 2-litre engine, had made its debut in the 1953 Italian GP. This was nicknamed the *Squalo* (shark) because its bulbous side tanks (Ferraris usually carried the juice in a tail tank) gave it a clean and mean appearance, but it was never to fulfil the promise of its looks.

During the two years of the Formula 2, 2-litre Grands Prix, Ferrari raced the Tipo 500 4-cylinder cars. This is Alberto Ascari, World Champion to be, on his way to victory in the 1952 British Grand Prix at Silverstone. (Guy Griffiths)

Although its suspension layout was broadly the same as on the Tipo 500, the front transverse leaf spring was under the chassis and attached to the lower wishbones and it was a shorter, more compact car — with a space-frame-*style* chassis. It still had a 4-cylinder engine, but while this derived from the 625 engine, it was in many ways a new unit with different head (and valves inclined at 10 degrees instead of 58 degrees), a new block and larger bearings. It was of 2496cc with markedly over square dimensions (100×79.5 mm) and it produced, so Ferrari said, 250 bhp at 7500 rpm.

The beginning of 1954 was a little like the Phoney War, for neither Lancia nor Mercedes-Benz were to enter the fray until later. Those early races were basically between Ferrari and Maserati with Gordini leading the supporting cast of privateers and ex-F2 cars.

First blood went to Maserati when Fangio won the WC Argentine GP, then Ferrari won at Syracuse (Farina, 625) and Behra's Gordini won at Pau. Gonzalez, who, with Maurice Trintignant, had joined the team, then won at Bordeaux (625). He had a 553 for the International Trophy and won his heat but could not start the final because his engine had seized solid. He took over Trintignant's 625 (winner of the other heat) to win the final.

Gonzalez won at Bari (625) and for the first European WC race, the Belgian GP, Ferrari entered 553s for Gonzalez and Farina and 625s for Trintignant and Hawthorn. Both the *Squalos* retired with engine pro-

blems and Trintignant finished second to Fangio's Maserati.

Ferrari had a problem, all the drivers much preferred the 625 even though it was not on a par with the new Maserati 250F. By contrast the *Squalo* was ill-handling and unreliable. A compromise was reached whereby a 553 head was mated to the block of a 625, given the cylinder dimensions of a 553, and run in a 625 chassis. Hawthorn had such a combination in the Rouen GP, where the crankshaft broke, while Trintignant won in a normal 625. This was a week after the French GP at Reims, where Mercedes-Benz had returned and confirmed everyone's worst fears, although Gonzalez had practised within a second of Fangio's pole. The three works cars, however, all broke in their effort to keep up in the race.

The improved 625s, however, ran in the British GP, where Gonzalez led all the way and Hawthorn inherited second place. For the rest of the season, Ferrari was overshadowed first by Mercedes-Benz, then by Moss in the Maserati 250F and finally by the appearance of the new Lancia D50. At the German GP another new engine type appeared, this being a 553 head and bores with the bottom end of the 735 sports car engine. With this unit, Gonzalez ran second to Fangio, but he had been shattered by the death in practice of his friend, the young Argentine Onofre Marimon and he handed over to Hawthorn, who drove superbly to take the car from fourth to second place, with Trinitgnant (625) third.

Froilan Gonzalez in his heat of the 1954 International Trophy at Silverstone with a Tipo 553 Ferrari. He drove a 625 in the final. (T. C. March)

Although still shattered by his friend's death, Gonzalez set pole in the Swiss GP in a 625 with a 553/735 engine and came home a fine second to Fangio's Mercedes after Moss' Maserati retired. Hawthorn and Trintignant, who both had 625-553/735s, retired with engine trouble, while Umberto Maglioli trailed in a distant seventh in a 553.

Since Lancia was still not ready to enter the fray, Ascari returned to the team at Monza and in a 625-553 he practised just a shade slower than Fangio's Mercedes and actually led at half-distance before the engine let go. Hawthorn in a 625-625/553 (Rouen-type) eventually came home second, a lap down on Fangio. Third was Gonzalez, who had taken over Maglioli's car, which was a 625 with a basic 625 engine, while fifth was Trintignant with a combination similar to Hawthorn's but with extra fuel tanks.

All this jiggling about with engines and chassis was a sure sign of a team unsure of its direction, and confirms Ascari's prognosis for the season, but Ferrari was not that far from Fangio's Mercedes-Benz in terms of pace (which shows that M.-B. was struggling rather than Ferrari was doing well), and the leading Ferraris were generally quicker than Fangio's team-mates. Just how close was shown at the Spanish GP, where Hawthorn scored a surprise win in the unloved *Squalo*.

This was actually yet another variation on the theme, since the engine had been beefed up with new con-rods and there were modifications to the breathing, but the most notable innovation was new front suspension by coil springs and wishbones plus an anti-roll bar. It was, however, Trintignant in a 625-553 who led the race after Ascari's new Lancia retired. His race, however, finished just after half-distance with engine trouble and, with Fangio's car overheating, Hawthorn ended the season on the best possible note.

It was to be a false spring, since Mercedes-Benz had further developments in the pipeline, and by signing Moss had another driver capable of winning. Ferrari pressed ahead with both a new straight-six engine and also Lampredi's V-twin. For the Argentine GP, Ferrari sent a team of 625s but with the *Squalo* coil spring and wishbone front suspension, 553 engines, 5-speed gearboxes and a modified rear end with the transverse leaf spring moved to over the top of the differential.

Hawthorn had decided to drive for Vanwall, and Harry Schell replaced him, while Farina, Gonzalez and Trintignant stayed on the strength with Umberto Maglioli as cadet driver. The Argentine GP was run in sweltering heat and most drivers succumbed to it. The result says it all: 1st, Fangio; 2nd, Gonzalez/Trintignant/Farina; 3rd, Farina/Maglioli/Trintignant.

Back in Europe Ferrari pressed ahead with the Tipo 555 *SuperSqualo*. This had a different chassis with two

Froilan Gonzalez scored a remarkable victory with the Tipo 625 in the 1954 British Grand Prix at Silverstone. (T. C. March)

large-diameter main tubes and a structure of smaller tubes to carry the body, tanks and rear suspension. It first appeared at Turin in late March, where Farina drove it in practice, without much enthusiasm, and switched to a 625. That race, ominously, saw a first win for Ascari's Lancia.

Trintignant and Farina had a pair of 555s at Bordeaux, but they were slower than the better Maseratis and both retired. Schell and Taruffi had 555s for the Monaco GP, with Trintignant and Farina preferring 625s, and when Fangio, Moss and Ascari all retired,

Trintignant scored a surprise win.

Shortly afterwards Ascari was killed during a routine test at Monza and that was to change the whole face of the 1955 season, for at the next race, the Belgian GP, there was only one token Lancia, for Castellotti, and that was the last time a works Lancia appeared. Ferrari decided to send only 555s to the race for Farina, Trintignant, Taruffi and the Belgian journalist/driver Paul Frère. For this high-speed circuit, the cars were fitted with long, tapering noses and Farina and Frère came home third and fourth.

Nino Farina with the Tipo 55 SuperSqualo in the 1955 Belgian Grand Prix. He finished third. (Louis Klementaski)

The week after the race came the horrific accident at Le Mans, which blighted the season and put the future of road racing in doubt, but the Dutch GP went ahead since it was on a purpose-built circuit. Farina had decided to retire because he was still suffering the aftermath of burns received the previous year, and Castellotti and Hawthorn were brought in alongside Trintignant. None of the cars showed well and the best finish was Castellotti in fifth, three laps down. The same three drivers had 625-555s for the British GP and again they were way off the pace, with the only finisher being a car shared by Hawthorn and Castellotti which was sixth, three laps down.

Ferrari was in a desperate position, since it was clear that not even the projects in the pipeline were up to the mark. He then wheeled and dealed in an Italian way. Cue violins. He would be forced to give up racing. He could no longer afford to carry the reputation of Italy, even if that did sell Italian cars abroad. It was a pity, but he had to face reality.

The Italian industry anxiously rallied round. The new owners of Lancia, which had come close to collapse, handed over all but one of the D50 F1 cars and along with them went Vittorio Jano, the transporters and spares. Fiat guaranteed a five-year subsidy. The day was saved. For the next two years Ferrari would become an entrant of modified Lancias but since these are not Ferraris, they are covered under Lancia-Ferrari.

There was one final race in 1955 for the *Super-Squalo*, at the Italian GP. Ferrari was determined to win, and entered Lancias for Farina and Villoresi, and no fewer than four 555s for Hawthorn, Castellotti, Trintignant and Magioli. The Lancias encountered tyre problems on the Monza bankings (Ferrari used Englebert, Lancia had used Pirelli) and so were withdrawn. None of the 555s was particularly fast, with the exception of Castellotti, who practised fourth fastest behind three Mercedes-Benz streamliners, and he drove well to finish third. *SuperSqualos*, including one with a Lancia V-8 engine appeared in the Argentine at the beginning of 1956, but that was the end of the line.

That, for the time being, was the end of Ferrari-originated cars in Formula 1, but the Lancias which were run during 1956 and 1957 were only a stop-gap, a chance to regroup. At the end of 1955, Lampredi left Ferrari, having designed, apart from the F1 cars, a series of highly successful sports and GT models.

In place of Lampredi, Vittorio Bellentini was put in charge of engine design and development and Alberto Massimino oversaw chassis design. Jano was officially a consultant, but in fact his was the biggest contribution to the F1 cars over the next few years. Ferrari, that old myth-maker, tells how his dying son, Alfredino, took an active interest in the development of the new engines and it was his decision to use a V-6 layout. In fact, before he left, Lampredi had already started designing a V-6, while Jano had been responsible for some fine V-6 engines for Lancia. The engine, however, was named 'Dino' in memory of Ferrari's son.

The first car, Tipo 156 (1.5 litres, 6 cylinders) was completed before the end of 1956. It had a 65-degree d.o.h.c. V-6 of 1489cc (70×64.5 mm) which developed a claimed 180 bhp (say, 160 bhp) at 9000 rpm and drove through a 4-speed gearbox in unit with the final drive. The two engine blocks were staggered and Jano had designed them to operate as three coupled V-twins.

In many ways the chassis was a scaled-down 1957 F1 Lancia-Ferrari with two large-diameter main tubes and with an additional superstructure of small tubes. Suspension by was coil springs, unequal-length wishbones and an anti-roll bar at the front, and a de Dion rear axle suspended on a transverse leaf spring.

The driver's seat was slightly off-set to the right to accommodate the angled prop-shaft and, an indication of intent, the fuel tank held a full 37 gallons, enough for a full Grand Prix distance and not just for an F2 sprint.

Luigi Musso debuted the car in the Naples GP at the end of April 1957, where he qualified and finished third behind his team-mates Hawthorn and Collins, driving F1 cars. The field was a thin one, but Musso was delighted with the car's handling and he was not much slower than the 'senior' cars.

It was tried in practice at the Monaco GP and then, in the hands of Maurice Trintignant, won the important F2 race at Reims – by a clear lap. That was its only F2 appearance in 1957, but versions with 1860cc (78.6×64.5 mm) engines appeared in the Modena GP in late September. Driven by Musso and Collins, and designated Tipo 196, they finished second and fourth respectively in both heats behind the works Maserati 250Fs of Behra and Schell.

In the final race of the year, the non-Championship Moroccan GP, Hawthorn had a Tipo 226 (2195cc, 81×71 mm, 250 bhp at 8500 rpm) and Collins had a Tipo 246 (2417cc, 85×71 mm, 270 bhp at 8300 rpm). Neither was particularly fast in practice, but Collins led the opening stages because he was carrying a lot less fuel than the opposition and the reason for this was that both Ferraris were running on Av-gas in anticipation of the 1958 regulations. Collins was unwell and crashed, and Hawthorn was eliminated by an electrical fault, but the progress of the new cars seemed most satisfactory.

To the first race of 1958, the Argentine GP, Ferrari sent three 2.4-litre cars and one with a 2.2-litre engine. The opposition seemed thin, for Maserati had officially

Peter Collins (Ferrari Dino 246) on his way to victory in the 1958 British Grand Prix at Silverstone. (T. C. March)

withdrawn (although it sent a car for Fangio) and the many private 250Fs were unhappy on Av-gas. Vanwall and B.R.M. were both busily converting their engines to the new fuel and there was otherwise only Moss in the 2-litre Cooper-Climax.

Moss demonstrated his brilliance by conserving his tyres and driving the whole distance without stopping, even though he was down to the canvas at the end. Too late Ferrari realized what he was up to, and although Musso gave chase he was still 2.7 seconds in arrears at the flag, with Hawthorn third.

Things looked promising in the early non-Championship races – Hawthorn won at Goodwood, Musso at Syracuse and Collins in the International Trophy at Silverstone, but in none of them did Vanwall appear. That happened at Monaco, where the fastest Ferrari in practice was Hawthorn in sixth place behind a Vanwall, a B.R.M. and three Coopers. At Monaco the cars had new rear brakes and a new cowl over the downdraught carburettors, which had the air intake at the rear, and two of the cars had revised, strengthened, chassis frames.

It was a race of attrition, but eventually Hawthorn battled with Moss' Vanwall until it retired with engine trouble. Hawthorn then led easily, but was side-lined by a broken fuel pump before half-distance. That left Trintignant's Cooper at the front but neither Musso nor Collins could catch him, so they had to settle for second and third.

The Ferraris did not handle well in the Dutch GP – they were tricky to drive at the best of times and summed up the basic Ferrari philosophy of 'make it powerful, make it strong, make it pretty, and paint it red' – and the best finisher was Hawthorn, fifth and lapped, behind a Vanwall, two B.R.M.s and a Cooper. The Belgian GP at Spa was a different matter and Hawthorn and Collins were fastest in practice. Moss' Vanwall led at first, but he missed a gear change and wrecked his engine, whereupon Brooks' Vanwall moved ahead to win from Hawthorn.

On the very fast Reims circuit Hawthorn had a pole to flag win from Moss, who was unable to do anything about the Ferrari's speed. New recruit Wolfgang von Trips finished a strong third with Collins back in fifth behind Fangio (Maserati), having his last race. There was tragedy though as Musso, burdened by gambling debts and under threat from heavies, tried too hard to win the large cash prize. His state of mind was not helped by a pre-race message from Enzo Ferrari telling him to win for the honour of Italy.

On lap ten he over-reached himself, crashed, and was killed. It would be many years before Italy produced another driver of his calibre.

It is hard to say what happened at the British GP at Silverstone, for none of the three cars were particularly quick in practice, but Collins made a blinding start from the second row and led all the way. Moss followed him until one-third distance and then his engine blew and this let Hawthorn up to second. Poor Collins was not to enjoy his win for long.

At the Nürburgring, Moss led the opening laps at a fantastic pace until a broken magneto put him out. This let Hawthorn and Collins ahead and the two friends swapped the lead until Brooks caught and passed them. In his efforts to get back on terms, Collins crashed fatally, and shortly afterwards Hawthorn's clutch went. Brooks won and the only Ferrari driver to finish was von Trips, who did well to finish fourth with no brakes left at all. Making his WC debut for Ferrari in the German GP was Phil Hill in an F2 car. He had a troubled race on this occasion, but later would become World Champion for the Scuderia.

Next up was the Portuguese GP at Oporto and there Moss drove a flawless race from Hawthorn. On the last lap Moss was about to lap him, but Mike pulled a face and Moss held station. Then Hawthorn, under pressure from Lewis-Evans, and with his brakes fading, spun and could not restart. Moss, on his slowing-down lap, signalled for him to push the car on to the pavement and start it down hill. Mike did so and was disqualified until Moss spoke up for him, pointing out he had driven against the flow of traffic, but *on the pavement*, not on the circuit. This gesture was to cost Stirling the Championship he so richly deserved

Brakes were becoming a problem and at Monza Hawthorn's Ferrari appeared with Dunlop discs which had originally been fitted to Peter Collins' own 250GT road car. The irony is that it is just possible that Collins might not have crashed had he had disc brakes at the Nürburgring. The Italian GP was a straight fight between Vanwall and Ferrari and the early laps were led by Phil Hill. Then the race became a Moss versus Hawthorn duel until Moss' gearbox went. As often happened, Brooks really started to motor when he assumed the role of team leader and he drove superbly to win, with Hawthorn second and Hill third.

The final race of the season, the Moroccan GP, would decide the Championship. To win the title, Moss had to win the race and set fastest lap and, if that happened, Hawthorn had to finish second. Both did what was required of them and Moss duly led all the way and set fastest lap. Hawthorn spent much of the race in third,

behind Phil Hill, but the American waved him through, and by coming second, Mike became the first British World Champion by a single point. He had only won one race to Moss' four, but a string of seconds scored points. Shortly afterwards he retired from the sport; he had been shattered by the death of Collins and had problems with his health. Three months after hanging up his helmet, he died in a road accident.

During the Moroccan GP, Stuart Lewis-Evans suffered mortal burns when he crashed after his gearbox seized. This led to the retirement of the Vanwall team and created a vacuum at the top. Most confidently expected Ferrari to fill it, but it would be Coventry Climax engines in Cooper cars which did so. 1958 was a turning point in F1 history with the loss, through retirement or death, of Fangio, Musso, Collins, Lewis-Evans and Hawthorn. It had also seen the growing strength of Cooper and Lotus, but Ferrari did not appreciate the significance of the newcomers.

Ferrari faced 1959 with cars which were basically the same as the previous year but with new bodies made by Fantuzzi, Dunlop disc brakes and tyres, a 5-speed gearbox and a new coil spring rear suspension, still with a de Dion axle. Telescopic shock absorbers, first Girling, then Koni, replaced the Houdaille lever-arm dampers which had previously been preferred.

At the previous year's Italian GP, a new engine had been tried. This was the 256, which had a capacity of 2451cc achieved by increasing the stroke by 1 mm. The exhaust pipes were relocated so that they went under the rear suspension instead of curling up over the rear wheels. Bonnet air scoops now faced forward again.

Drivers were Tony Brooks, Phil Hill, Jean Behra and Oliver Gendebien, who was a fine sports car driver but not quite an F1 ace. Cliff Allison was signed from Lotus and Ferrari would later call on Dan Gurney from the sports-racing team.

Ferrari's first F1 race of the year was the Monaco GP, where the cars had Vanwall-style stub noses. Behra led the early stages pursued by the Coopers of Moss and Brabham until his engine blew. The race eventually went to Brabham, with Brooks second and Hill fourth.

As in 1958 Ferrari struggled in the Dutch GP, which eventually fell to Bonnier's B.R.M. Ferrari could do no better than fifth (Behra) and sixth (Hill). Things improved in the French GP at Reims, where sheer power told and Brooks led Hill home to a Ferrari 1-2, with Gendebien fourth. During that meeting Behra had a huge row with the Ferrari team manger, Tavoni, over his status within the team. Behra thought he should be recognized as the Number One and given appropriate support. Things got out of hand and he thumped Tavoni. Had he been an ace he might have got away with it, but he was reckoned to be dispensible and so was dispensed with.

The problem stemmed from Ferrari's refusal to nominate a number one driver and was typical of the way the Old Man consistently played puppeteer with his drivers. He picked favourites and dropped them, encouraged rivalries, and, as in the case of Behra, stretched men beyond a reasonable point. He rationalized his actions, but none could call them admirable. Ultimately they were counter-productive as well.

A strike in Italy meant that the team missed the British GP. Then came the German race run on the ridiculous Avus circuit in two heats. On a circuit where power was even more at a premium than Reims, Brooks led Gurney and Hill to a 1-2-3, but it was not a race to be taken seriously. Sad to record, in a sports car race which preceded the main event, Jean Behra crashed his Porsche and was killed.

Coopers ruled the roost in the Portuguese GP, but Gurney managed third, a lap down. At Monza, which should have seen a Ferrari win, Moss again outsmarted the opposition by driving his Cooper without a tyre change to win from Hill, with Gurney fourth, Allison fifth and Gendebien sixth.

It was still possible for Brooks to win the World Championship at the last race, the American GP at Sebring. There he had a car with a slightly shorter chassis and double wishbone irs, which Chiti admits he copied from Cooper. On the first lap he collided with von Trips and called into the pits to check for damage. There was none, but although he drove from 15th to third, the race went to McLaren and the title went to Brabham with Brooks runner-up.

Cooper, a despised *garagiste*, won the Manufacturers' title quite easily from Ferrari, a *grand constructeur*. Times were changing, fast, and Ferrari was puzzled again.

Enzo Ferrari had once sworn he would never build a rear-engined car and loftily declared, 'from time immemorial, the horse has always drawn the cart and not pushed it'. He was still repeating it in 1959 by which time it was a silly statement which bore no relationship to reality. Apart from Cooper, Porsche had long demonstrated that a rear-engined car could be very effective. 1500cc Porsches had humilated much larger Ferraris on several occasions in sports car racing.

Apologists have suggested that Ferrari was resistant to any idea which his firm did not originate, and the late use of disc brakes is cited as an instance. If Ferrari was so insistent on original ideas the marque would not have got off the ground, for it has never, ever, introduced a new idea to motor racing.

Ferrari has always been a bastion of conservatism, although as these words are written a new car designed by John Barnard might alter that view. Enzo Ferrari himself liked to project a lofty image, but the truth is that, at the time, Ferrari was a team of special builders which happened to make its own components. The way in which variations were cobbled together from the parts bin on the off-chance they might work provides evidence of this view.

Still, the writing was on the wall for the traditional layout and a rear-engined Ferrari was slowly taking shape. Inside Maranello, Chiti had become more influential and was starting to put the team on a more professional footing. Brooks and Gendebien left to drive Coopers and Gurney joined B.R.M. Hill and Allison were retained, von Trips returned, and Richie Ginther and Willy Mairesse joined. There were new faces in the cars, but the machines remained much as before, although the new irs system finally put the old de Dion layout to rest. Such a modification, however, was only an Elastoplast, what was needed was major surgery. Chiti worked to supply it.

By 1960 the Dino was a dinosaur competing not only against vastly improved Coopers but the new Lotus 18 and the rear-engined B.R.M. Cliff Allison started promisingly enough with a second in the Argentine GP, but a better gauge came in the International Trophy at Silverstone, where Hill qualified over five seconds off Moss' pole and could do no better than fifth, and lapped.

At the Monaco GP, 'the Ferrari which would never be built' made its appearance. This was the rear-engined 246P, which was virtually a Dino with the engine put behind the driver. Just in case it proved a failure, it was given out that it was fitted with a 2.1-litre engine, but Ginther showed all was well by equalling Hill's practice time, although this was 2.3 seconds off pole. During practice Allison had a huge accident which put him out of racing for some time. In the race, Hill managed to inherit third while Ginther trailed home a distant sixth, 30 laps down, after breaking a ring-gear tooth. After that one race, Ferrari put the 246P away to concentrate on an F2 version, for the following year would see the 1½-litre Formula 1.

As usual the cars were poor at Zandvoort, where von Trips finished fifth, and lapped. The same result fell to Hill in the Belgian GP, but he had been battling for the lead when a small fire broke out on his car. Reims had always been a happy hunting ground for Ferrari, but although the cars were quick, and Hill even led, none of the three Ferraris finished as they all went out with transmission failure. Only two cars were entered for the British GP and they were comprehensively outclassed at

Tony Brooks drove this Dino 246 in the 1959 International Trophy at Silverstone but retired because of an engine misfire. (T. C. March)

Silverstone, with von Trips sixth and Hill seventh, and both two laps down.

The token entry of just two cars was significant. Ferrari had more or less written off the season as a bad job and everything became clear a week later when von Trips appeared in the F2 Solitude GP at the wheel of a rear-engined Ferrari, based on the 246P, which was clearly intended to be the base of the Scuderia's weapon in 1961. It had the 65-degree V-6 engine tweaked to give about 175 bhp at 9200 rpm. This version had dimensions of 73 × 58.8 mm (1477cc), which gave it a much shorter stroke than the first 1½-litre V-6. Von Trips won, but it was a narrow victory from Herrmann's Porsche, and then only after Clark's Lotus, which had dominated, had to pit to take on more water. It was a promising debut for the car, but was by no means a clear indication of the superiority the model would enjoy the following year.

Since the German GP was for F2 cars (Porsche was doing well at the time), Ferrari's next F1 race was in Portugal, where both Hill and von Trips qualified on the fourth row of the grid, but the German finally took fourth after recovering from a first-lap incident. To give Ferrari a chance, the organizers of the Italian GP included the

Monza bankings again, but the British teams decided this was too dangerous, and while they received criticism for this, the fact is that banked circuits were an anachronism in F1 and their cars were not designed to cope with them. Thus Ferrari had a hollow walk-over against an assortment of privateers and Hill led Ginther and Mairesse home for a 1-2-3.

It was Ferrari's only F1 win of the year and since the quality of any victory is determined by the strength of the opposition it accounted for nothing at all. It remains statistically interesting, however, for it was the first Championship win by an American and the last by a front-engined car, but as Disraeli observed, there are lies, damned lies and statistics.

Ferrari had not made a successful F1 car for seven years when the new 1½-litre formula began. It had not been *unsuccessful* to the degree of B.R.M., Gordini, or the front-engined Lotuses, but it had been a bleak period. Discarding wins with the Lancias, Ferrari had won only eight WC events in that time and they included the 1960 Italian GP, and the 1959 German race on the odd Avus circuit.

New moves were afoot at Maranello, however, and Chiti had even used a wind tunnel. Previously,

Phil Hill with the 65-degree V-6 Ferrari on his way to second place in the 1961 Monaco Grand Prix. The 'shark mouth' nose characterised 1961-2 Formula 1 Ferraris.

The simple multi-tubular space-frame of the 1961 Ferrari.

'aerodynamics' was a word to look up in a dictionary. Of long-term significance was the appointment of the designer Mauro Forghieri, who would uphold rational engineering values at Ferrari for many years.

The 1961 Dino 156 was a spectacular-looking car, low and clean with a mean look from its twin-nostril nose cone. It was a shame that the name *SuperSqualo* had already been used, for this was a car which could carry it. Initially it had the short-stroke 65-degree V-6 engine, which was mated to a 5-speed gearbox and installed in a rugged space-frame which had the now-usual suspension of coil springs and double wishbones all round. The Dunlop disc brakes were outboard at the front, inboard at the rear.

Chiti had also worked on a version of the engine with the banks set at 120 degrees. Externally, the main difference was that the 65-degree engine had a single fine mesh bubble over the carburettors, while the 120-degree engine had twin bubbles. Lampredi had sketched a 120-degree V-6 as long ago as 1951, but other projects took priority and, besides, so wide a unit was not suitable for a front-engined car.

Ferrari did not enter the earliest races of 1961, which were contested by the British and German 4-cylinder cars, but at the Syracuse GP there was a lone 156/65-degree for a virtual unknown, Giancarlo Baghetti, who got the drive through a national scholarship scheme. He won, against a field which included all the strongest non-Ferrari teams. Sharp intake of breath all round.

Porsche was still behind in preparing for the formula and the British teams were awaiting their V-8 Coventry Climax and B.R.M. engines. This allowed Ferrari virtually a clear run with a car whose power overcame an indifferent chassis.

Syracuse was followed by the Monaco GP, where Stirling Moss scored a famous victory in his Lotus-Climax. He was chased all the way by the Ferraris with Ginther in a 156/120-degree car proving the strongest challenge, but though he had a power advantage, his car did not have the handling to offset Moss' own advantage, genius. Behind Ginther came Hill and von Trips, both in 156/65-degrees. Von Trips actually crashed on his last lap, but was so far ahead of the rest of the field he was classified fourth.

Baghetti was given a 156/65-degree for the Naples GP, which he won by a lap against a field of privateers, and then battle was joined again in the Dutch GP. There all three Ferraris were 156/120-degrees and they occupied the front row of the grid. It might have been a Ferrari 1-2-3 except that Ginther had a throttle spring problem, but as it was, von Trips won by 0.9 seconds from Hill with Ginther in fifth.

Ferrari's next race was the Belgian GP, where the three regular drivers, none of whom were of the top drawer, were joined by Olivier Gendebien in a 156/65-degree car ostensibly entered by the Équipe Nationale Belge. The four cars dominated practice, and the race, and finally finished in the order Hill, von Trips, Ginther and Gendebien. It was the most complete domination of a race since Mercedes-Benz in the 1955 British GP.

After that it seemed pointless for anyone to turn up to the French GP at Reims, but although the finishing order was decided beforehand by Ferrari, von Trips had his engine break, Hill spun while leading and took ages to re-start and Ginther's car lost its oil pressure. Most of the leading non-Ferrari runners dropped out too and the race came down to the Porsches of Bonnier and Gurney and Baghetti, making his WC debut in a 156/65-degree car. The youngster kept his head and finally won the slipstream battle by pulling out from behind Gurney 300 yards from the finish line to win by a few feet.

It had been a Ferrari victory, but it remains an odd one since retirements had elevated mid-field runners. Of the three cars which battled at the end (Bonnier's went sick with two laps to go) only Gurney had even made the third row of the grid and then he had been nearly five seconds off the pace. Although Baghetti was celebrated for his win, and he had driven a sensible race, it was really that in a pond of small fry he had emerged as Boss Minnow

In the very wet British GP at Aintree, Moss gave the Ferraris a hard time until first he spun and then succumbed to a broken brake pipe. Thus von Trips led home Hill and Ginther for another Ferrari perfect score. Baghetti also had a works 156/65-degree car, but although he was slow, and crashed, he had been entered by the Scuderia Saint' Ambroeus so did not count as a works car, although it was.

The team seemed invincible, but at the Nürburgring Moss demonstrated there was still room for class and in a wet/dry race he took his Rob Walker Lotus to another superb win. Von Trips just managed to win the battle with Hill for second, Ginther was in eighth and Mairesse, back in the team with a 156/65-degree car, crashed, as so often he did, but Ferrari seemed to like his spirit.

At the Italian GP Ferrari fielded the three usual cars plus Ricardo Rodriguez in a 156/65-degree car. As expected the quartet dominated practice with Rodriguez being only a tenth off von Trips' pole. The event again used the bankings, but this time everyone turned up. As the field was in its second lap von Trips and Clark collided and the Ferrari ploughed into the crowd causing carnage. Fourteen spectators and von Trips himself died.

It overshadowed everything else. Hill won, and took the Championship, which might otherwise have gone to von Trips. The other Ferraris retired. Clark was accused of causing the accident, but was cleared, for it had been a typical racing incident and if anything it was the fault of the circuit owners for not providing adequate protection.

With both the Championships in the bag, Ferrari decided not to go to the final round, the US GP, a curious decision, since Ferrari is supposed to be so passionate about the purity of the sport. In America, Innes Ireland scored Lotus' first WC win.

1961 had been a Ferrari triumph and the emphasis had to be on the maker, for none of its drivers were very special and the cars flattered them. Ferrari himself knew that and began to negotiate with Moss on extraordinary terms. It was more or less a blank sheet of paper on which Stirling was to write his demands.

In the works, however, there was trouble. After the death of Dino, Ferrari had decided to officially recognize his illegitimate son, Piero Lardi (now Lardi-Ferrari) and this did not go down well with Laura Ferrari, who asserted her position as Queen Consort and began to stir the pasta everywhere. A number of senior, and serious-minded, citizens resented this interference and so, at the moment of triumph, Ferrari had to cope with a walkout of key personnel, led by Carlo Chiti, who found a welcome at the embryo A.T.S. concern.

It was a typical Ferrari incident, fuelled by passion,

and while such a defection would have destroyed many marques, Italy was packed to the gunwales with eager punters whose only aim in life was to work for Ferrari. In the short-term, however, it delayed development at the very time Ferrari needed it, for the new British V-8 engines were ready.

Richie Ginther left to join B.R.M. and so the team comprised Hill, Ricardo Rodriguez, Baghetti and Lorenzo Bandini. The youngsters all showed promise, but were short on experience, so it was a fairly weak line-up. Little was done to the cars, apart from a small increase in track. Ferrari announced his cars would have four valve heads, but these never materialized, although often Hill's car had a 6-speed gearbox located in front of the final drive and not behind.

Although Willy Mairesse opened the season on a high note by winning the Brussels GP in a 156/65-degree fitted with the new gearbox, it was not a reliable indicator, for there were many retirements.

The Pau GP was won by Trintignant in an obsolete Lotus 18 with Rodriguez (156/120-degree) second and Bandini (156/65-degree) fifth behind a couple of British privateers. It was not promising. Hill and Baghetti could do no better than third and fourth in the Aintree 200, a far cry from the previous year's dominance. A 156/65-degree was entered for Innes Ireland in the International Trophy at Silverstone in the name of UDT/Laystall as a tribute to Moss, who was then fighting for his life. Ireland,

Ricardo Rodriguez with the later 120-degree V-6 Ferrari in the 1962 Pau Grand Prix. He finished second.

a fine driver, could only finish fourth, and lapped.

The rest of the season followed the same pattern. Hill and Baghetti were third and fourth in the Dutch GP. Bandini and Mairesse then scored a 1-2 in the Naples GP, but the opposition was negligible. Monaco saw Hill and Bandini inherit second and third, but they had been way off the pace, then Hill and Rodriguez were third and fourth in the Belgian GP. Mairesse had, however, battled for the lead at one point, but when Clark took that slot he continued to battle for second with Taylor's Lotus. Then the two cars touched and both were destroyed. Neither driver was hurt, but Mairesse did not drive again until Monza. The French GP at Reims should have seen Ferrari's best chance of the year, but labour troubles prevented its appearance. Only one car, for Hill, managed to get to the British GP at Aintree and he qualified in the second half of the field, never showed in the race, and retired with valve trouble.

In the German GP Bandini had a new car, Tipo 156/62/P, which was to serve as a development machine for 1963. It had a modified frame and revised suspension geometry, and the driver sat low and reclining, as on the British cars. Its body was slimmer, due to modified tanks, and the distinctive twin-nostril nose gave way to a small oval intake, just like the British cars. The best Ferrari finish at the Nürburgring was Rodriguez in sixth. Bandini and Baghetti took a 1-2 in the Mediterranean GP, but there were no other works cars present. Ferrari made a big effort for the Italian GP and entered five cars, but none even qualified in the top ten and the best finishers were Mairesse and Baghetti in fourth and fifth.

Since the marque had no longer any interest in the World Championship, and was still beset by labour problems, it again did not send cars to the US GP. Thus it ended the year sixth in the Manufacturers' Championship behind B.R.M., Lotus, Cooper, Lola and Porsche. From being almost invincible it had sunk to the level of a make-weight. For the first time since 1951 it had failed to win a single WC race. Heads had to roll and Hill's was nominated. He and Baghetti left to join A.T.S., and ruin their careers. Ricardo Rodriguez was regrettably not available for re-selection since he had died at the wheel of a Lotus while practising for his home GP in Mexico.

For 1963 Ferrari engaged John Surtees, seven times a World motorcycling champion, who had made a spectacular switch to four wheels, Mike Parkes, a very gifted engineer and test driver, and Willy Mairesse, a wild man if ever there was one. Surtees and Parkes spent the winter developing a new car which had an upper transverse link and twin radius arms − very British. The experimental 6-speed gearbox of the previous year became standard fitting and the body followed the style of the 'Nürburg-ring' car. During 1963 only the 120-degree V-6 engine was raced.

There were two significant breaks with tradition, Bosch direct fuel injection replaced the much-loved Webers and, for the first time, alloy wheels with centre-lock nuts replaced the gorgeous Borrani wire wheels which Ferrari had continued to use long after every other team had switched to alloys.

Apart from their colour, Ferraris were now virtually indistinguishable from the British cars. The *grand constructeur* was imitating the *garagistes* and, it must be said, often did not understand what it was copying, with the result that sorting out such details as suspension geometry took a great deal of time in trial and error − the old Ferrari 'suck it and see' philosophy.

Thus Ferrari was not ready for the early season Italian races. The 156/63 made its debut at the International Trophy at Silverstone, where Surtees ran second until succumbing to an oil leak, and Mairesse crashed. Surtees ran second at Monaco, too, until oil on his goggles (from another car) caused him to drop back and he finished fourth, though set fastest lap. Mairesse set pole at Spa, but by the end of the first lap Clark's Lotus had 16 seconds on the whole field except Graham Hill's B.R.M. Mairesse spun, restarted, and later retired with gearbox trouble, while Surtees, who ran as high as third, retired with injection problems. In the Dutch GP Surtees had a new team-mate, Lodovico Scarfiotti, Ferrari having made a policy of entering just two cars per race. Surtees finished third, and lapped, and Scarfiotti was another lap down in sixth.

Scarfiotti crashed in practice for the French GP at Reims, but Surtees ran second in the early stages until retiring with a broken fuel pump. Only a single car, for Surtees, was entered for the British GP and he finally inherited second to Clark. Mairesse was back in the team for the German GP (he crashed on the first lap) and both cars featured new bolt-on alloy wheels. Surtees was on the pace all weekend and gave Ferrari its first WC win for 23 months.

He followed that with a win in the Mediterranean GP at Pergusa, against thin opposition, and was on top form at the Italian GP, where he set pole. This was done in an entirely new car intended to take a new 90-degree V-8 engine designed by Angelo Bellei. At Monza, however, Surtees had an uprated V-6 engine with transistorized ignition and new pistons which gave 210 bhp.

Bellei's engine, which would become standard kit the following year, had a capacity of 1487cc (64×57.8 mm), Bosch fuel injection and transistorized ignition, and gave 220 bhp at 11,000 rpm. The Tipo 158 featured a semi-monocoque with internal stiffening by a tubular

In 1963 Ferrari was still racing the V-6 cars in improved form. This is John Surtees with the V-6 in the International Trophy at Silverstone that year. (T. C. March)

structure and the engine and gearbox bolted directly on to the back of the rear bulkhead, forming a stressed member. Externally, the car even more closely resembled a Lotus with its inboard front suspension. Despite the fact that it was a brand new car, Surtees disputed the lead with Clark for the first 16 laps until his engine broke. Bandini, called back into the fold, retired with a broken clutch.

Surtees had the interim car for the US GP, but the engine blew in practice and he had to revert to a 156/120-degree car. He still managed to lead until, near the end, a valve spring went. Bandini came home a distant fifth, four laps down. In the final WC race of the year, the Mexican GP, Surtees was disqualified for receiving a push start after a pit stop and Bandini had his engine go.

The last Championship race of the year was the South African GP on 28 December, and Ferrari arrived early and entered the Rand GP as well. Both cars were 158s and gave Surtees and Bandini a morale-raising 1-2 when the works Lotuses both had fuel pump problems. Neither car ran as well in the South African GP itself, and the only finisher was Bandini in fifth.

Towards the end of the season Surtees had had a chance of finishing second in the Championship to Clark, but those hopes evaporated in the final races. Ferrari had done rather better than the year before and finished fourth in the Manufacturers' Championship behind Lotus, B.R.M. and Brabham, but Porsche and Lola had both dropped out and the depth of competition in F1 had contracted accordingly.

Ferrari has claimed that he was at the time more interested in sports car racing, where the marque had considerable success. The reason given is that sports car success sold road cars while GP success made drivers famous. That is actually a thin excuse for comparative failure for, in 1964, no fewer than six F1 cars would be prepared.

Two would have the up-rated V-6 engine, two the new V-8 and two would have a new flat-12 (T1512) developed by Forghieri. This latter was based on the 1948 1½-litre supercharged V-12 engine, which itself derived from the still-born Alfa Romeo 512 flat-12 engine. Full circle! It was made in two versions, one of 1498cc (55 × 52.5 mm) and the other of 1499cc (56 × 50.4 mm) which gave 225 bhp.

Surtees (V-8) and Bandini (V-6) gave Ferrari a 1-2 in the Syracuse GP against a second-string field and then Surtees (V-6) retired from the International Trophy at Silverstone without running higher than fifth. Neither car finished the Monaco GP because of gearbox trouble, although Surtees (V-8) qualified fourth. Both drivers had V-8s for the Dutch GP, where Bandini retired (fuel injector pump), but Surtees finished a strong second to Clark's Lotus. Neither finished in the Belgian GP, and only Bandini made it to the end of the French race, ninth and two laps in arrears. The British GP at Brands Hatch brought better fortune when Surtees came third and Bandini fifth. Then Surtees took second from a strong field in the Solitude GP.

The Nürburgring was a different matter, for Surtees was superb on that great drivers' circuit and he took pole, fastest lap and victory with Bandini third. Bandini was improving apace and he came into his own at the Austrian GP at Zeltweg, which received WC status for the first time. There he won. True, he was aided by many retirements, but he had been on the pace all weekend.

John Surtees (Ferrari 158) in the 1964 British Grand Prix at Brands Hatch. He finished third in what was to be his World Champion year. (**T. C. March**)

Ferrari then brought joy to the *tifosi* at the Italian GP with Surtees first (and pole and fastest lap), Bandini third and Scarfiotti ninth with a V-6. At Monza the flat-12 appeared in practice but did not race.

In retaliation for a tiff Ferrari had been having with the Italian racing authorities, the cars were entered by the North Amercian Racing Team in the US GP and pointedly painted in the white and blue of America. He also threatened never to race on Italian soil again, so there! Surtees (V-8) was on the pace and eventually finished second after a spin, while Bandini (1512) retired with a blown engine.

With only the Mexican GP remaining, Surtees and Ferrari both had a chance of winning their respective Championships. John retained his V-8, Bandini had the flat-12, and Pedro Rodriguez was given the V-6. Pedro was the older brother of Ricardo, who had been killed in practice for the race two years before. Bandini was marginally the faster in both practice and the race. The Championship looked lost, however, when Clark sailed imperiously into the distance. Then, on the last lap but one, Clark's car started to lose oil and his title drained away. Had Clark managed to limp to the finish ahead of Surtees, the drivers' title would have gone to Graham Hill, but his car expired on that lap. Bandini slowed to let his team leader by to take second from Gurney's Brabham.

Thus both Surtees and Ferrari won their titles. This was a bit tough on Hill and B.R.M., who had each grossed more points, but only the six best scores counted.

It would be interesting to know exactly how much Surtees' presence in the team had contributed to its success for, apart from being a brilliant driver, he was also a gifted engineer, who later ran his own team and built his own cars. It would be 11 years before Ferrari won the Manfacturers' Championship again and much of the reason then was the presence of Niki Lauda in the team.

Bandini and Surtees were retained for 1965 and the new World Champion (V-8) opened his score with a good second in the South African GP, while Bandini (1512) had ignition trouble and was unclassified. Surtees (V-8) appeared at the Race of Champions at Brands Hatch, but was off the pace, was sixth in heat one and retired in heat two.

Then Surtees (V-8) and Bandini (1512) came second and third to Clark in the Syracuse GP, and the same driver/car combinations came second and seventh in the International Trophy at Silverstone, won by new boy Jackie Stewart in his B.R.M. Monaco saw Bandini (1512) drive superbly to finish second to Hill with Surtees (V-8) fourth after running out of fuel on the last lap when he was in second place. Surtees was not pleased at seeing his afternoon's work evaporate and thus began the first hairline crack, which was to become a complete rift the following year.

At Spa Ferrari was off the pace. Surtees' V-8 gave up after only six laps and Bandini (1512) could only make ninth. Things improved at the French GP at Rouen, where both drivers were on the pace, but neither had an answer to the brilliance of Clark and Stewart. Surtees, however, finished third with Bandini eighth after losing a wheel. Surtees took third, too, at the British GP. In the Dutch race he took the flat-12 while Bandini had a V-8, but neither was on the pace and both finished out of the points. It had been 12 years since a Ferrari had gone well at Zandvoort.

John Surtees (Ferrari 1512) in the pits road at the 1965 British Grand Prix at Silverstone. He again finished third. (T. C. March)

The season was see-sawing, at one circuit Ferrari was in contention, at another it was yesterday's news. Surtees' chance of a hat-trick at the German GP went when his gearbox broke on the first lap, while Bandini (V-8) finished sixth. Both had flat-12s for the Italian GP and a V-8 was entered for Nino Vaccarella, the Targa Florio specialist. Surtees was in the leading bunch when he retired with clutch trouble, Vaccarella retired, but Bandini came fourth.

After Surtees had a huge crash in a Can-Am race, Bandini became team leader for the last two races of the year. In America he was joined by Rodriguez (1512) and the American Bob Bondurant (V-8), who were officially entered by the North American Racing Team. All finished, Bandini fourth, Rodriguez fifth and Bondurant ninth, four laps down.

Scarfiotti replaced Bondurant for the Mexican GP, the last race to the 1½-litre F1, but although he practised the car was taken over by Rodriguez for the race. Since

Rodriguez car was officially a N.A.R.T. entry the opportunity was taken to run it on Firestone tyres. In the race they had a huge duel until Bandini spun and damaged his nose cone. While it was being replaced, Rodriguez came in for a new battery. They rejoined, but finished in the last two places. It was a low note on which to end the 1½-litre formula. Ferrari ended the year without a WC win, again, and was fourth in the Manufacturers' Championship. It would be ten years before it would win the title again.

Given Ferrari's advantages, it should have dominated the period under review with the possible exception of 1955, but it was long on passion and gesture and short on intelligence, sound engineering and good management. By staying in the game, with a subsidy from Fiat, it occasionally was able to turn other's mistakes to its advantage, but apart from the latter end of 1951, with the 4½-litre cars, it never beat strong opposition. The fault lay at the very top.

The Alfa Romeo 158 dominated early post-war Grand Prix racing. This is Giuseppe Farina, winner of the first Driver's Championship in 1950, in that year's British Grand Prix which he also won. (Guy Griffiths)

In 1951 Froilan Gonzalez with a single-plug Ferrari Tipo 375 scored a remarkable victory in the British Grand Prix; the race saw the first defeat of the Alfa Romeo 158s for five years. (Guy Griffiths)

By 1952 the sleek lines of the V-16 B.R.M. had been marred by louvres and intakes. This is Ken Wharton at Goodwood. (Guy Griffiths)

Mike Hawthorn at the wheel of the Ferrari Tipo 500 4-cylinder 2-litre car with which he so convincingly won the 1953 International Trophy at Silverstone. (Guy Griffiths)

Mercedes-Benz completely dominated the 1955 British Grand Prix at Aintree with the W196 cars and took the first four places. Here the winner, Stirling Moss, leads Juan Fangio who finished second. (T. C. March)

Stirling Moss again, at Aintree in the 1957 European Grand Prix with the Vanwall which he retired before taking over Tony Brooks' car to win the race. (T. C. March)

1957 World Champion Juan Fangio at the wheel of Harry Schell's Maserati 250F during practice for the 1957 European Grand Prix at Aintree. (T. C. March)

Luigi Musso (Tipo 801 Ferrari) at Aintree in 1957. He finished second. (T. C. March)

In 1958 Mike Hawthorn (Ferrari Dino 246), destined to win the World Championship, finished second in the British Grand Prix. (T. C. March)

By 1958 the B.R.M. P25 was beginning to enjoy reliability. This is Harry Schell in the British Grand Prix in which he finished fifth. (T. C. March)

The first appearance of a mid-engined Formula 1 Ferrari was in 1960 at Monaco where Richie Ginther drove this car into sixth place. (David Phipps)

Jim Clark with his works Lotus 18-Climax in the Gold Cup race at Oulton Park in 1960. (T. C. March)

Another photograph from the Gold Cup race at Oulton Park, this time Graham Hill with his rear-engined B.R.M. (T. C. March)

One of the great disappointments of 1962 was the flat-eight Porsche 804. This is the British Grand Prix at Aintree and shows Dan Gurney who finished ninth. (T. C. March)

One of the most persistent (and persistently unsuccessful) teams was Signor Dei's Scuderia Centro-Sud. In 1963 the team ran a 1961 B.R.M. P57 chassis with V-8 engine for Lorenzo Bandini. Here he is seen before the British Grand Prix in which he finished fifth. (T. C. March)

During the years of the 1500cc Grand Prix Formula the fortunes of the Cooper team gradually declined. Here is Phil Hill in the 1964 British race at Brands Hatch in which he finished sixth. (T. C. March)

FERRARI-JAGUAR

In 1950 Clemente Biondetti, who had driven a works Jaguar XK120 in the Mille Miglia, obtained another Jaguar engine and mated it to a Ferrari Tipo 166S chassis. The chassis was designed as a sports car, but since the body had cycle wings, it was an easy matter to remove them and make it into an 'offset' single-seater. It was entered in the Italian GP, where Biondetti was slow in practice and retired after 16 laps with engine trouble.

The entity of this car still exists.

FRAZER NASH

Frazer Nash had long let it be known that it was willing to make single-seater versions of its Bristol-engined Le Mans Replica sports car, but it was not until 1952 that the offer was taken up. Peter Bell, an entrant who ran under the name 'Scuderia Franera', ordered a Mk II chassis for Ken Wharton to drive. This had a ladder-frame of two parallel 4½-in tubes, front suspension by transverse leafspring and lower wishbones and a live rear axle was suspended by longitudinal torsion bars and located by an 'A'-bracket. It was fitted with a tight body with a 'potato chipper' grill, a long air duct and Frazer Nash's usual disc wheels with knock-off hub nuts and from a distance could be mistaken for a Cooper-Bristol.

Bristol did most of the engine work and teased about 140 bhp from the unit. Like all Frazer Nashes it was beautifully made, but was heavier than the Coopers, shared their power disadvantage, and the road holding was limited by the live rear axle. Still, its brief career did include a World Championship points finish.

It first raced in the 1952 International Trophy at Silverstone, where Wharton finished sixth in his heat and seventh from 19 runners in the final, a promising debut, although neither Ferrari nor Maserati were present. In the Swiss GP Wharton was way down the grid, 23 seconds off the pace, but he plugged around steadily, and although lapped twice, finished fourth to take the only WC points of his career. He was then third in the Eifelrennen, although the major teams were absent, and ninth in

Ken Wharton at the wheel of Peter Bell's single-seater Frazer Nash in the 1952 International Trophy at Silverstone. (T. C. March)

his heat of the Monza GP, only to retire in the final when the A-bracket broke.

In the Belgian GP Wharton was dicing with Hawthorn's Cooper-Bristol for fifth place when he got into a slide and crashed. Car and driver were both repaired by the Dutch GP two months later, but at Zandvoort the back axle broke. Its only other appearance was in a minor race at Turnberry, when the engine gave up.

Also at Turnberry, however, was a second Frazer Nash single-seater built by the works for the Scottish amateur Bill Skelly. This had a markedly different (and much more handsome) body with a grille similar to that of the Le Mans Replica. A third car was built for the Irish enthusiast R. E. Odlum, but, like Skelly, he confined his racing to national events.

With acknowledgements to Denis Jenkinson's *From Chain Drive To Turbocharger* (published by Patrick Stephens Ltd).

GIAUR

When the first Continental F3 500cc designs appeared anyone could have told at a glance from which country they originated, for low-level racing derived from national traditions, unlike today's racing, which is based in the international currency of science. So the D.B. was typically French with its eccentric layout and excellent aerodynamics and the Giaur epitomized the Italian tradition, being a front-engined miniature F1 car.

With only 500cc and, at most, 50 bhp on tap, weight was of the essence in F3 and no Italian car could make up for the fact that it came to the line 50 per cent heavier than, say, a Cooper and suffered power loss through the drive train by being front-engined. It was not long before the Italians decided that being beaten by Cooper-Nortons was not their idea of fun, so the formula never caught on.

In its place, they created their own 'F3', but for 750cc cars which could use Fiat components. Giaur was one of the most successful of the small Italian makers and was a collaboration between Domenico Giannini and Bernardo Taraschi. Giannini had been tuning Fiats since 1925 and, indeed, had designed engines for Moto Guzzi. Taraschi was a driver/constructor who later entered Formula Junior with cars which, initially, were second in success only to Stanguellini.

Giannini made a clever d.o.h.c. head on a Fiat block, while Taraschi made a typical Italian ladder-frame chassis with coil spring and double wishbone front suspension and a live rear axle suspended on tiny coil springs and located by twin trailing arms.

When the 2½-litre F1 was announced, it carried with it a proviso for a 750cc supercharged equivalent. In 1954 Giaur was having an excellent season in Italian F3 and Taraschi decided to test the equivalence with a blown version of one of his 750cc cars in the 1954 Rome GP. There it proved to be both slow and unreliable and was quietly put aside.

The Giaur has its place in motor racing history, however, as being the first 750cc s/c F1 car and, with D.B., being one of only two marques which raced in this configuration.

GILBY

Sid Greene was 16 years old and an engineering apprentice when he was knocked off his bike by a bus and lost his left arm. Paradoxically, that was the making of him for thereafter he tried harder. Pre-war he raced cars at Brooklands and Donington, then he brazened his way into the R.A.F. and became a Spitfire pilot, nicknamed the 'Wingless Wonder'. When peace returned he continued to race and also built up a fairly large company, Gilby Engineering.

After retiring from active racing in 1953, when he was 47 years old, he became a notable entrant in British racing, but at the back of his mind was always the ambition that his son, Keith, would be able to achieve in the sport the heights his own disability had put beyond his reach. Keith, who later became a distinguished team manager, was a fairly good, but not top-level, driver, who happened to have an ambitious father eager to advance his career.

Ian Raby at the wheel of the Gilby-B.R.M. in the 1963 International Trophy at Silverstone. (T. C. March)

When the Lotus 17 that the Greenes had bought in 1959 proved to have a severe handling problem and when Lotus sacked its first assistant designer, Len Terry, Sid employed Terry to sort out the problem. From then it was a short step to a Terry-designed Gilby-Climax sports car, which raced with some success in 1960.

It was, again, a short step to making an F1 car. Though none could see it at the time, the employment of Len Terry was to signal a change in the infrastructure of motor racing, which was to make Britain the foremost nation in the sport. Previously a special builder would make a car for himself and, if it was successful, customers would knock at his door asking for replicas. Len Terry was the first of a long line of designers who began with Lotus or Lola and were then employed by others.

The Gilby was conventional, as it needed to be, since it was to be run by a small team from a little workshop. It had a light space-frame (59 lb) made of round and square ¾-in steel tubing, triangulated around the cockpit and with a detachable top member across the engine bay. Into this frame was fitted a Coventry Climax FPF engine, angled 18 degrees to the right, and mated to a 5-speed Colotti gearbox.

Front suspension was by coil springs and double wishbones, while the independent rear suspension was

by double wishbones, the leading edges of which formed twin radius arms. Girling disc brakes (10¼-in front, 9½-in rear) were used along with Cooper Elektron cast wheels, and the car, which weighed around 1000 lb, was covered by a pretty aluminium body.

In testing at Goodwood, Keith Greene showed his inexperience by lapping at about 1m 35s, but then Bruce McLaren was invited to drive it and he returned a time of 1m 28.9s, a tenth off the F1 lap record. That bucked everyone up, and motivated the driver. The team did not have sufficient funds to tackle a full season (the entire car had cost only £5000), but took in five British non-Championship races, the Danish Grand Prix and one Championship race, the British GP at Aintree. There Keith qualified 23rd (of 30) and finished 15th, six laps down on the winner. The car's best result was fourth in the late season Lewis-Evans Trophy sprint race at Brands Hatch.

1962 started on a better note, as the driver had more experience and a 6-speed Colotti gearbox was fitted. Fourth places were taken at the first three races of the year: the Brussels GP, the Lombank Trophy at Snetterton and the Lavant Cup at Goodwood. In May, Keith Greene took his best result with the car, third in the Naples GP.

Meanwhile the little team took delivery of its long-awaited B.R.M. V-8 engine. Len Terry had designed a new frame to accommodate it, but recalls, 'The engines which B.R.M. sold its customers were much less powerful than the works engines and I reckon our's was the worst of a poor bunch. In fact I reckon it gave hardly more power than the Climax it replaced.'

The second F1 Gilby qualified a whole minute off the pace for the German GP and retired with suspension failure, finished seventh in the Mediterranean GP at Pergusa and failed to make the grid for the Italian GP. Bruce McLaren had demonstrated that the car was not all that bad, so one must conclude that the weakness was in the cockpit.

Behind the scenes, however, Gilby Engineering had

been in difficulties and had been taken over by another company which had agreed to continue the racing team if it could prove itself financially viable. Of course it could not and was wound up at the end of 1962.

The Coventry Climax frame was sold to a special builder, while the second car went to Ian Raby, who had a typical privateer's season with it, the highlight of which was third in the Rome GP at Vallelunga, although he failed to quality for either the German or Italian races.

The car passed through various hands and finished up as a Buick-engined sand racer in Jersey. When last heard of, it was undergoing a rebuild, with a Coventry Climax FPF engine.

GLEED-M.G.

In early 1958, British motor racing magazines carried photographs of a new F1 car constructed by a Derbyshire enthusiast, Peter Gleed. It was designed to take advantage of the 750cc s/c option and was taken surprisingly seriously, with one magazine commenting, 'on paper it sounds fabulous.'

In fact the 'Gleed' was an elderly Cooper Mk IV (500cc F3) chassis fitted with a 750cc d.o.h.c. M.G. 'R' engine. The source of the magazine's enthusiasm seems

to be the claim that it had 180 bhp in a car weighing 4 cwt. This would have given it a power/weight ratio of 900 bhp per ton, roughly the same as a Lotus 49. Neither the quoted power nor weight would stand close scrutiny.

The Gleed-M.G. was entered in a race at Goodwood, but did not arrive, and nobody was sufficiently interested to enquire further.

GORDINI

In common with those other great French constructors, Ettore Bugatti and Antonio Lago, Amédée Gordini was an Italian and he made his name as a tuner of Fiats. In fact, in the days when engine tuning was popularly regarded as a black art, when *tuning wizards* apparently *breathed* on engines to extract more power, Gordini earned the rather silly nick-name, *Le Sorcier.*

In 1934 was formed Société Industrielle de Mécanique et Carrosserie Automobile, Simca, which made Fiats under licence. In order to advertize its wares, Simca commissioned Gordini to produce high-performance versions particularly of the 508 Balilla, and these, some with lightweight aerodynamic bodies, won five classes and two Indices of Performance at Le Mans during 1937-39.

After the war Simca continued to fund Gordini's racing activities (provided he used Simca components) and the first fruit of the collaboration was a 1098cc single-seater in 1946 with a Fiat-derived push-rod engine which produced 65 bhp. Although 65 bhp is nothing to write home about, the little car performed well, for it was installed in a lightweight frame with a dry weight of just 7 cwt, which gave it a better power/weight ratio than the pre-war 3.6-litre Delahaye 135s, which reappeared in 1946. Simca-Gordinis could embarrass a lot of cars on twisty circuits.

This car set the pattern for most subsequent Gordinis with its light tubular ladder-frame, front suspension by lower wishbones and upper transverse links which each operated on a coil spring immersed in an oil bath, and the live rear axle suspended by torsion bars.

A 1220cc engine appeared in 1947, and early in 1948 there was a 1430cc version with a new cylinder head with hemispherical combustion chambers achieved in the same way as B.M.W. on the 328 with a system of cross-over push-rods. With two Solex carburettors, this engine produced about 100 bhp, and although Gordinis gave away 570cc in F2 they acquitted themselves well on the tighter circuits and were often driven by such first-class drivers as Raymond Sommer, Jean-Pierre Wimille (when not driving for Alfa Romeo) and 'B. Bira'.

By 1950, capacity had risen to 1490cc and Gordini added a Wade Type RO15 supercharger to raise the output to 115 bhp in order to compete in F1. There followed a frantic season as Gordini entered the same cars in both F2 and F1 events by simply adding or subtracting the blowers and changing the bonnets (supercharged cars had air scoops on the nearside).

When blown, the cars were fairly fragile, but, driven by Robert Manzon, André Simon and Maurice Trintignant, they turned in performances far better than their specification might suggest. In addition to strong perfor-

mances in F2, notably a 2-3-4 in the F2 race supporting the Swiss GP, Manzon finished fourth in the French GP ahead of all the Talbots and this on the very fast Reims circuit. Manzon and Trintignant entered the Monaco GP and were both eliminated in the first-lap multiple pile-up and they both raced in, and retired from, the Italian GP. Using an 1100cc Gordini, Manzon also smashed, by 17 seconds, the record for the Mont Ventoux hill climb set by Hans Stuck in an Auto Union.

Despite these and other performances the Simcas were little more than plucky interlopers and there was no way they could sustain the effort. Gordini wanted to press ahead with a proper racing engine for 1951, but Simca, which was still struggling to get back into full production, was insistent on the need to relate the racing cars directly to its road cars. In the end a compromise was reached whereby Gordini was allowed to make a d.o.h.c. cylinder head.

Gordini had been very close to the Maserati brothers and it was no surprise to see that his engine was similar to Maserati practice, with the same dimensions of 1496cc (78 × 78 mm). With 155 bhp on tap, the new car was an altogether more serious proposition, but was still very fragile.

Again the team charged around Europe in 1951, putting on and taking off superchargers, but the blown cars were very unreliable. In F2 form, however, Trintignant, Manzon and Simon finished 2-3-4 in the Monza GP, and on the same day, Johnny Claes in one of the old push-rod models, won the Grand Prix des Frontières at Chimay. Its one F1 victory was at Albi, where Trintignant beat the Talbots of Rosier and Chiron.

Gordini was trying to spread his thin resources too far and his little team had no chance of preparing cars properly as they went from venue to venue arriving at races and retiring from them. Simca grew dissatisfied with its involvement and, at the end of the year, withdrew support.

Once he was on his own, Gordini responded rather like someone who cannot swim and yet falls into a pool. He had been seeking permission from Simca to build a pukka 2-litre engine; now, with the alternative of packing up or continuing, he went ahead with it. He had also covered himself, by liaising with the Maserati brothers, and was to have taken delivery of four of the eight O.S.C.A. 4½-litre V-12 engines which had been planned. In the event, he had one in his workshop and the new straight-six engine he made was inspired both by his own 4-cylinder engine and by one bank of the O.S.C.A.'s engine.

It had a capacity of 1498cc (75 × 75 mm), larger

valves than on the 'four', three double-choke Weber car-burettors and it produced 175 bhp. Gordini also made a new tubular frame, and while the suspension remained broadly the same, longitudinal torsion bars replaced coil springs at the front.

Manzon debuted the car in the Marseilles GP, where it retired, and when both Trintignant and Manzon were signed by Ferrari, Jean Behra and Harry Schell were taken on. In the International Trophy at Silverstone, Manzon won one heat and Behra finished second to Hawthorn's Cooper in the other. Both were well up in the early stages of the final, but neither finished.

In the first Championship race of the year, the Swiss GP, Manzon took third place on the grid, but retired with a split radiator, while Behra brought his car home third behind two Ferraris. Behra then won at Aix-les-Bains and Manzon took third in the Belgian GP, on the same lap as the leading Ferraris.

Then came the non-Championship race at Reims, where Behra scored a sensational win, by a mile from the Ferraris of Farina and Ascari. It was a Grand Prix win of equal stature to any WC race, indeed the Reims GP was over a slightly longer distance than the French GP which followed a week later, and it had a slightly fuller entry list. It was Gordini's finest hour, but it was never to be repeated.

Manzon and Trintignant (back in the fold) came fourth and fifth in the French GP at Rouen, but both retired from the British GP with broken transmission. In practice for the German GP, Trintignant and Manzon sat on the front row of the grid, splitting the four Ferraris, but Gordini had to be content with only fifth place (Behra). Manson and Trintignant were fifth and sixth in the Dutch GP, but were outclassed in the Italian. Along the way Trintignant and Behra scored a 1-2 in the Caen GP and Schell took second at Cadours.

In addition to the F2 programme, Gordini also made sports cars in several sizes, and although these were unreliable in long-distance events, Manzon scored a wonderful victory with a 1½-litre car in the 2-litre race at the Monaco (sports car) GP – and he battled with Moss' Jaguar C-type in the unlimited race until both were eliminated by a multiple crash.

At the end of 1952, against all odds, Gordini was maintaining a staff of 50 on a hand-to-mouth basis. Still, the marque could claim to be second only to Ferrari as a force in motor racing. Given the French penchant for throwing money at national projects to produce world-beating racing cars, one might have thought that Gordini would have received recognition and support at home. Not a bit of it, that national generosity was strictly reserved for Micky Mouse ventures and Gordini had to struggle on alone.

As a result the cars never repeated the bright promise they had shown in 1952, for Gordini had no money to undertake development and/or new designs and, worse, components which would normally have been replaced at set intervals were used until they broke. He also tried marketing road-going sports and GT cars, but the fiscal penalties the French government imposed on hand-

This Gordini driven by Johnny Claes in the 1952 International Trophy at Silverstone was a 4-cylinder 1.5-litre car, the old Formula 1 car with supercharger removed. (T. C. March)

The 6-cylinder 2-litre Gordini of Robert Manzon in the British Grand Prix at Silverstone in 1952.
(T. C. March)

made cars made them impossibly expensive and very few were sold. Perhaps Gordini was trying to do too much too soon with too little, but it is hard to see what else he could do, since he had built up a large workshop with the backing of Simca and then was left to run it himself.

As a result of these many constraints, Gordinis were not successful in 1953 and the reappearance of Maserati pushed the team down the order. Sixth places were taken by Behra in the Argentine GP (six laps down) and by Trintignant in the Dutch GP (three laps down). Trintignant also came fifth in the Belgian GP and in the Italian GP, but generally the cars were unreliable and slow, and they got slower as they became more tired during the season.

Most poignant of all was the return to Reims for the French GP, the circuit where Behra had given the marque its finest win the year before. There all the Gordinis qualified at the back of the grid with the best, Schell, 44.6 seconds off the pace. None finished. It is hard to think of any other team which has fallen so quickly.

Earlier in the season, when the cars were still fresh, Trintignant had won at Chimay and Cadours, Schell had finished third at Pau (behind two works Ferraris and over a full GP distance) and Fangio, who had driven Simca-Gordinis earlier in his career, made a brief return at Bordeaux, where he finished third.

When the 2½-litre F1 began, Gordini was reasonably well prepared, for he already had a 2473cc (80 × 82 mm) version of his straight-six engine which had finished fifth, and won its class, at Le Mans in 1953. This produced 210-220 bhp and was installed in a chassis very similar to the old F2 cars, except that the torsion bars were smaller and there was an anti-roll bar at the front.

Although it suffered a power disadvantage, at around 580 kg the T16 was the lightest car in F1, but, as before, the team had to struggle to get the machines in any sort of condition to make the start of each race, let alone be presented in top-class condition. Elie Bayol finished fifth in the Argentine GP, and Behra won at Pau over a full GP distance and against works teams from Ferrari and Maserati. Behra and Simon finished second and third at Silverstone in the International Trophy, which attracted almost a full WC field, and Behra was third at Bari, ahead of all the Maseratis.

These were all promising results, but, as usual, as the season progressed so the cars became more tired and less reliable. André Pilette was fifth in the Belgian GP, however, so Gordini was still presenting the biggest threat to the Italian teams, but then Mercedes-Benz entered the fray and everyone moved down the ladder. In the French GP at Reims, Behra came home sixth, but was five laps down at an average speed not much better than when he

Jean Behra with the 6-cylinder 2.5-litre Gordini leads the Maserati of Roberto Mieres in the 1954 French Grand Prix. (LAT)

won in 1952.

After taking over Jâcques Pollet's car, Behra finished third in the Caen GP and he also finished fifth at Pescara, but the only other notable finish was Fred Wacker's sixth in the Italian GP, five laps down. Quite often the cars were quick in practice but failed to make the finish. Gordinis were still capable of springing surprises, however, as at the Avusrennen, when the demonstration run stage-managed by Mercedes-Benz was overshadowed in the early stages by Jean Behra slip-streaming the W196 streamliners for lap after lap. It was a typically gutsy drive by the Frenchman, but, alas, equally typical was the result: retired, transmission failure.

1955 began with a blow to the équipe, for Behra accepted a drive with Maserati, but Manzon, a grossly under-rated driver, stayed on with the promise of a new car. Despite the team's poverty, it entered the Argentine GP, but no cars finished and that set the tone for the season, with the cars constantly retiring, generally with gearbox trouble, and by mid-summer all that Gordini had to show for his efforts were a couple of place finishes in minor events.

At Monthléry in July, Gordini unveiled an entirely new car, the first completely new Gordini formula car since links with Simca had been broken. It had a straight-eight d.o.h.c. engine of 2474cc (75 × 70 mm) which developed perhaps 240-50 bhp, but had lost the lightness which had always been such a Gordini feature. In fact of all 1955 GP cars, only the Mercedes-Benz W196 was heavier than the Gordini T32.

The most striking feature of the car was the smooth bodywork with fairings sweeping out from the nose ahead of the front wheels. Beneath the skin, Gordini retained a ladder-frame, a new design with larger side members, but suspension was independent all round by Watt links and torsion bars. There were, too, Messier disc brakes and a 5-speed gearbox.

It was intended to debut the car in the French GP, but that was cancelled following the Le Mans tragedy, and with so many European races suspended it was not until the Italian GP that the car appeared. Manzon was due to drive it, but had to cry off, and his place was taken by Jean Lucas. After a troubled practice, it started from last place on the grid and retired with engine trouble after seven laps. As was becoming the pattern, neither of the two older cars in the race finished.

Gordini was in a desperate state, with the T32 being a huge disappointment. Manzon drove one in the Richmond Trophy at Goodwood and finished a distant sixth. Pilette drove it in the International Trophy at Silverstone and in qualifying recorded the same time as Hermanos da Silva Ramos in a T16, but while da Silva Ramos finished a poor fifth, Pilette retired with a broken transmission. Then came an astonishing result, Manzon won the Naples GP against a small but select field which included two Lancia-Ferraris and Villoresi in a Maserati. It was an inherited win, for the fast boys retired, but it was a final twist to the Gordini story.

In the Monaco GP the old T16s of Manzon and da Silva Ramos ran fifth and sixth until close to the end, when Manzon's brakes failed and he crashed. He had done enough laps, though, to be a classified finisher, in sixth place behind his team-mate. This was better than the T32, which was 12 laps down at the end.

Amédée Gordini's final Formula 1 car was the rather odd straight-eight driven here by André Pilette in the 1956 International Trophy at Silverstone. (T. C. March)

Thereafter the cars either retired or finished so far down the field that it is kinder not to rub in the point. Another bright spot was Simon's second at Caen to Schell's works Maserati, but it was not a strong field.

By the end of 1956 it was felt that Gordini's best hope lay in F2, and he went some way towards making such a car, but it would have been hopeless since it was a heavy, front-engined design. There was, too, another attempt to build a road-going sports car, but that never got off the ground.

Early in 1957 Amédée Gordini finally gave up the unequal struggle, closed down his Équipe, and accepted a post with Renault, where he began to transform Renault road cars. The name 'Gordini' has since been synonymous with sporting versions of Renault cars.

With the departure of Gordini, France enjoyed no representation in Grand Prix racing for over ten years, until Matra entered in 1968 and Jackie Stewart won the World Championship the following year with a Matra-Cosworth. Then, when Renault appeared in F1 in 1977, the name 'Gordini' was stamped on its turbocharged engines. It was a pleasant acknowledgement to the memory of a man who had made a great contribution to the state-owned company and who, against all the odds, had struggled to keep the blue of France in the top levels of sports and formula racing. It remains a tragedy that in the fifties Gordini did not receive the support he deserved.

GUÉRIN

Although France was devastated by the war, motor racing enthusiasts were keen to get back into action as soon as possible, and the first post-war race meeting was run in Paris in September 1945, while Britain was still engaged in some unfinished business in the Far East. During 1945, an engineer named Enguerrand de Courcy had drawn up a new F1 car and he was able to persuade the aviation firm Société Guérin to build it.

De Courcy's design revolved around a d.o.h.c. straight-eight engine of 1487cc (59 × 68 mm), which was supposed to give 255 bhp. This was installed in a ladder-frame with independent suspension all round, and the 4-speed gearbox, which was mounted in unit with the final drive, featured a clutchless gear change.

For reasons which remain obscure, the Guérin-de Courcy never raced in its original form, but, fitted with a supercharged 1100cc (Simca?) engine, the car did appear in a few F2 races in 1947 and 1948

H. A. R.

At the beginning of 1952, Horace Richards, an enthusiast from Smethwick, showed his new Formula 2 car, built by his own engineering works. It had a Riley engine in a simple ladder-frame built of 3½-in chrome molybdenum steel tubes with sheet steel castles at both ends and the frame itself weighted just 80 lb. Suspension was independent all round by unequal-length wishbones and Salter laminated-blade torsion bars, which were adjustable to trim the car for, apart from the 2-litre Riley engine, Richards intended to install 1500cc and 1100cc units to make it a versatile car. Richards had an elektron casting made to house the differential and at the front of the casting were two spur gears which not only allowed the prop-shaft to run very low under the driver's seat, but

Horace Richards at the wheel of the H.A.R. in the 1953 International Trophy at Silverstone. (T. C. March)

by changing these spur gears gave a total of six final drive ratios.

It was a handsome, well-made car which reflected credit on its builder, at least in the paddock. When it raced it was invariably on the back row of the grid and generally last to finish. Since it was only ever raced by Richards, there is no way of knowing whether the fault lay with the car or the driver.

When the 2½-litre F1 came into force, Richards continued to enter his car in non-Championship British F1 events and the odd race still run to the old F2 until the end of 1955.

Even then its competition career was not over and as late as 1960 it appeared in an FJ race at Mallory Park. The H.A.R. never figured in the results but it gave its builder a lot of enjoyment and is still in existence.

A second chassis was built for Bertie Bradnack, and during 1952 and 1953 this was entered in a couple of races under the name 'Woden' and was apparently to be Bristol-powered. It did not actually appear in any races, however, and it is thought that the 'Woden' was never completed, although later the chassis was used as the basis of a sports car. It currently lives in Australia, where it is fitted with a Jaguar engine, and its owner describes it as very fast, but somewhat lacking in both handling and stopping power.

H. R. G.

When Formula 2 began in 1948, Peter Clarke, an enthusiast who had achieved some success with H.R.G. sports cars, commissioned Marcus Chambers to build a single-seater based on a cut-and-shut H.R.G. sports car chassis. It had a shortened wheelbase, but retained the Vintage-style H.R.G. suspension, with solid front and rear axles suspended on quarter-elliptical springs. Power came from a modified 1998cc Standard Vanguard engine, which gave, at most 115 bhp, and which drove through a Standard 3-speed gearbox. It was a lost cause even before it turned a wheel, although the bulbous body was nicely made by Cooper Cars. In 1949 it appeared in a handful of races entirely without distinction and was then put aside. Despite its history it was revived in 1952 and entered for Mike Keen. He brought it home 11th in the Lavant Cup at Goodwood and then took it to the International Trophy at Silverstone. It proved that a slow car does not get any faster for being stored and Keen, who was a more than commonly competent driver, failed to qualify.

Rodney Lord with the Standard Vanguard-engined H.R.G. single-seater at Goodwood in May 1950. (Duncan Rabagliati)

H. W. M.

Just after World War II two friends, George Abecassis and John Heath, found themselves competing for the small number of customers in the Home Counties who were interested in buying performance and racing cars. They therefore combined and formed Hersham and Walton Motors, H.W.M.

Abecassis had the distinction of winning the last race in England before the war and the first one after it. He is one of those men who thrive on danger and still maintains the best time of his life was flying bombers and dropping S.O.E. agents into Europe, which was even more dangerous work. It is not surprising then that, as a driver, what he lacked in natural ability he made up by sheer bravery.

Heath, a tall, aristocratic man, had trained as an engineer, although his chief delight was working with his hands. At the outbreak of war he was working in the experimental department of Lagonda, and since it was considered vital work, there he had to stay for the duration.

When the two men joined forces Heath had the chance to do what he liked best, but his partner's involvement in racing fired his enthusiasm and he began competing with a sports Alta. Before long his natural inclinations took over and he produced a tuned, streamlined version of the car, with which he enjoyed some success. Some trips to Europe opened his eyes, for there prize and starting money were so good that he had his sport and came home in profit. There was clearly money to be made from racing in Europe.

He set to and built a twin-tube chassis with off-set seating so it could run in either Formula 2 or sports car racing, with double wishbone and transverse leaf front suspension, with the steering coming from a scrapped Citroën and the front uprights and lower wishbones from a Standard 12. At the rear was a Lagonda Rapier axle suspended on quarter-elliptical springs and located by a torque arm.

It was axiomatic with Heath that a second-hand part was as good as a new one, and when H.W.M. became successful and firms gave it free components, these were often sold, while he used parts gleaned from a scrapyard. It is an attitude which accounts for some of his cars' reliability records.

Into the chassis, Heath installed his Alta engine and this he mated to an ENV differential and 4-speed preselector gearbox and the plot was completed with a slim aluminium body with cycle wings. Called the H.W.-Alta, it gave Heath a very successful season in 1949. In Formula 2 form he inherited a win in the Manx Cup and finished fifth in the Coupe des Petites Cylindrées at Reims. Running as a sports car, he finished an excellent second to Charles Pozzi's Delahaye in the French GP at Comminges. They were just the sort of performances to make the Continental organizers take notice and, besides, it was novel to have a green car on the grid.

While the elephantine B.R.M. project lurched along, generating a lot of hype and trying everyone's patience, Heath had rolled up his sleeves and got on with the job. His little special had not only gone abroad but had returned with pride.

For 1950, Geoffery Taylor produced a new version of his d.o.h.c. Alta engine with a much shorter stroke (83×90 mm compared to the previous 79×100 mm), and although it produced only about 115 bhp, it was fairly reliable.

For his part Heath 'designed' a new car with tubes and welding torch and when it was to his satisfaction, he made up three more like it. He kept the front suspension of the H.W.-Alta, but produced a new independent rear layout with double wishbones and a transverse leaf spring. An ENV differential was retained, but since ENV gearboxes proved hard to come by he used 4-speed preselector gearboxes made by Armstrong-Siddeley, which, like ENVs, were made to Wilson patents.

Since the team had an opportunity to run at Le Mans, the cars were built as 'dual-purpose' machines, but in the event the works ran them only in F2. In looks they resembled the first H.W.-Alta and their bodies were made by the nearby Leacroft concern.

One of the cars was sold to an amateur racer, Maurice Baring, who was a friend of the partners, while the other three were for Heath and Stirling Moss with the third to be driven by Abecassis, when he was not minding the store, or else hired out to some local hero. Now called H.W.M., the cars first appeared at the Easter Monday Goodwood Meeting, but did not shine, although Moss and Abecassis finished sixth and seventh in a Formule Libre five-lapper and Moss took second in a handicap.

Then the team set off to lead a gypsy life on the Continent, and apart from a tendency to lose wheels through broken hubs and half-shafts, they were fairly reliable. Compared to the best opposition they were still overweight and underpowered, but on tighter circuits their excellent handling came into its own and, of course, Stirling Moss was a huge asset.

Another asset was the chief mechanic, a Polé named Kovaleski, who changed his name to 'Alf Francis'. Alf became a legend among racing mechanics, wrote an extremely good autobiography, and pops up with some frequency in this book.

During the season the team competed in 26 meetings

in seven months and took two wins, three seconds and six thirds. Not only had H.W.M. flown the flag, but came home in profit even before it sold-on its team cars – again at a profit.

Of the season's highlights, there was the Rome GP, where Moss ran fourth to three Ferraris and set fastest lap. Then a front hub sheared and he lost a wheel. It was still rated a magnificent performance which won both driver and team a lot of friends in Italy.

Lance Macklin, whom Abecassis still believes had the potential to be a great driver if he had taken the sport seriously, joined Moss and Heath in the Coupe des Petites Cylindrées at Reims. The race was won by Ascari's Ferrari from André Simon's Simca, but next up were Moss, Heath and Macklin. Then Moss was in brilliant form at Bari, where he chased the works Alfa Romeos and finished third, ahead of the likes of Villoresi's Ferrari and Bira's Maserati.

H.W.M.'s exploits had made exciting reading to those at home and the B.R.D.C., organisers of the International Trophy at Silverstone, extended the team a special invitation to take part in the race, which was for F1 cars. That race saw the debut of the mighty B.R.M., which had cost over £200,000 and had been years in the making. It broke its transmission on the line. By contrast each H.W.M. had cost £1500, a team of four cars had been built in a tiny workshop in a few months, they had fulfilled their obligations to organizers and they had come back home with heads held high. It is difficult today to appreciate just what a morale boost to British racing H.W.M. had been.

For 1951 there were new cars, this time single-seaters, a move which in itself shed weight. In place of the independent rear suspension, which had led to problems with the half-shafts, a de Dion layout was adopted, and this was suspended on quarter-elliptical springs and located by radius arms. At the front, double wishbones were retained, but coil springs replaced the former transverse leaf and M.G. TD components replaced the former Standard Vanguard parts, which had proved

H.W.M.s. finished first and second in the 1952 International Trophy at Silverstone. This is the winning car of Lance Macklin. (T. C. March)

inadequate (the cars had shed a lot of wheels). The engines were dry-sumped and two twin-choke Weber carburettors helped raise power to 130 bhp.

The new car was a decided improvement and Moss opened the score for it at Goodwood when he won the Lavant Cup for F2 cars, with Macklin fourth. Then it was back to Europe, where the pattern was much the same as in 1950, except that the cars did not shed wheels and European drivers were often seen in them.

Again the team came home with the knowledge of a job well done and again there had been times when the cars, particularly when driven by Moss, had humbled more glamorous cars. To prepare for the arrival of the enhanced status of F2 H.W.M. enjoyed the direct help of Alta and the engines were prepared by Robin Jackson, a noted tuner. He came up with new con-rods, pistons, crankshaft and camshafts and succeeded in squeezing about 145 bhp from them. Lighter tubing was employed for the 1952 cars, the de Dion rear layout had torsion bar springing and the 11-in rear brakes were mounted inboard. ZF limited slip differentials were also fitted, the team making a detour on the way to Pau to obtain them.

Despite these improvements, the cars were still too heavy, being a good 2 cwt over the Cooper-Bristols, and were still short on power compared with Maserati and Ferrari. Moss left the team believing it would struggle, although he later drove occasionally, and his place was taken by Peter Collins. Lance Macklin and the Frenchman Yves Giraud-Cabantous were the other main drivers in 1952, and Abecassis and Heath also took the wheel on occasion.

At Pau the cars suffered brake trouble, but Macklin finished seventh. There was a total of five H.W.M.s in the International Trophy at Silverstone, and although outpaced by Behra's Gordini and Hawthorn's Cooper-Bristol, they proved more reliable and Macklin and Rolt scored a splendid 1-2. It is true that neither Ferrari nor Maserati had been present, but there was a full field and it was to be H.W.M.'s finest win. Unfortunately, from that moment onwards, the team began a steady slide.

Moss rejoined the team for the Swiss GP, where the cars started from mid-field, although the fastest, Collins, was over 12 seconds off the pace. When, in the race, both Abecassis and Collins lost wheels, Moss and Macklin were brought in by the team. New axle shafts were soon made and Macklin finished fourth in the Paris GP, behind three Ferraris. Moss came second, and Duncan Hamilton fourth, in the Eifelrennen at the Nürburgring behind Rudi Fischer's private Ferrari. In the Grand Prix des Frontières at Chimay, Paul Frère was invited to drive and he managed to snatch victory when Ken Downing, who had dominated in his Connaught, eased off too much in the closing stages.

The H.W.M.s were outclassed in the Monza GP, but on the same day, Macklin finished second to Behra's Gordini at Aix-les-Bains. H.W.M.'s first World Championship points were scored in the Belgian GP, when Frère brought one home fifth, albeit two laps down. Reims was a circuit which had been surprisingly kind to H.W.M. in the past, but in 1952 they were completely out of the picture and Cabantous was the highest finisher – a distant eighth. In the French GP at Rouen, Collins finished sixth, but he was five laps down. Collins had some luck at Les Sables d'Olonne when a multiple crash eliminated a fair chunk of the field and he finished second to Villoresi's Ferrari, but it was a fluke result.

Four H.W.M.s took part in the British GP at Silverstone, where only two months previously it had scored a 1-2. There they were completely outclassed and not only by the continental teams, but the best Cooper-Bristols and Connaughts were also much quicker. Macklin was the only one to finish, in 13th place and five laps down.

For the record Cabantous retired at Caen; Claes was tenth across the line in the German GP after a stop to fix a loose magneto, but he was three laps (of 18) down and unclassified; Cabantous was sixth in the Comminges GP; and Hamilton and Macklin a distant seventh and eighth in the Dutch GP. Slightly better was a fourth and fifth for Collins and Cabantous at La Baule, a long way behind the works Ferraris, but neither of the two entries qualified for the grid for the Italian GP, for they were simply too slow. Collins ran in the Modena GP, but retired, while Cabantous took fourth place at Cadours.

That ended H.W.M.'s 1952 season. By comparison with earlier years, it had been a poor showing and there were several reasons for it. One was that Heath simply was not good enough a designer to keep up with the competition. His cars handled well, they were far too heavy and had no compensating feature such as superior aerodynamics, brakes or power.

Another factor in H.W.M.'s decline was the way the team went racing, shunting from meeting to meeting across Europe and preparing the cars at the circuits. It may have kept the starting money flowing, but was no way to ensure reliability or to develop machines.

For 1953 the cars had slightly more power due to the use of Weber 40DCO carburettors and a new twin-pipe exhaust system and in this form they gave a claimed 160 bhp, although this is a figure I doubt.

What the cars did not have, but which Connaught did, was nitromethane in the fuel tank. The new fuel, which was perfectly legal, was kept very quiet by those who had latched on to it. In the latter part of 1953

Stirling Moss used it when he drove a Mk II Cooper fitted with an Alta engine and the result was phenomenal, for power approached 200 bhp.

Leaving aside the fact that Moss was Moss and the Cooper was much lighter, had H.W.M. discovered the secret its 1953 season might have been very different and that might possibly have led to a better start for 1954. As it was H.W.M. tinkered with details looking for small increases, not knowing that a huge increase could simply be poured into the fuel tank. So, a Jaguar C-type gearbox replaced the pre-selector unit, since Heath thought it might make for a quicker gear-change and save fractions of a second, and a Halibrand quick-change final drive, which gave an option of 38 different ratios, replaced the ZF unit. Heath also reduced the wheelbase slightly and increased the size of the brakes. Externally, the 1953 cars could be distinguished from earlier models by their oval air intake in place of the familiar vertical grille.

The team knew that the writing was on the wall for them in F2, and Abecassis had been at work modifying a spare chassis to take a Jaguar engine. This was the first works-originated H.W.M.-Jaguar sports car (Oscar Moore had already made an H.W.M.-Jaguar using one of the 1950 team cars as the basis) and the H.W.M. name was destined to survive longer, thanks to these cars. After some initial successes in British events, however, the H.W.M.-Jaguars soon became uncompetitive, although they were liked by their owners.

Once again the team started with the Easter Monday Goodwood Meeting, but it struggled. The cars retired from the Bordeaux GP and the International Trophy at Silverstone, but in the Ulster Trophy at Dundrod, Duncan Hamilton managed a second in his heat and a sixth in the final, largely thanks to his press-on driving. When the Crystal Palace circuit re-opened, H.W.M. entered a team in the Coronation Trophy, but Macklin could do no better than fourth, beaten by a Connaught and two Cooper-Bristols.

They fared better in the Eifelrennen at the Nürburgring, where Macklin and Collins took second and third behind de Graffenried's private Maserati, but there was little opposition. In the Dutch GP Macklin had an improved engine which gave a *reputed* 175 bhp, but since he was over ten seconds off the pace in practice this seems a dubious figure, for it is unlikely that any H.W.M. ever had much more than 150/55 bhp. Macklin was an early retirement with a broken throttle, but Collins managed eighth, six laps in arrears.

It was worse at Spa, where both cars were over half a minute off the pace and both were early retirements, and although both finished in the French GP at Reims, Collins was eight laps down and Cabantous was ten laps in arrears. Four cars appeared in the British GP and although Macklin qualified in the top half of the field, in 12th, none of them finished. At Aix-les-Bains, however, Macklin managed third on aggregate, but the opposition was thin and the race was won by Bayol's O.S.C.A., which shows just how far down the order H.W.M. had slipped.

Despite their showing in the Eifelrennen, the organizers of the German GP refused the team's entries, which must have been especially humiliating since no fewer than 33 starters were on the grid. They were welcomed at Les Sables d'Olonne, however, and while Cabantous and Collins finished fourth and fifth on aggregate, they were also in the last two places in a thin field. Only one of the four cars finished in the Swiss GP, that of local man Albert Scherrer, and he was ninth, having completed only 49 of the 65 laps.

Three cars made the start of the Italian GP and all were way off the pace. While they struggled, Moss was running in fifth place and giving Felice Bonetto's Maserati a hard time in a Cooper fitted with the same sort of Alta engine that H.W.M. was using, with the difference that Moss had something a little special in his fuel tank. Cabantous was the only H.W.M. finisher, 13 laps down, and though none knew it at the time, that was to be the last occasion on which an H.W.M. finished a World Championship race.

It had been a terrible season, but Heath was still keen to continue in the 2½-litre formula, although he had a profound problem, the lack of a suitable engine. Like some others, he had pinned his hopes on the Coventry Climax 'Godiva' unit, but that was not forthcoming, and even if H.W.M. had received the engine, it is highly unlikely Heath could have designed a car to do it justice, for Formula 1 was about to become an altogether more serious proposition. He could not even keep his relationship with Alta going, for Geoffrey Taylor had reached an exclusive agreement with Connaught.

It was an act of desperation then to enlarge the existing F2 Alta engines to 2464cc (84 × 106 mm) and even to fit fuel injection, but at best these gave little more than 200 bhp. This was much less than Connaught was to obtain after re-working the Alta engines and very little more than what Moss' 2-litre engine had been giving on nitro-methane. The enlarged engines were fitted into two 1953 works cars, one of which was sold to Ted Whiteaway, while the other was entered by the works for Lance Macklin.

Macklin managed fourth in the seven-lap Lavant Cup at Goodwood, but was beaten by McAlpine's F2 Connaught. He was then a slow qualifier for the International Trophy at Silverstone, a race he had won only

Jack Fairman with his H.W.M. in the 1953 British Grand Prix. He retired because of clutch trouble.
(**T. C. March**)

two years earlier, but he non-started due to mechanical trouble. Whiteaway finished his heat a long way down and retired in the final. Of the performances that Whiteaway was able to post in British F1 races, one can say he showed consistency: he was invariably last on the grid and retired in the race. Although Whiteaway was no ace, he was a better driver than his performances with the car would suggest.

Macklin appeared in the French GP at Reims and this was to be H.W.M.'s last works appearance in single-seater racing. There he was over half a minute off the pace and he trailed around in last place until his engine gave up after ten laps. The H.W.M.'s story was not quite over, for Ted Whiteaway persevered with his car in 1955 and even attempted to qualify in the Monaco GP, but

after qualifying slowly for the Albi GP in May, and blowing his engine in the race, he gave up the unequal struggle.

After H.W.M.'s ignominious swansong in the French GP, the firm concentrated on its Jaguar-engined sports cars, which were quite promising at first but, in typical H.W.M. fashion, were soon overtaken by the opposition. Then, in 1956, Heath decided to fulfil a long-held ambition and run in the Mille Miglia with one of his own cars. In the race he lost control of his car in the wet, it overturned, and Heath was crushed beneath it.

On the death of his partner, Abecassis retired from racing, but continued to enter cars until the beginning of 1957, by which time there was no longer any point in doing so and the marque quietly faded away.

HONDA

By 1962, Honda had established itself as the world's largest manufacturer of motorcycles and the most successful firm in bike racing. It then began to turn its attention to cars and Honda decided to set some of its brightest engineers an exercise from which they could learn, a Formula 1 car.

Most striking feature of the Honda RA272 was its engine, a d.o.h.c. 60-degree V-12 of 1495cc (58.1 × 47 mm) with four valves per cylinder and needle roller bearings. It thus followed Honda's bike engines and the common ancestry was further evident in the use of six twin-choke Keihan carburettors and the power take-off, which was in the centre of the transversely mounted engine in the same way as Colombo's Bugatti T251. The 220 bhp at 11,000 rpm this unit produced fed directly into a 6-speed gearbox in unit with the final drive.

While the engine was as good as any of the opposition, the chassis was less advanced, with a monocoque central-section and a tubular sub-frame carrying the engine and rear suspension. Mr Soichiro Honda admired Brabham's way of building chassis and insisted that his engineers followed suit.

Front suspension was by rocker arms, with inboard coil spring/damper units and lower transverse links and radius arms, while the independent rear layout had reversed lower wishbones, an upper link and twin radius arms. Dunlop disc brakes were fitted outboard all round, but, unusually, it was not to Dunlop that Honda turned for its tyres, but to Goodyear, which had entered F1 with Brabham at the beginning of 1964.

For a first try from a brand new maker, it was an impressive effort, even though, at 1155 lb, it was not a particularly light car. When it made its debut at the Nürburgring at the wheel was a young American called Ronnie Bucknum, who had been successful in sports car racing on the West Coast but who had never raced a single-seater.

Honda had decided to enter racing with the minimum of fuss so it could climb its learning curve without too much attention. If Bucknum won or showed well the car would get the credit, if he floundered everyone would blame the driver. An American was chosen because Honda was about to launch its 600 saloon in the States.

Years later Honda used a similar ploy when entering F2 with Ralt and chose a not particularly successful driver whose career was in the doldrums because he was their idea of an Englishman. His name was Nigel Mansell.

Bucknum was never an ace, but he drove sensibly. For anyone to make his single-seater debut in a Grand Prix at the Nürburgring *in the wet*, and perform well, is something deserving more credit than Bucknum has received. In practice for the German GP the car suffered from overheating and erratic brakes and Bucknum qualified last, nearly 20 seconds adrift of the field and nearly a minute off the pace. In the race, which was wet, he had worked his way up to 11th, and had overtaken some fancied runners, when his steering failed four laps from home. He was classified 11th from 22 starters.

The Austrian GP was given a miss and indirect fuel injection replaced the carburettors for Monza. Bucknum and the Honda were still off the pace, yet had moved up the grid (tenth from 20), but brakes and cooling were still a problem. In the race Bucknum got up to fifth before retiring with overheating problems and in the US GP Bucknum was 16th on the grid, but retired at half-distance with a blown head gasket.

For 1965 engine power was up to 230 bhp at 12,000 rpm, 60 lb had been shed and Bucknum was joined in the team by Richie Ginther, who was widely admired as a test driver. The team missed the South African GP, even though the South African government magnanimously classified the Japanese as 'honorary whites', and the two cars qualified in the last two places at Monaco. Ginther was out after a lap with a broken universal joint and Bucknum retired at one-third distance with a broken gear linkage.

Spa was a different story and there Ginther qualified fourth fastest and finished sixth, while Bucknum started from mid-field and retired at one-third distance with transmission failure. The French GP on the tricky Clermont-Ferrand circuit saw Ginther qualify in seventh place, with Bucknum on the back row, but both cars had retired with ignition troubles by quarter-distance. At Silverstone there was just one car, for Ginther, and he qualified third and led the race for a while, but then ran third only to drop out with injection problems. Only one car was entered for the Dutch GP, where again Ginther qualified third, and he led the first two laps until spinning twice, but eventually he came home sixth.

Germany was missed while the team incorporated some modifications which included a new crankcase, lower engine mountings and slimmer bodywork, but they were back in action at Monza, where Bucknum claimed sixth slot on the grid with Ginther 17th, but both cars were plagued by engine problems. Ginther qualified third at Watkins Glen (Bucknum 11th), but spun on the first lap. Since Ginther was a very reliable driver and that was the second time he had spun early in a race, it suggests the Honda was a problem when fully laden. He eventually finished seventh, and since Bucknum trailed

***Richie Ginther (Honda V12) leads Spence (Lotus 33), Amon (Lotus), McLaren, Rindt (both with Coopers),
Hill (B.R.M.) and Siffert (Brabham) in the 1965 French Grand Prix at Clermont-Ferrand. (David Phipps)***

home in 11th, it was the first time two Hondas had both finished a race.

Finally there was the Mexican GP, the last race to the 1½-litre F1. Both drivers qualified well (Ginther third, Bucknum tenth) and at the start Ginther shot off into the lead and stayed there until the end to score his only GP win, and Honda's first. Bucknum brought the second RA272 home in fifth, so it was a double cause for celebration.

As soon as Ginther crossed the finishing line, the car was obsolete, but Honda had learned some valuable lessons, one of which was the part a fuel injection system can play in success, for with the circuit at 5000 ft above sea level its system had been the decisive factor in the win. In recent years we have seen the fruit of that lesson.

Honda was back again in 1966 with a powerful but grossly overweight 3-litre car, but it did not appear until the Italian GP. Ginther raced the new model just three times, and Bucknum once, and neither scored any success. The following year, Ginther switched to the Eagle-Weslake team, but, due to problems, never got to race one of the cars, and he retired from the sport in mid-season. Bucknum's services were not sought in Europe and he returned to America to pursue a career as a journeyman driver.

J. B. W. - M A S E R A T I

Brian Naylor was an enthusiast with a penchant for slightly unusual cars which were built and/or prepared by his chief mechanic, Fred Wilkinson. He was the only English buyer of a Maserati 150S, and when the car was a disappointment, he had the engine transferred to a Lotus Eleven. This was followed by another Eleven fitted with a 2-litre Maserati engine, with which Naylor had a highly successful season. It is true that he concentrated on minor events, but from 22 starts he came home with nine wins and nine places.

Wilkinson then persuaded his 'guv'nor' to allow him to build a Lotus-style chassis to take the Maserati engine and this became the J.B.W.-Maserati sports car, which, again, was quite successful in British and European meetings. It was followed by a a less happy combination, the J.B.W.-Ferrari, which had a 3-litre 4-cylinder 750

Brian Naylor with the J.B.W.-Maserati in the 1960 British Grand Prix. (T. C. March)

Monza engine. These cars added interest to a grid and made Naylor a better-known driver than would have been the case had he achieved the same results with a proprietary chassis.

Wilkinson then designed and built an F1 car which closely followed Cooper lines, but had a 4-cylinder Maserati 250S engine and 5-speed transaxle. Its body was somewhat dumpier than a Cooper and the rear wheels were wires for easy changing. Since Naylor alone drove it, we have no way of knowing how good or bad the car was. In 1959 it was entered in just three races, all in Britain, and it retired in the International Trophy at Silverstone, ran as high as 11th in the early stages of the British GP before retiring with a broken transmission, and was a non-starter in the Oulton Park Gold Cup following a crash in practice.

Naylor undertook a fuller season in 1960, but it was blighted by retirements, and in no race was it other than a make-weight. Perhaps its best race was the British GP, where Naylor qualified 18th from 24 starters and finished 12th and five laps down. Naylor drove it in 1961 in the Inter-Continental Formula races, but it was slow in all of them and failed to finish in any.

Another J.B.W. appeared in 1961. This again was a Cooper-copy, this time with a Maserati 150S engine driving through a 5-speed Colotti gearbox. After being entered in some early races and failing to appear, it made the line for the Silver City Trophy at Brands Hatch where it was over 10 seconds off the pace and it retired with overheating problems.

It failed to make a couple of other races for which it was entered but did make the start for the Italian GP (in penultimate slot on the grid and over 20 seconds off the pace) but the engine gave up after six laps. In the Stewart-Evans Trophy at Brands Hatch, a race for F1 privateers, it qualified slowly in a pretty poor field and retired on the first lap with a broken rotor arm. Then it actually finished the International Gold Cup at Oulton Park, in ninth place but four laps down.

Not surprisingly, Naylor did not pursue the matter and the car was never seen again in an F1 race but it has recently raced in Historic events.

KHARKOV

In the 1950s the 'Iron Curtain' let very little light through, but from behind it from time to time came tantalizing glimpses of motor sport activity. So little information came out of Russia that the few scraps which did emerge were eagerly seized upon, and when the chief of the Moscow Automobile Club attended the 1958 International Trophy at Silverstone as a guest of the *Daily Express*, it got everyone excited, even though it was only a case of a beaurocrat enjoying a 'freebie'.

Then came drawings and news of the Kharkov Six, an aerodynamic 6-cylinder car which apparently conformed to F1 and had achieved an average speed of 175 mph 'on a six-mile course' in the hands of Soviet ace Valiery Nikitin. The Kharkov received a lot of publicity in Britain, not only in specialist magazines but also in the national Press.

The fact is that it was a special built for record-breaking and in that context 175 mph, even if true, was not exceptional for a car of 2½ litres if, indeed, it had a 2½-litre engine. As a Grand Prix car, the Kharkov is a myth.

KIEFT

Cyril Kieft was in his early twenties when he found himself managing one of the largest steel mills in Europe, but he left when the British steel industry was nationalized in 1948. Supported by a small foundry business of his own, he looked for a challenge for his energy and found it in motor racing.

He designed a simple ladder-frame 500cc car which was marketed as a 'Kieft', but it was heavy, ill-handling and gained little success. Most similar projects quickly folded, but Kieft was able to subsidize his ambitions and a flair for publicity made his outfit better known than it deserved to be. He was, after all, a professional businessman operating in a field of enthusiast special builders.

In late 1950 he was approached by Ken Gregory, Stirling Moss' manager, to take over a 500cc project conceived by Dean Delamont, John A. Cooper (Technical Editor of *The Autocar*) and Ray Martin, who intended to provide a car for Stirling Moss. £120 exchanged hands and Kieft found himself possessing an advanced design with all-independent suspension by rubber bands. He also found himself with a direct line to Moss, who became a director of Kieft Cars.

Unfortunately, production Kiefts were made to low standards and the only other driver who achieved any success with one was Don Parker, who insisted on building his own car from Kieft parts and his car was really a Parker Special. Still, the name 'Kieft' was kept in the public eye and Cyril pursued a number of projects. He had an A.J.B. flat-four engine fitted with Norton barrels and cylinder heads and talked of a Kieft F2 car and a team of cars to take on Porsche. Unfortunately, Kieft Cars could never install the engine so that it would not overheat, although nobody else had problems with A.J.B. engines. On the other hand, as a businessman he was able to talk to the heads of other firms and it was this level of personal contact which formed a relationship with Coventry Climax. So one of the firm's rather crude sports cars ran at Le Mans in 1954 with the very first Coventry Climax FWA engine. It retired, but the engine went on to become a mainstay of British sports car racing.

Also, in 1954, Kieft's designer, Gordon Bedson, drew an F1 car which was to have been driven by his old friend Alan Brown. This was designed around the Coventry Climax FPE 'Godiva' engine (q.v.) and was a fairly conventional front-engined design. It had a semi-space-frame chassis (ie it had the form of a space-frame but was not properly triangulated) with front suspension by coil spring and double wishbones and double wishbones and a single transverse leaf spring at the rear. Braking was by outboard Dunlop discs all round (still fairly unusual in 1954) and the wheels also came from Dunlop, being cast in magnesium-zirconium with knock-off central hubs nuts. An E.R.A. pre-selector gearbox and a ZF differential completed the package.

Coventry Climax provided a dummy unit for fitting, but the engine was not released. At the end of 1954 the steel industry was privatized and Kieft returned to his first love.

The Kieft F1 was ready to run had Coventry Climax released its 'Godiva' engine and, indeed, a second chassis had been built up, this time with the front and rear castles cast on to the chassis tubes. Running an F1 car might have given the restless Cyril Kieft the challenge he craved, but it has to be said that the chassis was probably too crude to have done its job.

The uncompleted Kieft designed to take the Coventry Climax Godiva engine.
(Duncan Rabagliati)

KURTIS-KRAFT

Throughout the 1950s there was a gradual coming together of the American and European traditions. Sports car racing became increasingly popular in the States, Indy roadsters raced at Monza in 1957 and 1958, the Cunningham and Scarab teams crossed the Atlantic to race in Europe, and America exported some fine drivers. By 1959 there was sufficient acceptance of European-style racing in the States to hold a round of the World Championship at Sebring.

This did not go down well among some of the 'good ole boys' of traditional American racing, who believed that the Brickyard was for real men and these funny little Grawn Pree cars and sports buggies were for faggots. Roger Ward, winner of the 1959 Indianapolis 500 (and of the 1962 race), was broadly of this school and he reckoned that a red steak eatin' All-American Boy in a real man's car could show the Europeans how it should be done.

A Quarter Oval midget racer complied with F1 regulations and so it was that the Leader Cards Kurtis-Kraft-Offenhauser became a Grand Prix car. A Kurtis-Kraft midget had a tubular space-frame with solid axles front and rear suspended by torsion bars. A 1.7-litre

d.o.h.c. 4-cylinder Offenhauser engine was fitted, together with a 2-speed gearbox and 2-speed differential, and while the car had disc brakes, they were of a fairly rudimentary level, since their main function while racing was to help put the car into a slide on loose surfaces.

Ward was not completely naive, for earlier in the year he had entered a meeting at Lime Rock with the car and won one of the heats. It had shown up well against a Maserati 250F driven by Chuck Daigh as well as some other decent machines, but the long straights at Sebring, and a top class field, saw Ward struggling.

His best practice lap was 43.8 seconds off the pace and, since Moss' pole time was three minutes dead, practice indicated the Ward could be lapped nine or ten times during the race. Today he would have been excluded under the 110 per cent rule, but the winner of the Indy 500 was a draw.

Ward knew before the start that his was a lost cause, but he plugged away, giving his all, for he was nothing if not a racer. He completed 20 laps before his humiliation ended with clutch trouble, and since he was a sportsman he took his drubbing in good part and came away with a rather different perspective on Formula 1.

Roger Ward was persuaded to enter this Kurtis-Kraft Quarter Oval Midget in the 1959 US Grand Prix at Sebring after having raced it against Chuck Daigh's Maserati 250F earlier in the year. He soon discovered that Daigh in an elderly Maserati was not the benchmark in F1. (LAT)

LANCIA

Vincenzo Lancia had been a successful racing driver for Fiat in the early years of the century, but when he founded his own firm he turned his face against the sport. Like a reformed alcoholic, he knew only too well what a drain on resources it could be, but he did make an exception in the case of the Mille Miglia. This policy did not seem to harm his firm, which became famous for engineering excellence.

By the 1950s, Vincenzo was long dead and his son, Gianni, was in charge, and he felt that Lancia would benefit from a successful showing in competition. On Lancia's staff was Vittorio Jano, the greatest of all Italian designers, and a sporting version of his Aurelia saloon, a sort of 1951 'hot hatch', had been spectacularly successful in competition.

On the crest of such a wave, it was a short step to asking Jano to design a series of sports-racers for the 1953 World Sports Car Championship with an assault on F1 to follow. Lancia's 1953 season was respectable for a debut year and the team was remarkable for the speed with which it responded to change.

Lancia was going about the business of building up a competitions department in a thoroughly professional way, while, by contrast, Ferrari's plans for the new F1 in 1954 seemed to be complacent and in essence was little more than uprating F2 cars. Alberto Ascari, who had enjoyed enormous success with Ferrari during 1952-3, was disturbed by rumours of what Mercedes-Benz was planning and when he squared his information against what he knew Ferrari had in mind, he was not convinced that staying with Ferrari was a bright idea. On the other hand, Lancia was thinking big and had Jano. So it was that Lancia was able to welcome one of the greatest of all drivers, and with Ascari came Luigi Villoresi, his close friend and mentor.

Jano's F1 design, the D50, had a d.o.h.c. V-8 engine of 2489cc (73.6 × 73.1 mm) which was angled in the chassis so that the drive ran diagonally across the cockpit via drop gears to a 5-speed gearbox mounted in unit with the final drive. Output was quoted as 260 bhp and it was soon clear that the Lancia D50 was as powerful as anything on the grid and, at 620 kg, among the lightest cars of its time.

More significantly, the engine was a stressed member of the space-frame. This was a feature which broke new ground in racing car design, although, as is the nature of things, more attention focused on the fuel tanks, which were carried in sponsons between the wheels. Front suspension was by double wishbones and a thin transverse leaf spring, with the upper wishbones having a rocker arm extension operating on inboard telescopic

dampers. Another transverse leaf spring suspended the de Dion rear axle.

Although Ascari first tested a D50 as early as January 1954, Jano was not satisfied and a lengthy development programme was undertaken, so that when the car appeared it would be right, and, in the meantime, Lancia instigated a crash programme of sports car racing using the 3.3-litre D24 version of its 1953 series, for it had signed up the cream of Italian driving talent and had to keep it gainfully employed. It turned out to be not a bad season for a last-minute programme and saw Lancia runner-up to Ferrari in the WSCC.

Finally, in the Spanish GP, the last F1 race of 1954, two Lancias appeared for Ascari and Villoresi. Some indication of the sort of development Jano had been undertaking can be inferred by the fact that in practice one car appeared with an engine with cylinder dimensions of 74 × 72 mm.

Ascari put his car on pole, a full second ahead of Fangio's Mercedes-Benz, and he led from the third lap. Villoresi, starting from fifth on the grid, was less lucky, for his race lasted only a lap before he retired with brake failure. After nine laps Ascari called in at the pits to complain of clutch slip. It could not be cured and he retired.

It had not been a dream start, but it was a promising one. For 1955 Ascari and Villoresi were joined by the rising star Eugenio Castellotti, and the team's first race was the Argentine GP, where Ascari qualified third and led laps 11 to 21 when he spun and crashed. His team-mates did not finish.

In the Gran Premio del Valentino at Turin in late March, the three Lancias faced most of the serious runners with the exception of Mercedes-Benz. Ascari set pole and won, with Villoresi and Castellotti third and fourth behind Roberto Mieres' Maserati. Ascari led the Pau GP as well until, after 90 of the 110 laps, he had to pit with a split fuel tank. So he had to be content with fifth, while Castellotti was second and Villoresi fourth. Ascari won the Naples GP, with Villoresi third behind Luigi Musso's Maserati. The European tally read: three races, two wins and a third victory lost by a silly fault, eight starts, eight finishes, and all in the top five. Lancia was beginning to flex its muscles and looking as though it would be a major force in 1955.

For the first European WC event, Monaco, the usual complement of drivers was enhanced by the veteran Louis Chiron, who had been one of the originators of the race. In practice, Ascari was between the Mercedes-Benz W196s of Fangio and Moss on the front row of the grid, with a time equal to Fangio's. The two Mercedes went

Alberto Ascari with the Lancia D50 on its debut in the 1954 Spanish Grand Prix. He retired because of a slipping clutch. (Geoffrey Goddard)

into the lead and Ascari found himself having to worry about the pace of young Castellotti. At just before half-distance Fangio retired with transmission troubles and Moss led Ascari by a minute.

On lap 80 of 100, Moss' engine burst and, as he slowed, Ascari effectively took the lead, for he headed the remaining runners. Before he could actually overtake Moss on the road, however, he overshot the chicane and his car plunged into the harbour. Ascari disappeared under the water, but was soon seen swimming back to safety. This drama overshadowed everything else, including the fact that Castellotti was second and Villoresi fifth.

Four days later Ascari, apparently recovered from his ducking, happened to call in at Monza, where Castellotti was testing his Ferrari 750 Monza. Of course *il maestro* could drive it. Ascari borrowed a crash helmet and set off for a routine run wearing his everyday suit. He crashed and was killed.

Ascari was the greatest of all post-war Italian drivers and perhaps the most undervalued of all World Champions (he made everything look too easy for his own reputation) and his death devastated Italy. All sorts of explanations were forwarded for his death, a workman had crossed the track, believing it to be clear, his tie had blown up in front of his eyes, he was not wearing his

'lucky' blue helmet, but the most reasonable explanation is that a rear tyre let go on a car which was anyway notoriously difficult to handle.

Whatever the cause, Ascari was dead. Lancia entered the Belgian GP with three cars for Villoresi, Castellotti and Piero Valenzano; then decided its heart was not in it and would withdraw from the sport. Villoresi felt the same and announced his retirement and although he later reconsidered and turned out for a few more races, his career really ended when his protégé died. Castellotti took the view that it was Lancia's patriotic duty to beat the Germans and so a single car finally showed up for him at Spa and that was ostensibly a private entry. Eugenio performed well, qualifying on pole half a second ahead of Fangio's Mercedes, and was running third when, just before half-distance, he had to retire with gearbox trouble.

In the background there were other movements. Lancia had been brought to the brink of bankruptcy and one of the factors had been its competition programme, which, of course, received a disproportionate amount of blame. While economists and financiers worked to make sense of the situation, the Lancia family sold its shares to a group of industrialists.

Enzo Ferrari, sensing an opportune moment,

declared he could no longer continue to uphold Italian honour, for to do so would ruin him. His ploy worked and the Italian industry rallied round. Not only did Fiat guarantee a five-year subsidy of £28,000 pa, but the new owners of Lancia passed over six of the seven Lancia D50s, all the spares and castings, the transporters, and Jano. Not only had Ferrari secured his future, but he had in his possession the very cars for which Ascari and Villoresi had left Ferrari to drive. It was a scenario which could not have been played out in any other country.

Under the banner of Scuderia Ferrari, cars were entered in the Italian GP for Farina and Villoresi (the Scuderia's best drivers had Ferraris), but while they prac-tised reasonably well, they ate up their Englebert tyres (Lancia used Pirellis) on the concrete bankings and they were withdrawn.

Two cars turned up for the 1955 Oulton Park Gold Cup and Mike Hawthorn used one to set pole and arrive at the flag only a few seconds behind Moss' works Maserati 250F. Castellotti encountered problems in practice, but managed to finish seventh.

That was really the model's last appearance, for the following year the cars were modified and raced as Lancia-Ferraris. Luckily, Gianni Lancia retained a D50 and this can be seen occasionally on demonstration runs.

LANCIA-FERRARI

When the Lancia D50 project was handed over to the Scuderia Ferrari its designer, Vittorio Jano, joined Ferrari as a consultant. After the Scuderia ran the car in its original form at the end of 1955, Jano set to work with Ferrari's other engineers to modify the car for 1956.

The engine underwent some significant alterations; coil valve springs and direct-acting camshafts replaced original hairpin springs and cam followers. A new block was designed, extensive work was undertaken on the porting, power increased from 260 bhp to 272 bhp and, for some unfathomable reason, the engine ceased being a stressed member of the frame.

Jano's original concept called for the fuel to be stored in sponsons mounted on tubular outriggers to maintain an even balance, and neutral handling, as it was consum-ed. This is the thinking behind today's centrally-mounted fuel tanks, but under Ferrari the fuel was moved from the side sponsons to tanks in the tail, their traditonal loca-tion. The vestiges of the original sponsons were retained, however, except they were hollow and the tops were faired into the main body as an aerodynamic aid.

Ferrari's driver line-up for 1956 was led by the three-times World Champion Juan Fangio with support from four promising youngsters, Peter Collins, Eugenio Castellotti, Luigi Musso and Olivier Gendebien. Musso and Fangio shared a car to win the Argentine GP and two weeks later Fangio won the non-Championship Buenos Aires GP. At Syracuse in April, Fangio led home Musso and Collins in a demonstration of superiority, but a shock was awaiting the team at the International Trophy at Silverstone. Two cars were entered, for Fangio and Collins, but first Mike Hawthorn's B.R.M. led until retir-ing, and then Stirling Moss in the new Vanwall took the lead to win. Both Lancia-Ferraris were out by one third distance.

In the second WC round, Monaco, Moss and Maserati led from flag to flag and Fangio bent his car try-ing to catch him. He then took over Collins' car and brought it home second. Musso and Gendebien both missed the Belgian GP, while entries were made for local drivers, Paul Frère and André Pilette. After Moss retired with a lost wheel and Fangio went out with transmission failure, both before one-third distance, Collins and Frère stepped into the breach to record a 1-2.

Collins won again in France, at Reims, where Fangio was delayed when a fuel line split, and Castellotti, apparently driving under orders, came second only three-tenths of a second behind. It was clear that the Lancia-Ferrari was the class of the field and Ferrari had chosen his young drivers well, although Harry Schell's Vanwall had run with them, a straw in the wind. From the French GP onwards the cars had new engines with the old 73.6×73.1 mm cylinder dimensions (2489cc) giving way to 76×68.5 mm (2490cc), which brought a small increase in power.

Fangio won the next two races, the British and Ger-man GPs, but the British victory was somewhat fortunate in that Moss' Maserati retired with the race firmly under control and Fangio's own car was ill-handling. Fangio was not having a happy time at Ferrari, which, after two years with Mercedes-Benz, must have been a shock to the system. He did not appreciate the intrigues of the Scuderia, believed his car was being sabotaged, and was diagnosed by a specialist as suffering from severe and debilitating anxiety. He requested a mechanic with sole responsibility for his car, but this was refused.

The Lancia-Ferrari with streamlined body tried in practice for the 1956 French Grand Prix. (LAT)

Peter Collins with the Lancia-Ferrari in the 1956 British Grand Prix at Silverstone. He retired this car, but took over from de Portago to finish second. (Geoffrey Goddard)

At the start of the Italian GP, the final World Championship round, the Lancia-Ferraris were in trouble with their tyres, a repeat of the previous year. Their Englebert rubber simply could not withstand the cornering forces imposed by Monza's banking and Musso, Castellotti and de Portago all had lucky escapes after blow-outs at high speed.

There was already a question mark over Ferrari's choice of tyres following both the previous year's race and Ascari's fatal crash at Monza. Then, in the 1957 Mille Miglia, 'Fon' de Portago was to die after another high-speed blow-out and that led to a protracted prosecution against Ferrari for alleged negligence in fitting inappropriate tyres. It took Ferrari four and a half years to clear his name and, by the time he did so, his Scuderia was once again on top of the world, a happy coincidence of fortune.

While Moss led the Italian GP, Fangio had to retire with a steering problem. The position at the top of the Championship table was so close that if Peter Collins did no more than maintain his third place then the title would be his. Suddenly Collins came into the pits and handed over his car to his team-leader. It was an act of sportsmanship without parallel in motor racing and Fangio went on to take second place and his fourth title. He immediately joined Maserati.

For 1957 there were further changes to the engine, which was now a notably 'over-square' unit with cylinder dimensions of 80×62 mm (2499cc) in which form it gave a claimed 285 bhp. This modification was the first exercise undertaken by a new recruit to the design staff, Carlo Chiti.

At the Argentine GP a new chassis appeared which followed Lancia practice, but had single large-diameter tubes in place of the smaller twin-tubes of the original and the bracing around the cockpit was completely changed. One of the cars had new front suspension by unequal-length wishbones and coil springs, and although this arrangement became usual once the European season started, occasionally cars appeared with the older set-up. The most obvious external difference was the removal of the dummy sponsons, which left the exhaust pipes exposed, so now the cars bore little external resemblance to their Lancia forebears and Ferrari signalled the changes by calling the car the Tipo 801. In the meantime work went ahead on a new series of V-6 engines.

1957 was not a successful year for Lancia-Ferrari, since the Tipo 801 was no improvement and the opposition had made strides. Most improved was Vanwall, and in Stirling Moss, Tony Brooks and Stuart Lewis-Evans it had one of the strongest driver line-ups ever assembled

by one team. Maserati had made advances, too, and the inclusion of Fangio was the deciding factor, for his genius was enough to alter the whole balance of the field.

Ferrari welcomed back Mike Hawthorn, a driver who could be brilliant on his day, but one whose performances were not consistent. The team suffered an early blow when Eugenio Castellotti was killed during testing at Modena. Castellotti had been the natural heir to the tradition of great Italian drivers and his loss was a huge blow to Italy.

In the opening races works Maseratis dominated both the Argentine GP and the non-Championship Buenos Aires GP. Back in Europe Collins and Musso scored a Lancia-Ferrari 1-2 at Syracuse, but only after Moss' Vanwall lost a secure lead while having a fuel pipe fixed. Collins, Hawthorn and Musso filled the first three places at Naples, but both Maserati and Vanwall were absent and the rest of the field was notable chiefly for the number of obscure cars which ran.

Among the obscure cars were the three Ferraris. Hawthorn's car had a 4-in longer wheelbase and *Super-Squalo* front suspension, Collins had a swing-axle independent rear layout, and Musso was giving the Formula 2 V-6 'Dino' its first race. Leaving aside the Dino, for that is another matter altogether, it was Ferrari's ability to constantly cobble together spares bin specials which characterized the team. So much of the chassis development was on a 'suck it and see' basis, whereas scientific designers such as Chapman aimed to get it right on the drawing board and thereafter make only small modifications.

The Lancia-Ferraris appeared to be at home at Monaco and after four laps Collins and Hawthorn were close behind the leader, Moss, when Stirling had braking problems at the chicane and rammed the barricades hard, scattering the telegraph poles which were acting as a safety device. It ended the race for the first three men, and Fangio sailed through to win with Brooks' Vanwall second.

In the French GP at Rouen, Fangio was in brilliant form and while Collins, Musso and Hawthorn followed him home, the maestro would probably have won had he been on roller skates. Musso scored a fine win the following week at Reims. This is often dismissed as a mere 'non-Championship' win, yet it was on a Championship circuit and over a full Championship distance. Musso (and Lancia-Ferrari) deserves as much credit for this win as for a WC race. It might also be remembered that he drove the oldest car in the team, one of the 1956 chassis.

Vanwall (Moss/Brooks) won the British GP, and Fangio turned in his legendary performance to win the German GP, after Hawthorn and Collins appeared to

1957 proved a dismal year for the Ferrari team and little success was gained by the modified Lancia-Ferraris. Here Luigi Musso is seen on his way to a rare victory in the non-Championship Reims Grand Prix.

have the race in the bag. Moss' Vanwall won the GPs of Pescara and Italy and Behra (Maserati) won in Casablanca. Some races had been cancelled due to an oil crisis in the wake of the Suez adventure, and so Pescara had been included in the Championship. Ferrari had intended not to go to Pescara due to legal wranglings which stemmed from de Portago's crash in the Mille Miglia. Finally the Scuderia relented and entered a single car for Musso, who held second to Moss between laps two and nine, but who retired with a cracked oil tank.

In view of previous tyre troubles, confined to Ferrari's Engleberts, and the continuing legal dispute, the Italian GP at Monza was run over the road circuit only. This accommodation was of little help to the Scuderia, and while new recruit von Trips finished third to Moss and Fangio, he was two laps down.

With the exception of Reims, races in 1957 were basically disputed between Vanwall and Maserati, and in an effort to stay in touch, the Lancia-Ferraris became over-stretched and, hence, less reliable. By the end of the season, the Lancia-Ferrari challenge was fading as most

of the Suderia's effort went into the new V-6 Dino cars, and towards the end of the year Dinos began to make their first F1 appearances in preparation for 1958.

Since the rules for the new season required cars to run on Av-gas, and not a 'free' mixture, it was decided not to undertake the extensive work to convert the V-8 to the new fuel, but to concentrate on the V-6. In the last race of 1957, the non-Championship Moroccan GP, Collins and Hawthorn both had Dinos.

The Lancia-Ferraris were therefore seen no more and, as though they were an embarrassing reminder of the way in which they had saved Ferrari when it had lost its way, they were sawn up and cannibalized. It was as though they were bastards in the family, a reminder of old indiscretions, cars which did not fit the myth Ferrari had woven around himself with the collusion of unquestioning hacks. They deserved better treatment, but fortunately Lancia had kept a D50, otherwise today we would have no remaining example of Vittorio Jano's great design.

LANCIA-MARINO

This obscure car made only one appearance in an F1 race, the 1957 Naples GP. It used Lancia Aurelia components and, driven by Marino Brandoli, it qualified tenth in a field of 15, albeit 26 seconds off the pace. It retired after nine laps with a burst water hose.

LANCIA-NARDI

Enrico Nardi had been a successful pre-war special builder and he not only played a part in the construction of the Auto Avio 815s (the first cars built by Enzo Ferrari after he severed links with Alfa Romeo) but he was a nominated driver on the cars' first competition appearance in the 1940 Mille Miglia. After the war he set up his own business making tuning accessories, steering wheels and sports cars, usually using Fiat components. Nardi's ideas were often in advance of other small Italian makers, but he rarely developed his ideas.

In 1952 he showed a new F2 car which not only used Lancia components but had some assistance from the company. The most startling thing about the design was that it was a rear-engined space-frame. The tubes of the frame were much larger than necessary and the bare frame weighed 109 lb.

The engine was a tuned 1991cc (72×81.5 mm) V-6 Lancia Aurelia with larger inlet valves and a higher compression ratio and this eventually produced a *claimed* 130 bhp and drove directly to a standard Aurelia gearbox/final drive unit which, on the original car, was mounted at the rear. Aurelia suspension was used, sliding pillars at the front and irs with a transverse leaf spring, the rear drum brakes were mounted inboard, while the front brakes had the drums on the *outside* of the centre-lock disc wheels. The car was tested in September 1952, was found to be underpowered, and so never ran in a race.

The chassis of the Lancia-Nardi with rear-mounted V-6 Lancia Aurelia engine.

LOLA

Eric Broadley had shared the driving of some clubbie specials when, fired by ambition, he decided to tackle Lotus in the hotly contested 1100cc sports car class. Trained as a civil engineer, he had a sound grasp of stress engineering, but he also nurtured the dream of becoming World Champion.

Built in a lock-up, the Lola-Climax was a superbly made little car and immediately established itself as the cream of the field with Broadley, no ace, becoming the first sports car driver to lap Brands Hatch in under a minute in the Lola's first race meeting.

Orders quickly followed and Broadley became a constructor. His second serious design, a front-engined FJ model, sold healthily but never won a race mainly due to the fact that Lotus had both the best engines and drivers. A third car, a rear-engined single-seater, bristled with new ideas, but was unsuccessful in both the market place and on the track. It began to seem that Lola was a star which would quickly burn out.

In the days before sponsorship was permitted in Europe, some companies had by-passed the rule by entering teams under their own name, and among them was the Yeoman Credit finance house. In 1961 and 1962 (in which year it became known as Bowmaker Racing), its racing operation was managed by Reg Parnell (Racing) and for 1962 it commissioned Eric Broadley to design an F1 car for its exclusive use, making it in effect the Lola works team. That decision probably kept Lola alive.

While the 1962 car was the first F1 Lola, in 1961

Hugh Dibley had put a 1340cc Ford engine into his Lola Mk 3 FJ car and ran it in the Lewis-Evans Trophy at Brands Hatch, a race for those who had not gone to the US GP. There he gave a fairly good account of himself, qualifying sixth from 13 starters and running strongly until a wheel bearing seized.

Broadley's Lola Mk 4 was fairly conventional: a compact space-frame with suspension front and rear by coil springs, wishbones and radius arms. The first car made had a 4-cylinder Coventry Climax FPF engine, as the new team had to wait its turn to take delivery of its Climax FWMV V-8 units, and this was entered for John Surtees in the early races of 1962, while his team-mate, Roy Salvadori, had the use of a Cooper T56-FPF until his Lola was ready.

Surtees debuted the car in the non-Championship Brussels GP, where he finished fifth in heat one but retired with engine troubles in heat two. In the Lombank Trophy at Snetterton he started from fourth on the grid, fastest of the 4-cylinder brigade, and he was lying fourth when his engine overheated.

Salvadori received his car in time for the Easter Monday Goodwood Meeting. In the Lavant Cup for 4-cylinder F1 cars, Surtees had just taken the lead when he tangled with a back-marker and crashed, while Salvadori overcame a fluffed start to finish second to McLaren's Cooper. In the feature event, the Richmond Trophy, Surtees had a V-8 engine in the back of a new chassis, but suffered a sticking throttle which eventually caused his retirement.

John Surtees on his way to second place with his Bowmaker Racing Lola-Climax in the 1962 British Grand Prix at Aintree. (David Phipps)

That race will always be remembered as the one which saw the end of Stirling Moss' career and the story is often told how Moss, after a long pit stop, went out again and broke the lap record because he never gave up. Less well remembered is that Surtees did exactly the same, and at the end of the day he and Moss shared fastest lap. The Lola was developing into a competitive car.

At the Aintree 200 Surtees was in third place on the grid with a lap time equal to Graham Hill in second and he ran second in the race until valve trouble eliminated him. He was third again on the grid for the International Trophy at Silverstone and finished third in the race, a performance overshadowed by Hill's great charge, which saw him snatch victory form Clark on the last corner.

Then came the Championship opener at Zandvoort and Surtees confirmed the Lola's potential by taking pole, but early in the race, when fourth, a wishbone broke and he crashed. Salvadori, who had at last got a V-8, was withdrawn. Monaco saw both men qualify below mid-field and while Salvadori retired with suspension trouble, Surtees soldiered on to take fourth, but a lap down on McLaren's Cooper.

Surtees had been expressing the opinion that the chassis was flexing, but he was still a new boy in car racing, so his opinions did not carry the weight they would do later. Besides, there was that pole position at Zandvoort which suggested that the car could not be all bad.

On 11 July there were two F1 races in Britain; most of the serious runners turned up at Mallory Park for the 2000 Guineas' race while the rest were at Crystal Palace. At Mallory Park Surtees was fourth on the grid behind Clark, Brabham and Hill, but at the start he simply sailed away into the distance to win Lola's first F1 race. At Crystal Palace Salvadori, who was not terribly happy in the 1½-litre formula and who would retire from single-seater racing at the end of the year, finished second behind Ireland's Lotus-B.R.M. and ahead of McLaren's Cooper.

In the light of that day's work, Surtees' comments about a flexing chassis were even less well received, but at the Belgium GP, where he could qualify no higher than 11th, a curious thing happened in the pits. One of the car's corners was jacked up and none of the other wheels moved — the frame had flexed to take up the slack! Some extra tubes were hurriedly welded into place and Surtees eventually came home fifth, albeit two laps down.

Once the problem had been highlighted, modifications were made, and in mid-season the team improved. In the non-Championship Reims GP Surtees led a full WC field until, at half-distance, he retired with a broken

valve, while Salvadori came home sixth. In the French GP Surtees qualified fifth and ended in the same slot, although two laps down because of an unhealthy engine. By this time Salvadori was an also-ran, doing justice neither to his car nor to his reputation.

In the British GP at Aintree Surtees qualified second and finished second, to Clark. Another second place came at the Nürburgring, this time to Hill's B.R.M. and only 2.5 seconds behind in a very wet race. It seemed that in the hands of John Surtees, the Lola was a top-rate car and would finish its maiden season with a win, but from that point on there was a downward slide.

With a new chassis, designated Mk 4A, Surtees took pole in the Kanonloppet at Karlskoga and led a second-string field until retiring with a broken valve spring. Salvadori finished second to Masten Gregory's Lotus 24, but, more significantly, only two-tenths of a second ahead of Jo Bonnier's 4-cylinder Porsche. In the Danish GP Surtees could qualify only third, behind Brabham and Masten Gregory and retired with a broken drop arm.

In the final races of the year, Surtees slipped further down the field and, apart from taking third place in the Rand GP, did not finish another race. It was the old story of a team running out of money, and at the end of the season Bowmaker was in a crisis of its own and withdrew from motor racing. Surtees, the man who gave Lola its brightest moments in 1962, was snapped up by Ferrari.

One of the cars was sold to the ex-motorcycle racer Bob Anderson, who struggled on a shoe-string and mainly concentrated on non-Championship events where he could attract decent starting money and keep his little team going. He finished third in the Imola GP and fourth at Syracuse, but in the Rome GP won against a fairly big field of F1 make-weights to score Lola's second F1 victory. When Anderson entered the odd race where he faced serious runners he was out of his depth (he later developed into a Grand Prix racer who really deserved a works drive) and would finish way down the field.

Reg Parnell (Racing) retained two Lolas for 1963 and entered them alongside the team's Lotus 24, but the cars which had threatened to win in 1962 were now also-rans. Chris Amon was the main driver, but he was then a 19 year old learning his craft, and not only did the car need development but the team needed more money. Amon struggled, and his best result, fourth in the non-Championship Austrian GP, was not even recognized, for he suffered loss of oil pressure and finished too far behind to be classified.

In World Championship races he managed a couple of sevenths, in the French and British races, but on both occasions he was at least two laps down. His season ended at the Italian GP, where he crashed.

By 1963 the Lolas were being raced under the banner of Reg Parnell Racing. This is Chris Amon in the British Grand Prix in which he finished seventh. (Nigel Snowdon)

Maurice Trintignant, Mike Hailwood, Masten Gregory and Lucien Bianchi also drove Lolas in 1963, but all of them struggled, and only Hailwood managed to finish and on both occasions he was several laps down.

Had there been the money to do the job properly, it is likely Surtees could have ended Lola's first F1 season with a World Championship win. Having been introduced, however, Surtees and Broadley later collaborated on a number of projects. His brush with F1 had taught Broadley a lesson and it was a long time before the marque would again compete in the formula.

LOTUS

The story of Lotus and Colin Chapman is virtually the story of post-war British motor racing. Chapman, indeed, did more than any other individual to make Britain the major motor racing nation, for apart from the brilliance of his own designs he attracted dozens of bright talents who went on to make their mark on their own account. They ranged from designers to welders and fabricators who were inspired by his optimism and by the way he made things happen against all odds.

From its earliest days, Lotus did not attract admirers, it attracted *fans*, and because Chapman had shown what could be done, others were fired to follow. They formed the backbone of the British motor racing industry whether they founded great firms such as Cosworth or small operations making chassis frames and wishbones.

By the time the first Lotus single-seater with a Lotus badge appeared, in 1957, Chapman had been building cars for less than ten years, beginning with Austin Seven specials, graduating to marketing kit cars, and then redefining design parameters for small capacity sports cars. It seemed that anything Chapman touched turned to gold, and when he announced he was entering the new

1½-litre F2 it was confidently expected by all the Lotus fans that his advance would be irresistible, but it took him three years to find his way in single-seaters.

First, though, we should make the point that Chapman's first single-seater was not the Lotus Mk 12 but a much earlier car with the original designation 'Lotus Mk 7', which is dealt with under the entry 'Clairmonte'. Even before the first single-seater to bear the Lotus name had appeared, Tony Vandervell had taken an inspired gamble and at the end of 1955 commissioned Chapman to design the chassis for the Vanwall.

The 1956 Motor Show at Earls Court saw the first public appearance of a single-seater Lotus, the Mk 12. Actually that 'prototype' was really only a show car, for the engine and gearbox were mock-ups and the frame had been tacked together and painted.

It had a light space-frame, with coil spring and double wishbone front suspension based on the geometry of the swing axles which Chapman had previously favoured, and the front arms of the top wishbones were joined to act as an anti-roll bar. At first, rear suspension was by a de Dion axle, sprung on coil springs and located by single trailing arms and a central pivot. Testing, however, showed up deficiencies in this layout and although the type made its early racing appearances with a de Dion rear end, this was soon changed to an independent layout featuring the Chapman strut, a combination of a single trailing arm, a non-splined drive-shaft and the coil spring and damper assembly all converging on to a single casting.

The Coventry Climax FPF engine was bolted rigidly into the frame, making it a semi-stressed member. In order to keep the prop-shaft as low as possible, Harry Munday (then Technical Editor of *The Autocar*) and Richard Ansdale, an ex-B.R.M. designer, collaborated with Chapman to design a gearbox which mated directly to a hypoid crown wheel and pinion and a ZF limited slip differential. ZF also cut the gear ratios and later made the complete unit for Lotus.

A drop of five inches in the drive line was achieved with this transmission, which had a motorcycle-style up and down change in a series of 'Zs'. At first the unit gave endless trouble and was soon known as the Lotus 'queerbox', the first of several to carry the name, but eventually a student who helped out in his vacations was taken on full-time to develop the gearbox; among the changes he made were a spiral-bevel crown wheel and pinion and eventually the transmission became quite reliable. The student's name was Keith Duckworth and his boss at the works was a mechanic-cum-driver called Graham Hill.

Girling disc brakes were fitted all round, inboard at the rear and bolt-on alloy disc wheels, with a distinctive 'wobbly web' pattern, replaced the centre-lock wire wheels which Lotus had previously favoured. Since the

W. H. Allen's Lotus 12 leads Chris Bristow's Hume-Cooper in the 1959 British Empire Trophy at Oulton Park, a Formula 2 race. (T. C. March)

car weighed less than 700 lb, it was assumed, rightly, that tyre wear would be low.

Frank Costin has often been credited with the design of the slim bodywork, but it was the result of a sketch by Chapman, drawing on his knowledge of Costin's work, and the eye experience of Charlie Williams of William & Pritchard, the Edmonton bodyshop which made so many Lotus shells.

Pete Ross and 'Mac' Mackintosh, who had designed the space-frame for the Lotus Mk 8 sports-racer, and Frank Costin, who had designed its body, had urged Chapman to consider a rear-engined car, and a monocoque to boot. Chapman resisted the latter idea because he felt that cars could not be built in quantity using monocoque construction, and as for the idea that they should be rear-engined the retort was 'What would John Cooper think!'

Thus the Mk 12 had to be front-engined and the enthusiastic little team accepted the boss' decision and in their imaginations cast Lotus in the role of Mercedes-Benz to Cooper's Auto Union. Nobody could have conceived that Lotus would win more Grands Prix than Mercedes-Benz and Auto Union combined.

Mk 12s did not often appear in 1957 and when they did they had to concede best to the better-driven Coopers. They might have been more successful if the gearbox had not played up, if drive-shafts had not broken and if the chassis had not cracked so often. Apart from a second and a third in minor races, the only notable result was Cliff Allison's second place in the Oulton Park Gold Cup, but that was virtually a British national event.

Chapman at the time was always trying to make his cars as light as possible and took the view that it really did not matter if they crossed the finishing line and then fell apart. Too often they started to fall apart before the finish (Lotus always took welding equipment to the races) and this gave them a reputation for fragility which stuck to the marque long after if was justified.

During 1957, Coventry Climax had made a 1960cc version of the FPF engine and, with this installed in the back of their Coopers, Jack Brabham and Roy Salvadori had taken in a few World Championship events. Then, in January 1958, Stirling Moss in Rob Walker's Cooper scored an extraordinary win in the Argentine GP. Chapman had been against moving up to F1, but his drivers were egging him to have a go and if there was any doubt left in his mind, the matter was settled by Cooper's win. The blacksmiths could not beat the scientist! Despite the 12's general unreliability, it was upgraded to F1.

Lotus' World Championship debut was at Monaco on 18 May, 1958, and it was a modest start to its Grand Prix career. Earlier, Allison and Hill had given some promising performances in non-Championship races, but at Monaco there were three Coopers among the top five qualifiers – and two Lotuses among the last four. At least, however, they made the grid and while Hill retired just after half-distance with gearbox trouble, Allison was classified sixth, and last, 13 laps down from Trintignant's winning Cooper.

Allison took another sixth at Zandvoort using a 2.2-litre engine after both cars qualified down the grid and, again, Hill's 2-litre car retired just after half-

Graham Hill's Lotus 16-Climax in the 1959 British Grand Prix. He finished well down the field. (T. C. March)

distance, this time with engine trouble. The two drivers had the same cars for Spa and Hill's retired with engine trouble just before the half-way mark while Allison survived to finish fourth. Had the race been one more lap he might have won, for none of the cars ahead of him was fit enough to have completed it.

Although Chapman had not been keen to get into F1 so soon, once he had made the commitment he tackled it in his usual full-blooded manner, and from the beginning of the year had been working on a new design. This was to be another front-engined car for he, like most other designers, had shrugged off Cooper's performances as a fluke. The Cooper with its curved tubes and crude suspension should not work and even though Coopers won the first two WC races of 1958, because they *should* not have done, they *could* not have done.

When it appeared, the Lotus 16 was immediately nicknamed the 'Mini-Vanwall' and its body was credited to Frank Costin, but, in fact, it was another collaboration beween Chapman and Charlie Williams. The 16's general layout followed that of the 12, but its frame was wider and stiffer and the engine was not only canted 62 degrees on to its side to gain a low bonnet height but it was slightly off-set from the centre to take the drive-line to the left-hand side of the driver and then to the latest version of the 'queerbox', which was off-set 8-in to the left of the differential (it had been 5-in on the 12). During the life of the 16, the position of the engine changed several times and, indeed, after initial testing, it first raced with the FPF canted over to a less radical 17 degrees. Suspension remained as before, except that the radius arms to the Chapman strut had been lengthened.

Whatever else the 16 was or was not, it was stunning to behold: the smallest, lightest, smoothest, and altogether most advanced front-engined F1/2 car ever. Unfortunately, that was a little like saying it was the most advanced biplane fighter ever made. Further, although it was theoretically a wonderful piece of design, it did have several practical drawbacks.

When Frank Costin designed the body for the Vanwall he carefully arranged ducts to keep the drivers reasonably cool in an almost enclosed cockpit, but the 16 had only an overall-ish Costin shape and none of his clever detailing, so the drivers often finished a race done medium rare. Then Chapman's obsession with ultimate lightness was counter-productive, the body shell often cracked and crazed and the record for a number of fractures appearing in a frame after a single race appears to have been 14!

The first 16 appeared during the Reims weekend of 1958, driven by Cliff Allison in the F2 race in which it retired. Later that day, Graham Hill gave the type its F1

debut and he too failed to finish. For the British GP, Allison had his 2.2-litre 12, while Hill and Alan Stacey both had 16s. Allison qualified quite respectably, in fifth place and over 2.5 seconds quicker than Hill's smaller-engined 16, but all three retired, the 12 with loss of oil pressure, the 16s both with overheating.

Allison had a 1.9-litre 16 for the German GP and ran as high as second after most of the small field had retired (there were only 12 F1 starters and the field was made up to strength by F2 cars). Then his radiator split, which ruined his race, but still he was classified fifth and last, two laps down. On the road, however, Allison came in tenth and had five F2 cars, led by McLaren's Cooper, ahead of him and all on the same lap as the winner.

During practice for the Portuguese GP, Allison crashed and destroyed his 16 and thereafter returned to his 12, while Hill kept his 16, now with a 2.2-litre engine. Both continued to be also-rans and while a power dis-advantage could be used as an excuse in comparison with the Vanwalls and Ferraris, the Coopers with the same engine were always quicker and more reliable.

Hill and Allison did manage, however, to finish the Italian GP in fifth and sixth places following the dis-qualification of the fourth-placed Maserati, but were, respectively, eight and nine laps adrift. It had not been a marvellous season, and even the F2 12s which had reached private hands fared little better, either in reliability or results

Cliff Allison's driving had impressed Enzo Ferrari, who offered him a contract for 1959. Innes Ireland moved up from the sports car team to be the number two driver to Hill, and Stacey remained number three.

For 1959 Coventry Climax had its new 2495cc FPF engine, which gave around 240 bhp, less than the best opposition but enough to be exploited by lightweight cars such as Cooper and Lotus. There were a number of detail changes to the 16, the front anti-roll bar was switched to the trailing edge of the top wishbone and Len Terry, who had joined Lotus as Chapman's assistant, added a lower wishbone to the rear suspension. Terry also added a new bulkhead at the front of the cockpit and to save the drivers from cooking, the exhaust pipe, originally faired into the body shell, was put out into the airstream.

These changes were an improvement, but not enough. Works or privateer, F1 or F2, the season was a disaster. More often than not the cars retired or, if they survived, finished way down the rankings. There were occasional flashes of promise during practice and quali-fying for races, but frames would crack, the suspension would break, the transmission would fail, and if there was any sheer bad luck floating in the air, it would invariably choose to settle on a Lotus.

In World Championship terms, the team's best and only points-scoring result was Ireland's fourth at Zandvoort and, at the end of the season, Graham Hill left in disgust to join B.R.M. Worse, Coopers dominated F2, most non-Championship F1 races, and carried Jack Brabham to his first World Championship.

Lotus was not only on the ropes in single-seater racing, its sports cars were being beaten in every category, and production of the Elite GT car was progressing painfully and expensively. It was a catalogue of trial and woe which would have destoyed many another small constructor, but Chapman buckled to and within a year took Lotus from the brink of disaster to the forefront of constructors.

At the traditional Boxing Day Meeting at Brands Hatch in 1959 most attention was focused on the first British Formula Junior race with a representative entry. There were new cars from Lola, Gemini, Cooper and Lotus. Any new Lotus was an event, but reaction to this one was sceptical, 'a shoe box with four dustbin lids' was how one correspondent described it.

It was the Lotus 18, Chapman's first rear-engined car, and it appeared that he had made a major blunder for, even with Alan Stacey behind the wheel, it was slow and its progress was not helped by a couple of spins. An Elva won and a Lola was second and both were front-engined cars, just like the successful European FJ cars. In fact its racing engine, made by the new Cosworth company, had blown up and it was using a makeshift unit and the springs were too soft.

The second appearance of the new model, now in Formula 1 form, came in the Argentine GP on 7 February, where (sensation!) Innes Ireland put it in second place on the grid and led the race until all sorts of troubles intervened. He eventually finished sixth with one brake not working and the steering deranged, but suddenly everybody had to take notice of Lotus.

The 18's space-frame was a properly triangulated affair using 18 and 16-gauge tubing with additional bracing from perforated panels around the scuttle and in the tail. A 22-gallon fuel tank was housed over the driver's legs and an additional 9½-gallon tank was behind his seat. Front suspension was by unequal-length wishbones and coil springs, while at the rear were non-splined half-shafts, reverse lower wishbones and twin radius rods. Anti-roll bars were fitted front and rear and the rear discs were mounted on each side of the 'queer-box'.

In a sense, Chapman had made a 'scientific' Cooper and, according to Stirling Moss, it was a much less forgiving car, but, within a more narrow envelope, it had better road holding and traction. Where Chapman really made his advance, and turned the fortunes of Lotus at a stroke, was by making a single model into a whole range of cars. By using different gauges of tubing the 18 would serve for F1, F2 and FJ. Moreover, Lotus had the cream of new talent for its works teams in the lesser formulae.

Thus at Goodwood on 19 March, 1960, in the first British meeting of the year, the Lotus 18 FJ car had its first win in the hands of a young Scot whose name was Jim Clark. That set the pattern for the year and by the end of the season the works Lotus FJ team of Clark, Trevor Taylor and Peter Arundell, with Cosworth engines, had won virtually everything in sight.

There had been over 100 makers of Formula Junior cars at the beginning of 1960 and they used 14 different types of engine, but by the end of the season Lotus, Ford and Cosworth had wiped most of them out. That one season destroyed the embryo racing car industries in every other country and in the long term changed the balance of power in the sport.

National headlines followed the 18's next F1 race, the Richmond Trophy at Goodwood, when Innes Ireland beat Moss' Cooper by nearly three seconds, and in the F2 Lavant Cup beat Moss' Porsche by six seconds. In a burst of media frenzy Ireland was hailed as a new star, while Moss' entrant, Rob Walker, quietly ordered a Lotus. Ireland won the International Trophy at Silverstone as well, but at Monaco Moss had his 18. In fact he also had his old Cooper and after trying both in practice, he elected to drive the Lotus, which he had put on pole. He won, but along the way had had to pit to have a plug lead replaced and had also felt severe vibration behind him – the engine mounts had broken and the front of the engine was being held on by the water hose!

Still Stirling Moss and Rob Walker gave Lotus its first WC win, just as they had opened the score for Cooper two years before. Moss and Ireland sat on the front row for the Dutch GP with Brabham in-between. Brabham led from Moss and Ireland, but on lap 17 one of his rear wheels dislodged some of the concrete kerbing and propelled it straight at Moss' car close behind. Since it weighed about 25 lb, it is lucky it only hit one of Stirling's front wheels, but that was enough to shatter the wheel and Moss lost two laps. Brabham won comfortably from Ireland, but Moss, as usual, was the star as he drove back to fourth place to finish on the same lap as Brabham.

Almost unnoticed was Jim Clark making his WC debut. He was not particularly quick in practice and he retired in the race, but it was less than six months before that he had first driven a single-seater, a Gemini FJ car, on Boxing Day.

The season was settling down to be a straight Cooper versus Lotus affair, with the new rear-engined B.R.M. P48s looking stronger all the time, when calamity struck at the Belgian GP. Mike Taylor had bought the prototype 18 and was making his bid in the big time when a weld in the steering column broke in practice and he crashed heavily, breaking his ribs, clavicle and neck. He survived, and later obtained settlement against Lotus, but his hopes of a serious career in racing ended. Also in practice, Moss had a rear stub axle fail and lost a wheel. Among the injuries he sustained were a broken nose, broken ribs and broken legs. Although he made a remarkable recovery, the incident changed the face of the season.

In the race itself the brilliant young Chris Bristow crashed his Cooper and was killed and Lotus' third works driver, Alan Stacey, a personable young man who managed to keep the fact of an artificial leg fairly quiet, was, it is said, struck in the face by a bird and crashed with fatal results. It was a black weekend for motor racing in general and Lotus in particular with the only bright spot being the distant sixth place taken by Clark.

Chapman had a reputation for building his cars as light as possible and in some people's minds lightness equated to weakness. The Lotus 16 frames had cracked frequently, and that weekend at Spa when essential items broke led to a myth that Lotus cars were inherently unsafe and some drivers refused to drive them. It was a reputation which was deserved − for a time. The fact is that after Spa 1960 and at least to the end of the period

under consideration, Lotus suffered no more structural breakages per car per race than any other top-line maker and it is high time the myth was laid to rest.

Brabham won at Spa, and he won too at Reims. Here, while Lotus was off the pace and Clark and Flockhart could finish no higher than fifth and sixth, and Ireland retired, Lotus had three Scotsmen in its team, a unique occasion in F1.

For the British GP, Lotus gave Surtees a drive and he responded by finishing second to Brabham, with Ireland in third place. Without Moss, Lotus was not looking as sharp as it had at the beginning of the year.

Moss was back for the Portuguese GP with a new Lotus 18, this time with a Colotti gearbox which necessitated outboard rear brakes. He was not on the pace, however, and had a troubled race even before a brake snatched and caused him to spin. Trying to get the car started again by going downhill on the pavement led to his disqualification. Surtees, however, added to his growing reputation by leading until leaking fuel covered his brake pedal and his foot slipped at a crucial time. Clark had crashed his car in practice, but it had been repaired and the body held together by masking tape; he took things easy and came in third behind the works Coopers of Brabham and McLaren.

With the Portuguese win Brabham secured his second World Championship. The British teams boycotted the Italian GP because of the Monza bankings and so Ferrari was able to take a win, the last in a WC event for a front-engined car. With the title decided in August, there was little excitement surrounding the US GP at Riverside. In the interim Ireland and Clark scored a 1-2 in the Lombank Trophy at Snetterton against a good field, and Moss

Jim Clark at the wheel of his Team Lotus 18 with patched nose after a practice crash in the 1960 Portuguese Grand Prix. He finished third. (David Phipps)

won the International Gold Cup at Oulton Park, again against a strong entry. At Oulton Park Clark qualified second only to Moss and before he was punted out of the race by a back-marker had set fastest lap. At Riverside Moss and Ireland rounded off Lotus' late season revival by taking first and second.

In one season Lotus had gone from 'Team Shambles' to a major force. It was clear, however, that the winning was likely to stop in 1961, at least until Coventry Climax came up with its promised V-8.

The Lotus 21 was both a logical development of the 18 and also drew on the new Mk 20 FJ car. Out went the old 'shoe box' body and in came a slim, low, slippery shape with the driver seated in a reclining position which was to establish a Lotus house style throughout the 1½-litre formula.

The fuel tank was removed from its dangerous position in the nose and in its place was a low-slung pannier, which helped lower the car's centre of gravity. Front suspension also established Lotus practice for the future since, following Alberto Massimino's work for Maserati in 1948, the coil springs were mounted inboard and activated by rockers from the top wishbone, an arrangement which cleaned up the airflow.

At the rear, an upper transverse link was added and the drive-shafts incorporated Metalastik rubber couplings. The 'queer-box', which wore out at an alarming rate, was replaced by a ZF 5-speed unit and the rear brakes were mounted outboard. The space-frame derived from the Lotus 18, but was wider and heavier, for the FIA had imposed a minimum weight limit of 450 kg for the new formula.

The car was late in making its debut, partly because development of the Lotus 20 FJ car had taken longer than expected (it turned out to be worth the wait) and partly because the 21 had been first designed around the Coventry Climax V-8, and when it was clear this was behind schedule, the rear end of the car had to be re-drawn to accommodate the 4-cylinder FPF engine.

Main drivers for the works F1 team in 1961 were Clark and Ireland, but because Moss was contracted to BP, and Lotus to Esso, Rob Walker was not able to buy a 21, so Stirling had to soldier on with his 18, although from mid-season on he was able to have an interim 18/21. Still, Moss was to turn in two of the greatest drives in history with his obsolete car. Among others to have Lotus 18s for the new season were the U.D.T.-Laystall team, and, after a false start with Emerysons, the Équipe Nationale Belge.

In the early non-Championship races of 1961, 4-cylinder cars had the field to themselves and the wins were shared among Cooper, Lotus and Porsche just as they had been in F2 the previous year, with Clark winning at Pau and Moss taking the Grosser Preis von Wien at Aspern. Then, at the Syracuse GP, the Ferrari 156 appeared and won in the hands of Giancarlo Baghetti on his F1 debut.

This gave everyone something to think about and Ferrari would have finished 1-2-3 at Monaco, except that Moss decided to demonstrate who was the greatest driver of the age, as he took pole and led for most of the race to win by 3.6 seconds from Ginther's Ferrari, which had something like a 20 per cent power advantage. Monaco also saw the debut of the Lotus 21 and Clark was on pole after the first practice session, but crashed. He therefore started from the outside of the front row and led the opening stages until dropping back with various troubles.

In the Dutch GP, the only Grand Prix in history which had no retirements, three Ferraris occupied the front row with the quickest Lotus qualifier, Moss, in fourth place. Ferraris came home first and second with Clark third and 13.2 seconds ahead of Moss in fourth place. With his car uprated to a specification half-way between an 18 and a 21, Moss was in slightly better shape for the Belgian GP, and while his was the fastest Lotus in practice, he was nearly nine seconds off the pace. He was the best Lotus finisher, too, back in eighth and lapped.

From the fast sweeping curves of Spa to the long straights of Reims, where Stirling was again the quickest Lotus in practice after slipstreaming von Trips' Ferrari. As was becoming usual, Clark was the quicker of the two works Lotuses and while he shared the second row with Moss, he had not yet the maestro's foxy ways and was 1.2 seconds slower. Moss was easily the quickest non-Ferrari in the race, but was to retire with brake problems, and while the finish was eventually between Baghetti's Ferrari and Gurney's Porsche, Clark and Ireland came home fourth and fifth.

At Aintree Moss was, in fifth place, the quickest Lotus on the grid and in a race run in very wet conditions, he harried the Ferraris. On lap 24 he spun on sheet water, but pirouetted a couple of times and continued as though nothing had happened. As the rain receded, Moss had a repeat of his Reims brake trouble and had to call it a day. The highest Lotus was Ireland's in tenth place.

Innes took his first 1961 win, however, at Solitude after a near photo-finish with Bonnier's Porsche, but everyone fell under Moss' shadow at the Nürburgring. There he decided to use Dunlop 'high hysteresis' rain tyres whatever the weather. These were softer, and more grippy, than Dunlop's normal 'dry' tyres and for once the Lotus' lack of power came into its own, for Moss knew he could go the whole distance on them, wet or dry. Once again Moss showed his genius and won from the Ferraris of von Trips and Hill with Clark in fourth.

Moss then won the Kanonloppet, the Danish GP and the Modena GP, in every case beating the works Lotuses. In the Italian GP, however, the whole Lotus contingent was out of luck. Moss had a V-8, but elected not to use it, and Ireland handed over his much quicker 21 to the maestro, who might have finished second but for a broken wheel bearing. The race was anyway overshadowed by the accident which befell poor 'Taffy' von Trips. While dicing with Clark for fourth, their cars touched and the Ferrari was launched into the crowd, killing 14 spectators and von Trips, who had been on his way to the world title.

Ireland won the Flugplatzrennen at Zeltweg (Moss was absent) and Moss the International Gold Cup at Oulton Park (Team Lotus absent). Moss had a V-8 for the US GP, but elected to use an FPF, and was still the quickest Lotus. He led too, after Brabham retired, but the engine chosen for its reliability ran its bearings. Ireland came home to win Team Lotus' first WC event, though, of course, Moss had already won four such races for the marque.

Not unreasonably, Innes thought he was secure at Lotus for 1962, but suffered the mortification of discovering he was sacked, and Chapman would not tell him why. It seems that Innes' raffish lifestyle spoke against him and Chapman preferred to deal with the shy young Clark, who sought fewer distractions. Trevor

Taylor was promoted from the Junior team to be No 2 F1 driver. From that decision came perhaps the greatest partnership in racing history, as Chapman increasingly existed to service his star, and two mighty talents merged into one. Clark had been the fastest of the works drivers, but his elevation to team leader gave him a new lease, and he was ready to take on Moss.

Team Lotus went to South Africa for the winter and Clark and Taylor put on a demonstration run in the Rand GP. In the Natal GP Moss arrived and, not having officially practised, started from the back of the grid. Clark won with Moss second, and Stirling set fastest lap. Still, the fact that he was not able to catch Jimmy was significant. Normally his superiority was such that a win would have been expected, even though his engine was not revving properly and Clark had a works car. Jimmy had emerged as the pretender to Stirling's crown.

He appeared to have his hands on it when he, again, beat Moss in the non-WC South African GP. Some claim that with that drive Jimmy became Stirling's master, but Moss was ill and it is a wonder he was able to race at all, let alone come second in an obsolete car.

Moss missed the Cape GP in January 1962, which completed the South African 'Temporada', and apart from the works Porsches and some European privateers, most of the field consisted of local drivers. Clark led and Taylor had to work up past several other drivers, but he eventually took the lead. Jimmy responded and regained the front, but his team-mate sat on his tail. Then Clark's attention slipped and he spun and although there was

In 1961 Moss scored two remarkable Grand Prix victories. Here at the Nürburgring with his rebodied Rob Walker 18 he beat the Ferrari team in the German Grand Prix. (David Phipps)

Jim Clark with the small, compact Lotus 21 is followed by Phil Hill with the, by comparison, lorry-like Ferrari V-6 in the 1961 Dutch Grand Prix. (David Phipps)

only 0.6 second in it at the end, Taylor took his first F1 win. Alas, it was to be his only F1 win.

There was a four-month gap before the next race, the Brussels GP, and there Clark had the first Lotus 24. It resembled the 21, but with a high engine cover to clear the taller Coventry Climax FWMV and the overall layout was refined 21. New cast front uprights replaced the old Triumph units, and there was a new steering system with the track rods mounted level with the rocker arms to clean up the air flow. At the rear, rubber doughnuts replaced the splined half-shafts, and to increase fuel capacity to cope with the thirstier V-8 an additional tank was mounted over the driver's legs.

Clark put it on pole on its debut, but suffered broken valve gear on the first lap of the first of three heats. Both Clark and Taylor had 24s for the Pau GP, where Jimmy was easily quickest in practice, but his gear-change became deranged and Taylor had so many problems that he was 28 laps down at the end. Still, a Lotus won as Maurice Trintignant, driving like a man inspired, led the field (including Clark) from lap 16 in one of Rob Walker's 18s.

On the same day, St George's Day 1962, Stirling Moss had his near-fatal crash at Goodwood in one of U.D.T.-Laystall's Lotus 18s fitted with a V-8 engine. He was never to return to top-class racing. When he crashed he was still the undisputed master, but, at the moment he crashed, Jimmy took over that position. *The king is dead, long live the king!*

The fact they did not race against each other throughout the 1960s gives the supporters of both grist for endless pub debates as to what the outcome might have been if they had. It is as well they did not, because one would have finished up the loser, but, as it is, we can enjoy the memory of their different brands of genius, and make out cases for both, and never actually *know*.

Jimmy dominated the Aintree 200 and demonstrated that Ferrari had no answer, as he was nearly four seconds quicker than either Phil Hill or Baghetti in practice and he dominated, too, the International Trophy at Silverstone until he relaxed at the end and Graham Hill caught him on the last corner and crossed the line, sideways, just ahead, in one of the most dramatic finishes in F1 history.

Both Surtees' Lola and Hill's B.R.M. were quicker in practice at Zandvoort, but Clark led until his clutch began to slip. Victory went to Hill, but almost as impressive was Trevor Taylor in second place. Unfortunately, the promise of that finish was not to be fulfilled, as Taylor suffered a terrible season. By the Dutch GP both Jack Brabham and U.D.T.-Laystall had taken delivery of Lotus 24s, but Chapman always gave his works drivers an edge and had rewritten the designer's handbook. From out of the Lotus transporter came the 25, the first modern Grand Prix car to use monocoque construction.

The principle had been known for 50 years and several competition cars had been built using it, indeed, the Jaguar D-type had a monocoque central section. Rodney Clarke had planned a semi-monocoque Connaught, the all-wood Marcos was a monocoque and it was common in the aircraft industry. It is often said that Chapman drew his inspiration for the 25 from the backbone chassis of the Lotus Elan, which was then in preparation, but Frank Costin tells a different story.

Costin, Peter Ross and 'Mac' Mackintosh (now chief designer for J.C.B.) had urged Chapman to consider a rear-engined monocoque in 1957, but had been overruled. At the 1960 Racing Car Show Costin sat with his new Marcos and was approached by a sceptical Chapman. Costin sketched his basic design, Chapman was thoughtful and went away. It may well be true that he later drew a scheme on a paper napkin in a café and that experience with the Elan had made him reconsider his ideas, but the fact remains that the overall layout of the 25 was essentially that of the Marcos.

By today's standards, it was a crude affair in that it consisted of two stressed pontoons joined by the undertray, front and rear bulkheads, a stressed panel carrying the instruments, and additional tubular cross-bracing at the front. The monocoque itself was full-length and the engine was cradled within it as a semi-stressed member.

Suspension was the same as on the Lotus 24.

The structure was lighter than the 24, with much of the saving coming by using rubber fuel bags inside the pontoons, but the big advantage was greatly increased rigidity. Since suspension deflection through the chassis flexing was reduced, it allowed Lotus to refine its suspension set-up with much more accuracy and also allowed softer springs to be used, which was an advantage in slower corners since they improved traction.

Many who copied the construction found themselves all at sea, because they were unable to tease out the potential gains in the suspension. The British Racing Partnership (which in 1961-2 ran the U.D.T.-Laystall team) is a case in point and its B.R.P. copy of the 25 went no better than its production 24. Between Chapman and Clark, however, there existed such empathy that they were able to explore the subtleties of the suspension and hone it to perfection.

At Monaco Clark put the new car on pole, but was involved in a fracas just after the start when Willy Mairesse barged his Ferrari into the lead and then braked too late for the hairpin. By the time everything was sorted out, Taylor was in the pits with damaged bodywork and Clark had lost several places. It took him some time to tiger up to third and then he slowed with a slipping clutch. The race was won by Bruce McLaren's Cooper.

At the Belgian GP Taylor diced for the lead with Mairesse in an incredibly close duel, while Jimmy started slowly. On lap 8, however, he moved up from fourth to first and sailed away into the distance to score his first World Championship win. Behind him his team-mate still diced with Mairesse until, on lap 25, the Ferrari nudged the Lotus up the rear and knocked it out of gear. This slowed Taylor and then Mairesse thumped him really hard. The Ferrari rolled and caught fire, but Mairesse suffered only minor injuries and Taylor only shock. It seems, however, that the crash had a long-term effect on Taylor, for he never again figured so prominently in a race.

In the Reims GP, a third Lotus 24, this time with a B.R.M. engine, was entered for Peter Arundell, who came from the Junior team. Clark took pole position, but retired when his engine lost its coolant. Then Arundell pitted to have a fuel pipe reconnected and Jimmy took over the car to try the B.R.M. engine – and soon ran out of fuel.

A new 25, R2, arrived for Clark for the French GP at Rouen and Taylor took over R1. Jimmy took pole position, but was unhappy with his front suspension, did not make his usual bid for the lead, and was soon out with a faulty ball-joint. As the race ended, Surtees' stricken Lola stopped and Trintignant, behind him, pulled out and into the path of Taylor, who was travelling at about 120 mph or 80 mph faster. So Taylor was involved in another huge crash, not of his making, although luckily neither driver was physically hurt.

At the British GP at Aintree, Clark led from pole to flag, while Taylor was delayed by a carburettor choke tube popping out. Problems in practice saw Clark 'only' third on the grid at the Nürburgring, he then forgot to switch on his fuel pumps so that his engine died and he set off a long way last. Driving brilliantly he worked up to fourth, but the conditions were so wet that he settled there, since the leaders were too far ahead. Poor Taylor

At Aintree in 1962 Jim Clark scored a fine victory with the new monocoque Lotus 25-Climax V-8.
(T. C. March)

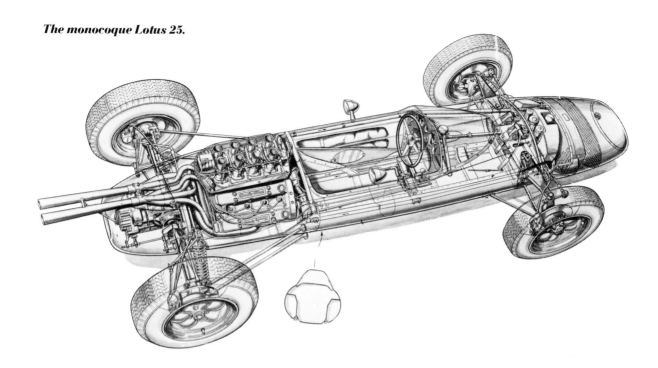

had his engine cough and splutter then suddenly it fired on all eight pots and caught him out. He went through a hedge, down a bank and into a tree. Taylor seemed jinxed and the irony is that in none of the accidents had he been at fault.

Clark sat on pole position for the Italian GP, but both he and Taylor retired with broken transmissions. Jimmy led from pole to flag in the US GP at Watkins Glen, apart from laps 12-19, which Graham Hill led, while Taylor's engine suffered from fluctuating oil pressure. In the non-Championship Mexican GP Jimmy sat on pole position but his car would not start and he was disqualified for receiving a push, so he took over Taylor's car, stormed through the field, and beat Brabham by 2.1 seconds.

Clark still had a chance of winning the Championship with only the South African GP to run. There he set pole just ahead of Graham Hill, who led the series. In the race he led Hill until the small bolt which located the jack-shaft worked out because someone had forgotten the locking washer. With only 20 laps to go Clark retired with loss of oil pressure and thus Hill and B.R.M. took both World Championships.

There had been many lesser F1 races throughout the season: Ireland (24-B.R.M.) won the Crystal Palace Trophy; Taylor (24) was third in the Solitude GP; Masten Gregory (24-B.R.M.) won the Kanonloppet and was second in the Danish GP, where Brabham won in his 24-Climax; Clark won the International Gold Cup at Oulton Park and the Rand GP.

By the end of 1962 there would typically be eight or nine Lotuses in a WC race and a dozen or more in the more important non-Championship events. If at the end of 1962 you had brought together every F1 Lotus 18, 21 and 24 in regular use and ran a race for them, you would not only have had a full grid, but you would have needed pre-qualifying sessions.

That position would decline over the coming season for a number of reasons. Even for non-Championship races you needed a V-8 to get among even the fag end of the prize money. Other cars, such as Lolas and Brabhams came on to the market. F1 became anyway more expensive, which weeded out some. Others felt that Lotus had been unfair in using the monocoque 25, while selling only the space-frame 24. Then, some punters who had put out money to have a taste of the big time would fade away.

So far as 1963 is concerned, the story is simply told. Lotus retained Clark and Taylor and the 25, but it was Jimmy's year. The season started with a race at Snetterton, where Clark took pole, but had to settle for second to Hill after a locking brake sent him into a multiple spin. He led from pole to flag at Pau with Taylor second, a tenth behind. It was another pole to flag win in the Imola GP, with second place going to Jo Siffert's 24-B.R.M. Siffert then won the Syracuse GP against a thin field. Clark took pole for the Aintree 200, but his car would not start, and he won the International Trophy at Silverstone with Taylor third.

Front row of the starting grid at the 1963 British Grand Prix with, from camera, Jim Clark (Lotus 25), Dan Gurney (Brabham BT7), Graham Hill (B.R.M. P57) and Jack Brabham (Brabham BT7). (Nigel Snowdon)

In the 1963 British Grand Prix Jim Hill drove this Lotus 24-B.R.M., but retired because of gearbox trouble. (Nigel Snowdon)

Thus Clark went to Monaco, the opening round of the WC, with three wins and a second from five races already under his belt. There he sat on pole, was slow away, took the lead on lap 18 and then had his gear selector break when the race was in the bag. In the Belgian GP he was on the third row, after gearbox trouble in practice, but was in the lead a mile after the start and won by five minutes with the second half run in a deluge.

Dutch GP: pole to flag win. French GP: pole to flag win. British GP: pole, a poor start but another win. German GP: pole, but the engine was not running cleanly so it was finally second place to Surtees' Ferrari. Italian GP: relatively slow practice (only fourth on the grid) but another win. US GP: second in practice, fuel pump played up throughout, third. Mexican GP: pole to flag win. South African GP: pole to flag win.

Where does one find adjectives to describe a season like that? Along the way he also won the Kanonloppet and the International Gold Cup. It was typical of his attitude that when experimental drive-shafts failed him on the line at Solitude he insisted new shafts be fitted so he could join in at about half-distance and give the fans value for money. He did too, and sliced 6.5 seconds off the old lap record!

Let the statistics speak for themselves. In 1963 Clark started in a total of 20 F1 races, took 14 pole positions, 11 fastest laps and 12 wins. In the ten World Championship races it was a case of seven pole positions, six fastest laps, seven wins, a second and a third. Play with the statistics as you will, it remains the outstanding season in the history of Formula 1.

By contrast Taylor had a dreadful time. Possibly he had lost his edge, but much was due to the fact that Lotus could not prepare two cars to an equal standard. At the end all he had to show was second in the Kanonloppet, third in the International Trophy at Silverstone and sixth at Monaco. Taylor's career helped feed a myth that being number two at Lotus was a short cut to oblivion, but very few teams have ever had equal results with two cars.

Innes Ireland in the B.R.P. 24 began the season well with a win in the Richmond Trophy at Goodwood and high finishes in other non-Championship races and then switched to B.R.P.'s 25-copy and began a drift down the grid. Peter Arundell had a works 25 on occasion and he took second in the Solitude and Mediterranean GPs.

For 1964 Lotus released Taylor, who teamed up with Ireland at B.R.P., and Arundell was brought in to replace him. Reg Parnell had been planning a Lotus 25 copy, but died suddenly. His son, Tim, who had been running his own team, took over Reg Parnell (Racing) and was able to buy two ex-works 25s, so the Parnell F1 car was converted into a sucessful sports-racer. These first privateer 25s had B.R.M. engines, Hewland gearboxes and outboard Metalastik couplings.

The biggest change for 1964, however, and one which affected everybody, was the introduction of a new type of Dunlop racing tyre which was wider and which ran on 13-in wheels. The introduction of this new tyre

Jim Clark scored his third successive British Grand Prix victory with the 25 at Brands Hatch in 1964. (**T. C. March**)

was to bring lap times tumbling and, indeed, start a trend towards ever wider tyres, but obviously they necessitated changes in suspension. Thus the 25B had new rear uprights, smaller rear disc brakes and a re-location of the lower radius arms' pick-up points.

While the 25 was being uprated, and indeed other detail modifications to the suspension produced 'C' and 'D' variants during 1964, work was proceeding on the Lotus 33. Len Terry had returned to Lotus and his brief was to refine the 25. Thus Terry went back to first principles to shed some of the weight which had accumulated during development and produced a simpler monocoque which used the revised (25B/C/D) suspension. The 33's chassis numbers reflected the fact that it was a 25 development − R1 to R7 were 25s, R8 to R14 were 33s.

Clark and Arundell headed the very wet *Daily Mirror* Trophy at Snetterton, but both retired, then took a 1-2 in the *News of the World* Trophy at Goodwood. Arundell shared the third place car at Syracuse with Mike Spence and also finished third in the Aintree 200 and the International Trophy at Silverstone. Brabham, however, had its revised BT7s working very well on the new tyres and was probably the class of the field.

Jimmy had the first 33 for the Aintree race and was disputing the lead with Brabham when a couple of backmarkers caused him to crash heavily, which meant both men had to rely on 25Bs for Monaco. Clark set pole and was in the lead when all sorts of troubles began and he was eventually classified fourth (and not running), one place behind Arundell. Clark won the Dutch GP (Arundell third) and then completed a hat-trick of wins at Spa. He set pole and led the French GP at Rouen until a piston broke, but Arundell came home a strong fourth.

Alas, the following weekend at Reims this promising driver was involved in an horrendous crash. Although he was later to return and Chapman kept his word and gave him back his old seat, he was never to regain his former brilliance. In the meantime Mike Spence took his place in the team. Let us look again at the myth which says the Lotus number two drive is a short cut to nowhere. Chapman kept his promise to Arundell in 1966 even though it was soon apparent he was not his former self. He had kept faith with Taylor, too, even though by the end of 1962 it was clear he was not the same man who had started the year − and his accidents were not the fault of either driver or car.

It is true that the number two car retired more often, but that is a different matter. Among the number two drivers who did not pass into oblivion are John Surtees, Graham Hill, Emerson Fittipaldi, Ronnie Peterson and Nigel Mansell. While Chapman was alive, Lotus introduced more drivers to F1 than any other team. The myth-mongers ignore the fact that Clark was once a *number three* driver at Lotus, the same Clark who took a Lotus 25 to a pole to flag win in the 1964 British GP, which was run at Brands Hatch for the first time.

Just over a week later Clark scored the 33's first win at Solitude in Germany. Jimmy retired from the German GP with broken valve gear, was beaten by an inspired Jo Siffert (Brabham) in the Mediterranean GP at Enna, but was to retire from the next three WC races, at Zeltweg, Monza and Watkins Glen. In the final round of the series, the Mexican GP, he looked set for a pole to flag win, and the Championship, when late in the race a split oil pipe on the scavenger pump cost him the race and the title. He finished fifth, and third in the Championship behind Surtees and Hill.

Of the other Lotus users in 1964, Taylor took third at Goodwood and sixth at Solitude, with B.R.P.'s 24-BRM; Spence took sixth at Monza with a 33 and fourth in Mexico with a 25. Walt Hansgen had a works 33 for the US GP and came home a distant fifth, while the Parnell cars had a poor reliability record, but Amon took fifth at Zandvoort, and Hailwood sixth at Monaco.

To the Rand GP in December Team Lotus sent cars for Spence and a youngster making his F1 debut, Jackie Stewart. Stewart set pole from Spence, but his transmission failed on the line in the first heat. Still he won the second heat and set fastest lap, and never again raced a Lotus.

Coventry Climax had a flat-16 engine on the stocks and in 1965 Lotus built a car (the 39) to take it. It was based on the 25/33, but had a much shorter monocoque at the rear. When the engine failed to appear, the chassis was put aside and later modified to take a 2.5-litre Climax FPF for Clark to drive in the 1966 Tasman series.

Lotus fielded only 33s in 1965 with Clark and Spence the drivers. Paul Hawkins was allowed to buy the first 33, R8. Parnell retained its 25s for, variously, Innes Ireland, Richard Attwood, Chris Amon and Mike Hailwood.

So far as the World Championship is concerned, Clark won in South Africa, missed Monaco because of Indianapolis (which he won) and then took his fourth successive win at Spa (in the wet). There following wins in the French, British, Dutch and German GPs − six starts, six wins, and World Championships for both driver and constructor. Then the season took a dive. At Monza he was in the tight leading bunch when a fuel pump failed; he retired from the lead in the US GP with a broken piston and was not long into the Mexican GP when his engine failed.

As for the rest of the year, Clark won the first heat of

Clark completely dominated the 1965 Dutch Grand Prix with the 33-Climax, leading the race from start to finish. (**British Petroleum**)

the Race of Champions at Brands Hatch, but crashed in the second when trying to pass Gurney, and also won the Syracuse GP and the *News of the World* Trophy at Goodwood, the last F1 race ever held on the Sussex circuit. In the Mediterranean GP at Pergusa, however, he was again beaten by a fraction by Jo Siffert's Brabham.

Spence had a typical Lotus Number Two season: lots of reliability problems. Still, he came fourth in the South African GP, first in the Race of Champions, third in the International Trophy at Silverstone, fourth in the British GP and third in Mexico. For most of the season Clark had the use of the four-valve Climax engine, while Spence usually had a two-valve engine.

The Parnell cars had a dreadful reliability record and Paul Hawkins' season, with his 25 entered by DW Racing Enterprises, ended at Monaco when he spun his car into the harbour, like Ascari ten years before. As on that occa-

sion the driver was uninjured and the car was retrieved.

Lotus had begun the 1960 season as a make-weight in Formula 1, but by the end of 1965 it had won 23 World Championship events, 38 other F1 races and a further 13 races in the Tasman series. The racing history of the 25 and 33 did not, however, finish with the end of the 1½-litre formula. Fitted with stretched FWMV and B.R.M. P56 engines, they formed the mainstay of Lotus's unsuccessful 1966 season and kept some privateers in the game as well.

Lotus was the team of the 1960s and 1970s and its achievements remain unequalled. Colin Chapman set the standards of design, performance and innovation for nearly 20 years and no other designer apart, perhaps, from Vittorio Jano deserves his name uttered in the same breath.

LOTUS-BORGWARD

Ex-Cooper 500 driver Kurt Kuhnke entered his Borgward-engined Lotus 18s as B.K.L.s in 1963 and the initials stand for *Borgward-Kuhnke-Lotus.* Kuhnke had driven an Autosport Team Wolfgang Seidel Lotus 18-FPF without success in 1962 and, half-way through the season, bought two of the team's cars and fitted them with Borgward 30 engines.

Borgward had introduced its 1488cc (80 × 74 mm) d.o.h.c. 16-valve engine in 1957 and, since it produced 150 bhp, it could have given Porsche a hard time, but the Borgward sports-racing chassis was relatively crude and the company's competition programme was spasmodic and poorly directed. The cars did, however, do well in the European Hill Climb Championship. In 1959 Moss had a fuel-injected Borgward engine in a Cooper chassis and with it he won four major F2 races from four starts. It was an exceptional engine.

By the time Kuhnke got his hands on the unit the Borgward company had gone to the wall and, of course, the Lotus 18 was obsolete. Kunhke entered his Lotus-Borgward in several races in 1962, but failed to arrive at any of them.

B.K.L. entered cars for Kuhnke and Ernst Maring in the 1963 Rome GP, but neither qualified. At Solitude both were over a minute off the pace and retired with engine problems. Kuhnke entered the German GP, but did not qualify (over 2½ minutes off the pace), but in the Kanonloppet Maring qualified tenth, only 8.3 seconds off the pace, and finished tenth in the first heat − and then crashed.

Two cars ran in the 1964 Solitude GP, one crashed on the first lap and the other finished last.

A Lotus 18-Borgward also raced in South Africa and in 1962 Helmut Menzler drove it in the Cape GP. The same car was driven by Vern McWilliams in the Natal GP, but neither performed with any distinction.

LOTUS-MASERATI

After struggling in 1960 with its unsuccessful Cooper-Maseratis, Scuderia Centro-Sud shoehorned one of its 250S engines into the back of its equally unsuccessful F2 Lotus 18 and entered it in the International Gold Cup at Oulton Park, the last race in Europe to the 2½-litre F1. Since the team missed official practice, the Lotus, driven by Ian Burgess, had to start from the back of the grid. It did not figure in the race and was out at quarter-distance with broken suspension.

This chassis was sold to Prince Gaetano Starrabba, who fitted a Maserati 150S engine, and it appeared spasmodically in minor races over the next three years, with its usual pattern of being slow in qualifying and retiring with engine trouble being interrupted only once. That was in the 1963 Rome GP, where, in a field of privateers, Starrabba qualified half-way up the grid and finished fifth on aggregate, albeit four laps down.

M. B. M.

M.B.M. first appeared at the 1960 Geneva Motor Show, where it displayed a rear-engined Formula Junior car. The initials stood for Peter Monteverdi, a Swiss sports car driver who later marketed luxury GT cars under his own name; Bâsle, where the cars were made; and Dr Mantzel, a German two-stroke engine specialist who prepared the D.K.W. units which powered the car.

In Formula Junior form they were made in small numbers, and were sold in America under the name 'Machan', but achieved little success. The first car, in fact, was very poor and was quickly replaced. By 1961, indeed, the initials 'MBM' stood for Monteverdi Binningen Motors, Binningen being the suburb of Bâsle where they were made, and some idea of the upheaval within the little company can be gauged by the fact that for a short time the final 'M' had stopped standing for Dr Mantzel and stood for Gerhard Mitter, another tuning specialist who was also a fair driver.

Switzerland's first post-war Grand Prix car, the M.B.M., seen during its only race, the 1961 Solitude Grand Prix with constructor Peter Monteverdi at the wheel. (LAT)

Peter Monteverdi in his M.B.M. at Solitude, 1961. The Porsche derivation is obvious from the wheels. (LAT)

In 1961, one of the latest Formula Junior chassis was strengthened and lengthened too take a Porsche RSK engine. Porsche had refused to sell Monteverdi an engine so he bought a complete car, removed the motor and had it tuned to give about 150 bhp. This was installed in a fairly conventional space-frame with front suspension by coil springs, lower wishbone and upper link, and coils and double wishbones at the rear.

Monteverdi himself drove it with some success in Swiss hill climbs and this prompted him to enter it in the 1961 Solitude GP. There he qualified last and retired after two laps with engine problems. That was the sum of M.B.M.'s F1 career, for although it was entered in the German GP, in the intervening period it was written off in a Formule Libre race at Hockenheim in a crash which Monteverdi was lucky to survive. The remains of Switzerland's only F1 car were later buried.

MASERATI

In the late 19th Century six brothers were born in Voghera, near Milan. They were Carlo, Bindo, Alfiero, Mario, Ettore and Ernesto Maserati and, with the exception of Mario (who became a painter) they all became motor engineers. The eldest, Carlo, had begun building motorcycles as early at 1897 and he himself won several important events with one of his machines, but he tragically died in 1910.

Ettore and Alfieri spent some time in the Argentine working for a subsidiary of Isotta-Fraschini and there they built, and raced, an IF special. They returned home to work for Isotta during the First World War, developing aero engines, and there they were joined by Bindo. In his spare time Alfieri designed a new type of sparking plug, which he marketed, and he created a prosperous business.

Alfieri, the most talented of the surviving brothers, built an Isotta special when peace returned and won several important events. This led Diatto, which built uninspired touring cars, to ask him to build a Diatto special to boost its image, and this too was successful. Impressed, Diatto commissioned a new GP car which had a blown 2-litre straight-eight engine, and this appeared in the 1925 Italian GP, where it retired.

Diatto was in financial difficulty, so Alfieri took over the project, reduced the engine to 1½ litres, to comply with the new GP regulations, and in 1926 formed Alfieri Maserati SpA, Bologna, and he was soon joined by Ettore, Bindo and Ernesto. Maserati was not an instant success, but from about 1929 onwards began to feature regularly in the results.

A works GP team was run in 1930 and was very successful, and Maserati 1100cc cars frequently won their class in the Mille Miglia. In 1932 the firm received a severe blow when Alfieri underwent an operation from which he did not recover. Ernesto then assumed the role of chief designer.

During the next few years, the marque did not enjoy huge success, but its cars were popular with privateers. The introduction of the Tipo 6CM *Voiturette* in 1936 changed that position and during the next three years it took 19 important wins.

Maserati was a small concern and money was tight, so when the wealthy industrialist Adolfo Orsi approached the brothers with a buy-out offer, they listened. Orsi was interested in the profitable sparking plug business, but reasoned that Maserati cars could add lustre to his empire. In their turn, the brothers welcomed financial security and the support of a large combine. In early 1938 the take-over was completed, the brothers signed a ten-year service contract and Adolfo's son, Omer, became managing director.

Voiturette racing had become dominated by the Alfa Romeo Tipo 158 and in 1939 Maserati's answer appeared, the Tipo 4CL. This had a d.o.h.c. 4-cylinder engine of 1490cc and was unusual for its 'square' dimensions of 78×78 mm and its four valves per cylinder, although this was by no means a 'first'.

After experimenting with two-stage supercharging, the brothers settled on a single Roots-type blower and in this form the 4CL produced 220 bhp at 6500 rpm. This was delivered through a 4-speed gearbox in unit with the dry sumped engine and drove to a rigid rear axle suspended on quarter-elliptical springs, which splayed out slightly and were located by radius arms.

Front suspension was by double wishbones with longitudinal torsion bars attached to the top wishbones, the same system that had been used on the successful 6CM, and the simple, cross-braced, channel-steel frame derived from the earlier car as well.

Maserati's reputation among privateers was such that a 4CL had been delivered to its first customer before the works had even given it a race debut. This servicing of customers was always a Maserati strongpoint and would continue to be the case for years to come.

The works debuted the car in the 1939 Tripoli GP, which was run to *Voiturette* rules. Italy had become tired of being beaten by the German teams in GP racing and so had turned to the junior category, where it could win. Libya was then an Italian colony and Italy looked forward to a win in a race which had achieved 'classic' status. One of the most frequently told stories in motor racing tells how Mercedes-Benz built two 1½-litre cars and upset the plan.

Maserati entered cars for Franco Cortese, Count Felice Trossi and Luigi Villoresi, whose car had an enveloping streamlined body designed and built by a German firm. This obviously worked, for Villoresi set fastest practice lap at 134 mph, which tends to confirm the claim that the car's top speed was 170 mph. Unfortunately, it went out on the first lap with gearbox trouble, while the other works Maseratis also retired on lap one, with broken pistons. It was a débâcle, but it is interesting to note there was a total of 25 Maseratis in the race, the privateer's friend indeed.

Later in the year, the model took several wins, with Villoresi winning the Targa Florio. The English privateer, Johnny Wakefield, went to Italy to collect his car and returned home via the Naples GP (which he won), the Picardy GP (first), the Coupe du Commission Sportive at Reims (second, after encountering brake trouble) and the Alibi GP (first). It was a terrific spell for a privateer, especially since he beat the works cars at Naples.

The model continued to give a good account of itself in the few races which were run before Italy joined the war in June 1940, although Alfa Romeo had the upper hand. When Alfa was absent, Maserati was the team to beat and Villoresi and Cortese took a 1-2 in the 1940 Targa Florio held on a closed circuit before war closed down the sport.

Work continued on the design throughout hostilities and when racing began again in Italy, in 1946, Maserati was ready for business once more. It no longer ran a works team, but privateers, notably Scuderia Milano, which later built its own Maserati specials, upheld works honour.

That year the cars won the Nice GP (Villoresi), the Marseilles GP (Sommer), the Grand Prix de Fôrez (Sommer), the St. Cloud GP (Sommer), the Albi GP (Nuvolari), the Nântes GP (Raph), the Coupe du Salon in the Bois de Boulogne (Sommer) and the Penya Rhin GP (Pelassa). All this was low-key stuff as you would expect in the circumstances. In fact the only significant win was Sommer's at St. Cloud, where Alfa Romeo was defeated, something which would not happen again for another five years.

1947 was a similar season and Maserati chalked up another 11 wins, with Villoresi being the most successful driver with six of them.

It was in 1948 that Maserati produced its next significant car, the 4CLT/48. As the name suggests, it was a development of the pre-war car and a large step forward.

It featured a lower, sleeker body which is one of the classic shapes of the period. Beneath the skin much was familiar, but there was two-stage supercharging which pushed power up to 260 bhp at 7000 rpm. There was, too, a new tubular chassis frame with 4-in main tubes which had first been seen the previous year.

By this time the Maserati brothers had left to form O.S.C.A. and Alberto Massimino was in charge of design; he came up with a rocker arm front suspension system using inboard coil springs. Many years later Lotus would rediscover and popularize the layout.

Maserati ran no works team, but had a relationship with Count 'Johnny' Lurani's Scuderia Ambrosiana similar to that which Alfa Romeo had once with the Scuderia Ferrari, i.e. it was a works team in all but name. Scuderia Ambrosiana entered the new cars for Villoresi and Alberto Ascari at the San Remo GP and, despite problems, Ascari won with Villoresi third. Alfa Romeo was absent, but it is always special when a new car wins first time out. In honour of that win the 4CLT/48 is usually called the 'San Remo'.

Throughout 1948 Maserati again won 11 races, and Villoresi again won six of them, including the inaugural post-war British GP. To put these statistics into perspective is virtually impossible. Almost anyone with a car could run in a 'Grand Prix', except if they were German. Everyone except Ferrari was using variants of pre-war designs. If Alfa Romeo deigned to appear, as it did four times a year, that race became important and Alfa Romeo won it.

'B. Bira' (Price Birabongse) at the wheel of his Maserati 4CLT/48 'San Remo' in the 1948 British Grand Prix. (Guy Griffiths)

It is in all the statistics that Villoresi and Ascari scored a 1-2 in the British GP at Silverstone, but the opposition was feeble on a circuit marked out on an airfield by oil drums and straw bales. So far as British racing was concerned, however, the race was important and started the post-war British renaissance in the sport.

In 1949 things changed, since Alfa Romeo temporarily withdrew from racing and the second string got a chance of glory. The season came down to a battle between Maserati, Ferrari and Talbot, but there were changes among the drivers. Ascari was growing in stature and he and Villoresi joined Ferrari. At a stroke Ferrari changed the balance in racing, for he had the established ace and the coming man.

A national scholarship scheme of the Argentine Automobile Club sent two Argentinians to race Maseratis in Europe and one of them was Juan Manual Fangio. In those races which attracted a full representative field, however, the issue was largely between Ferrari and Talbot, but in the minor affairs Fangio began to build his reputation, and his wins at Pau, Perpignan, San Remo and Albi, together with other fine performances, took him to an Alfa Romeo drive the following year. Again it

was an instance of Maserati being the privateer's pal.

Enrico Platé ran a private team of Maseratis and employed Bira and de Graffenried. Bira won the Swedish Summer GP (actually a short sprint) and, among other results, scored seconds at Albi, San Remo, Perpignan, Zandvoort and in the French GP at Reims, as well as third in the Italian GP. De Graffenried won the British GP (Ferrari was absent) and took seconds at Pau, Zandvoort and in the Jersey Road Race, and third at Lausanne and San Remo. Farina won at Lausanne, beating the works Ferraris, and was second in the International Trophy at Silverstone.

In terms of wins and places it was a respectable season, but in truth only Farina's win at Lausanne counted for much. The car was at the end of its development and there was nothing in the pipe-line. When Alfa Romeo returned the following year, and undertook an extensive programme, the Maseratis were relegated to make-weights.

4CLT/48s continued to race in F1 for some years more, but the marque was in a decline and the slide got steeper as time went by. Still, as late as 1951 Farina won the Paris Grand Prix in the Bois de Boulogne with a

In the 1948 British Grand Prix Alberto Ascari finished second at the wheel of another 4CLT/48 entered by Scuderia Ambrosiana. (Guy Griffiths)

4CLT/48.

While the car was outclassed in F1 some privateers adapted them for F2, the most notable effort being that of the Argentine team named for Achille Varzi, which put a Maserati A6G 2-litre s.o.h.c. sports car engine into a San Remo chassis. It was overweight but promising, and Fangio actually won a minor race with it.

As Maserati's parent company grew stronger there was a revival of interest in racing and for 1952 Vittorio Bellentani and Alberto Massimino produced a new F2 car, the Tipo A6GCM. This had been instigated before F2 became the World Championship formula and the thinking was much the same as behind the successful pre-war *Voiturettes* — if you cannot win at the top level, go for success in the number two category.

In general layout, and body style, it was similar to the 4CLT/48, although the wheelbase was markedly shorter (there was no need to make space for superchargers) and front and rear track were slightly wider. It used an engine based on Ernesto Maserati's last (sports car) design for the marque before he left and this, in turn, derived from his 6C *Voiturette* of 1936. As engineered for the new car, this was a d.o.h.c. straight-six engine of 1988cc (75×75 mm — classic Maserati dimensions) which produced about 165 bhp.

As a break with tradition, Maserati did not immediately sell the car to privateers, but entered the motorcyclist Nello Pagani in the Argentine races which began the 1952 season. It was far from fully developed and Pagani was no ace, but it was clear it was not on the pace with Ferrari.

Thus work continued and it was not until the Monza GP in June that the cars next raced. There the works entered Fangio, Gonzalez and Bonetto, while two, sold to the Brazilian private team Escuderia Bandeirantes, were driven by Chico Landi and Gino Bianco.

It was not a dream return, as the cars proved unreliable and unable to get near the Ferraris. The best finish was Bonetto, in seventh on aggregate, and even then he was not running at the end. Worse, Fangio, who started without practising after a long and tiring journey from Ulster where he had been attempting to tame a B.R.M., was washed out by his efforts, made an error of judgement, and crashed heavily. The reigning World Champion was badly injured and missed the rest of the season.

The private cars were entered in the French and British GPs, but neither showed any form, and a single works car, for Bonetto, lasted only two laps in the German GP. The season lurched on with the new cars unable to make an impression even in minor events and, more often than not, they retired.

By the Italian GP, however, there had been modifications to the engine to improve reliablity and power and most noticable of these was a twin-plug head. It now produced 177 bhp, but did not have sufficient fuel capacity to run the whole distance. Gonzalez shot off into the lead from the second row of the grid, but was passed by the Ferraris of Ascari and Villoresi while taking on more fuel. Eventually he finished second, and the 78 seconds he was down on Ascari at the end was perhaps less time than he had lost by having to stop.

Gonzalez came close to winning the final race of the year, the Modena GP, until he was badly baulked by an amateur, who let Villoresi's Ferrari by. It was not, however, the works cars but the 4CLT/48-based specials of Enrico Platé (q.v.) which did most to keep the marque's name alive in the entry lists during 1952. This brave effort was a stop-gap solution only and Platé took delivery of a pukka Maserati F2 car in 1953.

During 1952, Maserati was joined by Giaocchino Colombo, that brilliant but restless designer, who had left Ferrari having contributed so much to the team's fortunes, had joined Alfa Romeo to mastermind the *Disco Volante* sports cars, and had then accepted a new brief in Modena. He set to work on reworking the A6GCM and came up with an improved car which was as good as the best around (the Ferrari Tipo 500) in every department except roadholding.

Colombo specified 'over-square' (76.2×72 mm) dimensions, which gave a capacity of 1997cc and, with large Weber carburettors, gave a claimed 190 bhp. The chassis frame was made stiffer by a triangulated superstructure above the main tubes and the rear quarter-elliptic springs now ran parallel to the main tubes, and the rigid rear axle was located by an A-bracket; the car's handling deficiencies had stemmed from the rear suspension. Fuel capacity had been increased, and to accommodate the larger tank the rear bodywork became more bulbous, so, in profile, it closely resembled the contemporary Ferrari.

For the first time ever, a European works team comprised three Argentines: Fangio, Gonzalez and Oscar Galvez, at least in the Argentine, all of whom had 1952-spec cars. Fangio, returning to the sport after his crash, qualified a close second to Ascari (Ferrari) and ran second in the race until his engine blew, but Gonzalez brought his car home third, and Galvez was fifth.

Back in Europe, de Graffenried in Platé's car took a surprise win in the Syracuse GP when the works Ferraris all dropped out due to a faulty batch of valve springs, and then he won a couple of races at Goodwood. Fangio and Gonzalez finished second and third to Farina's Ferrari at Naples, beating the sister Ferraris of Villoresi and Ascari,

Froilan Gonzalez at the wheel of the twin-plug A6GCM Maserati which he drove into second place in the 1952 Italian Grand Prix. Gonzalez is seen during his refuelling stop. (Publifoto)

At Goodwood on Easter Monday in 1953 this interim 1952/3 A6GCM was entered by Enrico Platé for Emmanuel de Graffenried. (Guy Griffiths)

Juan Fangio on his way to second place with his works A6GCM Maserati in the 1953 British Grand Prix at Silverstone. (T. C. March)

and then de Graffenried won the Eifelrennen at the Nürburging, although the opposition was not of the first rank. Maserati was back in the picture and very close to Ferrari in performance.

In the opening European round of the World Championship, the Dutch GP, Fangio qualified second to Ascari, but retired with a broken rear axle, as did Gonzalez. Gonzalez, however, took over Bonetto's car and tigered up from ninth to third, while de Graffenried came home fifth. Fangio set pole in the Belgian GP, and Gonzalez, in third spot, recorded the same time as Ascari in the leading Ferrari. The two Maseratis led until a third-distance, when first Gonzalez, and then Fangio, retired with engine trouble. Fangio then took over Johnny Claes' car and got it up to fourth, but on his last lap he spun on some oil and crashed. Still the private cars of Onofre Marimon and de Graffenried finished third and fourth.

The French GP at Reims produced one of the greatest duels in racing history as Fangio battled for the lead with Hawthorn's Ferrari. This showed up an interesting contrast between the two cars, for the Maserati was marginally quicker in a straight line while the Ferrari scored on braking. Hawthorn won by a whisker, but, close behind, Gonzalez just pipped Ascari (Ferrari) for third after an equally close race. Much later Fangio was to claim he had lost the use of first gear so was hobbled at

the tight Thillois hairpin before the finishing straight.

Fangio took second place to Ascari in the British GP, the Ferrari driver having an untroubled race. Gonzalez was delayed, when he was wrongly black-flagged for dropping oil and eventually came home fourth, two laps down. Fangio then scored his third successive second place in the German GP, where Ascari was robbed of his fourth consecutive win at the Nürburgring when a wheel came off. This let the Maserati into the lead, but Farina, enjoying an 'on' day, came past to win for Ferrari, a minute ahead of Fangio. Bonetto and de Graffenried took fourth and fifth places for Maserati.

At the Swiss GP Fangio was again faster in practice and here the other works cars were driven by Bonetto, Lang and Marimon, but although Fangio led away, the Ferraris soon asserted their authority. Fangio eventually blew his engine, while Bonetto and Lang finished a distant fourth and fifth.

Maserati had been tantalizingly close to victory all season and it finally came in the last race of the F2 World Championship, the Italian GP. For much of the race there was a four-cornered fight between the Maseratis of Fangio and Marimon and the Ferraris of Ascari and Farina. This became a threesome when Marimon was delayed with a holed radiator, although after losing two laps he again joined the battling trio. On the very last cor-

Stirling Moss with his private Maserati 250F, 2508, in the wet in the International Trophy at Silverstone in May 1954. He retired because of a broken de Dion tube. (T. C. March)

ner Ascari led, just, but either made a rare error of judgement and spun and was rammed by Marimon or else, depending on which version you believe, was punted off by Marimon. Farina took to the grass, but Fangio slipped by to record a narrow victory.

It was Maserati's first Championship win and augured well for the coming 2½-litre formula. It was also the only time during the Formula 2 WC that Ferrari was defeated. The win, and a point for fastest lap, saw Fangio pip Farina for second place in the Championship, to Ascari, although Farina actually grossed more points.

Enzo Ferrari announced at Monza that he was to quit racing, which was his regular way of drumming up more money, and so Ferrari missed the Modena GP, which rounded off the season. On its home ground, Maserati had no real opposition and Fangio won from Marimon and de Graffenried.

For the new formula Maserati made what was to become recognized as one of the great classic designs, the 250/F1, which abbreviated to 250F. In truth, it broke no new ground and was not exceptionally successful, with only eight WC wins during the four years the works ran them.

It was, however, beautiful to behold, sold in large numbers to privateers, confirmed the stature of Stirling Moss and provided Fangio with perhaps his greatest drive, in the 1957 German GP. Further, 250Fs not only appeared in the first race of the 2½-litre formula, Argentine 1954, but also in the last, US GP, 1960. My own theory is that it achieved classic status after Fangio drove

it at Rouen in 1957. Photographs showing him holding it in a four-wheel drift on a long, sweeping, downhill curve caught everyone's imagination. It is the epitome of Grand Prix racing of the period.

Most of the design work was done by Colombo and Massimino before the former, restless as always, left to design the abortive Bugatti Type 251. The engine derived from the twin-plug A6GCM unit, but the bore was increased to give a capacity of 2493cc (84 × 72 mm) and a feature was that no gaskets at all were used, but metal to metal joints were sealed by a compound. In 1954 this unit developed 240 bhp at 7200 rpm and drove through a 4-speed trans-axle.

For the first time Maserati specified a space-frame-*style* chassis. Front suspension was by coil springs and unequal wishbones and at the rear was a de Dion axle located by radius arms and a central sliding guide and sprung by a transverse leaf spring. As usual, damping was by Houdaille vane-type shock absorbers mounted on the chassis and operated by lever arms.

Maserati received a lot of orders for the new car and in order to keep faith with customers prepared six A6GCMs and fitted them with the 2½-litre engine, but the extra power rather embarrassed the older design's rear suspension.

Eight of the 17 entrants in the Argentine GP in January 1954 had Maseratis, two of them 250Fs for Fangio and Marimon. The newness of the design showed up in severe lubrication problems caused by the oil overheating. The cars did not handle very well either, but some improvement was found by making the frame more flexible by cuttting out a couple of tubes in the cockpit section! It is as well they were not true space-frames or that could have caused real problems. In the event Marimon drove an interim car, but Fangio gave the lone 250F a debut win.

Lubrication problems beset the cars until mid-season, when they were solved by moving the oil tank from under the bonnet to the tail, a cooler location.

From April onwards cars began to reach customers and during 1954 no fewer than 19 Maseratis, 11 of them 250Fs, were seen in Grand Prix races. Most famous of all the privateers was, of course, Stirling Moss, who made the move reluctantly since he would have preferred to drive a British car, but by the end of the season he was Number One at Maserati and on his way to a glorious career in Formula 1.

The first European WC race was the Belgian GP, in late June, and there Fangio gave the model its second successive Championship win with Moss in third. Fangio had signed for Mercedes-Benz, which tactically delayed its debut until the French GP at Reims, but he was released to drive for Maserati. It is probable, however, that he would still have been World Champion had he driven for the Italian team all season, for Mercedes-Benz was only superior during 1954 when he was at the wheel.

Ascari and Villoresi were released from Lancia to drive for Maserati at Reims, and Moss lent the works his own car for Villoresi to drive. Reims was not the place for the 250F to display its virtues, which were mainly controllability and handling. Ascari still made the front row of the grid, but his engine went after a single lap. Bira came home fourth, however, and Villoresi fifth, but both were lapped by the Mercedes-Benz W196s, which scored a spectacular 1-2 on the firm's return to the sport.

Although Maserati had won two of the three WC races of the year, and its cars were performing well in minor events, it did have a problem in that it had no ace driver. Fangio and Ascari were spoken for and Ferrari had the pick of the rest. Its team therefore was led by young Onofre Marimon, who was promising, but had yet to make his bones

At the British GP Mercedes-Benz was all at sea and Gonzalez' Ferrari led from start to finish. In the early races of the year, Moss had set himself a rev limit because he could not afford a large bill, but, impressed by his progress, the factory offered to finance all his engine rebuilds. He was therefore free to drive his own race and got his car up to second when, with only ten laps to go, he was forced out with transmission trouble.

Moss qualified his car on the front row of the grid at the Nürburgring, ahead of three of the four Mercedes-Benz runners – and M-B's team manager, Alfred Neubauer, had refused him even a test drive on the grounds he lacked experience! Sadly there was a gap on the grid, for the popular and gifted Marimon was killed during practice. As a result, Villoresi withdrew from the race. Moss' engine blew on his second lap and the best Maserati finisher was Sergio Mantovani, a distant fifth.

After Marimon's death Maserati invited Moss to lead its team, using his own car (painted red instead of green) which the works would prepare. He repaid their faith by qualifying on the front row for the Swiss GP and running second to Fangio's Mercedes-Benz until his oil pump packed up. Roberto Mieres and Sergio Mantovani finished fourth and fifth, but both had been lapped twice.

The last WC race of the year was the Italian GP and again Moss sat on the front row of the grid, only three-tenths slower than Fangio's streamliner. When Ascari's Ferrari retired, Moss moved into the lead and pulled away from the field until an oil pipe broke only 12 laps from the end. It was a disappointment, but the race marked his arrival in the top rank.

An oil pump failed in the final race of the year, the Spanish GP, when Moss was in third place with a good chance of second or, even, a win. Luigi Musso eventually took second to Hawthorn's Ferrari, but the recurring lubrication failures were a disgrace. Maserati ignored them in the hope they would go away, but the solution was quite simple – the problem centred on too-rigid installation of components.

While the works had to be content with only just two wins, privateers took another seven in non-Championship F1 events: Moss won the Aintree 200, the Oulton Park Gold Cup, the Goodwood Trophy and the *Daily Telegraph* Trophy at Aintree; Marimon took the Rome GP, Luigi Musso the Pescara GP and Bira won at Chimay. Moss also won a couple of Formule Libre races and Maseratis took second or third places on 18 occasions.

For 1955 there was smoother bodywork, larger brakes and a single-pipe exhaust system. Moss left to join Mercedes-Benz, the second year running that the German team had robbed Maserati of its star, and that had an adverse effect on the whole team. In his place came the brave and forceful Jean Behra, who was supported by Mantovani, a gifted amateur, Mieres, yet another Argentinian, and Musso who would eventually become Italy's great hope.

Without a star and with the company also running a sports car programme, which sapped resources, Maserati was not in the best shape in 1955. In any case Mercedes-Benz had progressed to such a level that it seemed to be in a different sphere.

So far as Maserati was concerned the first race of 1955, the blistering hot Argentine GP, was something of a disappointment especially since no fewer than seven cars were entered by the team. Some of these were privateers under the works umbrella, for they were a long way from home, but the number remains a record for one team. Behra was fast in practice, but crashed on the third lap. He then shared in the driving of two other cars, one of which retired, and he finished sixth in Harry Schell's car, behind Mieres, who drove the entire distance.

Tragedy struck in practice for the Valentino GP at Turin, when Mantovani crashed heavily in practice and eventually had to have a leg amputated. He never raced again in Formula 1, but is still active in the sport. Mieres made some small amends by finishing second, preventing a Lancia 1-2-3.

By the time the next WC, the Monaco GP, came around Maserati had won four of the six non-Championship races in Europe. Behra was quick in practice, but despite swapping cars he did not finish and it was Cesare Perdisa, with whom he had swapped, who brought home the first 250F, in third place.

So far as Championship races were concerned the season was something of a disaster, although Behra was often quick in practice. Musso and Mieres were third and fourth in the Dutch GP, Musso was fifth in the British GP and Behra was fourth in the Italian. The car Behra drove at Monza was a streamliner, although the tops of the wheels were exposed. Unfortunately the exhaust pipe, which emerged from the body just behind the cockpit, had the unfortunate habit of setting fire to the paintwork.

It had been a disappointing season in WC events, but in non-Championship races, 250Fs were again very successful. Bira won the New Zealand GP, Behra took Pau and Bordeaux, Salvadori won races at Goodwood and Aintree, André Simon took Albi, Peter Collins the International Trophy at Silverstone, Moss the Oulton Park Gold Cup, and Bob Gerard and Mike Hawthorn with Moss' car both won minor F1 races in Britain. The car Collins drove had been bought by B.R.M. to keep in practice until its own cars were ready to run and it was identifiable by its Dunlop alloy wheels and disc brakes. Moss' own car was also fitted with disc brakes.

The unsuccessful streamlined Maserati, 2518, raced in 1955, seen here in unpainted form. (Corrado Millanta)

Juan Fangio in the 1957 British Grand Prix with 'lightweight' 250F, 2529. (T. C. March)

With the Mercedes-Benz withdrawal, the balance of power changed. Fangio went to Ferrari and Moss went to Maserati, this time as a super-star, for had he not won both the Mille Miglia and Targa Florio? Unfortunately Maserati was in a state of confusion. The poor 1955 season meant the F1 programme was under threat, for Maserati was tasting success in sports cars and its road car business was picking up. Perhaps this pressure had an unsettling effect, but whatever the reason there was no clear thought behind its development work. Different types of bodywork were tried, fuel injection put on and taken off, and then another type of injection used. Disc brakes were tried and then discarded.

Giulio Alfieri had taken over as head of design and he was a man of some imagination who could turn his attention to any part of a car, from engine to aerodynamics. Perhaps he was trying too hard to make an impression too soon. When he settled down he became a very able designer.

Mieres dropped out of racing for reasons connected with the overthrow of President Perón in his native Argentina. Behra stayed on as number two, and resented his position. He did not feel number two to Moss, but he was. At one time or another almost every available F1 driver raced under the works umbrella in 1956, including Taruffi and Villoresi.

No fewer than eight of the 13 starters in the Argentine GP were Maseratis, and the race was led by local man Carlos Menditeguy (250F) until about half-distance.

After his retirement Moss led until his engine went, but Behra eventually came second to Fangio, who had taken over Musso's Lancia-Ferrari.

Moss then had a flag to flag win in the Monaco GP, with Behra in third. That win shelved any thoughts of dropping from F1, but from then on the team tripped over itself. In the Belgian GP Moss finished third in Perdisa's car after his own had lost a wheel, and then Behra took third at Reims, where the Maserati drivers had no answer to the speed of either the Lancia-Ferraris or the new Vanwalls. The streamliner appeared in practice with fuel injection and disc brakes, but Moss describes it as 'a dead loss'. Moss set pole in the British GP and seemed set to win until first he had an ignition fault and then his gearbox broke. Behra finished third, a lap down. Moss then took second in the German GP with other Maseratis filling the next four places.

For the Italian GP Alfieri came up with new cars for Moss and Behra. These were lower, lighter and wider, and the engine was angled 5 degrees from the centre-line so that the prop-shaft ran diagonally across the floor from right to left. This arrangement had the effect of lowering the driver some eight inches in the car. The body had high cockpit sides, something which had been tried earlier, the radiator was fully ducted and the nose and tail were longer and tapered.

Moss drove an intelligent race, letting the Lancia-Ferrari challenge burn itself out, and despite running out of fuel (he was given a nudge to the pits by the Maserati of privateer Luigi Piotti) came home to win and finish second in the Championship.

As always there were wins in private races and Moss won the New Zealand, Mendoza and Australian GPs, the Aintree 200, and races at Goodwood and Crystal Palace. Harry Schell won the Caen GP, Reg Hunt won a couple of races in Australia and Horace Gould took the Aintree 100.

In view of the model's subsequent status, it is interesting to note that after three years it had won just four WC races, but by the end of 1956 no fewer than 21 had been completed with the majority in service with privateers. It was an ideal privateer's car, being practical, relatively simple and reliable, and strong and sweet to drive. Without it, it is hard to imagine what the state of F1 could have been like in the mid-1950s, especially the many non-Championship events.

1957 was to be the type's greatest year. Alfieri had calmed down and directed his considerable talent to constructive thinking. In fact, there had been a general reorganization. All the lessons learned from the previous three seasons were utilized and the latest cars drew heavily on the 'off-set' model with which Moss had won at Monza except that the engine reverted to its original 'straight line' position. The chassis were built from smaller-gauge tubes and moved closer to being true space-frames. Power was increased to 270 bhp at 8000 rpm, partly by adding nitromethane to the fuel. Even wider drum brakes were employed and the body was sleeker, rather like the Monza cars.

Moss left to join Vanwall and in his place came Fangio, who, despite his Championship, had been unhappy at Maranello. Behra stayed on as number two and Harry Schell, the ebullient Franco-American, joined the team.

Behind the scenes work was proceeding on a new V-12 engine and a new car to take it. This engine was a d.o.h.c. 'twin-plug' unit of 2476cc (68.5×56 mm) which apparently gave nearly 320 bhp at 9500 rpm. Unfortunately its power and torque curves were not of a satisfactory shape to say the least. Thus this complicated unit was virtually still-born, although Moss had a version of it in his 300S-based sports car in the 1956 Mille Miglia. V-12 engines were installed in two chassis, an old 250F and a 1957-type. They appeared in testing and practice, but only in two starts. Had Maserati continued into 1958, when Av-gas became mandatory, it is possible something could be made of them.

1957 was Fangio's year, and Maserati's, although in truth both had luck on their side, for the year should have belonged to Moss and Vanwall. The maestro opened his score with a win in the Argentine GP followed by Behra and Menditeguy. Moss also was in a works 250F (Vanwall had missed the race) and he had set pole by over a second, but was delayed for nine laps with a throttle problem. Since he finished only seven laps down, and with fastest lap, perhaps the result might otherwise have been different.

Maserati raced the V-12, in the 1957 Italian Grand Prix, in which it was driven by Jean Behra. The car was retired with engine problems. (**Publifoto**)

Fangio won the European opening round of the Championship too, after Moss' Vanwall had brake trouble, and in the ensuing crash, the Lancia-Ferraris of Hawthorn and Collins were eliminated as well. For different reasons both Moss and Brooks were too ill to race in the French GP at Rouen so Fangio had his main threat removed and he was able to deal with the Lancia-Ferraris and substitute Vanwall drivers. Behra finished second to Musso's Lancia-Ferrari in the Reims GP after Lewis-Evans' otherwise dominant Vanwall slowed when the newcomer had oil sprayed on his goggles and brakes. After three rounds, Fangio had three wins and had never had to race Moss to the line. Fangio did not shine in the British GP at Aintree, and he retired, but Behra might just have won had not his clutch let go 20 laps from home. As it was, Moss in Brooks' car, scored a glorious British victory.

At the German GP Fangio employed the trick of starting on half-full tanks, building up an early lead, losing time by refuelling, and then setting off again. It was by no means a new ploy, but he had not built up a dominant margin before his stop and he had to use his every resource, which was considerable, to overtake the Lancia-Ferraris of Hawthorn and Collins to win and clinch the title. Vanwall, on its first visit to the Nürburgring, was all at sea with its suspension settings and proved no threat.

In the remaining two races of a season blighted by a fuel shortage, the Pescara and Italian GPs, Fangio had to give best to Moss' Vanwall. His was not a hollow victory in the Championship race, his win in the German GP was magnificent, but he had had luck on his side.

The V-12's one race came at Monza, where Behra had one in a lightweight chassis. The engine's characteristics still made the car a handful, but Behra qualified fifth, behind the three Vanwalls and Fangio, and actually led for several laps early in the race. He was delayed by the need to take on water, new rear tyres and

Juan Fangio drove this 250F 'Piccolo', 2529 into fourth place in the 1958 French Grand Prix at Reims and then retired from the sport. Here he is being passed by Moss (Vanwall). (LAT)

extra fuel to feed the thirsty engine and finally went out with overheating. The engine's potential was demonstrated, however, and had Maserati continued into 1958, it is likely it would have fielded V-12s as its main weapon.

Behra rounded off Maserati's greatest season by winning the Moroccan GP, which, while it was a non-Championship event, attracted a representative field even if many drivers were suffering from Asian 'flu. It was the last time that Maserati officially ran an F1 team and so a works 250F had the distinction of winning both its first and last race, although private cars continued to appear.

Maserati's parent company had large investments in the Argentine and after President Péron's fall from power it had severe financial problems. These were heightened by a disaster in Venezuela when, with a chance to win the World Sports Car Championship as well, the team saw its hopes dashed as disaster after expensive disaster befell its cars. At the end of its most successful year, Maserati had to announce its withdrawal from racing.

Despite Fangio's Championship, other victories were thinner on the ground. Fangio won the Formule Libre Buenos Aires City GP and Behra won at Pau and Modena. 1958 would see Fangio winning the Buenos Aires race and Ross Jensen two races in New Zealand and that brought the tally of wins to a close until the cars began to appear in Historic racing.

Maserati did in fact provide Fangio with a car (entered under the banner of Scuderia Sud Americana) for the 1958 Argentine GP and he set pole, but the cars did not take kindly to running on Av-gas and they were prone to overheat. Fangio finished fourth, in the only 250F not to be lapped by Moss' Cooper, and he set fastest lap as well.

No fewer than nine 250Fs were entered in the Monaco GP, but only two qualified and neither finished. Three started in the Dutch GP, but only Bonnier finished, four laps down. Things had moved quickly and the Champion car of 1957 was completely outclassed in 1958.

Although Maserati was still officially out of the sport, the American privateer Temple Buell financed the building of a 1958 version, nicknamed the 'piccolo'. This had the wheelbase shortened by 1½ inches and a weight-shedding programme lost 160 lb. There was a smaller and lighter gearbox, the brakes were larger (although still drums) and there were detail changes to the suspension. There were new fabricated wishbones at the front, with larger coils, springs and Girling dampers, while at the rear Koni shock absorbers were used. Apparently the engine had been revised and was now

2473cc (80 × 81 mm), which, with a raised compression ratio, was said to develop 270 bhp at 7500 rpm. The car appeared in practice for the Belgian GP and was given to Fangio to drive in the French race. It was to be the maestro's last race, but such had been the rate of progress that he could make only tenth place on the grid, although he inherited fourth place at the end. It was the last time that a Maserati won WC points.

Thereafter Maserati faded quickly, although 250Fs were to continue to appear as make-weights until the end of the 2½-litre formula. Indeed, as many as five appeared in the 1960 Argentine GP, although none finished. A little afterwards, however, Gino Munaron and Ettore Chimeri finished third and fourth in the Formule Libre Buenos Aires City Grand Prix, which was the last time a 250F finished in the top three in an international race.

It fell to an otherwise obscure driver, an American, Bob Drake, to write the last lines in the 250F story, at least so far as Formula 1 is concerned. In the car which Fangio used in almost every race in 1957 he took part in the last race of the 2½-litre formula, the 1960 US GP at Riverside. He was outclassed, but was a classified finisher in 13th place.

Even that was not quite the end of the story, for Maserati engines were to be used by other makers, notably Cooper, until the late 1960s. Indeed, Cooper was to win two World Championship races using developed 3-litre versions of the V-12 engine.

Although Maserati officially pulled out of racing at the end of 1957, it never quite let go and before long there was the 'birdcage' series of sports-racers which sold in some numbers to privateers and while there was no official works team, the Camoradi USA team took over that function for a while. By the early 1960s, Maserati was a spent force in racing but Ing Alfieri was not quite finished.

In 1964 Maserati announced it was ready to supply F1 teams with a new engine, the Tipo 8/F1, together with a new 6-speed gearbox. This engine was a 1½-litre d.o.h.c. 60-degree V-12 (55.2 × 52 mm) designed to be mounted transversely in a car's frame and with the transmission, including the final drive, built into the crankcase. Lucas fuel injection feed through Dell'Orto carburettor bodies and it was claimed to give 180 bhp at 12,000 rpm.

So far as its potential customers were concerned, it was too little, too late, for both B.R.M. and Coventry Climax engines produced more power and had proven reliability records. With the 1½-litre F1 due to end the following year, it made no sense at all in adopting an untried engine which might, or might not, eventually become competitive and an engine, moreover, whose design dictated too many parameters to a designer.

Thus nobody was hurt in a rush to buy and the unit only ever ran on a dynamometer.

In retrospect it is as well that Maserati pulled out when it did because even had Fangio driven a works 'piccolo' throughout 1958 it is unlikely he would have enjoyed success beyond a few places. It would not have been a fitting end to his glorious career and neither would it have been a fitting end to Maserati works Grand Prix involvement. The reputation of the 250F has grown with the passing of time, but its total of WC wins, eight, was not extraordinary, particularly if one takes into account the number of starts the cars made. Still, more that any other car it epitomizes its period and Formula 1 would have been pretty thin fare without the dozens of private 250Fs which swelled the grids.

MASERATI-PLATÉ

Enrico Platé ran a private F1 team using Maserati 4CLT/48s with 'B. Bira' and Baron de Graffenried as his principal drivers. When Formula 2 became the World Championship category, he found himself unable to obtain suitable cars. He reasoned that if the Maserati unit could withstand two-stage supercharging, it would be reliable without. He had new blocks cast with wider bores and fitted long-stroke crankshafts.

The result was an engine of 1995cc (84×90 mm) which gave perhaps 140 bhp, and the rest of the car was pure Maserati 4CLT except that the wheelbase was shortened by eight inches to 7 ft 6½ in, similar to the Maserati A6GCM, this being possible once the plumbing for the superchargers had been removed. Externally, the main difference was a new radiator cowl.

Considering the cars were only a stop-gap, they were a decent enough effort, although they suffered from steering and braking problems. Overall, they were roughly on a par with H.W.M., make-weights in Championship races but welcome in the minor races, where, against other lesser lights, they might occasionally come away with some silverware. They were overweight and underpowered, but they kept Platé in racing during 1952. Originally Louis Chiron was to partner Baron Emmanuel de Graffenried, but in the first race of the year, at Syracuse, his car caught fire, he was badly burned and missed the rest of the season. Nello Pagani, a motorcycle racer, and Franco Cortese drove the second car, without success, in the early races of 1952, but eventually Harry Schell became the regular choice.

Pagani and de Graffenried showed pace in the Pau GP, but both retired, then de Graffenried came fourth in the Marseilles GP and third in the International Trophy at Silverstone. In the Swiss GP, his home race, he was well off the pace, but qualified ahead of Moss' E.R.A. and the H.W.M. team, and although four laps down at the end he

Harry Schell with one of the Platé-Maseratis in the 1952 International Trophy race at Silverstone. These cars, based on the 4CLT/48, were neither quick nor reliable. (T. C. March)

finished sixth. Schell, in the other car, was much slower and retired with engine trouble.

Schell was the quicker at Rouen for the French GP, but both cars retired with brake trouble at half-distance. In the only other WC race in which the team started, the British GP, they were late arriving and had to start from the back of the grid. Although both finished, they were over seven laps down. At Silverstone, however, the cars were about six seconds a lap slower than they had been at the International Trophy only two months earlier. The team did not have the facilities to keep two cars fettled, and as the season progressed they became increasingly slower and less reliable. To Platé's credit, however, he kept all his engagements, even though he must have been hard pressed to have done so. In general Maserati-Platé concentrated on the minor races, where the highlights were third places for de Graffenried at Aix-le-Bains and Cadours. Two car were entered for the Italian GP for de Graffenried and Eitel Crespo, but by then they were worn out and both failed to qualify.

Maserati started selling its A6GCM in 1953 so, their job done, the Platé cars were retired from racing and embarked on a new career as film stars. They were sold to 20th Century-Fox and starred as the 'Burano' GP cars in the film *Such Men Are Dangerous*. Afterwards they disappeared into the studio's garage of 'prop' cars. Enrico Platé continued to enter cars in 1953, but was killed in a pits accident in the Argentine early the following year.

MERCEDES-BENZ

After the Second World War, Germany was excluded from international motor sport until 1950. One effect of the ban was that the face of motor racing changed. The Alfa Romeo 158, a *Voiturette*, became dominant in Grand Prix racing. Cars such as Talbot-Lagos, which had once been make-weights, became promoted to contenders. Racing benefitted as a contest, but stepped back in time.

Daimler-Benz and Auto Union had other problems to deal with, such as a divided Germany and the rebuilding of shattered factories. In the boardroom of Daimler-Benz, however, the value of racing as a development exercise and publicity vehicle was seen as part of the strategy of rebirth. The question was not if the company would return but when, and the decision depended partly on the health of the company and partly on international politics.

In early 1951 Mercedes-Benz discreetly tested the water by sending a pair of 1939 3-litre supercharged W163s to the Argentine to compete in a couple of Formule Libre races. Karl Kling and Hermann Lang finished second and third in both, on each occasion beaten by Gonzalez' blown 2-litre Ferrari. It gave the company a small indication of the opposition, but, more importantly, there had been no outcry about their participation.

Soon afterwards the board of Daimler-Benz sanctioned a return to racing the following year with a sports car based on production components with a pukka GP effort to follow. Under the direction of that great engineer Rudolf Uhlenhaut, a team of Mercedes-Benz 300SL coupés was built for racing in 1952 and they acquitted themselves well, with the highlight being 1-2 at both Le Mans and in the Carrera Panamericana. This design was then retired, a production version was marketed, and a new F1 design was laid down for the start of the 2½-litre formula.

A design team led by Uhlenhaut and Hans Scherenberg produced a car which commanded respect rather than excitement. No matter how much money and personnel a team has, success can never be guaranteed or else Ferrari would have won every race in the last 30 years, but Daimler-Benz' W196 was extremely successful, so all credit to it. The interesting thing remains that it was not copied. The reason for this is that it was a complete *package* of a sort which could only be compiled by a major manufacturer.

On 4 July, 1954, Mercedes-Benz returned to GP racing at Reims with three cars for Fangio, Karl Kling and Hans Herrmann — one star and two second-string drivers who happened to be German. Externally, the cars were sensational, for they were clothed in gorgeous fully-enclosed aerodynamic bodies, ideally suited to Reims, which was a high-speed triangle of long straights with tricky corners at the end of each straight. This body has struck a chord in the imagination, although W196s did not race in this form many times and they were actually not that clever.

Under the shell was a properly triangulated spaceframe made up of small-diameter tubes which was as advanced as any GP car of its day, but was no more advanced than Colin Chapman's frames. The engine was a straight-eight, the last successful straight-eight in racing, and was chosen for lightness, but what advantage it had over a V-8 was negated when early testing showed up

Posed for the press: Karl Kling at the wheel of the streamlined Mercedes-Benz W196 in February 1954.

severe vibration which had to be cured by crankshaft dampers.

The Mercedes unit was made in two blocks of four cylinders with the timing gears and power take-off between them. A shaft then took the power via a dry single-plate clutch and a prop-shaft which passed beneath the rear axle line to a 5-speed gearbox mounted in unit with the final drive, which had Porsche synchromesh on the top four ratios. This 2496cc engine (76×68.8 mm) followed established M-B practice in that the ports and water jackets were welded on, but there were only two valves per cylinder and these were activated by a desmodronic system, i.e. the twin overhead camshafts both opened and closed the valves without the use of valve springs. The crankshaft ran in ten roller bearings and a new type of Bosch direct fuel injection was another feature. The engine itself was canted over at 37 degrees from the horizontal to achieve a low bonnet line. Initially a power output of 257 bhp at 8200 rpm was quoted and, unlike many power figures, this may be assumed correct. By the beginning of 1955, output had increased to 290 bhp at 8500 rpm.

Suspension was independent all round with torsion bars springing both the double wishbone front layout and the swing-axle rear. Swing-axles were chosen to maintain family resemblance, for production Mercedes-Benz cars used them. The choice of swing axles was a bit of an own goal, because there was no way that such a layout was optimum for a 1954 GP car and thus handling was marginal.

Massive drum brakes were mounted inboard front and rear. Like most German companies Mercedes-Benz has always been resistant to non-German ideas so chose drum brakes over discs despite the fact that Jaguar had proven their superiority. In 1955 Mercedes-Benz twice fitted air brakes (hydraulically operated flaps) to its 300SLR sports cars to try to match the braking power of discs, and although the solution was admired, it was a crude expedient. While mounting the brakes inboard reduced unsprung weight, there was another motive and that was the team's intention of eventually fitting four-wheel drive. Such a system would probably have kept the cars competitive had Mercedes-Benz stayed in racing past the end of 1955.

It was easily the heaviest car of its time and its power was not extraordinary, but it was reliable and everything worked in harmony. Having said that, it did require a top-class driver to make the most of it and while a second-string man could be flattered by it, there was no question of the car being so good it could make a winner of such, as the Ferrari 156 did for Giancarlo Baghetti.

Mercedes-Benz, however, had two huge advantages.

One was that Uhlenhaut was not only a brilliant engineer but he was also a superb driver who could have made a career in F1. The other was that it had produced an entirely new car for the new formula on time. Lancia's D50 was not ready, Ferrari was relying on an enlarged F2 design, Connaught and B.R.M. were not yet ready to race, the appearances of the Vanwall were spasmodic, Gordini was suffering its eternal problem, lack of cash, while the Maserati 250F, fine car though it was, was not quite good enough unless it had a star behind the wheel.

The Maserati was not far off, however, as Ascari proved at Reims, when he practised third fastest, 1.1 seconds slower than Fangio's pole, but only a tenth slower than Kling and five seconds quicker than Herrmann. Fangio and Kling sailed off into the distance and most of the serious opposition blew their engines trying to stay in touch. Helped partly by retirements, Herrmann was up to third when his engine let go on lap 16, but he did have the satisfaction of setting fastest lap, although it was 3.5 seconds down on Fangio's pole time.

So Mercedes scored a 1-2 on its return and the impact was heightened by a stage-managed finish, with Kling arriving only a tenth of a second down with Robert Manzon's Ferrari in third place, a whole lap behind. For a new design to win so convincingly on its debut was then so rare that the event made headlines around the world and thoroughly demoralized most of the opposition. There was a sense of inevitability in the statement, 'So there you are — they're back', which Rodney Walkerley wrote in *The Motor*.

That race has stuck in the popular imagination, but the rest of M-B's 1954 season was by no means as dominant. Overlooked at the time was that Reims was a clever choice to stage-manage a return, provided the cars finished, for with their streamlined bodies they were ideally suited to what was, after all, a freak circuit.

Some observers noticed that the cars looked a handful on the tighter corners at Reims and wondered how much aerodynamics had contributed to the win. The cars were quick, but so are aerodynamic record-breakers, which did not mean to say they will go round corners. Indeed, M-B was soon to discover a major problem in that to utilize the properties of the body, the suspension had to be set up in such a way that the car went from understeer to oversteer very quickly.

If the *stromlinienwagen* had been at an advantage at Reims it was a handicap at Silverstone, where the enclosed wheels made the car difficult to place in the corners and its handling was a problem. Fangio still set pole, but Kling, in the only other Mercedes entered, could do no better than sixth on the grid, three seconds off the pace. Suddenly Mercedes-Benz was reduced to human size.

Gonzalez' Ferrari led from flag to flag, and while Fangio ran second for a while, he had to be content with fourth place a lap down, and his car's battered bodywork told its own story. The lack-lustre Kling came in seventh, three laps down. Mercedes was not looking quite as good and the next race was at the Nürburgring in front of the home crowd.

Many have suggested that the width of the body made the car unsuitable for Silverstone but that is nonsense, Fangio could drive a sports car without hitting markers. The fault lay in the shape of the body and the unpredictable handling it generated. It is right to call it a 'streamlined' shell for there was no sensible application of aerodynamics.

In the two weeks between the races, the strength of M-B was demonstrated as open-wheeled cars were prepared for Fangio, Kling and the veteran Hermann Lang, while Herrmann had a streamliner. In contrast to the streamliners, on the open-wheelers no attempt had been made to include aerodynamics in the equation and they were not at all quick on a speed circuit. It is worth noting that Connaught did not have a problem with a fully enveloping body on a tight circuit. It took Frank Costin and Vanwall to apply aerodynamics to a Grand Prix car in a way which was both practical and which would work on any circuit.

Fangio set another pole position at the Nürburgring, but his team-mates were a long way behind. Lang had won the European Championship for Mercedes in 1939 so his inclusion was a pleasant gesture, but he was sadly lacking practice and was only a shadow of his former greatness. In fact, he practised over 12 seconds slower than Moss' Maserati and Moss had been told by M-B's Alfred Neubauer that he lacked sufficient experience to drive for the team! Fangio's brilliance gave M-B a home win, Lang spun off, Herrmann had a fuel pipe break when fifth, Kling with his great knowledge of the circuit led for a couple of laps at two-thirds distance, but had to stop for fuel and finished fourth. The record books show another win for Mercedes-Benz, but it was a win for Fangio more than anything.

Gonzalez took pole in the Swiss GP, from Fangio and Moss, with Kling and Herrmann down the grid, but although Fangio took the lead he was harried by Moss until the Maserati's oil pump failed. Kling spun on the first lap, charged back to third place at two-thirds distance, but retired with a broken fuel injection pump a few laps later. Fangio stroked home to win from Gonzalez with Herrmann third, and a lap down, following the retirement of all the other serious runners. This was another win for Fangio, not Mercedes-Benz, for he could equally have won with the Maserati with which he started the season.

Fangio set pole at Monza in a streamliner, but Ascari in a Ferrari was only two-tenths slower. Moss' Maserati was only at tenth slower than Ascari and quicker than Kling in another streamliner. Herrmann, in an open-wheeled car, could only manage eighth on the grid.

Kling led Fangio in the early stages until spinning. Then Ascari and Moss hounded Fangio, and Ascari actually took the lead between laps 6 and 23 until he retired. Moss then moved ahead and built up a lead of more than 20 seconds until, ten laps from the finish, his oil tank split and allowed Fangio a lucky win. With that drive Moss established himself not just as a top-level driver but as a driver of greatness. Even the myopic Neubauer had to recognize talent when it bit him on the leg. Herrmann finished fourth, while Kling had a lucky escape when an oil pipe broke and squirted lubricant in his face. He ran off the road and felled several trees, but escaped serious injury.

The non-Championship Berlin GP run on the fast Avus circuit was a Mercedes-Benz benefit against a thin field of privateers. The three streamliners swapped the lead without stressing themselves and Kling was permitted a politic win with Fangio half a second behind and Herrmann a further four-tenths down. The race was interesting for two things, one was Fangio's fastest lap with an average speed of 137.74 mph and the other was Kling's winning average, 132.66 mph. By contrast the record at what is now the fastest circuit, Silverstone, then stood at 100.16 mph and that was when Woodcote was a high-speed corner.

The final race of the year, the Spanish GP at Barcelona, saw Ascari put his new Lancia on pole, a full second ahead of Fangio, with Herrmann and Kling well down the order in ninth and twelfth places. Ascari was in the lead when, after nine laps, he retired with a slipping clutch. Thus the fierce battle for second between Harry Schell (Maserati, and running with a half-full tank to try break the opposition), Mike Hawthorn (Ferrari) and Maurice Trintignant (Ferrari) became the battle for the lead with Fangio biding his time and Kling and Herrmann outclassed as usual. At the finish the winner was Hawthorn from Luigi Musso's Maserati with Fangio's car third and not in peak condition. Waste paper had been sucked into his car's air intake and caused overheating. Kling finished fifth with a sick car, while Herrmann retired with engine trouble.

1954 saw Fangio win his second World Championship, deservedly so, but it is likely he would still have won had he stayed with Maserati, for whom he scored two victories before Mercedes-Benz entered the fray. So much garbage has been written about the

In the 1954 Italian Grand Prix Juan Fangio with the W196 leads Moss (Maserati). Moss retired because of a leaking oil tank when leading the race, and Fangio was the eventual winner. Note the disappearance of the Mercedes emblem from the air intake grill. **(Publifoto)**

'dominance' of Mercedes-Benz that it is high time the facts were examined.

In 1954, apart from M-B's dominance at Reims, the best one can say is that *Fangio* was marginally quicker than the opposition in *some* races, but then he would have been in a Maserati or a Ferrari. Neubauer's choice of drivers to back his star was guided by sentimentality and not hard-nosed professionalism, yet he is so often described as 'legendary'. Then again, Alberto Ascari, whom Fangio acknowledged as his master, spent most of the season on the sidelines waiting for his Lancia to appear, and the absence of the maestro was a key element in the season. If Mercedes-Benz enjoyed a power advantage it was more than offset by the weight of the cars, which were anyway not particularly sweet to drive. M-B also made some fundamental mistakes such as running streamliners at Silverstone.

On the other hand the company was sufficiently well organized and committed to respond to its errors very quickly, at least in the technical department. The team did *not* enjoy superiority in 1954, it had a small edge in performance and it had reliablity. It also had Fangio and that made the difference. Running such as Kling, Herrmann and Lang was a waste of time, money and effort.

Having said that, nothing can be taken away from Mercedes-Benz' 1955 season. It had learned from its mistakes, Fangio stayed on and was joined by Moss, so there were now two potential winners in the team. Engine power was increased to 290 bhp and the team produced both long-wheelbase (92.5-in) and short-wheelbase (87-in) versions. Later the 'short-wheelbase' type would be termed the 'medium-wheelbase', because an even shorter (84.6-in) version was prepared for Monaco. To save confusion they are here labelled retrospectively.

For the Argentine GP, run in searing heat, the cars had cooling holes cut in their bodywork, vents to take air into the cockpit and side plates which were meant to deflect hot air rising from the exhaust pipes from worrying the drivers (on the Vanwall, Frank Costin cooled his drivers by clever ducting — he did not have to add plates to the body). Fangio and Kling had mwb cars, while Moss and Herrmann had the older version. For once practice was very close, with only 1.8 seconds covering the first ten cars. Fangio was second behind Gonzalez' Ferrari, Kling sixth, Moss eighth and Herrmann tenth.

The heat took its toll as drivers made mistakes or simply handed over their cars, unable to continue. After quarter-distance Fangio led from Moss, but soon afterwards Moss' engine expired. After his exhausting session behind the wheel, Stirling lay down in the pits and was pounced on by ambulance men, who assumed he had

collapsed and took him away on a stretcher. He eventually escaped from the ambulance and took over the car in which Herrmann had started, but which Kling, who had crashed his own car, had taken over. Moss brought it home fourth, but two laps down on Fangio, who had driven alone, while the Ferraris which finished second and third each had had three drivers.

A fortnight later came the Buenos Aires Formule Libre GP and three W196s were fitted with 2979cc versions of the straight-eight engine which were then being prepared for M-B's assault on the WSCC. The race was run in two heats with victory in the first going to Farina's Ferrari from Fangio and Moss. Moss won the second from Fangio, but when the times were combined, Fangio emerged the winner with Stirling second.

Three short-wheelbase cars were entered at Monaco for Fangio, Moss and Herrmann and these had their front brakes mounted outboard for better cooling. Herrmann crashed heavily in practice and broke a leg, which kept him out of racing for some time. The Frenchman André Simon was drafted in to take over the team spare. Fangio and Moss sat on the front row of the grid with Ascari's Lancia between them. At the start Fangio got away first, but Castellotti slotted into second place from his fourth place on the grid. It took Moss four laps to get by the Italian's Lancia and a further 30 to catch his team-leader, whereupon they circulated in close convoy.

On lap 49 Fangio retired when an adjustment screw in the valve gear broke and it looked as if Moss was heading for his first GP victory, when, on lap 81, his engine let go for the same reason as Fangio's. A few moments later Ascari, who effectively led, had his famous dip in the harbour and it was left to Maurice Trintignant to score a fluke win in his Ferrari 625. André Simon retired from tenth place with a broken oil pipe after 24 laps.

The following Thursday, Ascari was killed in a private test session at Monza. His death hastened the withdrawal of Lancia, which anyway was close to ruin, and with Ferrari in a shambles, and Maserati without a star driver, that left the field to Mercedes-Benz. Had Ascari not been killed and had Lancia seen out the year, 1955 might have been a great season. As it was, it became something of a damp squib and any excitement has been generated in retrospect by hacks who have churned out starry-eyed accounts of Mercedes-Benz' walkover. It is true that Mercedes-Benz carried all before it for the rest of the season, but after Ascari's death the 'all' did not amount to much.

In practice for the Belgian GP at Spa, Castellotti's lone Lancia took pole from Fangio and Moss with Kling in sixth slot, nearly six seconds off the pace. All three M-B

Stirling Moss with the unstreamlined medium-wheelbase W196 on his way to his first Grand Épreuve *victory in the 1955 British Grand Prix at Aintree.* (Daimler-Benz AG)

drivers had lwb cars and at the start Fangio and Moss sailed into the lead to finish 1-2, while Kling retired with a broken oil pipe just after half-distance when fourth. Three cars were entered in the Dutch GP for Fangio, Moss and Kling, and they qualified in that order. Fangio had an swb, Moss an mwb, and Kling's mwb car had outboard front brakes. Fangio and Moss established themselves in the first two places and ran away from the field to finish in line ahead. Kling spun out from fifth place after 21 laps.

Following the tragedy at Le Mans, the French and German GPs were cancelled, so the team's next appearance was at Aintree for the British GP. Moss (swb) took pole by two-tenths from Fangio (swb) with Behra's Maserati in third slot and Kling (mwb) and Piero Taruffi (swb) in fourth and fifth. Moss came home to win by two-tenths from Fangio, with Kling third, 72 seconds behind, and Taruffi fourth, a lap down. It was Stirling's first WC win and if, as seems likely, Fangio allowed him a home victory, it was a generous gesture by a great sportsman and made up for Moss' disappointment in the 1954 Italian GP.

The tragedy at Le Mans blighted racing. Switzerland banned motor racing altogether, the Automobile Association of America washed its hands of the sport, there was outrage everywhere and many races were cancelled. Thus there remained only the Italian GP to complete the 1955 World Championship.

New to Monza were the bankings, and in August Mercedes-Benz tested there and decided that the best compromise would be a medium-wheelbase streamlined car. It also tried flip-up air brakes, but decided not to race with them. Two mwb streamliners with outboard front brakes were prepared for Moss and Fangio, and also taken to the race were a lwb streamliner and two open wheelers (one swb, one mwb). Then it was found that, since the test session, the bankings had been smoothed and the lwb car was best suited to the track. Daimler-Benz built two new lwb streamliners with outboard front brakes *in 30 hours* and rushed them to Italy on its fabled high-speed transporters, which had a 300SL engine and could exceed 100 mph. This was the true measure of M-B's strength. No other team before or since could have done that. Its racing department, headed by Walter Kostelezky, comprised 200 designers, engineers and mechanics and they had first call on the entire factory and all the best craftsmen.

No team in racing history has enjoyed such back-up, and while there was not an unlimited budget for the project, it was sufficient to provide no fewer than 15 chassis and 70 engines for what was to be a total of 14 races. Contrast that to the early 1960s, when the *total* number of Coventry Climax V-8 engines was less than half what M-B had. Then all that most teams took to a meeting were two cars and a spare engine. If anything explains why Daimler-Benz was successful when it went racing, it was this remarkable reaction and, please note, its leading drivers were already assured of a 1-2 in the World Championship.

So Fangio sat on pole with a brand new lwb streamliner and Moss was in second place with a similar chassis, but with the less svelte 1954 enveloping bodywork. Kling, in third slot, had an lwb open wheeler, while Taruffi, in ninth, had an swb open wheeler with outboard front brakes. After the start Fangio led from Moss with Taruffi third and Kling fourth, although these two swapped places on lap four. After 19 laps a stone from Fangio's wheels shattered Moss's windscreen. He pitted to have a new one fitted and dropped to 12th, where he still was when a piston broke eight laps later. Shortly after Moss retired, Kling disappeared from second place with a broken transmission. Nothing was to stop Fangio and Taruffi, however, and they cruised round in convoy to another Mercedes-Benz 1-2.

With the exception of the uncharacteristic engine failures at Monaco, Mercedes-Benz completely dominated the 1955 Grand Prix season. The cars raced only six times in F1, but won five, took three 1-2s and one 1-2-3-4, and over 30 years later Daimler-Benz still reaps the benefit.

Work was going ahead for 1956 when, on 22 October, Daimler-Benz announced it was withdrawing from motor sport. Its decision was perhaps prompted by the fact that it had been Pierre Levegh's Mercedes-Benz 300SLR which had exploded into the crowd at Le Mans. As some had been quick to point out, Levegh was an odd choice for a top team, but it had been another sentimental decision, since he had so nearly denied Mercedes-Benz victory at Le Mans in 1952.

This decision again left the field wide open, but it remains a moot point whether M-B could have sustained its dominance as Maserati and Lancia-Ferrari got into their stride and Vanwall loomed on the horizon. Since the team was likely to retain the services of Fangio and Moss, the answer must be affirmative, for they were enough to tip the balance.

MILANO

The organizers of the 1949 Italian Grand Prix offered particularly handsome starting money to any entrant of two cars to a new design. This inducement led the Scuderia Milano, run by the Ruggeri brothers, to take a couple of Maserati 4CLT/48s, refettle them, and enter them as Maserati-Milanos. Mario Speluzzi, who tuned Maserati engines for use in speed-boats, worked on the engines to tease out a claimed 290 bhp, which, if true, was 30 bhp more than standard. Much of the work appears to have been concentrated on the blowers, which operated at 44 psi instead of the more usual 28 psi. As for the cars themselves, they were Maseratis with shortened wheelbases and larger brakes, but AC Milano deemed them sufficiently novel to qualify for the bonus.

Driven by Giuseppe Farina and Piero Taruffi they proved fast enough — only the works Ferraris were quicker — and satisfyingly noisy, but neither lasted long in the race. Taruffi had a number of problems, and pit stops, and finished third, while Farina gave up in disgust after 18 laps because, poor dear, he was only in third place behind the Ferraris of Ascari and Villoresi. Had he continued at this pace he would have finished second. Still, the starting money was a welcome cash injection and the Ruggeris laid down two new chassis for 1950.

These were designed to take the Maserati engines and both chassis were large-oval-tube ladder-frames with double wishbone and torsion bar front suspension; at the rear the first chassis had a de Dion axle with a transverse leaf spring while the second had twin trailing links and transverse leaf irs. Both chassis took a long time to complete and, in the interim, Felice Bonetto was entered in one of the original Maserati-Milanos in the Swiss and French Grands Prix.

At Berne Felice Bonetto finished fifth, but two laps down. During a pit stop he suffered a fuel explosion — this did not delay him, but did demolish the pit! At Reims the car had a troubled practice and Bonetto retired with engine trouble at a quarter-distance.

For the non-Championship Grand Prix des Nations at Geneva the de Dion chassis ('1') was ready and was entered for the veteran Gianfranco Comotti, while Bonetto had a 1949 car. Comotti's car had a large single Roots-type blower in place of the two-stage system used on the 1949 cars, but it never ran properly and was withdrawn after eight laps, while Bonetto motored round to finish eighth. For the Freiburg Hill Climb, Scuderia Milano had the pre-war Auto Union driver, Paul Pietsch, in the 1949 car and he confounded expectations by setting ftd and

This Milano driven by Jover finished tenth in the 1950 Penya Rhin Grand Prix at Barcelona.

breaking the record. Fired by this performance, Bonetto gritted his teeth and finished third in the first car.

These performances suggested to the Ruggeris that there was nothing basically wrong with their cars, but the problem lay in the cockpit. In fact, in racing, the cars were simply not fast enough, because at Pescara Bonetto in '1' was timed at 152 mph and could only finish seventh, while Fangio's winning Alfa Romeo was timed at more than 30 mph quicker.

Three cars were entered for the Italian Grand Prix, but only '1', for Comotti, appeared. By this time there was a new Speluzzi cylinder head with two plugs per cylinder which gave a claimed 320 bhp. It retired after 16 laps. Two cars were entered for the Barcelona GP and were handled by local heroes Francesco Godia-Sales and

José Jover; the former had the 1949 car and retired, while the latter had '1', which finished a distant tenth, and last, in a sick condition.

That would have more or less spelled the end of the Milano cars, for the team withdrew in early 1951, except for two things. One was that in 1955 chassis '2', which had not been raced, was completed to form the basis of the Arzani-Volpini F1 car. The other was that the Ruggeri brothers teamed up with Enrico Franchini to create an entirely new car. This would have had a chassis similar to '2' except that Franchini's air-cooled flat-eight engine of 2490cc (72×76.5 mm) would have been transversely mounted behind the driver. It was designed to give over 300 bhp, but there was not the money to complete either frame or engine, although both are still in existence.

O. S. C. A.

In 1937 the three surviving Maserati Brothers, Ernesto, Ettore and Bindo, sold their eponymous company to Count Orsi, but were retained on a ten-year service contract. At its expiry they moved to Bologna and began work on a series of small sports-racing cars which achieved a great deal of success in the 1950s until first Porsche and then Lotus overshadowed them.

In 1951 the brothers produced an ambitious V-12 engine for Formula 1. This was a normally aspirated engine of 4472cc with the classic Maserati cylinder

dimensions of 78×78 mm. It was derived from Ernesto Maserati's 4-cylinder 1½-litre 4CLT engine, but was simplified in that it had only one camshaft per bank of cylinders and only two valves per cylinder in place of the 4CLT's four. It produced nearly 300 bhp, but that was already somewhat short of what was necessary to compete with the 4½-litre Ferraris.

A run of eight engines was projected and Amédée Gordini, who was working in co-operation with the Maseratis, was due to take delivery of half of them. In the

'B. Bira' in the paddock at Goodwood at the Easter Monday meeting in 1951 with his O.S.C.A. 4.5-litre car, based on the 4CLT/48 Maserati chassis. The car was a dismal failure. (Guy Griffiths)

event only four were made for, at the end of 1951, F1 was replaced by F2 as the World Championship formula, so the unit was redundant within months of its debut. One of the four engines was delivered to Gordini, who used it for evaluation purposes.

'B. Bira' took delivery of the first engine, which he fitted into his 4CLT/48 chassis which, of course, was designed by Ernesto Maserati, wearing a different hat. Bira won on his debut with the car at Goodwood, but it was only a five-lap race and the opposition was thin.

In the Italian GP, the penultimate WC race of the year, Franco Rol appeared with a second car which had an all-new ladder chassis with front suspension by coil springs and double wishbones and a de Dion rear axle suspended on torsion bars. Rol qualified more than 20 seconds off the pace, and though he was classified ninth in the race he was 13 laps in arrears. Rol drove the car occasionally in 1952, but with similar results, and it was put away. In 1956 it was converted into a central-seater sports car. Bira appeared with his car for the last WC event for which it was eligible, the Spanish GP. In practice he was 35 seconds off the pace and retired on lap one with engine trouble. After an adventurous life this car eventually ended up in the Donington Collection. A third Tipo 4500-G was sold to Cordero di Montezemole Paole, who appears not to have raced it, but instead had it converted into an rhd sports car.

It seems that the Maserati brothers considered

Louis Chiron with the 6-cylinder Formula 2 O.S.C.A. in the International Trophy at Silverstone in May 1953. The car was not competitive and the Monégasque driver retired because of a split fuel tank. (Guy Griffiths)

building a 2-litre V-8 engine for F2, but abandoned the idea after Gordini had built and scrapped a similar unit. Thus the O.S.C.A. F2 car which appeared in 1952 had a 6-cylinder d.o.h.c. engine of 1987cc (76×73 mm) which was very similar to Gordini's 2-litre unit, although with slightly different cylinder dimensions. The chassis was a scaled-down version of the second V-12 car except that the de Dion rear axle was suspended on quarter-elliptic springs. The car was overweight, but 170 bhp was claimed from the engine, and while this was probably over-optimistic it was perhaps not extravagantly so, for the cars went fairly well on speed circuits such as Reims and Monza. Since Gordini used a similar engine, but a completely different, lightweight, chassis, one is fairly safe in identifying the chassis as O.S.C.A.'s weakness. An O.S.C.A. engine in a Cooper frame might have been a clever combination in 1952.

Elie Bayol bought the first of the two cars made and because it took longer than expected to appear, he began the season with a stripped-down O.S.C.A. MT4 sports car, and while it was completely outclassed (it had a 1½-litre engine) it picked up a few place finishes, indeed Bayol finished fourth in the 1952 Pau GP with his sports car and fourth in the following year's race with his pukka F2 car. It was not until early August that the car was ready to race and Bayol had it for the Comminges GP, where he ran as high as fourth, but was disqualified for a technical infringement. In the Italian GP he qualified quite respectably, tenth from 25 starters and best privateer, but his gearbox gave up before he completed a single lap in the race. In the Modena GP, however, Bayol finished sixth behind works Ferraris and Maseratis.

It had been a fairly promising start and a second car was sold to Louis Chiron, who was in the twilight of a distinguished career. Between them, Bayol and Chiron garnered a few place finishes in non-Championship events and Bayol won at Aix-les-Bains, beating Rosier's Ferrari in the process. Chiron's best placing was second at Syracuse, but he was three laps down on de Graffenried's Maserati.

Both cars were entered in the 1953 French GP, where Chiron practised last and finished last, 17 laps down, while Bayol at least qualified ahead of the H.W.M. team, but retired before one-third distance. Both entered the 1953 Italian GP, too, and Bayol again qualified well, 11th from 28 starters and ahead of all the British cars, but he retired in the race. Chiron qualified near the back of the grid and plugged away to finish tenth, but he was 53 years old and racing only for his own amusement.

From then on O.S.C.A. concentrated on its sports cars, which were extremely successful until first Porsche took charge of the 1500cc class and Lotus did the same in 1100cc racing. The problem was that the Maserati brothers were essentially 'engine men' and had no answer to a new generation of chassis designers. Further they were all ageing, the youngest being over 60 by the end of the decade and in 1963, they sold their company to M.V. Agusta.

In 1960 Alejandro de Tomaso fitted one of the brothers' 4-cylinder 1453cc (78×76 mm) 'desmodronic' engines to a copy of a Cooper to make a de Tomaso-O.S.C.A. F2 car. It did not actually race in F2, but the following season turned up as an F1 car. Several of the six de Tomaso F1 cars made had O.S.C.A. engines and their sorry tale is told elsewhere.

PARNELL

After a long and distinguished career as a driver, Reg Parnell turned his hand to team management and was responsible for putting together the deal which combined Lola and John Surtees with finance from the Yeoman Credit (later Bowmaker) finance house. In 1963, after Bowmaker withdrew from the sport, he continued to run the Lolas for such as Hailwood and Amon and, towards the end of the year, added a Lotus 24-B.R.M. to the strength.

Parnell was not content simply to be a passive privateer, but actively pursued experimental work with both Coventry Climax and a new maker of racing transmissions, Mike Hewland. Before the end of 1963 he commissioned Les Redmond, who had designed FJ cars for Gemini and Heron, to lay down a new F1 car. In effect he was pursuing a similar path to B.R.P. in that the car drew heavily on the Lotus 25 with a similar monocoque and suspension and, indeed, the front and rear uprights were made by Lotus.

The car was being built when, at the beginning of 1964, Reg died suddenly after an operation. His son, Tim, who had been running his own racing team, took over Reg Parnell (Racing) and then found that Coventry Climax was unwilling to continue to supply the engines because it demanded exclusivity which he felt he could not guarantee. Besides, he was able to become the first private owner of a Lotus 25 when Chapman sold him the 1963 works cars.

There was no point in continuing work on a Lotus 25 copy when the team owned real Lotus 25s (which were fitted with B.R.M. P56 engines) so work on the car was abandoned and from its components Redmond created a space-frame sports-racer with a 2-litre B.R.M. engine. In the hands of Mike Spence, the Parnell-B.R.M. took several good wins.

PORSCHE

It was more or less inevitable the Porsche should enter F1 in 1961. Beginning with a special built from V.W. components, the company had built up an enviable reputation in the small-capacity sports car classes. Porsche had started in a shed, deprived of materials and severely restricted by regulations imposed by the occupying powers, but had, by sheer grit and guts got into production. From the start Porsche featured a competition programme, and the line of cars it made for the World Sports Car Championship, 1953-61 was arguably the most consistent and competent of the era.

When F2 was resurrected, Porsche was soon involved and began by running a stripped-down sports-racing RSK When this experiment was successful, it laid down a bespoke F2 car. At about the same time, Jean Behra commissioned Valerio Colotti to make him a single-seater based on Porche RSK components, but for various reasons this car was never given the opportunities it should have enjoyed. Pete Lovely became famous in America when he put a Porsche 356 engine in a modified Cooper 500 chassis to create the single-seater 'Pooper'.

Porsche did well in F2, but then so did Cooper-Climax, Cooper-Borgward, Ferrari, and Lotus. Cut it as you will, one is forced to the conclusion that no marque was superior.

Much is made of the fact that the British were caught wrong-footed at the start of the 1½-litre formula and allowed Ferrari a free rein in 1961. One does not often hear it mentioned that Porsche was in exactly the same position, except that it took even longer than the Brits to make its bespoke F1 car, and when the car did appear it was not up to scratch and Porsche cut and ran.

Porsche began 1961 with Jo Bonnier and Dan Gurney as its main works drivers and the ex-Formula 2 *Typ* 718 as its main weapon. This was basically a single-seater RSK with an air-cooled flat-four d.o.h.c. engine of 1498cc (85 × 66 mm) which developed about 155 bhp. It was installed in the rear of a space-frame chassis with front suspension by twin trailing arms and torsion bars and rear suspension by coil springs and wishbones.

Although in F2 form, a 6-speed Porsche gearbox was the usual fitting, the excellent power curve provided by Kugelfischer fuel injection meant that as F1 cars they frequently ran with 4-speed boxes. Just to confuse things further, quite often they ran with Weber carburettors, since the team encountered early difficulties in using fuel injection under racing conditions. Like most German companies, Porsche has consistently succumbed to the NIH (Not Invented Here) syndrome and so the cars still ran with drum brakes and were the last works cars in F1 to do so. Simultaneously, the company made the *Typ* 787, which departed from normal Porsche practice in that it had front suspension by coil springs and wishbones. This was designed to test ideas for a new car which was taking shape and which would use an air-cooled flat-eight engine Porsche had under development, although it took a long time before the flat-eight could be persuaded to perform significantly better than the flat-four.

Bonnier and Gurney took in some of the non-Championship races which began the season and it began promisingly enough when Bonnier set pole and won the first heat of the Brussels GP, only to be eliminated by an over-enthusiastic John Surtees in the second heat. Then Gurney and Bonnier finished second and third to Baghetti's Ferrari at Syracuse, beating all the leading British runners.

The team therefore looked in good shape when it arrived for the Monaco GP, clearly not a Ferrari-beater but possibly ahead of the rest. Bonnier had a new 787, while there were 718s for Gurney and Hans Herrmann. While Moss and the Ferraris had a private race at the front, Bonnier and Gurney led the remainder and, for a while, Bonnier even got into second place, but retired with a broken fuel injection drive. Gurney eventually finished fifth (scoring Porsche's first World Championship points) and Herrmann ninth.

For the Dutch GP where teams were limited to two cars each, the works entered 787s for Gurney and Bonnier while the Dutch amateur, Godin de Beaufort, did a deal with the works which secured him a 718 with

In the 1961 French Grand Prix at Reims the Porsches of Bonnier and Gurney harrass the Ferrari of the eventual winner, Giancarlo Baghetti. (**David Phipps**)

another for Herrmann under the banner *Ecurie Maarsbergen.* In this race of no retirements, the four Porsches were in the last six and all at least two laps down.

Blame for this sorry performance was officially put on the fuel injection, but some of it must have been due to the performance of the 787 chassis. At Spa not only were the engines back on Webers, but Bonnier and Gurney had reverted to 718s backed by de Beaufort's orange car. They were all a long way off the pace (de Beaufort was only ever a make-weight) and could do no better than sixth (Gurney) and seventh (Bonnier).

Three 718s were entered at Reims and after Moss and the quickest Ferraris had dropped out, Bonnier and Gurney disputed the lead with Baghetti in one of the fiercest battles seen in Grand Prix racing. Bonnier had the misfortune to have his engine go off song two laps from the end, and although Gurney led out of the last bend, Baghetti pulled from his slipstream to win by a length.

Bonnier raised a few eyebrows at Aintree by equalling

pole time, but in the streaming wet race conditions could finish only fifth with Gurney seventh. Porsche turned up in force for the Solitude GP with 718s for Bonnier, Gurney and Herrmann and a 787 for Edgar Barth. In the absence of the Ferraris, Bonnier and Gurney qualified fastest and became embroiled in another monumental dice, this time with Ireland's Lotus. Innes used every ounce of his considerable skill at the very last corner and scrambled by Bonnier to win by half a length with Gurney two-tenths behind. Herrmann came home sixth and Barth eighth.

Barth's car was an interim model and was to share many characteristics with the flat-eight Type 804. Its cooling fan was placed horizontally on top of the engine, instead of vertically as had been the practice, the frame was longer to accommodate the flat-eight which would eventually go into it, and for the first time there were disc brakes, made by Porsche, but incorporating Dunlop patents.

The same driver/car line-up appeared in the German GP, but Gurney's car was fitted with disc brakes. Herrmann held third in the early stages, then fell back to have a race-long duel with Clark until delayed by a slipping clutch. None of the other Porsches were in contention and the best finish was Gurney's seventh place. As Denis Jenkinson wrote at the time, 'At Solitude they lost with honour, at Nürburgring they just lost.'

Bonnier had a 718 for his home race, the Kanonloppet at Karlskoga, and came second to Moss, and he came second to Moss in the Modena GP as well, with Gurney just behind in third. Gurney and Bonnier had 'horizontal fan' engines in their 718s for the Italian GP. After Clark and von Trips crashed and all the Ferraris bar Phil Hill's retired, Gurney scrapped with Moss for second and when the Lotus ran a wheel bearing Gurney stroked home in second.

Bonnier managed a third at Zeltweg, and in the US GP, which Ferrari missed, Gurney in a 'vertical fan' 718 came a fine second just 4.3 seconds behind Ireland's Lotus, with Bonnier down in sixth. For a first season in F1, and then with a make-shift car, it had not been too bad a performance. Porsche finished third in the Manufacturers' Championship and Gurney fourth in the Drivers' Championship, with an equal score to Moss, but Stirling had won two races.

To round off the season, Bonnier and Barth took part in the South African 'Temporada' with a pair of 718s. The opposition came mainly from Team Lotus and, in a couple of races, Stirling Moss, with the rest of the grid being mainly local cars and drivers. They finished according to the form book: Bonnier third and Barth fourth in the Rand GP, the same in the Natal GP, third and fifth in the South African GP and third and sixth in the Cape GP.

The team cars were then sold; one 718 went to Count Volpi's Scuderia Serenissima Republica di Venezia and was driven by Bonnier, when team duties allowed, and by Carlo Abate, when Bonnier was absent; another went to Wolfgang Seidel, a third was bought by Heinz Schiller and Ben Pon bought a 787.

In the curtain-raiser events of 1962, Bonnier took second in the Brussels GP and third in the Lombank Trophy at Snetterton and the only emergence from total obscurity for the others was Seidel's sixth in the Lombank Trophy at Snetterton.

So far as the works was concerned the season opened with the Dutch GP, where the flat-eight (*Typ* 753) engine made its debut in the *Typ* 804 chassis. The engine had d.o.h.c. on each bank of cylinders, twin-plug ignition, and a horizontal fan. It was of 1494cc (66 × 54.6 mm) and, running on Webers, delivered 180 bhp at 9000 rpm. It was mated to an all-synchromesh 6-speed Porsche gearbox in unit with a ZF final drive. The spaceframe was broadly the same, but slightly narrower than

the interim 787 which Barth had driven in 1961, but suspension front and rear was by double wishbones and longitudinal torsion bars and telescopic dampers. Porsche disc brakes were mounted outboard all round. In point of fact the engine had, in 2-litre form, made its debut in the Targa Florio, where it had powered a modified RS61 to third behind two Ferraris.

With Porsche's towering reputation, much was expected from the new car, but the British V-8s were out in force and Gurney could qualify no higher than eighth. Still, he ran as high as third until pulling the gear lever out of its mounting (Dan could be a bit ham-fisted), while Bonnier was seventh after a pit stop to check the rear suspension. At Zandvoort Porsche had improved 1.7 seconds over 1961; the best Coventry Climax-powered car had improved by 3.7 seconds.

Porsche very nearly withdrew from Monaco after that performance, but Gurney persuaded the team to relent. Only one 804 was released, however, the other being used for testing, and while Gurney had his normal car, Bonnier had to borrow the Venezia car. Thus a works Porsche entry came to the line painted red! Gurney went well in practice, only to crash on the first lap in an incident sparked off by Mairesse, while Bonnier, with a 6-speed gearbox fitted, was lucky to qualify and he plugged round to finish fifth, seven laps down.

During 1961 Bonnier had sometimes been Gurney's superior in matched cars and even when the American had the upper hand, Jo was not far behind. For some reason that position changed in 1962 and Bonnier was completely outshone by his team-mate.

The Belgian GP was missed while work continued on the cars, and when they appeared at Rouen they had 183 bhp at 9300 rpm. The problem stemmed from the engine layout. In order to keep the vestiges of a family resemblance with Porsche's road cars, it had to be an air-cooled boxer unit. Temperature control being so much more difficult on an air-cooled engine, power was always going to be limited by comparison to a liquid-cooled engine and apparently this also precluded the option of four valves per cylinder. Many engine designers are of the opinion a boxer engine is inherently less efficient than a 'V'.

Gurney, the quicker in practice, was still 3.5 seconds off the pace, but most of the fast men encountered troubles and retired and he eventually inherited the lead, with Bonnier retiring with a broken fuel pump. So Porsche won its only World Championship victory but not its only GP win, for that came in the next race at Solitude, where three 804s were entered, the third for Jo Siffert. It was not, however, a strong field except for Team Lotus, and while Clark would normally take a pole to flag

Dan Gurney on his way to Porsche's only Grand Épreuve *victory in the 1962 French Grand Prix at Rouen.* **(British Petroleum)**

An overhead view of Gurney's Porsche at Rouen. **(David Phipps)**

win, his engine was off-song and anyway he crashed in the rain. Gurney not only gave Porsche a second win in a week, but Bonnier followed him home.

After two celebrations in eight days, things were back to normal for the British GP, where the cars were on the third row of the grid. Gurney ran strongly in the early stages and then encountered clutch trouble, which dropped him back to ninth, and Bonnier retired with a broken crown wheel and pinion. At the Nürburgring, however, Gurney demonstrated his class, but the result of a race-long three-car battle was a win for Hill's B.R.M., Surtees' Lola second and Gurney third with 4.5 seconds covering them. Bonnier was seventh, 4½ minutes behind.

Bonnier was loaned an 804 for the Kanonloppet, but could only finish third behind the B.R.P. Lotuses of Ireland and Gregory, a dismal showing for a works car. Gurney ran stongly at Monza, but retired with a broken rear axle, while Bonnier finished sixth. In the US GP, Gurney came home fifth, but Bonnier had so many problems he was unclassified.

Thus ended Porsche's Formula 1 works involvement, since the team decided not to take in the South African GP. In the final reckoning, Gurney and Porsche both finished fifth in their respective Championships.

Porsche realized that it would need a much better chassis and another 15-20 bhp to be competitive and since the company insisted on making F1 cars to a 'family' design, there was no hope of that, so it withdrew and concentrated on sports cars. The 804 engine was adapted and powered the 904 coupé.

With the works out, Godin de Beaufort still ran his two 718s. They were astonishingly reliable, too, and almost invariably finished. One of them competed in 46 races and covered over 10,000 racing miles, so de Beaufort quite often inherited decent finishes, such as sixth in the 1963 Belgian and US Grands Prix, and Gerhard Mitter used one to finish fourth in the German GP. Heinz Schiller and de Beaufort took third and fourth in the 1963 Pau GP, but a long way down, de Beaufort finished second in the Syracuse and Rome Grands Prix, although neither race attracted works entries, and he was third in the Austrian GP, but that was also last place and he was five laps down. His appearances were more spasmodic in 1964 and it was a sad loss to the F1 circus when he lost control of his car during practice for the German GP and died of his injuries.

That really was the end of Porsche in F1 and every time the question of a return was raised, Porsche would sniffily declare either that there were no technical benefits or that it had become so oriented towards driver personality that it wanted no part of it. Both excuses were nonsense, there has always been a personality cult in racing, which is why Stirling Moss is still a household name, and his career ended before the Porsche 804 made its debut. The truth is that Porsche could not live at the top level of racing, but it was able to be successful in sports car racing, where technical standards and the overall level of competition were lower than in F1.

R. R. A.

There were three F1 cars made by Geoff Richardson which used the initials R.R.A. (Richardson Racing Automobiles). The first was based on a Riley special built by Percy Maclure before the Second World War which was sometimes known as the 'IFS Riley Special'. Maclure had taken a Riley chassis and fitted it with André-Girling front suspension, an independent system utilizing transverse links, coil springs and radius arms, and he had also replaced the Riley engine with a supercharged E.R.A. unit of 1488cc (57.5 × 95.2 mm).

Richardson bought the car in 1948 and re-bodied it, and the following year he replaced the Riley frame with a new box-section chassis. He raced this for a number of years, mainly in club events, and although he did not score any notable successes, he at least enjoyed himself.

When the 2½-litre F1 arrived, Richardson respond-ed by fitting first a Riley engine, and then a 2-litre Alta unit, but, naturally, was always outclassed. Then Richardson bought the chassis of the single-seater special which Aston Martin had cobbled together for the 1955-56 Tasman series. Into this he fitted a 2.4-litre Jaguar engine and in the only important race he entered, the 1957 International Trophy at Silverstone, he did not exactly disgrace himself, qualifying eighth of the 14 starters in his heat. He retired after seven laps when his oil pressure vanished. This car was eventually sold on, and since the chassis had originally been a DB3S-style frame which had been narrowed, the new owner widened it again and created a new DB3S.

The last R.R.A. was a Cooper T43 fitted with a Connaught version of the 2½-litre Alta engine and this first appeared in the Silver City Trophy at Brands Hatch on

Geoff Richardson at the wheel of the original E.R.A.-powered R.R.A. Special in a Formule Libre race at Silverstone.

1 August 1960. With Richardson at the wheel it was slow in qualifying and finished 14th, and last, five laps down on the winner after 50 laps of the Club circuit. Undeterred, Richardson entered his car in the Lombank Trophy at Snetterton and the International Gold Cup at Oulton Park. In both races he qualified slowly and failed to finish.

In 1961 the car became eligible for Inter-Continental Formula races and it was entered in both the Lavant Cup and the International Trophy but in both races Richardson was the slowest qualifier. At Goodwood, where there were no retirements, he finished last, while at Silverstone he spun out after two laps.

ROVER

In 1948 three development engineers at the Rover Car Company, Peter Wilks, George Mackay and Spencer King, built an F2 car from Rover components. Its engine was a 1996cc (63.5 × 105 mm) version of the 2.1-litre straight-six unit which powered the new Rover 75 and had overhead push-rod inlet valves and side exhaust valves. It was installed in a box-section chassis using production Rover ifs (coil springs and wishbones) and a de Dion rear axle suspended on quarter-elliptic springs.

It began as a hobby but soon received official interest, since it was realized that the car was a useful experimental vehicle with special application to the handling and road holding of the company's road cars. The three friends drove it in minor British races until 1951 and then it was sold to Gerry Dunham, who was better know for his Alvis special. Dunham re-christened the car the D.H.S. (Dunham and Haines Special, after

his motor business) and entered it in a number of F2 races. It was never a winner, but Dunham drove it well and often qualified and finished ahead of more recently made cars.

It appeared in two minor 1954 F1 races, and in one, a five-lapper at Goodwood in June, Dunham brought it home fourth. It was a thin field, but he did beat the Emeryson-Alta, Turner-Alta and Whiteaway's ex-works H.W.M. Later it was handed over to Frank Lockhart, who had been a salesman at Dunham and Haines, and Lockhart and the Rover have been a popular feature of the Historic racing scene for years.

Another Rover special was built by Ron Searles, who at one point installed a B.M.W. 328 engine, but either the car or the driver was slow, and it did not figure in even the few minor F2 and F1 races in which it was entered up to the end of 1954.

SACHA-GORDINE

In 1952 French motor racing could be summed up by one word, 'Gordini'. It is true that there was a plethora of small companies making small-engined cars which contested the Index of Performance at Le Mans, but at a serious level there was only Gordini and, despite his brilliance, he lurched from financial crisis to financial crisis and was never able to do full justice to his ideas.

This situation rankled, especially since France had once had a sporting tradition to match any in the world, but for various reasons, mostly governmental fiscal measures, the old great marques had died. Attempts at building a French national team had ended in ignominy. What was needed was an individual of wealth, commitment and imagination. Enter M. Sacha-Gordine.

Gordine was a racing enthusiast who competed in rallies and was also a successful film producer. To put France back in the frame he set up his own company and to avoid confusion with Gordini, put a hyphen between his forename and surname.

His project might have succeeded had he been able to restrain his imagination. It seems that the French film producer thought in the same way as a Hollywood mogul. Not content with starting with a single car and engine his programme included simultaneous development of 1½, 2, 2½, 3 and 4½-litre V-8 engines, some of which were to be blown, and cars for F1, F2 and Le Mans. It is worth noting that though F1 still officially existed it had become a minor category, more or less a type of Formule Libre, and anyway would be phased out at

the end of 1953, yet here was Sacha-Gordine building a new car for it.

As if this were not enough, the cars were all unconventional, being rear-engined, their execution was undertaken without regard to cost, and for the 1953 World Championship season not one, not two, but *five* cars would be prepared. Someone should have told the film producer that not even Cecil B. de Mille managed to build Rome in a day.

Gordine's designer was a M. Vigna, who had trained with Porsche, and clearly Porsche's Cisitalia GP design had influenced him. Like the Cisitalia he specified torsion bar and trailing link front suspension and a rear-engined layout but more conservatively plumped for a ladder-chassis and de Dion rear axle, although this was again sprung on torsion bars located by twin trailing arms. Its wheelbase (8 ft 5½ in), front track (4 ft 5½ in) and rear track (4 ft 4 in) were all very close to the Cisitalia's dimensions.

In F2 form the d.o.h.c. V-8 engine had a bore and stroke of 70×64 mm (1969cc), and was fed by four twin-choke carburettors. The block was also finned to give additional cooling, although cooling was actually by glycol. Power was claimed to be 191 bhp at 8000 rpm, which, if true, would have made it the most powerful car in F2. This was transmitted through a 5-speed gearbox with a motorcycle-style shift (as on the Cisitalia). The engine itself made extensive use of magnesium and this expensive metal featured everywhere else: the gearbox

A model of the V-8 2-litre Sacha-Gordine and, below, the first chassis under completion. Although completed the car never raced.

casing, de Dion tube, trailing arms, brake back-plates, air scoops. If something could be cast in magnesium, it was.

The car's brakes were huge, with 16-in drums at the front, 14-in drums at the rear while the 17-in wire wheels stood well proud of the bonnet line, for it was the lowest single-seater of its capacity made up to that time. With twin-nostril front air intakes which fed two small radiators, it uncannily presaged the 1961 F1 Ferrari. Fuel was carried in two bulbous pannier tanks.

Estimates of its weight vary and they range from 470 kg, which was only marginally heavier than contemporary Gordinis, to 636 kg, which would have seen it win the heavyweight title in F2. The lower figure is surely closest. All in all, it was an extraordinary project and with two of the five cars nearly complete, Gordine unveiled them early in 1952 and filed an entry for the Pau GP in April, with a sports car predicted for Le Mans. Then M. Gordine's bean counter must have had a hard look at the costs, for Gondine realized that he was frittering away his fortune and abruptly closed down the project.

Of all the GP failures this was one of the most intriguing, because the design itself was so radical that if only the project had been taken one step at a time we might at least have seen the car race. Who knows, the name Sacha-Gordine might be uttered today in the same breath as Ferrari. A story circulated for some time that the cars were stored on an island in the Seine, but now nobody seems to know what became of them.

SADLER

In the late 1950s, Bill Sadler, a Canadian, made a name for himself in North American racing with a series of Corvette-engined sports cars and ran one of these in the 1957 Mille Miglia. Like Lance Reventlow and his Scarab project, Sadler nurtured an ambition to enter F1 and work began on a car in 1958. The chosen power unit was a Maserati 250F engine (apparently with more power squeezed from it) which was set at an angle of 7 degrees in the front of the frame and inclined at 16 degrees from the vertical.

The chassis itself was a space-frame using square chrome molybdenum tubes with coil spring and wishbone front suspension and a low-pivot swing axle rear system sprung on Koni coil spring and damper units and located by twin radius arms. Girling disc brakes were used all round and the gearbox/final drive unit was Sadler-designed (and patented).

It was, then, a fairly similar concept to the Tec-Mec. Work progressed slowly but during 1959 it became clear that the writing was on the wall for the front-engined car and the Sadler never appeared in any F1 race.

In late 1960, however, Sadler made a rear-engined Formule Libre car with a Chrevolet engine which had so much torque that a gearbox was initially dispensed with, instead the power went through a Halibrand quick-change centre-section and an hydraulically actuated clutch. For the rest it was a fairly conventional car, with coil spring and double wishbone suspension all round, discs on all four wheels (inboard at the rear) but to offset the rearward weight bias, it had a huge front anti-roll bar which gave understeer.

It was entered for Peter Ryan in the 1960 Formule Libre Watkins Glen Grand Prix and in practice was driven by Stirling Moss who commented that in some parts of the circuit it handled better than his Lotus 18 but, predictably, was slow coming out of corners.

In the race Ryan ran as high as fifth before encountering problems. We have been unable to find any other instance of the car running in an international field and it was left to Stebro (q.v.) to become the first Canadian car to run in a WC race.

SCARAB

By anyone's standards, Lance Reventlow was a wealthy young man. He was the Woolworth heir, who on his 21st birthday inherited the equivalent in today's money of $60-70 million, but even before then had enjoyed a large allowance. Like many another young man born to wealth, he enjoyed spending his money and was not out of his teens before he had the reputation of being something of a playboy. Also like many a young man who has not had to make his way in the world, he needed a personal challenge and he found it in motor racing. While still only 19, two years below the SCCA's 'legal' age, he bought a Cooper-Climax T39 'Bobtail' and a Maserati 200S and entered racing with some success. His ruse was rumbled, however, and he was banned for a year.

Nothing daunted he came to Europe in 1957 and wrote off the Maserati at Snetterton. He also took time to visit some racing car constructors and was astonished to see how apparently backward they were. His reaction on seeing a Lister chassis at the Cambridge works was, 'Hell, I could build a car better 'n *that!*' He was confirmed in his view by a later visit to Maserati, which was run in a typically Italian way, in a state of apparent chaos.

Since Archie Scott-Brown's Lister-Jaguar was regularly beating everything in sight in Britain and Maserati was taking Fangio to his fifth World Championship, as well as making the fastest car in the WSCC, it was easy to draw the conclusion that Good Ole American Know-How, properly financed and directed, could stand the racing world on its ears. Why, when the Indy boys travelled to Monza to take part in the 'Two Worlds 500' race that year, the only Europeans who turned up to take them on were the Ecurie Ecosse D-types.

In August 1957 Lance established Reventlow Automobiles Incorporated and recruited the best available talent. R.A.I. would start with a sports-racer, and since there was no capacity limit the car would use a modified Chevrolet Corvette engine, as it was a known factor and could be tweaked to give adequate power. Warren Olson would oversee the project. The car would be designed and developed by Dick Troutman, Dick Barnes and Ken Miles, while Chuck Daigh, who would be No. 1 driver, was also the chief mechanic and expert on fuel injection.

Work had begun and then suddenly the FIA announced there would be a 3-litre limit in the WSCC from

Chuck Daigh with the uncompetitive Scarab in the 1961 Inter-Continental Formula International Trophy at Silverstone.

the start of 1958. Reventlow apparently explored the idea of buying 3-litre Maserati V-12 engines, but Maserati withdrew from racing for financial reasons and this avenue closed. He therefore decided to press ahead with the Chevvy-engined car and run it in SCCA races, while preparing for Formula 1.

The resulting car was lovely to look at, superbly crafted and prepared and was called the 'Scarab'. The name was a private joke, for a scarab is a dung beetle, as low a creature as you could find, and was a deliberate reaction against the exotic and macho names other cars were called. As the two cars run by the works for Daigh and Reventlow steam-rolled the opposition in the 'B' Modified class, the name 'Scarab' itself became macho and exotic.

After a single, great, season the sports cars were sold on, and continued their winning ways, while R.A.I. decided to concentrate on F1 for 1960. The team had explored the idea of a WSCC season by running a 3-litre Offenhauser engine in one race, but Reventlow was so buoyed by success that he decided the time was ripe to tackle the Europeans at the highest level.

It was ironical in view of the débâcle the F1 project turned out to be that the 3-litre car was not much slower than the 5½-litre Chevvies, although whether the team had either the experience or the driving talent to undertake long-distance racing is another matter.

Troutman and Barnes drew a front-engined space-frame car with independent suspension by coil springs and double wishbones, front and rear. Leo Goossen, an Offenhauser engineer, designed a 4-cylinder engine of 2441cc (85.25×85.73 mm) which had d.o.h.c. and desmodronic valve gear and was fed by Hilborn fuel injection. This engine gave about 230 bhp and was canted over in the frame, virtually on to its side, to keep the bonnet line low and to make for a low drive train alongside the driver.

A 4-speed Chevrolet gearbox was fitted, although a 4-speed box within a Corvette casing was under development, but the most unusual feature of the original design was the braking system. This was to have aircraft-style 'bladder' brakes at the front (i.e. expanding bladders within conventional drums, and a special disc brake on the final drive (whole plates would press against the disc rather like a clutch). All this was taking time to develop, and the rear brake proved impossible to cool, so it was decided to simplify matters by adopting conventional Girling discs all round. While it was a wise decision, it was not made without some heart-searching, for Reventlow had hoped his car would be entirely American and the use of an English brake system went against the grain.

When the F1 Scarabs appeared at Monaco, the opening round of the 1960 World Championship, they were greeted with interest and respect. As with the sports cars, the finish and construction were immaculate and Scarab's achievements in American sports car racing had been well documented by the motor racing press. In his attempt to be all-American, Reventlow had decided on Goodyear tyres, but he and Daigh quickly found they were much too hard for Monaco and switched to Dunlops, whereupon times improved but neither looked like qualifying. Moss was persuaded to try one and he was 7 seconds a lap quicker than either Daigh or Reventlow, but even his best time was only 1 minute 45 seconds, while his pole-winning time was 1 minute 36.6 seconds and the slowest qualifier was 1 minute 39.1 seconds.

Reventlow was later to claim that his car was two years late and had he tackled F1 in 1958 the Scarab would have been competitive, but when one looks at Monaco qualifying times in previous years one discovers that he and Daigh would have only just been on the grid in 1954.

Scarabs next appeared at the Dutch GP, where Reventlow and Daigh both qualified but not in the top 15. Since the organizers were prepared to pay starting money only to the top 15, Scarab withdrew. Both cars qualified for the Belgian GP, and Reventlow was the quicker in 4 m 9.7 s (Daigh did 4 m 18.5 s) but nearly 20 seconds off Brabham's pole.

Reventlow retired after three laps when a con-rod broke, while Daigh soldiered on for 17 laps, bog last, when his engine began to drop oil. They turned up for the French GP at Reims, where Richie Ginther was released by Ferrari to drive Reventlow's car. In practice,

however, the cars encountered problems, used up their stock of spares, and called it a day. The cars went home.

Back home, R.A.I. moved to a new factory and Goossen began drawing a 4-cylinder 1½-litre engine for the new F1, but it was never completed. Ferrari showed the way with its V-6 and then was overtaken by the V-8s from B.R.M. and Coventry Climax. There was no point in completing it.

British manufacturers had woken up late to the realities of the 1½-litre formula and, in 1961, attempted to upstage it with a 3 litre alternative called the 'Inter-Continental Formula' in an attempt to use existing F1 and Tasman cars. R.A.I. shipped a Scarab to England for Daigh to drive. The car was no more competitive, and though Daigh finished seventh in the wet International Trophy at Silverstone he was three laps down.

Then came the idea of Formula 366, a precursor of F5000, which allowed stock-block 5-litre engines or racing engines of 3-litres. R.A.I. designed a rear-engined car with an alloy Chevvy engine for this formula, but the class never got off the ground and the car's sole appearance was in a race in Australia.

By this time Reventlow had lost heart and, anyway, under American law a loss-making company can be written off against tax for up to five years, so before R.A.I. reached its fifth birthday he wound it up. He had been fooled by the apparent disorder of the European constructors he had visited, for it had hidden years of experience and expertise. It had, however, been a brave try. Reventlow cut himself off from racing and was killed in a light aircraft crash in 1973.

SCIROCCO

Hugh Powell, a wealthy young American, had bought in-to Emeryson Cars Ltd to provide the means by which his guardian, Tony Settember, could go motor racing. For 1963 the team changed its name to Scirocco-Powell and moved into a lock-up behind the Seven Stars pub in the Goldhawk Road, London, a fact celebrated by the team incorporating seven stars in its badge. It is perhaps the only time in Grand Prix history that a pub has been so honoured. If so, it is Scirocco's only distinction.

New chassis were built for 1963 and these broadly followed the team's Emerysons except that the frame was changed behind the driver to accommodate V-8 B.R.M. engines and was strengthened around the cockpit, the rear suspension had lateral upper links, the body was

restyled and was much slimmer, and different wheels were used. Aiden-Jones, who had modified the Anglo-American Aiden-Cooper, was retained as a consultant.

The highlight of the Scirocco's career came in the non-Championship Austrian GP at Zeltweg, when Tony Settember brought his car home second to Jack Brabham. Actually he qualified nearly 6 seconds off the pace and although he did finish second he was one of only three classified finishers and was five laps down.

A photograph taken at Copse Corner, Silverstone, during the British GP is revealing. Settember is ahead of Dan Gurney's Brabham, but while the Brabham is low on its hunkers, with the whole car looking for grip and ways to exploit its power, the Scirocco is high on

The 1963 Scirocco-B.R.M. was based on the Emeryson Mk 2. Its one moment of glory came in the non-Championship Austrian Grand Prix where Tony Settember brought his car home second, but he was one of only three finishers and was five laps down at the finish. (LAT)

its springs with its wheels pointing in every direction. It is a perfect illustration of the sort of car you would expect to come from a lock-up behind a pub in the Goldhawk Road.

Entries for two cars were filed for both the International Trophy at Silverstone and the Monaco GP, but neither appeared. Settember in the first chassis (SP-1-63) made the grid for the Belgian GP, but was over half a minute off the pace, and although classified eighth his race finished after 25 laps when he crashed.

Scirocco missed the Dutch GP and a single car was entered for Settember at Reims, where, again, he was on the last row of the grid and lasted five laps before retiring

with a broken rear hub. Ian Burgess had a car (SP-2-63) for the British GP, but the story was as before, both were well off the pace and both retired. The story was repeated at the Nürburgring, then there came the 'triumph' in Austria. In the Italian GP Settember failed to qualify, even though he practised faster than Baghetti's A.T.S. but the organizers had reserved places for Italian entries.

The team's final appearance was in the Oulton Park Gold Cup, where Burgess qualified quite respectably and finished eighth, four laps down, while Settember's last drive for the team ended after five laps with a broken valve. Hugh Powell had grown tired of throwing money

Seen in the rain-soaked **Daily Mail** *Trophy race at Snetterton in March 1964 is the ex-works Scirocco, newly fitted with Coventry Climax V-8, driven by André Pilette and entered by Équipe Scirocco Belge. Despite the damaged nose-cone, Pilette finished, albeit seventh and last, four laps in arrears.* (T. C. March)

away on a lost cause so he wound up the team and both cars were sold on. A third chassis was later converted into a sports car.

Burgess' race car was sold to André Pilette, who really should have known better, since he once owned an Emeryson and had been painfully slow in it. Pilette installed a Coventry Climax FWMV engine and entered under the name Équipe Scirocco Belge. His usual qualifying position was last (in the German GP he failed to qualify at all) and though he was classified as a finisher in three non-Championship races he was always several laps down, in fact on average he was lapped every eighth lap he raced his car.

It is not surprising then that the name 'Scirocco' disappeared from the entry lists at the end of the season.

SOUTH AFRICAN SPECIALS

For reasons of geography and economics, Rhodesia, South Africa and other countries in the southern part of the continent developed their own forms of racing. In the early 1960s the South African Gold Star Championship catered for 4-cylinder 1½-litre single-seaters and quite often local builders made their own chassis which they fitted with modified production engines. These cars were not built primarily for Grands Prix but for national racing, which is why they are grouped together.

When the Europeans arrived for the South African 'Temporada', which was run to Formula 1, not Gold Star, rules, many of the locals joined in and while most confined themselves to the non-Championship Natal, Cape and Rand Grands Prix, several ran in the South African GP, although without giving the visitors many problems for, apart from anything else they were restricted by their engines.

South Africans quite often bought European chassis into which they fitted, say, Alfa Romeo engines and these I have ignored except when they made an appearance in a World Championship event. An exception to this rule is the Lotus 7 driven by Brausch Niemann in 1962, for Niemann's performances in it were so exceptional that its inclusion is utterly irresistible.

In the case of specials, I have included only those cars which ran in F1 races when European works teams were present. Quite often, however, these were more successful than many bought-in cars because the men who made them were the local tuning experts. It is interesting to note that many were copies of Cooper models even when Cooper was on the slide. This was partly because southern Africa was always a year or two behind European developments, and partly because Cooper made the sort of cars which a special builder might imitate without making problems for himself which is a double-edged comment on Cooper.

A note on the races might be useful. In 1961-2 four events, all non-World Championship, where run to F1 regulations and these were the Rand GP at Kyalami, the Natal GP at Westfield, the South African GP at East London and the Cape GP at Killarney. These attracted a small number of European teams, chief among them being the works Lotuses and Porsches, and Stirling Moss.

In 1962 the South African GP was a World Championship event and it was supported by the Rand and Natal Grands Prix.

1963 saw just the Rand GP and the South African GP, while the following year saw only one race, the Rand GP on 12 December. The South African GP, however, followed on 1 January, 1965, thus establishing its slot in the calendar, the first race of the year. While it appears that South Africa had missed a running of its World Championship round so soon after getting it, in fact there was only a year and three days between the 1963 and 1965 races.

Regular WC contestants were guaranteed starts, while the locals had to qualify for the remaining places; thus for the 1965 South African GP there was a total of 31 entries and 20 starters. Local drivers fought for the four 'free' places, so to get on to the grid at all was an achievement.

In 1965, the South African Championship was run to a 3-litre formula and while this appears to be anticipating F1 by a year, in fact it was only by a few weeks, since the season began late in the year.

Alfa Special:

Piet de Klerk worked his passage to England in 1958, a demonstration of determination which appealed to Colin Chapman, who gave him a job at Lotus. While there he absorbed the principles of racing car design and when he returned home after a couple of years he constructed his own car with the help of Doug Serrurier and Ernest Pieterse.

Like its name, the finished car was a no-nonsense

device, an attractive, well-made special which reflected credit on its builder. It was built around a space-frame with all independent suspension by coil springs and wishbones (wide-based at the rear) and, of course, an enlarged and tuned Alfa Romeo Giulietta engine.

Its cause was helped by the fact that de Klerk was a good driver, who later drove for Porsche at Le Mans. In the 1962 Rand GP it started 13th from 21 runners and finished seventh, 3 laps in arrears, but de Klerk applied the lessons learned and, at the next race, the Natal GP, he was fourth on the grid from 16 runners in his heat. At the flag he was fourth, beaten only by two works Lotuses and a B.R.M. In the final, which Trevor Taylor won from Jim Clark, de Klerk was seventh.

By the time the Europeans returned the following year, driver and car had improved, and in the first heat of the Rand GP de Klerk started from fourth spot, quickest of all the locals, and he went on to finish third, and on the same lap as the works Ferraris of Surtees and Bandini. He was fourth in the second heat and on aggregate was placed third behind the Ferraris.

In the South African GP he qualified 11th, by 2.5 seconds the fastest of the locals, and within 0.8 second of McLaren and Maggs in the works Coopers. This fine effort unfortunately came to an end at two-thirds distance with a broken gearbox.

By 1964 the car was starting to show its age, but de Klerk was still one of the quickest locals in the Rand GP and he took sixth in heat one but retired after a spin in the second heat. The South African GP followed, and although starting from 17th in a field of 20 does not sound a remarkable achievement, de Klerk was in a three-year-old special with a production-based engine in a WC event. He was quickest of all the locals in both qualifying and the race and though six laps in arrears at the finish, was classified tenth.

It is a pity that de Klerk did not bring his car to Europe for he would probably have done well in non-Championship races and perhaps even have earned enough to have fitted a V-8 engine. As it was, with a 2.7-litre Brabham BT11-FPF he finished only 6 seconds behind Jack Brabham's identical car in the 1965 Rand Grand Prix.

Assegai:

Designed and driven by Tony Kotze, the Assegai was a very slim car with a conventional space-frame, a 4-cylinder 1493cc Alfa Romeo engine and a 5-speed Colotti gearbox. Its chief claim to fame, however, was that it was claimed to be four inches lower than any previous F1 design, with a ground clearance of only 3½

in. It was entered for Kotze in the 1962 Rand GP at Kyalami, but failed to qualify.

Cooper-Alfa Romeo:

A 1961 T53 chassis fitted with an Alfa Romeo engine was entered by Mike Harris in the 1962 South African GP. Harris qualified third from last and retired with engine trouble just after one-third distance.

Heron:

The English enthusiast and amateur racer Jim Diggory employed Les Redmond, designer of the first Gemini FJ cars, to draw a rear-engined FJ car which he named the 'Heron'. It was a conventional design (space-frame, coil spring and double wishbone front suspension, etc.) which looked not unlike a contemporary Cooper. In FJ form it made little impact, but the prototype was sold to Tony Maggs, who took it to South Africa, and there it was fitted with an Alfa Romeo engine.

Entered by Scuderia Alfa and driven by Ernest Pieterse, it qualified mid-field in the 1961 Rand GP and finished sixth, albeit three laps behind Jim Clark's Lotus. Pieterse qualified it in mid-field for the Rand GP, but retired with overheating. In the South African GP it again qualified in mid-field, but was an early retirement, this time with gearbox troubles. In the final race of the South African Temporada, the Cape GP, Pieterse again qualified respectably and finished eighth, two laps behind Trevor Taylor's Lotus. Since Pieterse won the South African Championship with a Lotus the following year, one is fairly safe in suggesting there was no fault in the cockpit.

It was not until December 1964 that the Heron appeared again in an F1 race and this time it was driven by David Hume in the Rand GP. It qualified 14th from 22, finished 11th in the first heat, 13th and unclassified in the second, and on aggregate was a nominal 13th, but again unclassified.

Jennings:

Bill Jennings was the South African Champion in 1954, 1956 and 1957 with a Riley Special derived from the car with which Freddie Dixon twice won the Tourist Trophy. In 1958 he built a two-seater powered by a Porsche RS engine, but the authorities did not consider that a one-off constituted a sports car as defined by their regulations and so he used some of the running gear to make a single-seater to race for fun, since he regarded his serious driving career at an end.

Suspension was by coil springs all round with wishbones at the front, and the car seems to have followed the general lines of Pete Lovely's Cooper-Porsche, the 'Pooper'. In 1961 Jennings finished 11th in the Rand GP (8 laps down), ninth in the Natal race, and 12th (but not classified) in the South African GP. In the Cape GP it started last and retired with a broken valve.

L.D.S.:

L.D.S. 'Doug' Serrurier, a former speedway champion and a leading South African driver in the 1950s and 1960s, made a total of 13 L.D.S. specials. He began in 1956 with a front-engined 1100cc FWA-engined car and followed this with a copy of a 1957 F1/2 Cooper frame with his own modifications. Front and rear suspension were by coil springs and unequal wishbones.

This first single-seater '2', built for Serrurier's own use but soon bought by Sam Tingle, was fitted with an Alfa Romeo engine (incorporating Giannini parts) which produced 140 bhp and drove through a Cooper 4-speed gearbox. It was probably the most successful car of the L.D.S. series, but was never quite up to de Klerk's Alfa special. Tingle raced it from 1961 to 1965 (it was still racing years after that) but did not have a great deal of luck in the non-Championship races.

On the other hand he did manage to qualify for the South African GP on two occasions. In 1964, starting from 17th place (of 20) on the grid, his race ended after two laps with a broken half-shaft. The following year, he just managed to make the grid, but was not classified at the end.

Fanie Viljoen had an FPF engine in L.D.S. '3' (originally built for Errol Hamman who used it in Formula Junior) but he was never as quick as Tingle. Viljoen finished a distant eighth in the 1961 Rand GP and 12th in the 1962 Cape GP, on both occasions five laps down. Later, in 1962, he was ninth in the Rand GP and 12th in the Natal race. The car was driven by Dave Clapham in the 1963 Rand GP, but he was unclassified in both heats.

It next appeared in the hands of Jack Pretorious, who practised way off the pace for the 1964 Rand GP and failed to make the start. He attempted the 1965 South African GP, but did not get beyond pre-qualifying.

John Love had a Porsche RSK engine and gearbox in the back of L.D.S. '4' and in the 1962 Cape GP qualified quickest of all the locals and only 0.2 seconds behind Tony Maggs in one of the Parnell Coopers, but a troubled run saw him finish only ninth. By the end of the year he had a Cooper-FPF. Although no spring chicken, Love raced with distinction in Europe (he won the British Saloon Car Championship in 1962) and came close to winning the 1967 South African GP in a 2.7-litre Cooper-FPF.

L.D.S. '5' had an Alfa Romeo engine and was supplied to Dave Hume, who sold it on to Gene Bosman. In the 1962 Rand GP Bosman qualified in the middle of the local drivers (no fewer than 14 locals failed to qualify) but was 12th, and unclassified, at the end. The following year saw a better result as he finished ninth from 14 classified finishers. Steve Mellet had it for the 1964 Rand GP and was the slowest in the field.

Doug Serrurier himself had '6', which was the first L.D.S. Mk 2. This was based on the 1961 'low-line' Coopers and was fitted with an Alfa Romeo engine and a Hewland 5-speed gearbox. Serrurier rolled this in its first race and then re-built it and sold it to Sam Tingle.

He then built a similar car for his own use '7' and finished sixth in the 1962 Rand GP and tenth in the Natal GP. He qualified for the South African GP (ahead of de Beaufort's Porsche 718) but was not to finish. A good grid position for the 1963 Rand GP translated into fifth in the first heat, and on the same lap as the works Ferraris, but in heat two problems saw him finish down the order. For the second year running he qualified for the South African GP and, though eight laps down, was classified 12th.

Serrurier took sixth in the 1964 Rand GP, but failed to qualify for the 1965 South African GP.

Cars '8' and '9' were both Mk 2 models which were supplied to Gene Bosman (Alfa Romeo engine and gearbox) and Fanie Viljoen (Coventry Climax 1½-litre FPF engine and Cooper gearbox). Both drivers concentrated on their home series and neither entered Formula 1 events.

A completely new model, L.D.S. Mk 3 '10' was a copy of the Tasman Brabham BT11A made with the co-operation of the Brabham works, which supplied uprights, etc., because Sam Tingle had just been beaten to buying the last of the line. These gave a particularly good account of themselves in the 1965-6 Temporada. Sam Tingle, indeed, qualified L.D.S. '10' with a 2.7-litre FPF engine on the grid for the 1967 South African GP and was ahead of Graham Hill, Jo Siffert and Piers Courage. Unfortunately he did not finish.

Later Serrurier made a car to his own design '11' which was run with a 2-litre FPF engine in the 3-litre 'Gold Star' series. The L.D.S. line came to an end in 1965-6 with a pair of cars based on the Brabham BT16 F2 car, one of which was fitted with a Ford FJ engine and the other with a 2-litre FPF.

Serrurier than bought a Lola T70, which he raced from 1966 until 1969, when he decided to retire from driving. He is still actively involved with racing, however, and kindly assisted with this brief profile of his cars.

Lotus 7:

Brausch Niemann entered his Lotus 7, powered by a 1500cc version of the Ford 105E engine, for both the Rand and Natal GPs in 1962. It ran without front mudguards or lights, but in case anyone thinks it was a joke, it should be said that in the Rand GP it was clocked at 127 mph and, though last on the grid, at least it made the race, which is more than can be said for 13 other entries which included a Cooper-Maserati and a Cooper-Alfa Romeo. Niemann finished 11th, and last classified runner, and although he was 5 laps down on Clark's Lotus he had a couple of FPF-powered Lotuses behind him.

In the Natal GP he actually qualified 20th of 32 runners, but retired. It was a performance which makes one wish he had brought his car to Britain.

Lotus 22:

This was a Formula Junior car with an enlarged Ford engine which had to carry 140 lb of ballast to qualify for F1. Driven by (who else?) Brausch Niemann it qualified eighth of a field of 22 for the 1963 Rand GP, and despite losing a wheel on the last lap of the first heat was classified tenth of 16 finishers, though the problem ended his day's racing. Niemann then entered it in the South African GP, where he qualified 15th from a field of 21. Had he not encountered endless problems in the race it is likely he would have made a finish in the top ten.

In the following year's Rand GP he managed to finish fifth on aggregate, with the same number of laps as the winner, Graham Hill, but he just missed the cut in qualifying for the South African GP. Niemann later faded away from the scene, became 'bush happy' and returned to his remote farm. It was racing's loss, for he seems to have been made of the right stuff.

Netuar:

This Cooper-copy had a Peugeot engine, was made by Rauten Hartmann (Netuar = Rauten spelled backwards), and appeared in the Rand GP in the years 1961 to 1964.

In 1961, Hartmann qualified last and retired with engine trouble after 11 laps. He failed to make the grid the following year, but qualified last again in 1963 and finished 14th on aggregate, the last classified finisher. In the car's 1964 appearance, Hartmann again qualified near the back, finished 15th from 15 classified finishers in the first heat, but retired in the second with engine problems.

Quodra:

Don Philp, a Stellenbosch motor dealer, had successfully raced an F2 Cooper-Climax and was reckoned by some to be the best South African driven of his time. Many of the parts from his Cooper were used in the Quodra, which followed the lines of the 1960 works Cooper 'low-lines' but with a space-frame designed by Philp himself. He drove it in the 1961 Rand and Natal Grands Prix, where it qualified in mid-field and retired on both occasions. In the non-Championship South African GP he started 11th from a field of 23 and finished 14th, but out of classification.

Realpha:

Built by Rays Engineering Ltd in Rhodesia and driven by Ray Reed, the Realpha was a slim Alfa Romeo-engined Cooper-copy which appeared in the 1964 Rand GP. Reed qualified it 17th from 24 and was classified 14th in the first heat. Unfortunately the car's big ends had gone and so it did not appear for heat two. It was entered in the 1965 South African GP under the name 'R.E.' but failed to appear. Reed himself died soon afterwards in an air crash.

****

Motor racing in Southern Africa was particularly rich in the 1960s and there were many other cars which fall outside my brief (e.g. Scorpion-Alfa and Citrun-Climax) and there were, too, many fine drivers (such as Bruce Johnstone and Syd van der Vyver) who also slip through my brief. It remains a pity that no comprehensive history has yet been published on African racing during this period.

SPEED V-8

When the 2½-litre F1 was announced in 1952, Leslie Brooke, a noted Riley exponent and special builder, reasoned that if a suitable engine was available, then it would assist builders such as Cooper, H.W.M., Connaught and Kieft to make the transition to F1 and achieve what B.R.M. had failed to do.

In 1952 Brooke approached Alderman Harry Weston, Managing Director of Machine Tools Ltd and Lord Mayor of Coventry, with a scheme to provide such an engine. Coventry was then the centre of the British car industry, the largest in Europe, and Weston saw the project as an ideal way to promote the city. With his considerable influence he was able to persuade a number of local firms to contribute, although many recalled B.R.M. and contributed on a limited basis.

Among the companies which gave their approval was the Rootes Group. Nobody recalls Rootes being in the van of engine design, but it did have a number of fairly advanced engine projects running in single-cylinder form. It therefore gave its blessing to two of its designers, Bill Oliver and Ron Dalton, assisting on a part-time basis while having access to Rootes experimental work.

Brooke and Weston set up a company, Speed Engines Ltd, although the V-8 which resulted has popularly been known as the 'Brooke-Weston' engine. Oliver and Dalton came up with an over-square design (81.30 × 61 mm) which, since it used wet liners, could easily have been taken out to 3 litres or more for use in sports cars. Its block and crankcase were cast in RR50 alloy and while it naturally used d.o.h.c., it was unusual in that it had three valves (two inlets) per cylinder. It had, too, a five-bearing crankshaft and dry-sump lubrication.

At 13:1 the compression ratio was unusually high and the pistons had what Ron Dalton describes as 'radius scallop' crowns. Twin Lucas magnetos provided sparks for two plugs per cylinder, and although carburation was initially by four twin-choke downdraught Solexes, it was planned to fit CAV fuel injection. Drive to the camshafts and twin water pumps was by a fairly complicated cluster of bevel gears. Wills rings were used at the cylinder head face and interconnecting water channels between block and head were dispensed with.

The prototype engine was shown to the Press in late 1955, but the Press did not hail it with great enthusiasm, for it did not look at all promising. Each cylinder had been spaced widely from the next, with the result that the lump was no less than 37½-in long (the Coventry Climax 'Godiva' was 24-in long) and weighed 400 lb, which was stretching the imagination even for installation in a front-engined car. When the project died, the Press did not even mention the fact.

What happened was this: the prototype engine was installed on a dynamometer and driven by an external source for several hours to check that everything did what it was supposed to do. Everything seemed to be in order and the engine was fired and ran at 3000-4000 rpm, and then it seized. The tappets had been hardened, but in machining the chilled faces had been taken off and the cams gradually ate into the soft metal until they locked on to the tappets. The seizure wrecked the bevel gears in the drive chain. Although some firms in Coventry had undertaken to assist the project with components and machining, Brooke had put a lot of his own money into it and had no more to spare. There was simply none left to rebuild the engine and to try again.

Bill Oliver is now deceased, but Ron Dalton still works for Jaguar and his estimation is that running at a maximum of 8000 rpm, the engine's target output of around 230 bhp would easily have been achieved, and indeed he would have wagered serious money on seeing 250 bhp, then a competitive output. That is in the realms of 'what might have been', for a sub-contractor's machinist made an error and caused the project to fold after a single run on a dynamometer. In truth, however, the chance of such a long and heavy engine ever working in a racing car, no matter what its power output, must have been slim.

The engine is still in existence and when last heard, the owner had plans to rebuild and modify it, and install it in the Kieft GP car (q.v.) which he also owns.

STEBRO

Stebro has the distinction of being the only Canadian car to compete in a WC race, although that is a little like being the world's tallest dwarf. The car which in the 1963 US GP was a Stebro Mk IV FJ car fitted with a 1500cc version of the Ford 105E engine, with Weber carburettors giving around 110 bhp.

It was a very low car built around a conventional space-frame with wide-based double wishbone and coil spring front suspension and a rear layout consisting of a lower wishbone, upper transverse link and twin radius rods. Two Stebros were entered, but only one turned up, and to the surprise of nobody, Peter Broeker qualified it last, 15.1 seconds off the pace, but only 3.4 seconds slower than the hapless Baghetti in the appalling A.T.S. Broeker actually managed to finish seventh, 22 laps in arrears and unclassified, with the winner, Graham Hill, lapping him every five laps.

The following year Broeker and a Stebro appeared in a couple of F2 races, but the combination was embarrassingly slow.

The only Canadian car to appear in a World Championship event was this modified Formula Junior Stebro which Peter Broeker drove to a surprise seventh place in the 1963 US Grand Prix, but he was 22 laps down at the finish. (LAT)

TALBOT-LAGO

To Antonio Lago, Venetian by birth, French by adoption and an Anglophile by inclination, fell the task of keeping alive the last vestiges of the great pre-war French tradition of making quality sporting cars. In the 1920s he had been based in London, where he became well-known for his 'LAP' o.h.v. conversions. After a spell with the Wilson Self Changing Gear Company, Lago joined the old Sunbeam-Talbot-Darracq firm, and when the company failed in 1935 he was able to raise the capital to salvage part of it and so form SA Automobiles Talbot.

Lago looked to racing to enhance Talbot's image and together with Walter Becchia, he designed a 6-cylinder 4-litre engine with long and short rockers and cross-over pushrods. Lightweight sports versions were entered by the works in a number of races and won the 1937 Tunis GP, took a 1-2-3 in both the Marseilles and French GPs and first and second in the Tourist Trophy at Donington Park.

As a result he received a grant from the Racing Fund Committee which was set up by the Automobile Club of France to encourage French racing teams. Talbot then began work on a 3-litre supercharged engine and entered stripped down sports cars with engines of 4467cc (92 × 112 mm) in GP racing with neither success nor hope of success, but at least the *Tricolor* was being waved.

In 1939 Talbot built a single-seater version with an engine of 4483cc (93 × 110 mm) which gave 210 bhp. Although outclassed by the German teams, the Talbot did not entirely disgrace itself and took thirds in the Pau

In the 1948 Grand Prix at Silverstone 'Phi-Phi' Etancelin with his Talbot-Lago leads John Bolster (E.R.A.). (**Guy Griffiths**)

and French GPs.

Sports car or single-seater, Talbots all bore a family resemblance, with a channel-section chassis, front suspension by wishbones and transverse leaf, and a live rear axle suspended on semi-elliptic springs. Transmission was via a 4-speed Wilson pre-selector gearbox. They were never light, either, the single-seater weighed 850 kg or 18 cwt – an Auto Union D-Type weighed about the same, but produced 485 bhp. They were, however, durable and more economical than their rivals, covering up to five times the distance on the same fuel.

After the war both money and materials were tight, but the car was resurrected, and provided it did not have to take on the works Alfa Romeos, it gave a good account of itself. Louis Chiron won the French GP, came second to a Maserati in the Marne GP at Reims and Louis Rosier won the Albi GP. These races were Grand Prix in name and length, but were basically glorified national events,

for Europe was still smoking after the fires of war had been doused and it was a wonder racing was taking place at all.

For 1948 Talbot became known as Talbot-Lago (later it would be Lago-Talbot) and Lago and his new chief engineer, Carlo Marchetti, produced the T-26C, which had the same general chassis layout and engine dimensions as the single-seater but featured revised valve gear. Lago could not afford the cost involved in producing a d.o.h.c. head, but achieved hemispherical combustion chambers by high-mounted camshafts, similar to Riley and Lea-Francis. This car was even heavier, 915 kg, but it produced 240 bhp. By comparsion, the Alfa Romeo 158 weighed 700 kg and developed 310 bhp.

Lago intended to make a run of 20 cars and while that was over-ambitious, he did achieve about half that number, a good effort for the time. They were rugged, reliable cars which were ideal for a privateer. Ferraris and

Maseratis might be quicker, and more temperamental, but Talbots offered variety on a grid, which was an important consideration when negotiating starting money.

At Monaco, with Alfa Romeo absent, Chiron finished second to Farina's Maserati, but in the 1939 single-seater. Rosier had debuted the T-26C, but retired. A second T-26C was on hand for the Swiss GP, which was dominated by Alfa Romeo and Maserati, but the cars of Comotti and Raph were fourth and fifth behind the Alfa Romeo team in the French GP, Rosier took fourth in the British (Alfa Romeo was absent and he was beaten to third by Bob Gerard's E.R.A.), Raph was second in the Comminges GP and Chiron and Rosier were second and third at Albi, behind Villoresi's Maserati.

With Ferrari becoming a force in racing, every other team was pushed further down the rung, but the marque did manage one win, in the Coupe du Salon at Monthléry, where Rosier led Levegh and Giraud-Cantabous for a 1-2-3, but the opposition was negligible.

Alfa Romeo withdrew from racing for 1949 and its absence gave everyone else a chance. Lago-Talbot's first major race, the British GP, did not attract a strong entry, but even so Rosier could only manage third and then behind Gerard's venerable, and brilliantly driven, E.R.A., while Phillipe Etancelin could manage only fifth, behind David Hampshire's E.R.A.

At the Belgian GP, however, a combination of the car's strength and economy allowed Rosier to score an impressive win over the Ferraris of Villoresi and Ascari. Ferrari's reaction was to learn the lesson, decide the days of the supercharged car were numbered, and commission work on the 'long-block' V-12.

Ferrari was back on top in the Swiss GP, but Sommer and Etancelin came third and fourth. For the French GP Etancelin had an engine with a twin-plug head, which gave another 14 bhp, and while he retired, Chiron came home to give Lago-Talbot a second major win, and the day was made complete by Rosier and Sommer in fourth and fifth places. Etancelin had the new cylinder head for the Italian and Czechoslovakian GPs and finished second in both to add to the second he had taken earlier at Marseilles.

It had been a surprisingly successful year for Lago-Talbot and one which would never come again. Lago dreamed of making a V-16 supercharged engine, but financial reality meant it would never be built. Instead Lago-Talbot soldiered on with its T-26C, but with twin-plug ignition as standard, three Zenith 50HN carburettors which were mounted horizontally and, thanks to better fuel, a raising of the compression ratio from 8:1 to 11:1, up to 280 bhp was produced and there was even a 5 kg reduction in weight.

It was too little too late, for Alfa Romeo was back and Ferrari was growing stronger. Still, Giraud-Cabantous and Rosier were fourth and fifth in the British GP behind the Alfa Romeo team, but they were both two laps down. Neither of the two cars entered finished at Monaco. Rosier managed third in the Swiss GP after the works Ferraris both retired, but he was lapped by the Alfa Romeos, which came first and second. At Spa, however,

Engine view of a Talbot-Lago, showing the six single exhausts merging into twin tail pipes and the tubular air intake of early post-war engines. (Guy Griffiths)

Eugène Martin at the wheel of his Talbot-Lago in the European Grand Prix at Silverstone in May 1950.
(T. C. March)

the cars were fairly competitive and Sommer qualified fifth, with the same time as Villoresi's Ferrari, and Etancelin was sixth and ahead of Ascari's new 3.3-litre Ferrari.

The grid at Spa would have been pretty thin without Lago-Talbot, for the company had built exactly half of the 14 starters. Of the works cars, only Rosier's survived to the end and he finished a splendid third, less than 2½ minutes behind Fangio's Alfa Romeo. Qualitatively,

it was perhaps Lago-Talbot's finest Grand Prix performance.

A week later Rosier won Le Mans in a T-26C converted to sports car trim, with a narrow body and cycle mudguards, and he drove for all but two laps, when he handed over to his son. The model thus became the only one in history to win both a classic Grand Prix and Le Mans.

At Reims for the French GP Ferrari was absent and

Lockheed hydraulic brakes with 16-in alloy drums were fitted to the Lago-Talbot.
(Guy Griffiths)

246

***In 1951 British driver Duncan Hamilton ran a Lago-Talbot. Here the irrepressible Hamilton is seen at Silverstone.* (Guy Griffiths)**

the works Lago-Talbots provided Alfa Romeo's main opposition, but in the midsummer heat one by one the cars dropped out with overheating and only Etancelin struggled round to finish, in fifth place and five laps down. The WC season ended at Monza, where the cars were trounced, and while Rosier and Etancelin were fourth and fifth, they were both five laps in arrears.

In non-Championship events, Rosier, who at 45 was the baby of the team (Giraud-Cabantous was 46 and Etancelin 54!), had a highly successful time. He won the Albi GP, ahead of Gonzalez' Maserati, the Dutch GP ahead of the Ferraris of Villoresi and Ascari, and split the Alfa Romeos of Fangio and Fagioli at Pescara. Georges Grignard won the Paris GP in his private car.

The writing was on the wall for Lago-Talbot, for the venerable design could not be stretched any further. The engine might have carried the team through if installed in a new chassis with the shedding of three of four hundredweight, but there simply was no money to do it. The

French luxury car market was small and it was shared between a number of makers who formed the remains of the pre-war French tradition and, as for exports, few wanted to buy a pre-war design when the Jaguar XK120 was cheaper.

Then there were new fiscal measures imposed by the French government. In addition to car tax and a road tax system related to engine size, which made large cars extremely expensive to keep on the road, the government imposed a levy on employers of 48 per cent of a worker's wages.

The aim of the levy was to encourage automation and productivity, and it worked, but it cut the ground from under firms such as Lago-Talbot, which were labour intensive, and one by one the great names of the French motor industry disappeared. Lago-Talbot would be the last, absorbed by Simca in 1959.

Early in 1951 Antonio Lago announced his firm's withdrawal from Grand Prix racing, although it was to continue in sports cars, making repeated attempts to win Le Mans until 1956. Existing Lago-Talbot GP cars continued to appear, however, although the best World Championship result was to be the fourth, fifth and sixth of Rosier, Giraud-Cabantous and Pilette at Spa. Unlike the previous year, however, Rosier was lapped twice.

1951 was all about the battle between Ferrari and Alfa Romeo, but without the Lago-Talbots some of the fields would have been sparse (six of the 13 starters at Spa, for example). On all but the long circuits, however, they were completely outclassed and the best finisher would generally be five or more laps down.

Away from the World Championship, however, Rosier rounded off the marque's GP history with another win in the Dutch GP, from Etancelin and Moss' F2 H.W.M. He was second in the Albi GP (Chiron in another Lago-Talbot was third), but was beaten by Trintignant's little Simca. Other second places came at Pau (behind Villoresi's Ferrari, but ahead of Farina's Maserati) and at Pescara, where he followed home Gonzalez' Ferrari with Etancelin in third.

When the 4½-litre F1 lost its Championship status at the end of the year many of the cars sprouted mudguards and continued as sports cars.

TATRA

Czechoslovakia has suffered more than most countries from the fortunes of politics and war, but it has a sturdy, independent tradition of engineering and motor racing and it remains the only Eastern bloc country to have built cars which have competed at Le Mans. In 1949 an Aero-Minor won the 750cc class at Le Mans and Skoda ran there in 1950. Skodas are common in the West, but there is another Czech manufacturer, Tatra, which began as a carriage maker in the 19th Century and which, these days, builds military and commercial vehicles and saloons for Party officials. In the 1950s, Tatra made several racing prototypes, including a 2-litre, 4-cylinder, sports car with which Bruno Sojka finished ninth in the

1949 Brno (Formule Libre) GP and a rear-engined single-seater, the T607 'Monopost', which was said to conform to the 2½-litre F1.

It was based on production components and was said to feature a modified engine taken from the 603 saloon and reduced to 2490cc (75 × 70 mm). As on the saloon version, the overhead valves were operated by unequal-length push-rods activated by a single, centrally-located, camshaft, an arrangement which allowed hemispherical combustion chambers. Two downdraught Solex carburettors were used and the whole car weighed 606 kg.

Articles about the cars appeared in the Western press

The rear-engined Tatra T606-2 in record breaking form with coupé top. (Jan Tulis)

in the late 1950s and early 1960s with inevitable speculation about 'what might have been' and these articles give the impression that the car was built with the 2½-litre formula in mind, although no date of construction was ever given.

It is a shame to spoil a good story, but the two versions of the T607 were made in 1950 and 1951, when the 1½-litre supercharged/4½-litre unblown formula was in force. Further, their cylinder dimensions are actually (75 × 72 mm), which gives a capacity of 2545cc. It is therefore clear that Formula 1 had not entered anyone's mind and that the T607 was simply a test bed for ideas which took part in a few local races and made some record attempts.

Following normal Tatra practice, suspension was independent all round, with swing axles at the rear and double wishbones at the front, and both ends were sprung by torsion bars. One thing which is interesting, however, is that the T607 had a properly triangulated space-frame, something which was very unusual in 1950,

and it gives some idea of the competence of the engineers who made the cars. Further, the top three gears in the 4-speed box were fitted with synchromesh, which, again, was an unusually advanced feature.

Bruno Sojka drove T607-1 in the 1950 Formule Libre Brno Grand Prix and in very wet conditions brought it home second to Vaclaw Hovorka's Maserati. In 1953 Adolf Vermirovsky took a national speed record of 129.98 mph in T607-2 and two years later this was upped to 134.37 mph. These figures tell their own story – the car was a long way short of being competitive in F1 – though they are respectable enough for a production-derived special.

Since the Tatra T607 was never intended as a Grand Prix machine, and did not even comply to F1 regulations except in the sense that a 2.6-litre car notionally qualified for the 4½-litre formula, strictly speaking it has no place in this book, but is included in order to nail the myth. Both T607s are currently on display in the Tatra Museum in Koprivince together with other prototypes.

TEC-MEC

After Maserati pulled out of racing at the end of 1957, Valerio Colotti, the team's chief chassis and transmissions engineer, decided it was time for him to leave and set up his own studio. This was an unusual move for a top-class Italian engineer for, in the same circumstances, most would have simply moved to one of the major manufacturers, where they would have been welcomed.

One of Colotti's first commissions was a gearbox for Rob Walker's team, which had bought a Cooper for the use of Stirling Moss. Stirling had come to know Colotti well in his days at Maserati and appreciated his talent, hence he pointed Rob Walker to Colotti's Studio Tecnica Meccanica.

Transmission failures during 1959 cost Moss the World Championship and labelled him a car breaker, which he was not. The popular press had a high old time writing about the Moss 'jinx'. There was, in fact, nothing wrong with Colotti's design, the faults were all traceable to the sub-contractors who made and assembled the parts.

Later Colotti gearboxes were to occupy a similar position in F1 to Hewland today, a provider of good reliable transmissions to anyone who did not want to go to the complication and expense of making his own. That was in the future, however. Back in the early days of Tec-Mec Colotti was approached by Giorgio Scarlatti, an

amateur driver who had made appearances in Maserati works cars, to build him a successor to the Maserati 250F. The result centred on a lightweight space-frame which Colotti had on his drawing board when at Maserati. Coil spring and wishbone front suspension, similar to that on the 250F, was used, but the de Dion rear set-up was replaced by an independent system using a transverse leaf spring and wishbones. Girling disc brakes replaced the large drums which Maserati favoured.

Money was tight and progress was slow, indeed much of the early construction of the car took place in the front room of the ex-Maserati mechanic entrusted with the job. While the car was proceeding, Scarlatti sold his interest in it to an American domiciled in Italy, Gordon Pennington, and then Colotti sold Pennington the studio he had founded and went off to form Gear Speed Development SpA in partnership with Alf Francis, It was this company which made the production Colotti gearboxes.

Pennington changed the name of the studio to Tec-Mec Automobili, acquired a well-used 250F engine, and went testing. At first the car was terrible, but Tec-Mec persevered and eventually produced a reasonably competent car, but all this had taken time. Had it been ready during 1958, the Tec-Mec F415 might have made a decent showing, but by late 1959 you needed a lot of

horsepower or a Cooper chassis.

An entry was made for Giorgio Scarlatti in the car at the Italian GP, but it was not ready. Still, the last round of the World Championship that year was at Sebring in December and there the Tec-Mec was entered for the in-experienced Brazilian Fritz d'Orey. It is difficult to know how much of the car's poor showing was due to the driver, the car or the engine for that was well past its best.

In fact when the car was wheeled off the boat the engine lacked compression on two cylinders. Not surprisingly, d'Orey's best practice lap was 33.4 seconds slower than Moss' pole time and he managed to complete just six laps before the engine expired in a gush of oil.

Later the car was used in a record attempt, but the engine again blew up. Pennington lost interest and the Tec-Mec mouldered away until rescued and restored by Tom Wheatcroft.

TURNER

Jack Turner is a perfect example of the typical post-war British special builder. After coming out of the Armed Forces, he was involved in engineering and began to compete in events with an M.G. Then he decided to build his own car, which followed the Cooper's layout, a ladder-frame with independent suspension all round by transverse leaf springs. Someone else saw it, liked it, and asked to buy a replica and so Turner found himself becoming a constructor.

To his workshop came one John Webb, who had bought the ex-Reg Parnell M.G. K3 Magnette which had been fitted with a unique d.o.h.c. head designed by Laurence Pomeroy and he asked Turner to convert the car into a single-seater. By degrees Turner also obtained more power from the engine and Webb was sufficiently impressed to commission an F2 car for the 1953 season, for he had in the back of his mind the idea that he might take in a few Grands Prix.

The result was similar to Turner's sports specials with its lozenge-shaped ladder-frame and transverse leaf springing. Its wheelbase was 7 ft 6 in, 11-in Girling drum brakes were fitted all round, and the rolling chassis was completed by cast alloy wheels which Turner made for his own cars and sold to other constructors such as Tojeiro.

One of Turner's sports cars had been sold to Ken Rose, son of Lea-Francis' chief designer, Hugh. Through this connection Turner was able to have Lea-Francis' 1767cc iron block engine recast in aluminium. Enlarged to 1960cc (76 × 100 mm), which was the same as Connaught's LeaF engine, and with two plugs per cylinder and S.U. fuel injection, Jack Turner says his engine gave 145 bhp at 6000 rpm. This was transmitted via an Armstrong-Siddeley pre-selector gearbox and an ENV differential mounted on the chassis.

John Webb was some way from being an ace and he

John Webb with the Lea-Francis-powered Formula 2 Turner in the 1953 International Trophy at Silverstone. (T. C. March)

confined his activities to minor British F2 events in 1953, where the car was always at the tail end of the field. The following year he tried a 2½-litre Alta engine, but the story was the same. Perhaps its best performance was in the 1954 International Trophy at Silverstone, when Jack Fairman drove it to finish sixth in his heat and 13th in the final. Most of its races that year ended with mechanical failure.

Turner made a number of other Lea-Francis-based engines, and one was used by Kieft at Le Mans in 1955 without success. A 4-cylinder d.o.h.c. 500cc engine was also made, but it failed to live up to expectations, although the head performed well on a BMC Series 'A' engine. In 1954, however, Turner went into production with a little BMC-engined sports car, effectively an Austin-Healey Sprite, nearly three years before the Sprite appeared.

With various engines, this stayed in production for 11 years and around 800 were made, with some enjoying a fair degree of competition success in British and American club events. Finally ill-health caused Turner to close his factory and he now enjoys retirement in his native Wales, while his one single-seater is also in Wales.

V. M.

One of the saddest stories in motor racing is that of the V.M. *Monoplace.* Little is known about the car, which was a special created by one Viglielmo Matozza, except that it was based on Tatra components.

Matozza, who had last competed in 1935, filed an entry for the 1954 Grand Prix des Frontières, but as the deadline loomed the car was not ready and so he had to put in some 'all-nighters'. Alas, he was so stretched that he fell asleep after he arrived at Chimay and by the time he awoke it was too late for practice. Thus the car did not appear there and nor was it entered in any other F1 race.

VANWALL

When the B.R.M. project was floated, one of its first supporters was Guy Anthony 'Tony' Vandervell. Vandervell had himself raced cars and motorcycles in the 1920s and had later made a fortune by securing the European rights to 'Thin Wall' engine bearings. He was a forthright man and when the B.R.M. muddled along he decided to give it a boost by buying a Grand Prix car so the team could gain some experience of running a car.

Since he always wanted the best, he tried Alfa Romeo and got a refusal, then turned to Ferrari, with whom he was on good terms. Vandervell Products had helped sort out bearing problems on the firm's V-12 engine and Ferrari was happy to sell him a 1½-litre supercharged Tipo 125 Grand Prix car.

This arrived just before the 1949 British GP, where it was entered as the 'Thin Wall Special' Ferrari. Raymond Mays had an unhappy drive and handed over to the reserve, Ken Richardson, who crashed it. It was typical of Vandervell that, although he had not raced for over 20 years, he had nominated himself as reserve driver, but the RAC refused to accept him. The RAC also reacted to the car's name (trade advertising), but as usual Vandervell got his way. The car had been delivered only just before the race and afterwards 'GAV', as he was known in his firm, carried out a detailed inspection. He was not at all impressed, and made his feelings to Ferrari quite plain, while also suggesting numerous, sensible, improvements.

The car was sent back and a second Tipo 125, with two-stage supercharging and a longer wheelbase, was delivered. Again entered as a 'Thin Wall', Ascari drove it in the 1950 International Trophy at Silverstone until a downpour caught him out and he spun. This car, too, was inspected, found wanting, and returned.

In the interim Vandervell, who was also a director of Norton motorcycles, had instigated a project to make a 4-cylinder engine for Norton based on the B.R.M. V-16. This lurched along with the same speed, competence and commitment as the B.R.M. project itself and in the end Vandervell divorced himself from B.R.M., making his feelings for the project very clear indeed. Then he set up a racing department in his factory at Acton, which would begin by running another Ferrari.

The second Tipo 125 was rebuilt at Maranello with a 4½-litre unsupercharged engine with single-plug heads and the latest de Dion rear axle (making it Thin Wall No. 3) and it was delivered in time for Reg Parnell to drive it in the 1951 International Trophy at Silverstone. A storm of monsoon proportions caused the final of the event to be abandoned after only six laps and since Parnell was in the lead at the time, he collected the prize money. Nine days later Parnell took it to Goodwood, where he won the Festival of Britain Trophy, then he finished second to Farina's Alfa Romeo in the Ulster Trophy at Dundrod. This was all very encouraging, so the team entered the French GP, where Parnell finished fourth. Parnell was on duty for B.R.M. at the British GP, so Peter Whitehead drove and plugged around to finish ninth.

As the team learned about its car, so it set about improving it. The first area to receive attention was the braking system, and while Vandervell accepted a three-shoe Girling system as a short-term improvement, he made an arrangement with Goodyear's aircraft division for the supply of disc brakes adapted from Goodyear's aircraft system, although these specially developed units did not materialize until 1953. It was typical of GAV to decide before anyone else that the day of the drum brake was over. The team's first season rounded off with Parnell taking a couple of seconds (to Farina's Alfa Romeo) at Goodwood and a win in a Formule Libre race at Charterhall.

As 1951 ended so the car was effectively demoted, but far from abandoning F1, Vandervell continued with the development of his car and in 1952 took delivery of a long-wheelbase 'Indianapolis' chassis and the latest specification engine complete with twin-plug heads, and a body built in England.

This fourth 'Thin Wall Special' became one of the most famous cars in Britain as it provided the main opposition to B.R.M. in F1 and Formule Libre sprint races in Britain, which were very popular. GAV enjoyed these races, for he nurtured a personal rivalry with B.R.M., and because he did things properly, the Thin Wall was driven by stars such as Gonzalez, Taruffi, Farina and Hawthorn. In it Farina became the first driver to lap Silverstone at over 100 mph and it was still winning races in 1954, when a promising youngster named Peter Collins drove it.

Quite apart from the pleasure he had from quite often beating B.R.M., patriot that he was, he began to nurse a dream of beating 'those bloody red cars'. This was why B.R.M. had been formed and it is a small irony that he was competing against the British 'world beater' with a red car, except Thin Walls were always painted green. The green Ferrari rarely ventured abroad, but was retained to keep Vandervell in the swim and the racing team both in practice for a new project which was to be known as the 'Vanwall Special'.

GAV had been impressed by the results gained by special water-cooled Norton 500cc engines which he had had made for B.R.M. during the days of the abortive B.R.M./Norton project. Even running on inferior petrol, they had delivered 47 bhp, which, thanks to better cooling, was more than Norton's air-cooled engines. It was also close to the 'magic' 100 bhp/litre normally achieved using brews based on methanol.

Vandervell conceived the idea of a 2-litre F2 engine based on the Norton 'double knocker' complete with hairpin valve springs. VP had all the resources to design and build the engine, and GAV himself had all the contacts to hurry along the programme, but it still took longer than anticipated, largely due to problems sealing the cyinder head, and it was not until 1954 that the Vanwall Special made its debut.

GAV had become very friendly with John Cooper, in whom he recognized a kindred spirit, and he commissioned Cooper Cars to design a chassis with the brief that it should accept Ferrari-copy suspension, hubs, steering and gearbox, since these were all known elements. Consequently the car had double wishbone and transverse leaf front suspension and a de Dion rear, also with a transverse leaf, located by twin radius rods. As on the Thin Wall, Goodyear single-pad discs were fitted (inboard at the rear) and the 4-speed gearbox, a copy of Ferrari's, was mounted in unit with the final drive.

Externally, the body followed general Ferrari style except that there was no radiator intake, but the cooling was externally-mounted Clayton-Still 'Wire Wound' tubing. The thinking behind this unusual layout was to keep hot air away from the four Amal carburettors which fed the 1998cc (86 × 86 mm) engine, which was developing

about 200 bhp. Back at Acton, work was in hand to use Bosch fuel injection, since GAV had decided that that was where the future lay.

Since all the stars were spoken for, GAV asked Alan Brown, a journeyman driver, to give the car its debut in the 1954 International Trophy at Silverstone. In very wet conditions and, despite a spin, Brown brought it home sixth in his heat, and best 2-litre car, and was lying sixth in the final, and on his way to the F2 prize, when an oil pipe broke. Despite this the car received a favourable impression because, like all Vanwalls, it was superbly made.

By the time it next appeared, at the British GP, the engine size was 2236cc (91 × 86 mm) and this time there was a ducting panel over the external 'radiator'. At Silverstone, Peter Collins put it 11th on the grid and was running in eighth place (and ahead of Kling's Mercedes) when he had to retire on lap 17 with a cracked cylinder head.

Although a full 2490cc (96 × 86 mm) engine should have been in the car for the Italian GP, it broke a valve in testing and Collins had to have the 2.3-litre engine. Worried about the higher ambient temperature at Monza, the team fitted a conventional radiator in the nose, and since this did not affect the carburation, was retained thereafter.

In the Vanwall team was Derek Wooton, who drove the truck, but he was more than just a lorry driver, he was a died-in-the-wool racing nut. He it was who had fired up Colin Chapman when they were National Servicemen

Alan Brown at the wheel of the Vanwall Special, in 2-litre form and distinguished by its externally mounted radiator, on its first appearance in the International Trophy at Silverstone in 1954. (T. C. March)

By the 1954 British Grand Prix, where it was driven by Peter Collins, the Vanwall Special had a ducted panel over the external radiator.

in the RAF and he had remained close to Chapman thereafter. GAV warmed to enthusiasts and, being an excellent judge of men, he listened when Wooton told him he should bring in Frank Costin to look at the cars.

Costin it was who re-located the radiator and he also designed the high wrap-round perspex windscreen which Vanwall used at Monza and afterwards. He also designed some shrouds for the front suspension specifically for Monza, but there was not sufficient time to make them.

Collins qualified on the penultimate row of the grid, finding that while the engine was the equal of a number of full 2½-litre cars, the chassis left something to be desired in the faster corners. In the race he was in sixth place when the pipe to the oil gauge broke and he had to pit to have it sealed. Still, he finished seventh and although five laps down at least it was a finish.

Then came a couple of British races, this time with a full 2½-litre engine. At Goodwood Collins finished second to Moss' Maserati and well clear of Salvadori in the Gilby Engineering 250F. In the *Daily Telegraph* Trophy at Aintree, Mike Hawthorn had the car and again came second to Moss, this time with several private Maseratis behind at the end. Finally there was the Spanish GP, but there Collins wrapped the prototype around a tree in the first practice session so that was that.

For 1955 GAV planned a two-car team, now called simply 'Vanwall'. The chassis remained broadly the same, although coil springs were used at the front, just like the latest Ferraris, and the bodywork was tidied up with a longer nose, but a lot of work was done on the engines. Leo Kuzmicki, a Norton engineer who had been working on camshaft design for Vanwall, joined the team full-time to oversee engine development. The Bosch fuel injection system was ready and its injectors were mated to Amal carburettor bodies and throttle slides.

Vandervell hoped to sign Hawthorn and Collins, and although he got the former, who liked driving for Ferrari but hated living in Italy, Collins had signed for B.R.M. Unfortunately he did not disclose this until after nearly four months of hollow 'negotiations' to drive for Vanwall. This left the team in the lurch and Ken Wharton, a gifted all-rounder, but not an ace, was taken on the strength.

The team's first appearance was in the International Trophy at Silverstone and, while Hawthorn equalled Salvadori's pole time in practice, he never ran higher than fourth in the race. After 15 laps a leak in the gearbox both saturated him and caused his engine oil pressure to drop. Wharton had been well back on the grid and was making good progress when he pitted to have his throttle seen to. Then he was forced off line going into Copse corner and his car hit one of the marker drums, which ruptured the fuel tank. Although Wharton was able to jump from his blazing car, he was badly burned. To round off the catalogue of disaster, the race was won by Collins in the Owen Racing Organisation's

Maserati 250F, for the B.R.M. was not yet ready.

With Wharton in hospital, just one Vanwall, for Hawthorn, ran in the Monaco GP, but was not near the pace and retired with a broken throttle linkage. Things were not much better at Spa, where the lone Vanwall was nearly 15 seconds off the pace and retired with another oil leak from the gearbox. Hawthorn was upset by the way things were going and had had overtures to re-join Ferrari. After Mike had demonstrated *in vino veritas* (in his case pints of bitter), GAV opened the door for him and he chose to go through it and back to Maranello.

Hawthorn was right to be upset. He had missed first practice because his car was in the pits having its clutch changed. Vandervell had insisted on driving the car to the circuit, and in the traffic on the public road had cooked the clutch. GAV was unrepentant, his cars were *his* after all, they were his toys, and he would do as he liked.

Vanwall missed the Dutch GP, but appeared at Aintree with entries for Wharton and Harry Schell. Schell, a Franco-American, was a cheerful, exuberant man, and while not a top-line driver, was just the sort of character the team needed as it went through its difficult learning process.

Although Schell qualified well (seventh), he fluffed the start and finished the first lap in 18th position. He then drove like a man possessed and was up to eighth (and ahead of Hawthorn's Ferrari!) when in his excitement he pushed his accelerator so hard it came away from its mounting. Wharton, who had been playing himself in, had an oil pipe break and called at the pits to have it fixed. Schell took over, and although he finished last, at least the engine was still running.

With so many races cancelled after the Le Mans tragedy, a car was entered for Schell in the London Trophy at Crystal Palace, where he finished 1.4 seconds down on Hawthorn in Moss' Maserati. Then Schell and Wharton took a 1-2 in the RedEx Trophy at Snetterton, with Moss in his 250F well beaten in third place – a significant result especially since among the also-rans were the Maseratis of Salvadori and Rosier and Fairman's Connaught B-series.

Neither car was very fast in the last WC race, the Italian GP, and both were early retirements with problems related to the pounding they received on the bankings. Three cars were entered for the International Gold Cup at Oulton Park, but Wharton had been injured in the Tourist Trophy and so only those of Schell and Desmond Titterington started, but they started from the second row beaten only by two works Maseratis and two Ferrari-entered Lancia D50s. Schell retired, but Titterington came home third behind Moss (Maserati)

and Hawthorn (Lancia). To round off the season, Schell led from pole to flag in a minor F1 race, the Avon Trophy at Castle Combe.

On the evening before the Oulton Park race, GAV had been sinking a few drinks in the pleasant company of Frank Costin. They strolled over to the garage, where the chief asked Costin what he thought of the car. 'Wonderful engine, horrible chassis,' was the reply. 'Could you do better?' asked GAV. 'Yes,' said Frank, 'but Colin Chapman would do it even better, you need Chapman to do the chassis and me to do the body.'

Derek Wooton had long been urging a case for Chapman to be brought in on the project and Costin's reinforcement of the argument appears to have done the trick. One thing led to another, Chapman appeared at Acton, did his best to be diplomatic about the Cooper chassis, then found that words failed him and spoke his mind. He came away with a commission to design a new frame, with Costin to design the body.

Chapman designed a light space-frame which retained the previous front suspension with the addition of an anti-roll bar, and while the rear suspension remained similar in concept, the de Dion tube was lighter and the transverse leaf spring mounted higher and a Watts linkage was added to the twin radius arms to locate the tube. Despite its apparent bulk the Vanwall was lighter than any car of 1956 with the exception of the B.R.M. P25, which did not count.

Costin's problem was that the four-pot Vanwall engine was a tall unit and his solution was a startling teardrop body which he designed by calculation alone and which needed no alteration whatsoever. Unlike earlier aerodynamic bodies in GP racing, the underside of the car was included in the equation, the exhaust system was faired into the body and there was a ducting system to keep the driver cool. Moss was sceptical about the ducting until in a test session he pulled off one of the ducting pipes and found his head nearly blown off.

Meanwhile Kuzmicki undertook a careful development programme on the engine, which improved its power curve and raised output to a competitive 270 bhp with the added advantage that Costin's body made the most of it. A 5-speed gear cluster, with synchromesh on the top four ratios, was made by Porsche to fit the existing case, which, again, was mounted in unit with the final drive.

Vandervell's problem was to find drivers to do justice to his car, but most of the stars were spoken for and so he plumped for Schell and Trintignant. Moss had tested the car, been impressed, but had justified doubts about its reliability and Maserati offered a sports car programme as well as F1. He did, however, offer to drive when his commitments with Maserati permitted.

Since Maserati did not enter the International Trophy at Silverstone, Trintignant stepped down for Moss, who put the Vanwall on pole with Schell alongside and Fangio's Lancia-Ferrari third. Hawthorn's B.R.M. made the best start, but after it retired, Moss led effortlessly (with Schell third until an injector pipe broke) and both Lancia-Ferraris broke while chasing the green car. Yes, the Scuderia Ferrari had had to chase a green car and had failed in the attempt.

Coming so soon after Tony Brooks' win in a Connaught at Syracuse, it seemed as though Britain might have turned the corner, especially since Connaughts were second and third. It was a wonderful moment in British racing history, but the International Trophy was little more than half the distance of a full Grand Prix and the Vanwall had beaten only two of the *bloody red cars*.

At Monaco Schell qualified on the second row and Trintignant set an identical time, but Schell crashed on lap three trying to avoid Fangio's spinning Maserati and Trintignant bumped into the rear of another car and crumpled his nose cone, which finally led to his retirement through overheating. Schell took fourth at Spa (Trintignant's engine blew up) and in the process proved the Vanwall was the quickest car in a straight line if

deficient in high-speed corners. On the ultra-fast Reims circuit, however, the Vanwalls came into their own. Trintignant was released to drive the Bugatti, and Hawthorn, whose B.R.M. did not appear, took over. A third car was entered for Colin Chapman, who would have started from the second row alongside Schell, but his car was damaged when his brakes failed and he rammed Hawthorn in the tail at the Thillois hairpin. Thus ended Chapman's Grand Prix career.

In the race Schell had gearbox trouble and over-revved his engine. Hawthorn had driven in the 12-hour sports car race and so had been up all night and was driving comparatively slowly. Schell took over his car in seventh place and sensationally he drove up to second, breaking the lap record on the way. Schell stayed in the slipstream of the leader, Fangio, for four glorious laps, which was then easily the best performance by a British car in a WC event. The three Lancia-Ferraris tried every trick in the unwritten book to intimidate him, but it was a joint in the injector pump which put paid to the effort.

Trintignant and Schell were joined by Gonzalez for the British GP and they all qualified well. After Reims much was expected from the team, but Gonzalez broke a drive-shaft on the line, then (woe) two B.R.M.s led, but Schell mixed it with the red cars until a rear shock ab-

Part of the starting grid for the 1956 British Grand Prix, showing Harry Schell, Vanwall (No. 16), Froilan Gonzalez, Vanwall (No. 18), Tony Brooks, B.R.M. (No. 24), Archie Scott-Brown, Connaught (No. 19) and Desmond Titterington, Connaught (No. 20). (T. C. March)

sorber broke and had to be replaced; then he and Trintignant both had fuel starvation problems.

The German GP was missed (and so was the Vanwall Trophy at Snetterton) so the problems could be attended to, and at Monza, the last race of the year, Piero Taruffi joined the team. Despite the car being uncomfortable on the bankings, Schell ran second for 20 laps (and even led one), but again the gearbox started to leak oil and then seized. Taruffi also had a gearbox leak and Trintignant's front suspension broke.

Even with second-string drivers the cars had shone, and though Moss still wanted to race a British car he still had doubts about reliability. These were allayed by long-distance test sessions and after a traumatic year with B.R.M. Tony Brooks was delighted to join Stirling in the team. Brooks was at least Moss' equal in terms of talent and, a quiet, modest man was the ideal number two. From the beginning of the season it was felt that a three-car team made sense, but a decision on a third driver was deferred for the time being.

As a result of experience, numerous small changes were made to the package, the most obvious being the fitting of coil springs at the rear and patient work increased power to 285 bhp. There is a myth that the only non-British part of a Vanwall was the Bosch fuel injection, but the brakes were by Goodyear, the gearbox internals by Porsche, it ran on Pirelli tyres (until the end of 1957), there were Fitchel & Sachs shock absorbers and Scherdal valve springs, and GAV was in constant contact with other suppliers, mostly German, about other components – after all VP supplied the whole of the European motor industry with bearings.

Vanwall missed the Argentine GP, but entered Syracuse, where, against strong opposition, Moss and Brooks ran first and second until Moss had a fuel pipe break and Brooks a water pipe. Moss was able to rejoin and finish third. On hearing the news other firms offered possible solutions, and while these were being evaluated the cars ran at Goodwood, where, while easily the quickest, both suffered broken throttle linkages due to vibration in the system.

All the problems were solved by the Monaco GP, where the cars appeared with stub noses and bars across the air intakes, and while Moss crashed out of the lead on lap five (he maintains his front brakes failed), Brooks finished second to Fangio's Maserati, despite the fact he had to drive most of the way without a clutch. The Vanwall's gear-change was not good at the best of times and Brooks' left gear-change hand finished up like raw steak.

Money squabbles led to the cancellation of the Dutch and Belgian GPs, and by the time the French GP at Rouen came along, Brooks was out of action following a

crash at Le Mans and Moss had severe sinusitis. Their places were taken by Roy Salvadori and Stuart Lewis-Evans. Neither of the substitutes was particularly fast at Rouen, Salvadori retired with a broken valve spring and Lewis-Evans with a cracked cylinder head. Reims followed a week later and there Vanwall had its superb Costin-styled streamlined car, but neither of the subs were up to getting the best from it and it never did race. Lewis-Evans, however, qualified second in a standard car and calmly pulled away from a full WC field until, after 20 laps, oil started to blow from the engine on to his goggles and rear brakes, but he kept his cool and eased to compensate, finished third, and became the third member of the team.

At the British GP Moss sat on pole with Brooks, not fully recovered from his accident, on the outside of the front row. Moss swept into the lead, but after 20 laps his engine began to misfire. Brooks, far from race fit and running fifth was called in and Moss took over. He won. For a time Moss and Lewis-Evans lay first and second, but Lewis-Evans had his throttle control fail and had to be content with seventh.

But a Vanwall, driven by Moss and Brooks, had won a World Championship GP. Dammit, a green car had won! Those *bloody red cars* had been beaten at last. So far as British racing was concerned, it was the most important breakthrough but it was not isolated. In a few heady weeks there had been Aston Martin's triumph in the Nürburgring 1000 Kms, a Jaguar and Lotus whitewash at Le Mans, and domination by Cooper in F2. All the years of struggle and excuses, and the national humiliation which followed B.R.M.'s failure, seemed to be over. Shortly afterwards Behra's B.R.M. won the minor Caen GP, the twinkle dust seemed to be speading everywhere.

Hard reality followed Vanwall's first appearance at the Nürburgring, where the suspension was found to be far too stiff and gave their drivers a very rough time indeed. Lewis-Evans spun after gearbox oil sprayed on to his rear tyres, but Moss came home fifth and Brooks ninth, a lap down and severely dehydrated.

After the cancellation of the Belgian and Dutch Grands Prix, the FIA made up the World Championship by the introduction of the Pescara GP, run on a 15.9-mile road circuit, the longest in the Championship's history. Moss led from the second lap to the flag, Brooks retired with engine trouble after one lap and Lewis-Evans came fifth after tyre trouble. It was the first time a British car had won a major race on Italian soil, but, of course, the ultimate goal was to beat the *bloody red cars* at Monza.

After practice for the Italian GP the grid was changed from 3-2-3 to 4-3-4 so that Fangio's Maserati could start

Stirling Moss with the Vanwall that he had taken over from Tony Brooks scored an historic victory in the 1957 European Grand Prix at Aintree. (T. C. March)

from the front row alongside Lewis-Evans (pole), Moss and Brooks. To many Englishmen that typically Italian gesture meant more than the fact that the three green cars disputed the lead with Fangio and Behra. Brooks lost a lot of time with throttle trouble, Lewis-Evans retired with water loss and Moss sailed on his majestic way to win by over 40 seconds from Fangio. As Moss took the flag, Britain became the dominant force in Grand Prix racing and has remained so ever since.

The year ended with the non-Championship Moroccan GP over near-WC length. Moss contacted Asian' flu and withdrew, and Brooks and Lewis-Evens sat on the front row with Behra's Maserati in-between. During practice they had had the use of a brew containing nitromethane, which boosted power to 295 bhp, but were back on usual racing fuel for the race. Brooks was an early retirement and Behra won from Lewis-Evans. It was Maserati's last F1 win.

All three drivers, one of the strongest teams in GP history, were happy to stay with Vanwall for 1958. Supplies of Pirelli tyres finally ran out (the company had officially retired from the sport) and Vanwall switched to Dunlops. A late change in the rules meant that Av-gas had to be used for 1958, but the engines still gave around 270 bhp, a simple statement to make but something which took months to achieve. Since the cars were much more economical, all the fuel could be carried in the large rear tank and the subsidiary tanks on each side of the cockpit were removed. Because of this work Vanwall missed the Argentine GP and released Moss to drive Rob Walker's Cooper, and Moss, having heralded one revolution with Vanwall, heralded another with the Cooper.

Vanwall decided only to contest World Championship rounds in 1958 and so did not race again until Monaco in mid-May. When they appeared, apart from

the short nose, which was for Monaco only, the cars had a restyled tail section. Throughout the year the drivers spent time trying out combinations of the old Borrani wire wheels, with alloy rims, and new central-lock alloy wheels with a 'wobbly web' pattern. The exhaust system was made even more flush with the body and experiments were to be made with an outer cover of the exhaust pipe, designed to give a ram effect, which seemed similar to some of the cheap exhaust boosters on the market at the time.

Brooks put his car on pole and ran a strong second to Behra's B.R.M. until a sparking plug blew out of the head. Lewis-Evans was down among the Ferraris in midfield when a cylinder head joint started to leak, the water system became pressurized and the header tank expanded and fouled the steering column, one of the things which had happened in his troubled race at Rouen on his debut for the team.

Moss hit the front on lap 33 but retired soon afterwards with valve gear trouble. It was thus left to the Coopers of Brabham and Trintignant to star, and although the Australian retired, 'Trint' won.

The front row of the Dutch GP was altogether brighter with Lewis-Evans on pole and Moss and Brooks alongside him. Brooks retired with severe handling problems from a deranged rear axle, Lewis-Evans held second at first until passed by Schell's B.R.M. and then he lost third soon after half-distance, when a valve dropped, but Moss led from start to finish.

Twelve months before Britain had not won a WC race, three races into 1958 and British cars had taken three out of three and at Zandvoort a Vanwall won followed by two B.R.M.s, a Cooper, a Ferrari and a Lotus. Ferrari was in good shape at Spa, however, and Hawthorn and Musso were fastest in practice. Moss from the outside of the front row took the lead, but on his second lap over-revved his engine. Brooks, who felt his place was not to contest the lead with his number one, duly took over and won, with Lewis-Evans third. Tony Brooks talent was sublime and he won almost every race he drove at Spa.

In the French GP at Reims, a circuit where Vanwalls had made such splendid showings in the previous two years, both Ferrari and B.R.M. were superior and Moss had to settle for second to Hawthorn's Ferrari, with neither of the other Vanwalls finishing. Moss set pole at the British GP, but could run only second to Collins' Ferrari until his engine blew at one-third distance, whereupon Hawthorn took over second. Lewis-Evans could only finish fourth (beaten by Salvadori's Cooper) and Brooks was off form in seventh place..

On the team's second visit to the Nürburgring, Vanwall had everything sorted out with revised steering and suspension settings, but engine shortages meant there was no car for Lewis-Evans. Moss shot off into the lead, pulverizing Fangio's lap record, but his race ended after four laps with a broken magneto. Brooks, on another difficult circuit on which he excelled, then steadily moved up to overtake the leading Ferraris and win. Peter Collins, who had so featured in the history of GAV's cars, crashed fatally while trying to catch the Vanwall.

For the Portuguese GP, the cars had extra vents in their noses for their oil coolers and there Moss won, Lewis-Evans came third and Brooks, who had had a troubled race, eventually crashed. Mike Hawthorn, who finished second, should have been disqualified, for on his last lap he spun, stalled his engine, and on Moss' friendly advice, restarted by driving down the pavement against the flow of traffic. Stirling spoke up for Hawthorn when the stewards wanted to disqualify him and this sporting geature was to cost him the World Championship.

At Monza in 1957 Moss (Vanwall) leads Behra (V-12 Maserati), Lewis-Evans (Vanwall) and Brooks (Vanwall). **(Publifoto)**

The Vanwall in its 1958 form.

Three Vanwalls were among the four cars on the front row at Monza and Moss battled with Hawthorn until a bush in his gearbox seized. Brooks then did his duty and moved ahead to win, while Lewis-Evans retired with overheating. An interesting tweak was tried in practice, a Plexiglas bubble top over the cockpit, the very first commission undertaken by a new company, Cosworth Engineering, but the drivers stewed and it was discarded.

At the last race of the year, the Moroccan GP, Moss had to win and set fastest lap to take the Championship provided Hawthorn finished third or lower. In order to try to break the opposition, Brooks car was fitted with a lower final drive and he was instructed to act as the 'hare'. Brooks ran strongly, trading third place with Hawthorn, but his engine blew just after half-distance.

Moss did what was required of him and Hawthorn finished second, after being waved through by his faster team-mate, Phil Hill. Hawthorn thus became Britain's

The 1958 Vanwall engine. (Guy Griffiths)

first World Champion with a single win and a string of seconds, while Moss, with four wins and a second was runner-up. Poor Lewis-Evans crashed when his engine seized. His fuel tank was ruptured, his car caught fire, he inhaled the fumes, and despite the best medical attention Tony Vandervell's fortune could buy, he died a week later.

The death of the frail little driver, a man who was like a bantam cock and of whom GAV was particularly fond, took the stuffing out of Vandervell. He had succeeded in beating the *bloody red cars*, Vanwalls had taken nine wins from the 14 races since the British GP the previous year, and was the first recipient of what we now call the Constructors' Cup. The man who had stormed out of the B.R.M. project vowing to better it had done so. The man who had written long letters to Enzo Ferrari, pointing out the manifold shortcomings of his cars, had reduced Italy to second place. His health was anyway failing him and

on medical advice he issued a statement in January 1959 to the effect that he was retiring from the sport.

It was final, but not quite final, and his project was to continue, although in skeleton form because he could not let go of it. It was a shame it did so, for subsequent appearances detracted from the lustre of the Vanwall name. Even had Vanwall had Moss and Brooks on the strength for 1959 it would probably have struggled, for there was no lightweight rear-engined car in the pipeline.

Work did continue, however, and when Ferrari did not enter the 1959 British GP, Vandervell offered Brooks a ride in a lightweight car with lower bodywork. Moss had already tried it, found it did not handle well, and refused an invitation to drive it. Brooks qualified the car near the back of the grid and over six seconds off the pace. He did no better in the race and was the first retirement, with a misfiring engine.

Nine months went by until another Vanwall ap-

Tony Brooks with his Vanwall in the 1958 British Grand Prix. He was off-form and finished seventh, a lap in arrears. (T. C. March)

By 1960 the Vanwall featured much lower bodywork, alloy wheels all round, a Colotti gearbox and independent rear suspension. Brooks is on the grid at the French Grand Prix. (Eoin Young Archive)

peared, at Goodwood in the hands of Brooks. It was an interim development of the final front-engined car which would appear later. Brooks qualified some way down the small field, but not far off the pace, and in the race had to pit to have a plug lead replaced. He finished seventh and last, a lap down.

Brooks was back for the French GP at Reims and this was a new car with much lower bodywork, alloy wheels all round, a Colotti 5-speed gearbox mounted behind the final drive, and independent rear suspension. Its day was long gone, however, Brooks was over six seconds off the pace and retired early with transmission problems, possibly caused by being rammed from behind at the start.

Vanwall had taken delivery of a Lotus 18 chassis and installed its own engine into it, which should have made it a winner, for it was much more powerful than the usual Climax FPF unit, even if it did not have so muscular a power curve. Brooks was entered in the Lombank Trophy at Snetterton in September 1960 (the 2½-litre formula was only weeks away from ending), but valve trouble in practice meant it did not start.

Vanwall's final appearance was in the 1961 International Trophy run to the Inter-Continental Formula. There John Surtees had a 2.6-litre rear-engined car which was based on the Lotus 18, but with distinctive bodywork. Like all Vanwalls it was beautifully finished. Surtees did not qualify well, but in the race, which was wet, he took the lead briefly, was delayed by a spin and finished three laps down in fifth.

These late, unsuccessful, appearances were due to the fact that GAV was an autocrat who, while broadly accepting his doctor's advice, was making his own gesture of independence and was both not running a racing team but still was. Vandervell had always had a conflict, on the one hand his cars were his toys, on the other they represented a more serious ambition. The ambition won through, but in the last years his racing department was his playroom again.

Tony Vandervell died in 1967, ten years after he changed motor racing.

With acknowledgements to *Vanwall* by Denis Jenkinson and Cyril Posthumus (published by Patrick Stephens Ltd).

VERITAS

Veritas was the most successful of the West German constructors which used the B.M.W. 328 as its base, and well it might be because the cars were built by B.M.W. engineers Ernst Loof and Lorenz Dietrich. In 1948 it was no easy matter to build a car in Germany and so, together with Schorsch Meier, who had driven for Auto Union, they had to scour Germany to find the components to get started.

The first Veritas was a 2-seater sports car based on the tubular chassis of the special 'Brescia' 328s which had dominated the 1940 Gran Premio di Brescia, which is usually given the honorary title of 'Mille Miglia'.

Pre-war B.M.W. had been streets ahead of any other maker in aerodynamics and from the start Veritas cars had very slippery bodies and, apart from competition cars, a number of closely related road cars were also built. Loof began to develop the engine and some were made with roller bearings, and these apparently gave 125 bhp on the poor commercial fuel then available.

Despite the fact that there was a ban by France on importing German cars, several French enthusiasts lusted after these fast and competent machines which were made at Messkirch in the French sector of Germany. To get around the ban some cars were taken apart, imported as spares, and appeared in France under other names.

In 1948, in the first year of his company's existence, Loof built a single-seater and also designed a new engine. The *einseitzer* still had a ladder-frame chassis, but suspension was independent all round by double wishbones and longitudinal torsion bars. B.M.W. hydraulic brakes were used, with large drums, and B.M.W.-style disc wheels with knock-off hubs hinted at its ancestry, but the Veritas had developed a long way from Munich and there was, too, a new 5-speed gearbox in the pipeline.

Loof's new engine followed the broad lines of the B.M.W. 328, but had a single overhead camshaft which activated a similar push-rod layout to the 328. It had a capacity of 1988cc with 'square' cylinder dimensions (75×75 mm), and in competition trim, with three Solex carburettors and running on methanol, it gave 140 bhp. The block and cylinder head were cast in light alloy, but production of them was beyond the resources of the company, so they were built by Heinkel.

Veritas was nothing if not ambitious, and alongside its 2-litre road and competition cars, it also made a 750cc car using Panhard components. Perhaps it was trying to do too much, for it ran into financial difficulties in 1950 and closed. Shortly afterwards it revived, Dietrich left, and Loof began operating from a small workshop behind the grandstand at the Nürburgring.

At the 1950 Paris Salon Veritas unveiled a single-seater with an all-enveloping body and de Dion rear axle,

The Veritas of Paul Pietsch at the 1952 International Trophy at Silverstone. (Guy Griffiths)

designed to gain an advantage at the high-speed Avus and Hockenheim circuits.

By 1952, Veritas had probably done more than any other company to generate a revival of motor sport in Germany, and driven by such as Hermann Lang, Paul Pietsch, Karl Kling, Hans Klenk, Hans Herrmann and Wolfgang Seidel they had been immensely successful in German national racing and elsewhere. By the time F2 was elevated to Championship status, however, the drive had gone out of the marque and it was struggling.

Thus WC events rarely saw a Veritas, although the Belgian amateur Arthur Legat entered his home GP in 1952, but was extremely slow. Five cars started the German GP, but only one finished, that of Fritz Riess in seventh and two laps down. The year's best result came at the Grenzlandring, when Veritas filled the first three places (Ulmen, Klenk and Peters) while Klenk and Riess came second and third in the Avusrennen behind Rudi Fischer's Ferrari, but both races were effectively little more than national events.

Legat had his car in the Belgian GP in 1953, but was again very slow in practice and retired after one lap with engine troubles. Six cars started the German GP, including one driven by Loof himself, and although three finished, they were in ninth, 12th and 16th places. In the Avusrennen, however, Hans Klank, Theo Helfrich and Hans Herrmann finished 2-3-4 behind Jacques Swaters' Ferrari Tipo 500, but there were no works teams present. During 1953 Loof could see that there was no way he could keep pace with new developments and so he shut down his shop and went back to work for B.M.W. Sadly, he died of a brain tumour three years later.

WALKER-CLIMAX

In 1959 Rob Walker found himself in the extraordinary position, for a privateer, of being the entrant of the world's number one driver, Stirling Moss and also employing the most famous mechanic of the period, Alf Francis. The relationship between Moss and Francis went back to 1950 when both were in the H.W.M. team and apart from their mutual trust, they were both always looking for an extra edge.

Having run Coopers with great success, Francis, who always fancied himself as something of a designer, felt that he could refine and improve the basic Cooper concept. He set to work with Valerio Colotti's studio in Modena and by mid-1959, design had been completed and work had begun building the car.

Francis felt that tyre wear was becoming a crucial factor on some circuits and, indeed, quite often the Walker Coopers had run with wire wheels in place of the standard Cooper bolt-ons. Thus the Walker-Climax was designed from the start with Borrani knock-on wheels. The space-frame was a properly triangulated affair unlike the 1959 curved-tube Cooper and front and rear suspension was by coil springs and double wishbones with twin radius arms at the rear. In other words, it was fairly similar in concept to the 1960 'low-line' works Coopers.

The Coventry Climax 2½-litre FPF engine sat vertically making for a high (37-in) engine cover and the pannier fuel tanks (designed by an aerodynamacist) were held in place by rubber bands. As with the Walker Coopers, a 5-speed Colotti gearbox was used.

For one reason or another, work was suspended on the car at the end of 1959 and it was not in fact completed until early in 1961. In the interim Moss had lost interest in it for while it was probably a significant advance on customer Coopers, the Lotus 18 he had in 1960 made the Walker redundant. By the time it was finished the 1½-litre formula was in force and the Walker was too big and heavy to be competitive.

It was tested by Jack Fairman at Silverstone and behaved impeccably over 50 laps of the circuit and fulfilled one of Alf Francis' objectives which was to be a rugged, trouble-free, car. There was some talk of entering it in Inter-Continental Formula races but, in the event, Moss opted for his Cooper and the category was anyway short-lived. Thus the Walker never raced, though still exists.

A second, much lighter, chassis frame was made which might have been suitable for the 1½-litre formula, but Moss was content to stick with his Lotus, and this never became a complete car. Since Moss won no fewer than seven F1 races in 1961 (the same as Ferrari) which included his epic wins at Monaco and the Nürburgring, his decision was entirely vindicated.